First World War

and Army of Occupation

War Diary

France, Belgium and Germany

16 DIVISION
47 Infantry Brigade
Connaught Rangers
6th Battalion
18 December 1915 - 31 July 1918

WO95/1970/2

The Naval & Military Press Ltd
www.nmarchive.com
Published in association with The National Archives

Published by

The Naval & Military Press Ltd

Unit 10 Ridgewood Industrial Park,

Uckfield, East Sussex,

TN22 5QE England

Tel: +44 (0) 1825 749494

www.naval-military-press.com

www.nmarchive.com

This diary has been reprinted in facsimile from the original. Any imperfections are inevitably reproduced and the quality may fall short of modern type and cartographic standards.

Contents

Document type	Place/Title	Date From	Date To
Heading	WO95/1970 16 Div-47 Inf Bde 6 Connaught Rangers Dec 1915-Jul 1918 (No Diary For Mar 1918 reported Missing)		
Heading	16th Division 47th Infy Bde 6th Bn Connaught Rangers Dec 1915-jly 1918		
Heading	6th Connaught Rangers Vol I 31.12.15-31.12.15 Jan 16		
War Diary	Le Havre	18/12/1915	18/12/1915
War Diary	Hesdigneul	19/12/1915	26/01/1916
War Diary	Philosophe	27/01/1916	31/01/1916
Miscellaneous	6th (S) Bn. The Conn. Rangers Operation Orders Appendix I	06/01/1917	06/01/1917
Miscellaneous	6th (S) Bn. The Connaught Rangers. Casualties To 31st January, 1916, Inclusive. Appendix. I.	31/01/1916	31/01/1916
Heading	6th Connaught Vol 2		
War Diary	Philosophe	01/02/1916	08/02/1916
War Diary	Houchin	09/02/1916	09/02/1916
War Diary	Marles Les Mines	09/02/1916	09/02/1916
War Diary	Bellery	10/02/1916	12/02/1916
War Diary	Febvin Palfart	13/02/1916	28/02/1916
War Diary	St Hilaire	29/02/1916	29/02/1916
Miscellaneous	6th (S) Bn. The Connaught Rangers. Appendix III	01/02/1916	01/02/1916
Miscellaneous	Acts of Distinguish Conduct by N.C.O. and men of 6th Bn the Connaught Ranger between January Appendix III	26/01/1916	26/01/1916
Heading	6th Connaught Vol 3 16th Div		
War Diary	Annequin Fosse	01/03/1916	03/03/1916
War Diary	Annequin	03/03/1916	06/03/1916
War Diary	Annequin Fosse	06/03/1916	11/03/1916
War Diary	Fouqueruil	12/03/1916	17/03/1916
War Diary	Allouagne	17/03/1916	24/03/1916
War Diary	Philosophe	25/03/1916	31/03/1916
Miscellaneous	6th (S) Bn. The Connaught Rangers. Casualties In Action. Appendix IV		
Miscellaneous	6th (S) Bn. The Connaught Rangers. Casualties Appendix V	03/04/1916	03/04/1916
Miscellaneous		04/05/1916	04/05/1916
War Diary	Noeux Les Mines	01/04/1916	05/04/1916
War Diary	Hullech [Right] Sector	06/04/1916	09/04/1916
War Diary	Philosophe	10/04/1916	12/04/1916
War Diary	Hulluch Section [Support	13/04/1916	15/04/1916
War Diary	Hulluch [Right] Sector	16/04/1916	20/04/1916
War Diary	Mazingarbe	21/04/1916	28/04/1916
War Diary	10th Avenue	29/04/1916	30/04/1916
Miscellaneous	6th (S) Bn. The Connaught Rangers. Casualties Appendix No VI	27/04/1916	27/04/1916
War Diary	10th Avenue	01/05/1916	03/05/1916
War Diary	Loos	04/05/1916	07/05/1916
War Diary	Loos	07/03/1916	07/03/1916
War Diary	10th Avenue	08/03/1916	11/03/1916
War Diary	Loos	12/03/1916	17/05/1916

War Diary	Noeux Les Mines	18/05/1916	25/05/1916
War Diary	10th Avenue	26/05/1916	28/05/1916
War Diary	In The Trenches	29/05/1916	31/05/1916
Miscellaneous	6th (S) Bn. The Connaught Rangers. Casualties. Appendix VII	04/06/1916	04/06/1916
Miscellaneous	Appendix VIII		
War Diary	In The Trenches	01/06/1916	05/06/1916
War Diary	Philosophe	06/06/1916	06/06/1916
War Diary	In The Trenches	07/06/1916	10/06/1916
War Diary	Mazingarbe	11/06/1916	17/06/1916
War Diary	Philosophe	17/06/1916	20/06/1916
War Diary	In The Trenches	21/06/1916	24/06/1916
War Diary	Philosophe	25/06/1916	29/06/1916
War Diary	In The Trenches	30/06/1916	30/06/1916
Heading	War Diary 6th (S) Bn The Connaught Rgrs. 1st July to 31st July 1916 Volume 8		
War Diary	In The Trenches	01/07/1916	03/07/1916
War Diary	Noeux Les Mines	04/07/1916	10/07/1916
War Diary	In The Trenches	11/07/1916	31/07/1916
Heading	War Diary 6th Connaught Rangers Month Of August, 1916 Volume 9		
War Diary	Mazingarbe	01/08/1916	09/08/1916
War Diary	In The Trenches	09/08/1916	31/08/1916
Heading	War Diary 6th Connaught Rangers Month Of September 1916 Volume 10		
War Diary		01/09/1916	30/09/1916
Map	Rough Sketch		
Heading	War Diary Month Of October, 1916. Volume 11 6th Connaught Rangers.		
War Diary		01/10/1916	31/10/1916
Heading	War Diary For Month Of November, 1916 Volume 12 6th Connaught Rangers		
War Diary		01/11/1916	30/11/1916
Heading	War Diary For Month Of December, 1916 Volume 13 6th Connaught Rangers		
War Diary		01/12/1916	31/12/1916
Heading	War Diary For Month of January, 1917 Volume 14 6th Btn The Connaught Rangers.		
War Diary	In The Field	01/01/1917	31/01/1917
Miscellaneous	6th (S) Bn The Conn Rangers Operation Orders Appendix III	12/01/1917	12/01/1917
Miscellaneous	6th (S) Bn The Conn. Rangers. Operation Orders Appendix IV	20/01/1917	20/01/1917
Miscellaneous	Operation Orders 6th (S) Bn Connaught Rangers. Appendix V	24/01/1917	24/01/1917
Miscellaneous	6th (S) Bn. The Conn. Rangers. Operation Orders. Appendix VII	28/01/1917	28/01/1917
Miscellaneous	6th (S) Bn. Conn. Rangers. Operation Orders. Appendix VIII	30/01/1917	30/01/1917
Miscellaneous	Operation Order By Lieut Colonel R.C. Fielding D.S.O. Commanding 6th Bn The Connaught Rangers.	30/01/1918	30/01/1918
Heading	War Diary For Month Of February, 1917 Volume 15 6th Connaught Rangers.		
War Diary	In The Field	01/02/1917	28/02/1917
Miscellaneous	6th (S) Battn Operation Orders Appendix I	01/02/1917	01/02/1917
Miscellaneous	6th (S) Bn. The Conn. Rangers Operation Orders	05/02/1917	05/02/1917

Miscellaneous	6th (S) Bn. The Conn. Rangers Operation Orders Appendix III	13/02/1917	13/02/1917
Miscellaneous	6th (S) Bn. The Conn. Rangers Operation Orders Appendix IV	17/02/1917	17/02/1917
Miscellaneous	6th (S) Bn. The Connaught Rangers Operation Orders Appendix V	21/02/1917	21/02/1917
Heading	War Diary For Month of March, 1917 Volume 16 6th Btn Connaught Rangers		
War Diary	Locre (Currach Camp)	01/03/1917	01/03/1917
War Diary	Bde. Reserve	02/03/1917	05/03/1917
War Diary	Left Subsector (Spanbroek. Set)	06/03/1917	06/03/1917
War Diary	Left Subsector	06/03/1917	10/03/1917
War Diary	Bde Support	11/03/1917	12/03/1917
War Diary	Berthen	13/03/1917	30/03/1917
War Diary	Locre	31/03/1917	31/03/1917
Miscellaneous	6th (S) Bn. The Conn. Rangers Operation Orders. Appendix I	01/03/1917	01/03/1917
Miscellaneous	6th (S) Bn. The Conn. Rangers Operation Orders. Appendix II	05/03/1917	05/03/1917
Miscellaneous	Operation Order Appendix III	07/03/1917	07/03/1917
Miscellaneous	6th (S) Battn The Connaught Rangers Operation Orders Appendix IV	09/03/1917	09/03/1917
Miscellaneous	6th (S) Bn The Conn. Rangers Operation Orders. Appendix V	11/03/1917	11/03/1917
Miscellaneous	Operation Orders. 6th (S) Bn The Conn. Rangers.	30/03/1917	30/03/1917
Heading	War Diary For Month Of April, 1917 Volume 17 6th Connaught Rangers		
War Diary	In The Field Ref Map Sheet 28.3W E3.5A.1/20000	01/04/1917	30/04/1917
Miscellaneous	6th (S) Bn The Conn Rangers Operation Orders.	31/03/1917	31/03/1917
Miscellaneous	6th (S) Bn The Conn Rangers Operation Orders Appendix II	04/04/1917	04/04/1917
Miscellaneous	Operation Orders by Lieut Col R.C. Fielding Commanding 6th (S) Bn Connaught Rangers Appendix VII	18/04/1917	18/04/1917
Miscellaneous	Operation Orders 6th (S) Connaught Rangers. Appendix III.	06/04/1917	06/04/1917
Miscellaneous	Operation Orders By Lieut Colonel R.C Fielding Commanding 6th (S) Bn Conn. Rangers Appendix IV	09/04/1917	09/04/1917
Miscellaneous	Operation Orders By Lieut-Col. R.C. Fielding Commdg The Conn. Rangers Appendix V	14/04/1917	14/04/1917
Miscellaneous	Operation Orders 6th (S) Connaught Rangers Appendix VI	16/04/1917	16/04/1917
Heading	War Diary Volume 18 For Month Of May, 1917 6th Connaught Rangers		
War Diary	In The Field Ref Sheet 28.S.W. 1/2000 Hazebrouck	01/05/1917	31/05/1917
Miscellaneous	Operation Orders By Lieut-Col R.C. Fielding Commanding The Conn Rangers Appendix I	04/05/1917	04/05/1917
Miscellaneous	Operation Orders By Lieut. Col. R.C. Fielding Commanding 6th (S) Bn. The Conn. Rangers. Appendix II	09/05/1917	09/05/1917
Miscellaneous	Operation Orders By Lieut-Col. R.C. Fielding Comndg 6th (S) Bn. The Conn. Rangers. Appendix III	10/05/1917	10/05/1917
Miscellaneous	Operation Orders By Lieut. Col. R.C. Fielding Commanding 6th (S) Bn. The Conn. Rangers. Appendix IV	15/05/1917	15/05/1917

Miscellaneous	Operation Orders By Lieut. Col. R.C. Fielding Commanding 6th (S) Bn. The Conn. Rangers. Appendix V	16/05/1917	16/05/1917
Miscellaneous	Operation Orders By Lt. Col. R.C. Feilding Commdg 6th (S) Bn. The Conn. Rgs. Appendix VI	17/05/1917	17/05/1917
Miscellaneous	Operation Orders By Lieut-Col. R.C. Feilding Commanding The Conn. Rangers. Appendix VII	23/03/1917	23/03/1917
Miscellaneous	Operation Orders By Lieut. Col. R.C. Feilding Commanding 6th (S) Bn. The Conn Rangers. Appendix VIII	28/05/1917	28/05/1917
Miscellaneous	Operation Orders By Lieut. Col. R.C. Feilding Commanding The Conn. Rangers. Appendix IX	29/05/1917	29/05/1917
Miscellaneous	Operation Orders By Lieut. Col. R.C. Feilding Commanding The Conn. Rangers. Appendix X	30/05/1917	30/05/1917
Heading	2 Lt. H Chamer		
Heading	War Diary For Month Of June 1917 Volume 19 6th Connaught Rangers.		
War Diary	In The Field	01/06/1917	30/06/1917
Miscellaneous	Operation Orders By Lieut. Col. R.C. Feilding Commdg 6th (S) Bn. The Conn Rangers Appendix I	01/06/1917	01/06/1917
Miscellaneous	Operation Orders By Lieut. Col. R.C. Feilding Commanding The Connaught Rangers Appendix II	04/06/1917	04/06/1917
Miscellaneous	Operation Orders By Lieut. Col. R.C. Feilding Commanding The Conn Rangers	04/06/1917	04/06/1917
Miscellaneous	? Of Artillery Programme	05/06/1917	05/06/1917
Miscellaneous	Stokes Mortar Programme For Enterprise Of Connaught Rangers On Night	04/06/1917	04/06/1917
Miscellaneous	Raid By 6th Connaught Rangers Night	05/06/1917	05/06/1917
Miscellaneous	H.Q. 47th Inf Bde Appendix No A-T-I	09/06/1917	09/06/1917
Miscellaneous	Operation Orders By Lieut-Col R.C. Feilding Commdg The Conn. Rangers Appendix III	05/06/1917	05/06/1917
Miscellaneous	Operation Orders By Lieut-Col. R.C. Feilding D.S.O. Commanding 6th Bn The Conn. Rangers. Appendix IV	09/06/1917	09/06/1917
Miscellaneous	Operation Orders By Lieut-Col R.C. Feilding D.S.O. Commanding The Conn. Rangers Appendix V	12/06/1917	12/06/1917
Miscellaneous	Operation Orders By Lieut-Col R.C. Feilding Comdg The Conn Rangers Appendix VI	16/06/1917	16/06/1917
Miscellaneous	Operation Orders By Lieut-Col R.C. Feilding D.S.O. Comdg 6th (S) Bn The Conn Rangers Appendix VII	18/06/1917	18/06/1917
Miscellaneous	Operation Orders By Lieut-Col R.C. Feilding D.S.O. Commanding 6th (S) Bn The Conn Rangers Appendix VIII	19/06/1917	19/06/1917
Miscellaneous	Operation Orders By Lieut-Col R.C. Feilding D.S.O. Commanding 6th (S) Bn The Conn Rangers Appendix IX	21/06/1917	21/06/1917
Heading	War Diary For Month Of July, 1917 Volume 20 6th Connaught Rangers		
War Diary	In The Field	01/07/1917	15/07/1917
War Diary	In The Field Sheet 27aSE	16/07/1917	17/07/1917
War Diary	Cormette Ref Sheet France 27A S.E	18/07/1917	22/07/1917
War Diary	Winnezeele Ref Sheet 27	23/07/1917	24/07/1917
War Diary	Watou K.12 6.4.9 Sheet 27	25/07/1917	26/07/1917
War Diary	Watou Ref Sheet 27	27/07/1917	28/07/1917
War Diary	Brandhoek Area Ref Sheet Belgium 28.NW	30/07/1917	31/07/1917

Operation(al) Order(s)	Operation Order No. 23 By Lieut-Colonel J.D. Mather Commanding 6th Bn The Connaught Rangers. Appendix I	21/07/1917	21/07/1917
Operation(al) Order(s)	Operation Order No. 93 By Lieut-Colonel J.D. Mather Commanding 6th Bn The Connaught Rangers. Appendix 2	24/07/1917	24/07/1917
Miscellaneous	Night Operations 28-7-1917 Refernce Steenvoorde Training Area Map. General Idea Appendix 3	26/07/1917	26/07/1917
Operation(al) Order(s)	Operations Orders No. 25 By Lieut-Colonel J.D. Mather Commanding 6th Bn The Connaught Rangers Appendix IV	29/07/1917	29/07/1917
Heading	War Diary For Month Of August, 1917 Volume 21 6th Connaught Rangers		
War Diary	In Line N.E. of Ypres Ref Sheets Belgium 28 N.W. and N.E.	01/08/1917	06/08/1917
War Diary	St Lawrence's Camp Brandhoek G.II.c, Ref Sheet Belgium 28 N.W.	06/08/1917	06/08/1917
War Diary	St Lawrence's Camp. Brandhoek	09/08/1917	10/08/1917
War Diary	St Lawrence's Camp G.II.c Ref Sheet Belgium 28 N.W.	11/08/1917	14/08/1917
War Diary	Vlamertinghe Area No 3 Ref Sheet Belgium 28 N.W.	15/08/1917	16/08/1917
War Diary	Black Line Ref Sheets Belgium 28 N.W. & N.E	17/08/1917	17/08/1917
War Diary	Vlamertinghe No 3 Area	18/08/1917	18/08/1917
War Diary	Watou Ref Sheet Belgium 28 N.W. & 27	19/08/1917	19/08/1917
War Diary	Steenvorde	20/08/1917	23/08/1917
War Diary	Gomiecourt Ref Sheet France 51 C Ervillers	24/08/1917	26/08/1917
War Diary	The Line Ref Sheet Bullecourt 51B S.W.4	26/08/1917	31/08/1917
Miscellaneous	G.O.C. 47th Infantry Brigade Appendix 2	06/08/1917	06/08/1917
Miscellaneous	O.C., 6th Battalion The Connaught Rangers. Appendix 3	05/08/1917	05/08/1917
Miscellaneous	Summary of Casualties 3rd Battn of Ypres Appendix 4		
Miscellaneous	Table of moves of 47th Inf. Bde. Appendix 5		
Heading	War Diary For Month Of September 1917 Volume 22 6th Connaught Rangers.		
War Diary	The Line Ref Sheet Bullecourt 51B S.W. 4	01/09/1917	01/09/1917
War Diary	Ervillers Ref Sheet France 57c N.W.	03/09/1917	30/09/1917
Heading	War Diary For Month Of October, 1917 6th Connaught Rangers Volume Number 23		
War Diary	Theiss Line Ref Map Bullecourt 57BS.W.4	01/10/1917	01/10/1917
War Diary	Ervillers Ref Sheet 57C N.W.	02/10/1917	16/10/1917
War Diary	The Line Ref Sheet Bullecourt 51 BS.W.4	17/10/1917	31/10/1917
Miscellaneous	Operation Orders By Lieut Colonel R.C. Feilding D.S.O. Commanding 6th Bn The Connaught Rangers Appendix I	17/10/1917	17/10/1917
Miscellaneous	Operation Order By Lieut Colonel R.C. Feilding D.S.O. Commanding 6th Bn The Connaught Rangers Appendix 3	20/10/1917	20/10/1917
Operation(al) Order(s)	Operation Order No 35 By Lieut Colonel R.C. Feilding D.S.O. Commanding 6th Bn The Connaught Rangers Appendix 2	18/10/1917	18/10/1917
Operation(al) Order(s)	Operation Order No 37 by Lieut Colonel R.C. Feilding D.S.O. Commanding 6th Bn The Connaught Rangers Appendix 4	24/10/1917	24/10/1917
Operation(al) Order(s)	Operation Order No 38 by Lieut Colonel R.C. Feilding D.S.O. Commanding 6th Bn The Connaught Rangers Appendix 5	28/10/1917	28/10/1917

Heading	War Diary For Month Of November, 1917 Volume 21 6th Connaught Rangers		
War Diary	In The Line Ref Sheet Bullecourt 51 B S.W.4	01/11/1917	02/11/1917
War Diary	Ervillers Ref Sheet 57C N.W.	03/11/1917	18/11/1917
War Diary	In The Line Ref Sheet Bullecourt 51 B.S.W.4	18/11/1917	26/11/1917
War Diary	Ervillers Ref Sheet 57c N.W.	27/11/1917	30/11/1917
Operation(al) Order(s)	Operation Order No. 34 By Lieut Colonel R.C. Feilding D.S.O. Commanding 6th Bn The Connaught Rangers. Appendix I	01/11/1917	01/11/1917
Operation(al) Order(s)	Operation Orders No 35 By Lieut Colonel R.C. Feilding D.S.O. Commanding 6th Bn The Connaught Rangers. Appendix 2	17/11/1917	17/11/1917
Operation(al) Order(s)	Operation Order (No.1) by Lieut Colonel R.C. Feilding D.S.O. Commanding 6th Bn The Connaught Rangers. Appendix 3	18/11/1917	18/11/1917
Miscellaneous	Headquarters, 47th Infantry Brigade. Appendix 4	25/11/1917	25/11/1917
Miscellaneous	Headquarters, 47th Inf Bde. Appendix 4	27/11/1917	27/11/1917
Miscellaneous	Headquarters, 16th (Irish) Division. Appendix 5	22/11/1917	22/11/1917
Operation(al) Order(s)	Operation Orders No 36 By Lieut Colonel R.C. Feilding. D.S.O. Commanding 6th Bn. The Connaught Rangers. Appendix 6	22/11/1917	22/11/1917
Operation(al) Order(s)	Operation Orders No. 37 By Lieut Colonel R.C. Feilding. D.S.O. Commanding 6th Bn. The Connaught Rangers. Appendix 7	23/11/1917	23/11/1917
Operation(al) Order(s)	Operation Orders By Lieut Colonel. R.C. Feilding. D.S.O. Commanding 6th Bn. The Connaught Rangers. Appendix 8	25/11/1917	25/11/1917
Miscellaneous	Headquarters 16th (Irish) Division O.C. 6th Connaught Rangers.	25/11/1917	25/11/1917
Miscellaneous	Operation Orders By Lieut Colonel. R.C. Feilding. D.S.O. Commanding 6th Bn. the Connaught Rangers. Appendix 9	26/11/1917	26/11/1917
Operation(al) Order(s)	Operation Order No. 40 By Lieut Colonel R.C. Feilding D.S.O. Commanding 6th In The Connaught Rangers. Appendix 10	29/11/1917	29/11/1917
Heading	War Diary For Month Of December 1917 Volume 27 6th Connaught Rangers		
War Diary	Ervillers Ref Sheet France 57c. N.W.	01/12/1917	01/12/1917
War Diary	Gomiecourt	02/12/1917	02/12/1917
War Diary	Beaulencourt Ref Sheet France 57c	03/12/1917	04/12/1917
War Diary	Tincourt Ref Sheet France 62c	06/12/1917	09/12/1917
War Diary	Lempire Ref Sheet France 62.c.	11/12/1917	20/12/1917
War Diary	In The Line Ref Sheet France 62c	21/12/1917	23/12/1917
War Diary	Tincourt Ref Sheet France 62c	23/12/1917	28/12/1917
War Diary	Bde Reserve Ref Sheet France 62c	29/12/1917	30/12/1917
Operation(al) Order(s)	Operation Order No. 40 Lieut Colonel R.C. Feilding. D.S.O. Commanding 6th Bn The Connaught Rangers.	02/12/1917	02/12/1917
Operation(al) Order(s)	Operation Order No. 42 Lieut Colonel R.C. Feilding. D.S.O. Commanding 6th Bn The Connaught Rangers.	05/12/1917	05/12/1917
Operation(al) Order(s)	Operation Order No. 43 Lieut Colonel R.C. Feilding D.S.O. Commanding 6th Bn The Connaught Rangers.	11/12/1917	11/12/1917
Operation(al) Order(s)	Operation Order No. 45 By Lieut Colonel R.C. Feilding D.S.O. Commanding 6th Bn The Connaught Rangers.	16/12/1917	16/12/1917
Operation(al) Order(s)	Operation Order No. 46 Lieut Colonel R.C. Feilding D.S.O. Commanding 6th Bn The Connaught Rangers.	20/12/1917	20/12/1917

Operation(al) Order(s)	Operation Order No. 47 by Lieut Colonel R.C. Feilding D.S.O. Commanding 6th Bn The Connaught Rangers.	22/12/1917	22/12/1917
Operation(al) Order(s)	Operation Orders No. 48 By Major H.M. Raynsford Commanding 6th (S) Bn The Connaught Rangers	28/12/1917	28/12/1917
Miscellaneous			
Heading	War Diary For Month Of January, 1918 Volume 26 6th Connaught Rangers.		
War Diary	Ref Sheet Epehy 67.C.N.E.2	01/01/1918	04/01/1918
War Diary	Ref Sheet Epehy 62.C.N.E.2 Front Line	05/01/1918	10/01/1918
War Diary	Villers Faucon Ref Sheet Epehy 62 C.N.E. 2	11/01/1918	21/01/1918
War Diary	Ronssoy	22/01/1918	28/01/1918
War Diary	Vempire Ref Sheet 62C N.E.2	28/01/1918	31/01/1918
Operation(al) Order(s)	Operation Order No. 50 By Major R.M. Raynsford Commanding 6th Bn The Connaught Rangers.	03/01/1918	03/01/1918
Operation(al) Order(s)	Operation Order No. 51 By Lt Col R.C. Feilding. D.S.O. Cmdg 6th (S) Bn Connaught Rangers.	09/01/1918	09/01/1918
Operation(al) Order(s)	Operation Order No. 14 By Lieut Colonel R.C. Feilding D.S.O. Commanding 6th Bn. The Connaught Rangers	21/01/1918	21/01/1918
Operation(al) Order(s)	Operation Order No. 15 By Lieut Colonel. R.C. Feilding D.S.O. Commanding 6th. Bn. The Connaught Rangers	27/01/1918	27/01/1918
Operation(al) Order(s)	Operation Order No 16 By Lieut-Colonel R.C. Feilding D.S.O. Commanding 6th Bn The Connaught Rangers.	31/01/1917	31/01/1917
Heading	War Diary For Month Of February, 1918 Volume 27 6th Connaught Rangers		
War Diary	Front Line Ref Sheet Lempire	01/02/1918	02/02/1918
War Diary	St Emilie	03/02/1918	07/02/1918
War Diary	Front Line	08/02/1918	28/02/1918
Operation(al) Order(s)	Operation Order No. 17 By Lieut Colonel R.C. Feilding D.S.O. Commanding 6th Bn The Connaught Rangers.	02/02/1918	02/02/1918
Operation(al) Order(s)	Operation Order No. 18 by Major R.M. Raynsford Commanding 6th Bn The Connaught Rangers.	07/02/1918	07/02/1918
Operation(al) Order(s)	Operation Order No. 20 by Major R.M. Raynsford Commanding 6th Bn The Connaught Rangers.	13/02/1918	13/02/1918
Operation(al) Order(s)	Operation Order No. 21 by Major R.M. Raynsford Commanding 6th Bn The Connaught Rangers	16/02/1918	16/02/1918
Operation(al) Order(s)	Operation Order No. 22 By Major R.M. Raynsford Commanding 6th Bn Connaught Rangers.	20/02/1918	20/02/1918
Operation(al) Order(s)	Operation Order No. 24 by Major R.M. Raynsford Cmdg 6th Conn Rangers	28/02/1918	28/02/1918
Heading	47th Brigade. 16th Division. The War Diary is missing; this file contains the Report by O.C. Battalion 21st-27th March 6th Battalion Connaught Rangers March 1918		
Heading	6th Connaught Rangers 1918 21st-28th March Official Report Rendered To Brigade By Lieut-Colonel R.C. Feilding April 1918		
Miscellaneous	Epehy Sheet 62.C.N.E. 2 Edition 2A France Sheet 62.D. Edition 1		
War Diary	Hubigny	01/04/1918	01/04/1918
War Diary	Hamelet	02/04/1918	02/04/1918
War Diary	Baleux	03/04/1918	03/04/1918
War Diary	Blanchy	04/04/1918	04/04/1918
War Diary	Framicourt	05/04/1918	09/04/1918
War Diary	Wardrecques	10/04/1918	10/04/1918
War Diary	Merck St Lievin	11/04/1918	12/04/1918
War Diary	Drionville	13/04/1918	13/04/1918

War Diary	Remilly Wirquin	14/04/1918	26/04/1918
War Diary	Blequin	26/04/1918	30/04/1918
War Diary	Blequin Ref Map Hazebrouck 5A	01/05/1918	14/05/1918
War Diary	Desvres Ref Map Calais	15/05/1918	18/05/1918
War Diary	Doudeauville	18/05/1918	31/05/1918
War Diary	Doudeauville Ref Map Calais 13	01/06/1918	30/06/1918
War Diary	Doudeauville Ref Map Calais 1/100000	01/07/1918	31/07/1918

WO95/1970

16 Div – 47 Inf Bde

6 Connaught Rangers

Dec 1915 – Jul 1918

(No Diary for Mar 1918 – reported missing)

16TH DIVISION
47TH INFY BDE

6TH BN CONNAUGHT RANGERS

DEC 1915-JLY 1918

DISBANDED 2. 8 18

16 DN

47/76

6th Connaught Rangers

Vol I

~~8~~ 31 12.15 – 31.12.15

Jan 16

(1) Confidential

Dec '15 Sly '18

47/16

1

Instructions regarding War Diaries and Intelligence Summaries are contained in F. S. Regs., Part II. and the Staff Manual respectively. Title pages will be prepared in manuscript.

WAR DIARY
or
~~INTELLIGENCE SUMMARY.~~
(Erase heading not required.)

Army Form C. 2118.

6TH (S) Bn. CONNAUGHT'S RANGERS

Place	Date	Hour	Summary of Events and Information	Remarks and references to Appendices
LE HAVRE	18/12/15	6 AM	The Battalion under the command of Lt. Col. J. S. W. LENOX CONYNGHAM disembarked 36 officers and 952 other ranks and remained in a rest camp for that day until 6 P.M. when it entrained for HESDIGNEUL near BETHUNE, arriving there at 6 PM on 19th December. At the station the men heard the sound of the guns in the firing line for the first time. The journey from England to HESDIGNEUL was uneventful and the move worked smoothly except that hot water was not available along the railway route in FRANCE as arranged.	
HESDIGNEUL	19-12-15		Resting in billets	
	20-12-15		Resting in billets and attending to sanitation	
	21-12-15		Route march attempted but spoiled by weather	
	22-12-15		Arrangements made for attending the front line trenches for instructional purposes by Drafts	
	23-12-15		Draft of 25 all ranks proceed to trenches for 2 days. Remainder of Battalion march to BRUAY for bathing	

I. E.

#353 Wt. W2544/1454 700,000 5/15 D. D. & L. A.D.S.S./Forms/C. 2118.

2

Instructions regarding War Diaries and Intelligence Summaries are contained in F. S. Regs., Part II. and the Staff Manual respectively. Title pages will be prepared in manuscript.

WAR DIARY
or
INTELLIGENCE SUMMARY.

(Erase heading not required.)

Army Form C. 2118.

6th (S) Bn. The Connaught Rangers

2

Place	Date	Hour	Summary of Events and Information	Remarks and references to Appendices
HESDIGNEUL	25. 12. 15.	4.50pm	Draft of 416 all ranks under CAPT. W. B. LAMBERT – forming a Working Party left here in lorries. They were engaged on improving O.B.1. Sq 4 C. Trench Map 36.C. for one night	
HESDIGNEUL	26-12-15		Second draft of 25 all ranks proceed to front line trenches for two days for instructional purposes. This party happened to be in the trenches one mile N.E. of ~~[illegible]~~ MERVELLE about Sq 84 C. Trench Map 36.C. when the Germans exploded a mine under ~~our~~ front line trenches. Our machine Gun ~~officer~~ Sergeant was buried for some time but was extricated after about half-an-hour. 2nd LIEUT BOR our machine Gun Officer dug up a buried machine gun and had it ready for action during the night. LIEUT O'BRIEN with some bombers of the Battalion on duty (17TH LONDON REGT) held the crater of the mine during the night but the Germans did not attempt to advance and the position was consolidated next day.	
	27-12-15 to 30-12-15		The Battalion was engaged in fatigue duties at HESDIGNEUL	

#353 Wt. W2544/1454 700,000 5/15 D. D. & L. A.D.S.S./Forms/C. 2118.

3

Army Form C. 2118.

Instructions regarding War Diaries and Intelligence Summaries are contained in F. S. Regs., Part II. and the Staff Manual respectively. Title pages will be prepared in manuscript.

WAR DIARY
or
INTELLIGENCE SUMMARY.
(Erase heading not required.)

6th (S) Bn. CONNAUGHT RANGERS

Place	Date	Hour	Summary of Events and Information	Remarks and references to Appendices
HESDIGNEUL	31-12-15 to 3-1-16		The Battalion continued to be employed in supplying working parties under orders of the 4th Corps. these parties were employed at HESDIGNEUL AUCHEL and MINX. Major J. P. B ROBINSON ROYAL DUBLIN FUSILIERS reported for duty with the Battalion on the 3-1-16	
"	4-1-16 to 9-1-16		Working parties still employed. No opportunity therefore of continuing military training except for small parties of grenadiers under instruction.	
	10-1-16 to 14-1-16		B and C Companies of the Battalion were attached to the 173 Company R.E. at NOEUX LES MINES. A + D Companies continue to supply working parties at HESDIGNEUL AUCHEL and MINX under orders of the 4TH CORPS	
"	15-1-16		B + C Companies return from NOEUX LES MINES and rejoin their Battalion at HESDIGNEUL after having provided some mining parties in the LOOS salient under the R.E's. During this work one of C Company No 2723 Private P McTernan was wounded in the leg, being the first battle casualty of the Battalion	
	16-1-16		The Battalion is attached for instruction to the 15th Division and for administration to the 46TH Brigade. The Battalion continues to provide working parties for the 4TH CORPS.	

Army Form C. 2118.

Instructions regarding War Diaries and Intelligence Summaries are contained in F. S. Regs., Part II. and the Staff Manual respectively. Title pages will be prepared in manuscript.

WAR DIARY
or
INTELLIGENCE SUMMARY.
(*Erase heading not required.*)

6th (S) Bn THE CONNAUGHT RANGERS

Place	Date	Hour	Summary of Events and Information	Remarks and references to Appendices
HESDIGNEUL	16-1-16		2nd LIEUT. A HARBORD of the 4TH Battalion. CONN RANG reported for duty with this Battalion on the 15th instant and was taken on the strength of the Battalion as from that date.	
HESDIGNEUL	16-1-16 to 25-1-16		The Battalion continued to supply working parties to the [illegible] Corps. On the 21-1-16 2nd LIEUT MAC CORMACK reported for duty and was taken on the strength of the Battalion as from that date	
HESDIGNEUL	26-1-16		The Battalion moved up into the trenches in front and to the left of LOOS – in the PUITS No 14 bis sector. The Battalion was attached to the 46th INFANTRY BRIGADE and was distributed over that BRIGADE in the following manner. A Coy attached to the 7TH K.O.S.B.s. B Coy to 8TH K.O.S.B.s. C Coy to 12TH H.L.I. and D Coy to 4/ Suffolks. These Companies took up their respective positions in the trenches on the night of the 26/27. A and B being in the firing trenches for the period 26th to 29th with C Coy in immediate reserve and D Coy in BRIGADE reserve	

2353 Wt. W2544/1454 700,000 5/15 D. D. & L. A.D.S.S./Forms/C. 2118.

Army Form C. 2118.

Instructions regarding War Diaries and Intelligence Summaries are contained in F. S. Regs., Part II. and the Staff Manual respectively. Title pages will be prepared in manuscript.

WAR DIARY
or
INTELLIGENCE SUMMARY.
(*Erase heading not required.*)

6TH (S) BN. THE CONNAUGHT RANGERS

Place	Date	Hour	Summary of Events and Information	Remarks and references to Appendices
PHILOSOPHE	27-1-16	,	The Headquarters of the Battalion moved into PHILOSOPHE. The 46TH INFANTRY BRIGADE to which the Battalion is attached relieved the 44TH INFANTRY BRIGADE took over trenches extending along the front from G 36 d. 4 2 to VENDIN ALLEY (G 19 a 1. 8.) known as PUITS 14 bis section, which is ~~sub~~divided into three subsections as follows: Right subsection G 36 d 4. 2 to H 31. a. 3. 8. Centre Subsection H 31. a. 3. 8 to H 25 a 9. 3½ Left Subsection H 25. a 9 3½ to H 19. c. 1. 8.	
			The Companies were attached to the battalions as detailed on 26-1-16 above. The 7 K.O.S.B's with A Coy 6TH CONNAUGHT RANGERS holding the right sub sector from 26th to 30th January. The 8 K.O.S.B's with B Coy attached holding the centre subsection for the same period, The 4TH Suffolks with D Coy attached being in immediate reserve in NORTHERN SAP REDOUBT and 65 METRE POINT REDOUBT and the 12TH H.L.I. with C Coy attached being in Brigade Reserve at PHILOSOPHE also for the same period. The machine gun section of the Battalion took over the ~~Right~~ Left Subsection ~~which~~ which was held by the 10TH SCOTTISH RIFLES.	
			On the afternoon of this date the enemy's	

8353 Wt. W2544/1454 700,000 5/15 D. D. & L. A.D.S.S./Forms/C. 2118.

6

Army Form C. 2118.

Instructions regarding War Diaries and Intelligence Summaries are contained in F. S. Regs., Part II. and the Staff Manual respectively. Title pages will be prepared in manuscript.

WAR DIARY
or
INTELLIGENCE SUMMARY.
(*Erase heading not required.*)

6TH (S) BN THE CONNAUGHT RANGERS

Place	Date	Hour	Summary of Events and Information	Remarks and references to Appendices
~~[illegible]~~ PHILOSOPHE	27-1-16		artillery was very active along our front and support lines between VENDIN ALLEY and BROADWAY and considerable damage was done. At about 5 P.M the enemy left his trenches opposite the left sub-section and advanced on our lines but were soon stopped by our machine gun fire; our machine gun section helping considerably in this; LIEUT BEATTY the machine Gun Officer being much commended for the way he handled his guns in this his maiden effort against the "bosch".	
			The centre and right subsections also suffered from the enemies artillery but no attack was attempted against them.	
"	28-1-16.		During this day B Company in the centre sub-section had to undergo severe handling by the enemy's artillery. Our men behave well under fire for practically the first time the casualties in B Company ~~that~~ being two killed and thirteen wounded.	
"	29-1-16		The bombardment of our positions during this day was again reduced to the normal. and casualties were slight	

#353 Wt. W2544/1454 700,000 5/15 D. D. & L. A.D.S.S./Forms/C. 2118.

7

Army Form C. 2118.

Instructions regarding War Diaries and Intelligence Summaries are contained in F. S. Regs., Part II. and the Staff Manual respectively. Title pages will be prepared in manuscript.

WAR DIARY
or
INTELLIGENCE SUMMARY.
(Erase heading not required.)

6TH (S) BN. THE CONNAUGHT RANGERS

Place	Date	Hour	Summary of Events and Information	Remarks and references to Appendices
PHILOSOPHE	30-1-16,		Nothing unusual happened during this day. and the usual reliefs were carried out on the night 30/31. A Coy now coming back into immediate reserve. B into Brigade Reserve. C taking up its position in the Centre sub-section, and D the right sub-sector. The total casualties during the four days 26th to 30th were Officers NIL. Other ranks five killed and seventeen wounded. The plan of subdividing the battalion throughout a brigade, a company to a battalion, a platoon to a company, and a section to a platoon works well from an instructional point of view. but the issue of rations and water is thereby much complicated and it was found more expedient to hand over rations in bulk to the Battalions to which our several companies were attached leaving the subsequent subdivision to those Battalions. It would also seem to be advisable that a reserve of rations and water be stored in the front line trenches	

#353 Wt. W2544/1454 700,000 5/15 D. D. & L. A.D.S.S./Forms/C. 2118.

Army Form C. 2118.

Instructions regarding War Diaries and Intelligence Summaries are contained in F. S. Regs., Part II. and the Staff Manual respectively. Title pages will be prepared in manuscript.

WAR DIARY
or
INTELLIGENCE SUMMARY. 6th (S) BN. THE CONNAUGHT RANGERS
(Erase heading not required.)

Place	Date	Hour	Summary of Events and Information	Remarks and references to Appendices
PHILOSOPHE	30-1-16		in case of a temporary failing in the nightly supply of rations which under the most carefully thought out arrangements is bound to occur occasionally.	
"	31-1-16		The reliefs on the night of the 30/31 were carried out smoothly. During the day the normal conditions prevailed, and casualties were neglegible. Further reports bring the casualties from the 25th to 31st up to seven killed and 29 wounded	List of casualties annexed. APPENDIX.I
			[illegible] Lt. Col. Commanding 6th (S) Bn. The Conn. Rang.	
			1st Feb 1916.	

#353 Wt. W2544/1454 700,000 5/15 D. D. & L. A.D.S.S./Forms/C. 2118.

Appendix I

SECRET

6th (S) Bn. The Conn. Rangers.

COPY NO

OPERATION ORDERS

(1) The Battalion will relieve the 6th Royal Irish Regt. in the right sub-section tomorrow.

(2) On completion of relief the companies will be disposed as under:-

3 platoons D Coy and 1 platoon C Coy	-	FRONT LINE
3 " C Coy and 1 " D Coy	-	S.P. 6
B COMPANY	-	R.E. DUG-OUTS
2 platoons A COMPANY	-	GALWAY DUG-OUTS
2 " A "	-	Orders as for disposal will be issued later

(3) C Company will reinforce Front Line with one platoon each night

(4) B Company will relieve D Company and one platoon C Coy in Front Line on 9-1-17.

(5) Companies will move off in above order, the leading platoon of D Company to be at entrance to KINGSWAY at 4 p.m.

(6) Movements East of DERRY HUTS will be by platoons at 200 yards interval

(7) Lewis Guns will be relieved in daylight. All arrangements to be made between officers concerned.

(8) Completion of relief will be reported in code to Battn Hd. Qrs.

(9) Copies of Trench Store receipts will be handed into Orderly Room by 11 a.m. 6-1-17.

(10) Gum Boots will be taken over, they must be carefully checked and the attached receipt forms completed and handed in with Trench Store receipts

(11) Company Commanders will render to Orderly Room half-an-hour before departure, a certificate that the huts occupied by their companies and the surrounding area are in a thoroughly clean and sanitary state

(12) Officers Kits and mens packs will be stacked outside the Guard Room ready for removal by Transport by 2 p.m.

(Sd) F. W. S. JOURDAIN, Lieut

4-1-17 a/Adjt. 6th (S) Bn. The Conn. Rangers

APPENDIX. I.

6TH (S) 'BN. THE CONNAUGHT RANGERS.
****

CASUALTIES TO 31st JANUARY, 1916, INCLUSIVE.
****

		KILLED.		Date.
6/2442	Pte.	Lavery	J.	27-1-16.
6/4650	"	Moran	A.M.	28-1-16.
6/3627	"	McNamara	E.	28-1-16.
6/1562	Sgt.	Murray	J.	28-1-16.
6/4372	Pte.	McCartan	W.J.	28-1-16.
6/4104	"	O'Neill	J.	29-1-16.
6/1465	"	Adamson	J.	31-1-16.

WOUNDED.

6/4044	L/C.	Keegan	T.	26-1-16.
6/4088	Pte.	McHale	P.	26-1-16.
6/ 243	L/C.	Maguire	D.	27-1-16.
6/2197	Pte.	Sweeney	J.	27-1-16.
6/2205	"	Burns	B.	27-1-16.
6/2364	"	Canavan	J.P.	27-1-16.
6/2444	"	Donnelly	O.	27-1-16.
6/ 569	"	Moffatt	P.	27-1-16.
6/2430	"	Maynes	H.	27-1-16.
6/1707	"	Molloy	P.	27-1-16.
6/4347	"	Corbett	D.	27-1-16.
6/4524	"	Hogg	R.	28-1-16.
6/2410	"	Dempsey	J.	28-1-16.
6/2612	"	Kierans	T.	28-1-16.
6/2629	"	Rowan	J.P.	28-1-16.
6/1026	"	McAndrews	P.	28-1-16.
6/4713	"	O'Donnell	J.	28-1-16.
6/1466	"	O'Neill	P.	28-1-16.
6/4726	"	Smyth	P.	28-1-16.
6/4096	"	McGuinness	J.	28-1-16.
6/4659	"	Tuohy	J.	28-1-16.
6/4001	"	Diver	J.	28-1-16.
6/2456	L/Sgt.	Bennett	J.	30-1-16.
6/1536	Pte.	Dowling	E.	31-1-16.
6/3177	"	Dunne	M.	31-1-16.

ACCIDENTALLY WOUNDED.

6/2587	L/Sgt.	Molloy	W.J.	27-1-16.
6/4090	Pte.	Meehan	T. (S.I.)	28-1-16.
6/2550	Cpl.	Neeson	C.	30-1-16.
6/2404	Pte.	McLoughlin	P.	30-1-16.

Lieut. Colonel.
Commdg. 6th (S) 'Bn. The Conn. Rangers.

1st Feb 1916

16

6th Connaughts

Vol 2

47 4/24

9

Army Form C. 2118.

Instructions regarding War Diaries and Intelligence Summaries are contained in F. S. Regs., Part II. and the Staff Manual respectively. Title pages will be prepared in manuscript.

WAR DIARY
or
~~INTELLIGENCE SUMMARY.~~ of 6TH (S) Bn. THE CONNAUGHT RANGERS

(Erase heading not required.)

Place	Date	Hour	Summary of Events and Information	Remarks and references to Appendices
PHILOSOPHE	1-2-16		The position of the Battalion this day was as follows. A Company attached to the 7TH K.O.S.B were in immediate reserve in 10TH AVENUE. B Company attached to the 8th K.O.S.B's were in Brigade Reserve at PHILOSOPHE. C. Company attached to the 12TH H.L.I. were in the [illegible] sub section. and D Company attached to the 11th SUFFOLKS in the right sub-sector. with Nos 13. 15. and 16 platoons in the firing line and No 14 platoon in support in the cellars of LOOS. The latter company were bombarded about 8.30 P.M on this date but casualties were slight. A and B Companies supplied working parties and ration parties to the other two companies.	M

8353 Wt. W2544/1454 700,000 5/15 D. D. & L. A.D.S.S./Forms/C. 2118.

10

Army Form C. 2118.

WAR DIARY
or
~~INTELLIGENCE SUMMARY.~~
(Erase heading not required.)

Instructions regarding War Diaries and Intelligence Summaries are contained in F. S. Regs., Part II. and the Staff Manual respectively. Title pages will be prepared in manuscript.

6TH (S) BN. THE CONNAUGHT RANGERS

Place	Date	Hour	Summary of Events and Information	Remarks and references to Appendices
PHILOSOPHE	1/2/16.		The situation in our Section PUITS bis. remained normal during this day and casualties were slight, two wounded, a new firing trench running from G25a 9 9 to G31a 4.9 which was commenced by the 10TH GORDON'S was improved, firesteps being revetted with sandbags and rifle rests, ammunition stores, bomb stores, latrines, being added and parapet strengthened. The enemy opposite our front has been recently engaged in digging saps, the use for which has given rise to much conjecture. They are shallow trenches with a circular sap head 6 or 8 feet deep and six feet diameter. the earth is levelled off at the sap head and recent patrols report that small wooden frames are being placed near the sap head. They can hardly be required for joining up and forming a new trench. but it is possible that it is contemplated to place either gas cylinders or flammenwerfer in them in the event of the Germans making an attack with the help of such agencies. It has been the endeavour to hamper as much as possible with the help of the artillery and the employment of trench mortars	

11 ~~10~~

Army Form C. 2118.

Instructions regarding War Diaries and Intelligence Summaries are contained in F. S. Regs., Part II. and the Staff Manual respectively. Title pages will be prepared in manuscript.

WAR DIARY
or
~~INTELLIGENCE SUMMARY.~~

(Erase heading not required.)

Place	Date	Hour	Summary of Events and Information	Remarks and references to Appendices
			rifle grenades, and bombing raids. In spite of these efforts the saps appear nightly and multiply. It would appear necessary to have loop-holes prepared low down in our parapet which could be opened by pulling out some sandbags so that if flammenwerfer were employed by the Germans in an attack our men could fire from low down in their trench where they would be more or less immune from the flames and not over the top of the parapet where they could not long remain against such an attack.	
			Reports do not speak in the highest of terms of the order maintained during the reliefs on the nights of the 30th/31st. Of course the enemies Artillery, which was active proved a disconcerting agency and caused touch to be lost between platoons in many instances. The guides provided did not prove always reliable with the result that some of the reliefs were not completed until the following morning	WM

8353 Wt. W2544/1454 700,000 5/15 D. D. & L. A.D.S.S./Forms/C. 2118.

12

Army Form C. 2118.

Instructions regarding War Diaries and Intelligence Summaries are contained in F. S. Regs., Part II. and the Staff Manual respectively. Title pages will be prepared in manuscript.

WAR DIARY

or

~~INTELLIGENCE~~ SUMMARY.

(Erase heading not required.)

Place	Date	Hour	Summary of Events and Information	Remarks and references to Appendices
PHILOSOPHE	2-2-16		The dispositions on this day were as on the 1-2-16. The enemy indulged in an intermittant bombardment during the day and No 16 platoon received perhaps more than its share. The companies in the front line did much wiring and patrol work and the companies in immediate and Brigade Reserves supplied the usual working parties.	AM
"	3-2-16		The dispositions remained unchanged and nothing unusual happened, except that D Company in the ~~centre~~ right sub-sector was exposed to a bombardment by the enemy, though casualties were light. 2nd LIEUT BOWEN was wounded.	AM
"	4-2-16		There was an interchange between the Companies on the night of the 3rd-4th. A Company moved up into the left sub-sector. B Company into the right sub-sector. C Company remained where it was in the centre sub-sector and D Company moved back into immediate reserve in 10TH AVENUE.	

353 Wt. W2544/1454 700,000 5/15 D. D. & L. A.D.S.S./Forms/C. 2118.

Army Form C. 2118.

WAR DIARY

or

~~INTELLIGENCE SUMMARY~~.

(Erase heading not required.)

Instructions regarding War Diaries and Intelligence Summaries are contained in F. S. Regs., Part II. and the Staff Manual respectively. Title pages will be prepared in manuscript.

Place	Date	Hour	Summary of Events and Information	Remarks and references to Appendices
PHILOSOPHE	4-2-16		The reliefs were again very slow and the companies much scattered, touch having been often lost. For instance No. 13 Platoon of D Company arrived at 10TH AVENUE at 3.30 A.M. Nos 14 and 15 at 6 AM. and No 16 not till 8.30 A.M. No 2 Platoon of B Company was heavily shelled but fortunately there were no casualties. At night the usual patrols and wiring parties were sent out.	
"	5-2-16		Dispositions as on the fourth. The enemy indulged in the usual desultory bombardment but casualties were comparatively slight C Company having three men killed and D Company three men wounded	RM
	6-2-16		The dispositions remained unchanged and nothing unusual occurred. Some men of B Company took part in a bombing raid against one of the German Saps heads	RM

14

Army Form C. 2118.

Instructions regarding War Diaries and Intelligence Summaries are contained in F. S. Regs., Part II. and the Staff Manual respectively. Title pages will be prepared in manuscript.

WAR DIARY
or
~~INTELLIGENCE~~ SUMMARY.
(*Erase heading not required.*)

Place	Date	Hour	Summary of Events and Information	Remarks and references to Appendices
PHILOSOPHE	6/2/16		Unfortunately the party were discovered early before they had an opportunity of inflicting much damage to the enemy and were forced to retire after throwing five bombs. The officer of the 8TH K.O.S.B. in command of the party being wounded.	
PHILOSOPHE	7-2-16		In our centre sub-section there was a heavy bombardment by the enemy and CAPTAIN G S R. STRITCH was unfortunately killed. He had shown a fine fighting spirit during his short service in the trenches and his loss so early in the battle history of the Battalion is a distinct loss. He was buried in the Cemetery at NOEUX LES MINES.	Appendix II Casualties (Killed) between 1st & 8th Feb 1916
"	8.2.16		The Battalion was relieved on the night of the 7th 8th and assembled at 10 AM on the CHURCH SQUARE NOEUX LES MINES. B Company having billeted for the night at MAZINGARBE and A C and D Companies in NOEUX LES MINES	

8353 Wt. W2544/1454 700,000 5/15 D. D. & L. A.D.S.S./Forms/C. 2118.

15

Army Form C: 2118.

WAR DIARY

or

~~INTELLIGENCE~~ SUMMARY.

(*Erase heading not required.*)

Instructions regarding War Diaries and Intelligence Summaries are contained in F. S. Regs., Part II. and the Staff Manual respectively. Title pages will be prepared in manuscript.

Place	Date	Hour	Summary of Events and Information	Remarks and references to Appendices
PHILOSOPHE	8-1-16		During the attachment of the Battalion to the 46TH INF BDE for trench warfare instruction the men showed a fine soldierly spirit, and bore up bravely under the heavy bombardments the Germans indulged in on the LOOS salient during the period 26-1-16 to 7-2-16. The officers of the battalions to which we were attached were very complimentary in their reports on both officers and men of this Battalion, and it would seem that we had reached a degree of training which would put us at any time to take over and hold, and perhaps add to, any sector of the line that the Higher Commands might assign us.	AH
			There were many individual acts of gallantry (see Appendix III annexed). None perhaps of outstanding brilliancy and daring, but what is more satisfactory they were divided throughout all ranks showing that not	Appendix III Rewards for distinguished conduct

·16

Army Form C. 2118.

Instructions regarding War Diaries and Intelligence Summaries are contained in F. S. Regs., Part II. and the Staff Manual respectively. Title pages will be prepared in manuscript.

WAR DIARY
or
~~INTELLIGENCE SUMMARY~~.
(Erase heading not required.)

Place	Date	Hour	Summary of Events and Information	Remarks and references to Appendices
PHILOSOPHE	8-2-16		one soldier but many throughout the battalion were worthy to uphold the fighting traditions of their regiment and their country. Annexe is a list of Killed and during the period 1-2-16 to 7-2-16 (Appendix II and also of names of men who distinguished themselves. The private soldier is always a critic and our men were heard to criticise, not without reason the quality of our artillery ammunition. The "duds" (shells which did not explode) were too many to inspire confidence in the care exercised in their manufacture. All were however loud in their praise of the shooting ability of our gunners. The water supply was bad and men were forced to drink water from wells in the trenches which were not of the best quality with the result that many men suffered from diarrhoea.	[initials]
			Opinions of Company Commanders seemed to differ on the question of holding the line strongly or weakly during a bombardment. It would seemed	

17

Army Form C. 2118.

Instructions regarding War Diaries and Intelligence Summaries are contained in F. S. Regs., Part II. and the Staff Manual respectively. Title pages will be prepared in manuscript.

WAR DIARY

or

~~INTELLIGENCE SUMMARY.~~

(Erase heading not required.)

Place	Date	Hour	Summary of Events and Information	Remarks and references to Appendices
PHILOSOPHE	8-2-16		only reasonable to suppose that the enemy cannot attack through his own artillery fire and that the sensible course to follow would be to withdraw our men, leaving only sentries, to some place of safety near by from which they could be quickly thrown into the fighting line and meet an enemy attack. Men treated with this consideration would be in better spirits for fighting than if their morale was shaken by exposure to shell fire. The only point is, can they be got up in time after the enemies bombardment has ceased to meet an infantry attack? The answer would appear to be if they cannot suitable arrangement should be made, by digging more communication trenches, to make this possible.	PM
HOUCHIN			The Battalion moved to HOUCHIN CAMP where the night 8TH-9TH was spent	
	9-2-16		The Battalion paraded at 9 A.M. and marched to	

8353 Wt. W2544/1454 700,000 5/15 D. D. & L. A.D.S.S./Forms/C. 2118.

Instructions regarding War Diaries and Intelligence Summaries are contained in F. S. Regs., Part II. and the Staff Manual respectively. Title pages will be prepared in manuscript.

WAR DIARY

or

~~INTELLIGENCE SUMMARY.~~

(Erase heading not required.)

Army Form C. 2118. 18

Place	Date	Hour	Summary of Events and Information	Remarks and references to Appendices
MARLES LES MINES	9-2-16		MARLES LES MINES where it billeted on the night of the 9th 10th	
BELLERY	10-2-16		marched to BELLERY which was reached about 1 P.M. Billeted there on night of 10-11	AM
"	11-2-16		A and B Companies bathed and refitted at the DIVISIONAL LAUNDRY.	
"	12-2-16		C and D Companies bathed and refitted.	
FEBVIN PALFART	13-2-16		The Battalion marched to FEBVIN PALFART arriving there at 12 noon and settled down into billets and prepared for drill and general instruction on the following day	AM
"	14-2-16		Squad drill with and without arms was indulged in to shake off the lethargy of trench warfare. A draft of 5 N.C.O.'s and 48 men joined from the Base. Many of these men have served with the 1st and 2nd Battalions of this regiment in this campaign and some with the	

2353 Wt. W2544/1454 700,000 5/15 D. D. & L. A.D.S.S./Forms/C. 2118.

19

Army Form C. 2118.

Instructions regarding War Diaries and Intelligence Summaries are contained in F. S. Regs., Part II. and the Staff Manual respectively. Title pages will be prepared in manuscript.

WAR DIARY
or
~~INTELLIGENCE SUMMARY.~~
(*Erase heading not required.*)

Place	Date	Hour	Summary of Events and Information	Remarks and references to Appendices
FERVIN PALFART	14-2-16		5th Battalion in the DARDANELLES. and should prove a useful addition to the fighting strength of the battalion.	
"	15-2-16		Drill, musketry, and inspections in billets.	
"	16-2-16		Same as on yesterday D Coy proceeded to LAIRES for work with 16TH DIVISION SCHOOL of Instruction	
"	17-2-16		The G.O.C 16TH DIVISION inspected A Company and expressed himself as highly pleased with the smartness and steadiness on parade He congratulated the Commanding officer. the officers and the men of the battalion for their good work in the trenches from 26-1-16 to 7-2-16. Drill etc continued.	M
"	18-2-16		Drill. musketry. B Company route march.	
	19-2-16		Same as on 18-2-16 A Company on route march.	
	20-2-16		A draft of 2 NCO.s and 27 men joined the battalion today Drill etc continued	
"	21-2-16		The Battalion was inspected together with some other units of the Brigade by 1st CORPS Commander. GENERAL. SIR. HUBERT GOUGH. on the HURTEBISE - WESTREHEM ROAD. and were complimented on their smart appearance and soldierly	M

2353 Wt. W2544/1454 700,000 5/15 D. D. & L. A.D.S.S./Forms/C. 2118.

Army Form C. 2118.

Instructions regarding War Diaries and Intelligence Summaries are contained in F. S. Regs., Part II. and the Staff Manual respectively. Title pages will be prepared in manuscript.

WAR DIARY
or
~~INTELLIGENCE SUMMARY.~~
(Erase heading not required.)

Place	Date	Hour	Summary of Events and Information	Remarks and references to Appendices
FEBVIN PALFART	21-2-16		leaving	
	22-2-16		Drills etc as usual, also the special classes of young N.C.O's snipers scouts and grenadiers continued.	
	23-2-16		Drills as on the 22-2-16. B. Coy relieved D Coy at LAIRES the latter returning to the battalion	
	24-2-16		Parades and classes as usual	
	25-2-16		The battalion was inspected by the 1st Army Commander GENERAL MUNRO on the HURTEBISE - WESTREHEM ROAD at 3.45 PM. A snow storm rather spoiled the inspection but the parade was carried out in a determined fashion in a perfect blizzard.	
	26-2-16		Parades as before, musketry being the most important work done	
	27-2-16		Divine Services and inspections of Kits and mobilisation stores by Commanding Officer.	

8353 Wt. W2544/1454 700,000 5/15 D. D. & L. A.D.S.S./Forms/C. 2118.

21.

Army Form C. 2118.

Instructions regarding War Diaries and Intelligence Summaries are contained in F. S. Regs., Part II. and the Staff Manual respectively. Title pages will be prepared in manuscript.

WAR DIARY
or
INTELLIGENCE SUMMARY.

(Erase heading not required.)

Place	Date	Hour	Summary of Events and Information	Remarks and references to Appendices
FEBVIN PALFART	28.2.16		Parades as usual. B Coy returned from LAIRES	
St HILAIRE	29-2-16		The Battalion moved with the 47TH INF BDE to new billeting area. and billeted the night at ST HILAIRE moving next day to ANNEQUIN preliminary to going into the trenches. A draft of 1 NCO and 29 men joined the battalion this day.	
~~ANNEQUIN~~				
			MAJOR. G.F BROOKE left the battalion to take over command of the 9th ROYAL DUBLIN FUSILIERS on the 26-2-16.	

[signature] LIEUT. COLONEL,
COMDG. 6th (S) Bn. THE CONNAUGHT RANGERS.

$353 Wt. W2544/1454 700,000 5/15 D. D. & L. A.D.S.S./Forms/C. 2118.

Appendix III

6TH (S) BN. THE CONNAUGHT RANGERS.

*** **********

CASUALTIES FROM 1st TO 7th FEBRUARY, 1916, INCLUSIVE.

***** *********

		KILLED.		COY.	DATE.
6/3566	Pte.	Barr	H.	D.	3-2-16.
6/4600	"	Costello	J.	C.	5-2-16.
6/11139	"	Regan	M.	C.	5-2-16.
6/2609	"	Henry	M.	C.	5-2-16.
	Captain	Stritch	G.S.R.	C.	7-2-16.
6/3620	Pte.	McCormack	P.	C.	7-2-16.

DIED OF WOUNDS.

6/2364	Pte.	Canavan	J.P.	B.	3-2-16.
6/3780	"	Heaney	J.	C.	8-2-16.

[signature] ....LIEUT. COLONEL,

COMDG. 6th (S) Bn. THE CONNAUGHT RANGERS.

Appendix III

Acts of Distinguished Conduct by N.C.O.'s and men of 6th (S) Bn The Connaught Rangers between January 26th and February 8th 1916.

No 2281 Sergeant JAMES J. POLLOCK distinguished himself by fearless patrol work. On two occasions he got through the enemies wire and examined their saps. He has been recommended for the D.C.M. and been granted the Certificate for bravery of the G.O.C. 16TH DIV.

No 1571 Sergt JAMES MCMANUS and ~~Private~~ No 2343 Pte HENRY CASH of the Machine Gun Section by their devotion to duty and good example kept up the morale of their comrades during an intense bombardment by the Germans on the 27th January when the infantry on their flanks had withdrawn as the trenches had been badly damaged. Private CASH was sentry at one of the guns and as his periscope was damaged he had to expose himself unduly. When the Germans followed up their bombardment by an infantry attack Sergt MCMANUS so skilfully worked his guns that he helped very materially in driving back the enemy. They have

Appendix III
continued

both been recommended for honours.

No 3568 Corp DONAGH. (PATRICK. A.) and
No 2126 Private ~~EDWARD~~ PETER. F.W DUFFY signallers of D Coy volunteered to take a message through a heavy bombardment and succeeded in doing so They have been awarded the D.C.M. and the Certificate for bravery of the G.O.C 16TH DIV

No 6/3620 Private McCORMACK (PATRICK) volunteered to repair signallers wire during a heavy bombardment. He was Killed in doing so. He has been awarded Certificate for bravery of the G.O.C 16th Div

No 4729 Pte DANIEL HARKIN received the Certificate for bravery from the G.O.C 16TH DIV for his brave conduct during several days bombardment by the Germans.

Lieut ERIC EDGE BEATTY has been recommended for Honours for the way he managed his machine guns on the 27th. He practically held the line himself and beat back a German attack following an intense bombardment.

[signature] LIEUT. COLONEL,
COMDG. 6th (S) Bn. THE CONNAUGHT RANGERS

6th
Connaughts
Vol 3

16th Div

H.E.

22.
Army Form C. 2118.

Instructions regarding War Diaries and Intelligence Summaries are contained in F. S. Regs., Part II. and the Staff Manual respectively. Title pages will be prepared in manuscript.

WAR DIARY
~~or~~
~~INTELLIGENCE SUMMARY.~~
(Erase heading not required.)

6TH (S) Bn. THE CONNAUGHT RANGERS

Place	Date	Hour	Summary of Events and Information	Remarks and references to Appendices
ANNEQUIN FOSSE	1-3-16		The Battalion marched from ST HILAIRE and billeted the night of 1st - 2nd at ANNEQUIN FOSSE. Placed under orders of 36TH INF BDE	
"	2.3.16	7AM to 5PM.	A B + C Coys furnished carrying parties for 36TH INF BDE under orders of ROYAL ENGINEERS. D Coy moved to VERMELLES at 9 AM and took over billets and guards from the 8TH ROYAL FUSILIERS They supplied carrying parties to ROYAL ENGINEERS during the afternoon	
		11 PM	The Battalion was ordered to move up into the trenches in the HULLUCK SECTOR A Coy and D Coy were sent to reinforce the right of the 36TH INF BDE. A Coy in Reserve Trench SACKVILLE STREET and D Coy with one platoon in tees off GORDON STREET, one platoon in front line trench BIGGER WILLIE and two platoons in support in ANCHOR TRENCH.; both Companies under the orders of the 11TH MIDDLESEX REGT. B and C Companies were sent to reinforce the left of the 37TH INF BDE and moved into RESERVE TRENCH astride QUARRY ALLEY. both under orders of 7TH SUSSEX REGT. We had sprung five mines on the Germans at 5.45 PM on this date and the fight for the craters which we	

\#353 Wt. W2544/1454 700,000 5/15 D. D. & L. A.D.S.S./Forms/C. 2118.

Army Form C. 2118.

Instructions regarding War Diaries and Intelligence Summaries are contained in F. S. Regs., Part II. and the Staff Manual respectively. Title pages will be prepared in manuscript.

WAR DIARY

~~or~~

~~INTELLIGENCE SUMMARY.~~

(Erase heading not required.)

Place	Date	Hour	Summary of Events and Information	Remarks and references to Appendices
			occupied waxed fast and furious during the night of the 2nd 3rd MARCH B and C Companies were employed in carrying duties - principally grenades during that night.	
ANNEQUIN FOSSE	3-3-16		The Battalion Headquarters remained in ANNEQUIN FOSSE. At-noon A Coy took over line of trench from C Coy 11TH MIDDLESEX REGT from CLIFFORD ST to E end of BIGGER WILLIE. — ARCHWAY B Coy relieved A Coy of 7TH EAST SUSSEX in STICKEY TRENCH. QUARRY ALLEY and MUD TRENCH and NORTHAMPTON TRENCH between NORTHAMPTON TRENCH MUD TRENCH No 8 Platoon in reserve in and Nos 5 6 and 7 platoons holding the firing line from left to right respectively. The enemy renewed their attack on the craters on this night and bombers from B Coy were sent into the crater on their right to reinforce where they remained during the night and did good work, the Germans being beaten off after reaching our parapet, their trenches from the far lip of this crater being only fifteen yards away. C Coy remained in RESERVE TRENCH during the 3rd with	

#353 Wt. W2544/1454 700,000 5/15 D. D. & L. A.D.S.S./Forms/C. 2118.

2 3 [illegible]

Army Form C. 2118.

Instructions regarding War Diaries and Intelligence Summaries are contained in F. S. Regs., Part II. and the Staff Manual respectively. Title pages will be prepared in manuscript.

WAR DIARY
or
~~INTELLIGENCE SUMMARY.~~
(Erase heading not required.)

Place	Date	Hour	Summary of Events and Information	Remarks and references to Appendices
ANNEQUIN	3.3.16		one platoon thrown forward into NORTHAMPTON TRENCH astride GUILDFORD TRENCH. they were engaged in carrying duty during the day. D. Coy. took over from 11TH MIDDLESEX a line extending along ALEXANDRA TRENCH and KINK right on RIFLEMAN'S ALLEY left on ARCHWAY, The 11TH MIDDLESEX were relieved by 6TH BUFFS ~~under~~ whose orders D Coy came.	
"	4.3.16		The dispositions of the Companies were the same as on the previous day. Nothing unusual happened.	
	5.3.16.		A mine was blown up by us in front of A. Coy trenches and we occupied the near lip of the crater, the enemy making no attempt to attack. B Coy remained in the same trenches as on the 3rd and 4TH. C Coy were relieved and returned to billets in ANNEQUIN D Coy was relieved ~~in~~ the afternoon by 6TH QUEEN'S and returned to LANCASHIRE TRENCH with one platoon in JUNCTION KEEP. On this date the 36TH INF BDE was relieved by 37TH INF BDE under whose orders the Battalion now came	
	6.3.16.		A Coy had a German mine sprung on them at 8.45 A.M. burying	

8353 Wt. W2544/1454 700,000 5/15 D. D. & L. A.D.S.S./Forms/C. 2118.

25.

Army Form C. 2118.

Instructions regarding War Diaries and Intelligence Summaries are contained in F. S. Regs., Part II. and the Staff Manual respectively. Title pages will be prepared in manuscript.

WAR DIARY
or
~~INTELLIGENCE SUMMARY.~~

(Erase heading not required.)

Place	Date	Hour	Summary of Events and Information	Remarks and references to Appendices
ANNEQUIN FOSSE	6-3-16		nine of their men. Corp KEARNEY displayed great courage in helping to release those men all of whom were dug out and sent to hospital without any serious injuries. We sapped out to the lip of the crater and commanded it from the near lip.	
			A Coy was relieved at 12.30 P.M. by 6TH QUEENS and returned to RESERVE TRENCH — LANCASHIRE TRENCH	
			B Coy were relieved by 7TH EAST SURREY REGT and returned to billets in ANNEQUIN FOSSE.	
			C Coy provided carrying parties as before	
			D Coy. did likewise.	
	7-3-16		A + B Companies provided working and carrying parties for 37TH INF BDE. C Coy. under orders of 6TH BUFFS relieved 6TH QUEENS of front line trench BIGGER WILLIE and KAISERINE TRENCH on 6TH BUFFS being relieved they came under the orders of the 6TH WEST. KENTS.	
			D. Coy relieved the 6TH QUEENS in the same trenches as ~~they~~ held on the 3rd to 5TH and came under the orders of the 6TH WEST KENTS	

#353 Wt. W2544/1454 700,000 5/15 D. D. & L. A.D.S.S./Forms/C. 2118.

26.

Army Form C. 2118.

WAR DIARY
or
~~INTELLIGENCE SUMMARY.~~
(Erase heading not required.)

Instructions regarding War Diaries and Intelligence Summaries are contained in F. S. Regs., Part II. and the Staff Manual respectively. Title pages will be prepared in manuscript.

Place	Date	Hour	Summary of Events and Information	Remarks and references to Appendices
ANNEQUIN FOSSE	8.3.16		A + B contined to supply carrying parties. C + D held the trenches as indicated on the right of the 37TH INF BDE	
	9-3-16		As on the 8TH. Nothing unusual occurred.	
	10.3.16		A + B provided carrying parties and C + D Coys were relieved. A. C. + D returning to billets in ANNEQUIN FOSSE.	
			The casualties during the period 1st - 10TH were 10 killed 31 wounded and about 50 men sent to hospital suffering from exposure. Though our men were not severely tested under fire during this period they bore the extreme hardships of almost continuous fatigues through trenches in many places knee deep in mud and the long nights standing in that mud during cold wet and almost arctic weather with great fortitude and endurance.	Appendix 4 List of casualties 1st to 10th
			The reliefs in this sector were carried out during the day and there was none of the confusion which existed in the LOOS sector where reliefs were ~~made~~ carried out at night	

27

Army Form C. 2118.

Instructions regarding War Diaries and Intelligence Summaries are contained in F. S. Regs., Part II. and the Staff Manual respectively. Title pages will be prepared in manuscript.

WAR DIARY

~~or~~

~~INTELLIGENCE~~ SUMMARY.

(*Erase heading not required.*)

Place	Date	Hour	Summary of Events and Information	Remarks and references to Appendices
ANNEQUIN FOSSE	11-3-16		The Battalion marched to FOUQUEREUIL where it billeted for the night The men were in excellent spirits notwithstanding the hardships they endured during the proceeding ten days	
FOUQUEREUIL	12 3-16		The Battalion marched to ALLOUAGNE and billeted there.	
"	13 3-16		Inspections of kit and the men were rested A draft of 4 N.C.O.s and 56 men joined from the BASE. Classes of instruction were organised.	
"	~~14-3-16~~			
"	14-3-16		The Battalion bathed by Companies at FOSSE No 3. AUCHEL in the morning. In the afternoon. bombing and wiring was practised. and other parades were held.	
"	15/3/16		Drills and special classes.	
	16/3/16		As on 15/3/16	
	17/3/16		St PATRICK'S DAY. was celebrated by giving the men a	

#353 Wt. W2544/1454 700,000 5/15 D. D. & L. A.D.S.S./Forms/C. 2118.

Army Form C. 2118.

Instructions regarding War Diaries and Intelligence Summaries are contained in F. S. Regs., Part II. and the Staff Manual respectively. Title pages will be prepared in manuscript.

WAR DIARY
or
INTELLIGENCE SUMMARY.
(Erase heading not required.)

Place	Date	Hour	Summary of Events and Information	Remarks and references to Appendices
ALLOUAGNE	17/3/16		holiday. Brigade Sports, in which the Battalion had its due proportion of successes, were held in the afternoon and at night a successful Battalion concert was held. A draft of 21 men joined today.	
"	18/3/16		The Battalion practised the assault from trenches in the morning. In the afternoon classes and drills as usual	
"	19/3/16		Church Parades. Half the Battalion was employed in work under the Royal Engineers on the ALLOUAGNE - BURBURE road.	
"	20/3/16		Drill and classes as usual. special attention being given to bombing. it being the aim that every man in the battalion understands the mechanism of and is practised in throwing live grenades.	
	22/3/16		The Battalion parade for Assault practise had to be postponed	

29 Army Form C.2118.

Instructions regarding War Diaries and Intelligence Summaries are contained in F. S. Regs., Part II. and the Staff Manual respectively. Title pages will be prepared in manuscript.

WAR DIARY
or
INTELLIGENCE SUMMARY.
(Erase heading not required.)

Place	Date	Hour	Summary of Events and Information	Remarks and references to Appendices
ALLOUAGNE	20/3/16		on account of the weather. In the afternoon classes as usual	
"	21/3/16		Route march. Classes in the afternoon	
"	23/3/16		Drill under company arrangements	
"	24/3/16		Classes, especially bombing. The battalion has now all been excercised in throwing hand grenades.	
PHILOSOPHE	25/3/16		The battalion together with the rest of the Brigade took over PUITS No 14 BIS ~~right~~ sector of trenches from the 45TH INF BDE. The 6TH CONNAUGHT being in the battalion in brigade support with one (D Coy) company in PHILOSOPHE two A+B companies in 10TH AVENUE and one company C Coy in GUN TRENCH. The 6th ROYAL IRISH REGT were holding the right s sector from GORDON ALLEY to near RAILWAY ALLEY. The 7TH LEINSTERS from RAILWAY ALLEY to POSEN ALLEY and the	

2353 Wt. W2514/1454 700,000 5/15 D. D. & L. A.D.S.S./Forms/C.2118.

80

Army Form C. 2118.

Instructions regarding War Diaries and Intelligence Summaries are contained in F. S. Regs., Part II. and the Staff Manual respectively. Title pages will be prepared in manuscript.

WAR DIARY
or
INTELLIGENCE SUMMARY.
(Erase heading not required.)

Place	Date	Hour	Summary of Events and Information	Remarks and references to Appendices
PHILOSOPHE	25/3/16		8TH ROYAL MUNSTER FUSILIERS in Brigade Reserve at PHILOSOPHE. The relief of the 11TH A + S HIGHLANDERS was carried out without a hitch and was not interfered with by artillery fire	
	26/3/16		Same dispositions as on the 25th. The day was quiet and much good work in clearing up trenches and dug-outs was accomplished.	
	27/3/16		MAJOR BROOKE rejoined the battalion on this date. All quiet. The dispositions remained the same. A draft of 20 other ranks joined today	
	28/3/16		The battalion relieved the 6TH ROYAL IRISH REGIMENT in the right sub sector. D Company on the right of the line from GORDON ALLEY to midway between SCOTS ALLEY and ENGLISH ALLEY. A Coy from left of D Coy to 20 yards south of RAILWAY ALLEY	

2353 Wt. W2514/1454 700,000 5/15 D. D. & L. A.D.S.S./Forms/C. 2118.

31

Army Form C. 2118.

Instructions regarding War Diaries and Intelligence Summaries are contained in F. S. Regs., Part II. and the Staff Manual respectively. Title pages will be prepared in manuscript.

WAR DIARY
or
INTELLIGENCE SUMMARY.
(*Erase heading not required.*)

Place	Date	Hour	Summary of Events and Information	Remarks and references to Appendices
PHILOSOPHE	28/3/16		C Coy in support trenches and B Coy in RESERVE TRENCH. Battalion HeadQuarters were in LOOS. The situation was quiet and the relief satisfactory. The 2nd Royal MUNSTER FUSILIERS were on our right and the 7th LEINSTERS on our left.	
	29/3/16		Dispositions as on 28th. Only slight artillery and rifle grenade activity on both sides casualties slight. 2nd LIEUT SEMPLE and a draft of 65 other ranks joined on this date. nearly all from the reserve battalion	
	30/3/16		Dispositions remained unchanged. and the situation quiet. Our snipers had some successes.	
	31/3/16		The Battalion was relieved by the 8TH ROYAL IRISH FUSILIERS and returned to rest billets in NOEUX LES MINES. The relief worked smoothly. During our six days in the trenches there was little artillery activity on both sides	

2353 Wt. W2544/1454 700,000 5/15 D. D. & L. A.D.S.S./Forms/C. 2118.

32.

Army Form C. 2118.

WAR DIARY
or
INTELLIGENCE SUMMARY.
(*Erase heading not required.*)

Instructions regarding War Diaries and Intelligence Summaries are contained in F. S. Regs., Part II. and the Staff Manual respectively. Title pages will be prepared in manuscript.

Place	Date	Hour	Summary of Events and Information	Remarks and references to Appendices
PHILOSOPHE	31/3/16		but a good deal of rifle grenade and trench mortar activity. Casualties 2 killed and seven wounded.	
			Annexed is appendix of killed and wounded between 25-3-16 and 31-3-16.	Appendix V.
			It is apparent that some system of continuing work commenced by one battalion in the line should be adopted. At present the battalion taking over start work on their own judgment and do not in many case know of work being done or continue the work of their predecessors. Work is therefore often of a patchy nature when a battalion remains in the line only for a short time	

[signature] LIEUT. COLONEL
COMDG. 8th (S) Bn. THE ... [illegible]

2353 Wt. W2514/1454 700,000 5/15 D. D. & L. A.D.S.S./Forms/C. 2118.

APPENDIX IV

6TH (S) BN. THE CONNAUGHT RANGERS.

****

CASUALTIES IN ACTION.

****

	Reg.No.	Rank & Name.			Coy.	Date.
KILLED	4347	Pte.	Corbett	D.	B.	4-3-16.
	4122	"	Lavin	E.	A.	4-3-16.
	2248	"	Mallon	T.	A.	4-3-16.
	2386	"	McKinney	F.	B.	5-3-16.
	4640	"	Crawford	J.	A.	5-3-16.
	2314	"	Logan	J.	A.	5-3-16.
	1580	"	O'Hare	J.	D.	8-3-16.
	1393	L/C.	Carr	W.	D.	9-3-16.
	10563	"	Worth	J.	C.	9-3-16.
	4308	Pte.	McCrossan	F.	D.	10-3-16.
WOUNDED	2109	Pte.	Callanan	J.P.	D.	3-3-16.
	6503	"	Moores	J.	D.	3-3-16.
	3731	"	Darragh	T.	C.	4-3-16.
	5164	"	Mathews	J.	C.	4-3-16.
	3916	"	Kelly	P.	B.	4-3-16.
	4731	"	Dempsey	J.	B.	4-3-16.
	2336	"	Fogarty	R.	B.	4-3-16.
	4709	"	Davis	C.	B.	4-3-16.
	2590	"	Black	J.	A.	4-3-16.
	4607	"	Donnelly	J.	A.	4-3-16.
	4242	"	McCusker	H.	A.	4-3-16.
	2311	"	Rafferty	C.	A.	4-3-16.
	4156	"	Rogers	W.	D.	5-3-16.
	2351	"	McGuinness	J.	B.	5-3-16.
	4069	"	Shortt	A.	A.	5-3-16.
	4532	"	Craven	J.	B.	5-3-16.
	3924	"	Coughlan	J.	B.	5-3-16.
	5860	"	Malia	J.	A.	5-3-16.
	4171	"	Carden	C.	A.	6-3-16.
	4172	"	Conlon	J.	A.	6-3-16.
	3942	"	Gawley	P.	A.	6-3-16.
	4664	"	Keaney	P.	A.	6-3-16.
	4679	"	McLoughlin	T.	A.	6-3-16.
	4107	"	O'Brien	J.	A.	6-3-16.
	6529	"	Ralph	J.	A.	6-3-16.
	4485	"	Sweeney	P.	A.	6-3-16.
	3607	"	Kearney	P.	A.	6-3-16.
	4657	"	Shaw	G.	A.	6-3-16.
	4585	"	Kennedy	J.	B.	7-3-16.
	3658	Sgt.	O'Donovan	D.J.	C.	8-3-16.
	3560	Pte.	McKenna	J.	C.	9-3-16.
ACCIDENTAL (S.I.)	4669	Pte.	Brown	J.	B.	5-3-16.

[illegible signature] Lieut. Colonel.
Commdg. 6th (S) Bn. The Conn. Rangers.

APPENDIX V

6TH (S) BN. THE CONNAUGHT RANGERS.
****

C A S U A L T I E S.
****

Reg.No.	Rank & Name.			Casualty.	Date.
6/2411	Pte.	Burns	J.	KILLED in action.	25-3-16.
6/2329	"	Runaghan	J.	" " "	28-3-16.
6/3621	C.S.M.	Johnston	J.	WOUNDED in action	29-3-16.
3/3100	L/Cpl.	Swinburn	W.	" " "	29-3-16.
6/2759	Pte.	Rush	J.	" " "	29-3-16.
6/3677	"	Ryan	J.	" " "	29-3-16.
6/4608	"	McCarthy	C.	" " "	30-3-16.
6/3940	"	Brown	J.	" " "	30-3-16.
6/1507	"	Brogan	J.	" " "	31-3-16.

Lieut. Colonel.
Commdg. 6th (S) Bn. The Conn. Rangers.

3rd April, 1916.

To

Officer i/c A. G. Office.

Base.

Herewith War Diary of this Battalion for the month of April.

G. F. Brooke

Major

Comm'g. 6th Conn. Rang.

4 - 5 - 16.

XVI 33

Army Form C. 2118.

Instructions regarding War Diaries and Intelligence Summaries are contained in F. S. Regs., Part II. and the Staff Manual respectively. Title pages will be prepared in manuscript.

WAR DIARY ~~or~~ ~~INTELLIGENCE~~ SUMMARY.

(*Erase heading not required.*)

6TH (S) Bn. THE CONNAUGHT RANGERS

Vol. 4

Place	Date	Hour	Summary of Events and Information	Remarks and references to Appendices
NOEUX LES MINES	1/4/16		Kit inspections. Men were rested. Classes of instruction were organized.	
"	2/4/16		CAPT. R. J. TAMPLIN proceeded to AIRE on Artillery Course. Classes paraded for instruction in Grenades, Wiring, Sniping. The battalion bathed by companies. Steady Drill and Handling of arms were practiced.	
"	3/4/16		Drill and Special classes	
"	4/4/16		Drill and Special classes. C.O. and Company Commanders proceeded to PHILOSOPHE to reconnoitre trenches in HULLUCH [RIGHT] sector.	
"	5/4/16		Special Classes. Companies were occupied in making preparations for move into trenches.	
HULLUCH [RIGHT] SECTOR	6/4/16		Took over from 8th R.D.F. in front line. Relief was timed to commence at 3.30 p.m. but was delayed one hour owing to heavy hostile bombardment taking place. We found that the trenches were slightly damaged. This damage was repaired by us during the night. DISTRIBUTION – Front line from POSEN ALLEY to HOLLY LANE held by 'B' Coy. on the RIGHT and 'C' Coy on the LEFT. 'D' Coy occupied SUPPORT LINE from HOLLY LANE to	5.E

T2134. Wt. W708–776. 500000. 4/15. Sir J. C. & S.

Instructions regarding War Diaries and Intelligence Summaries are contained in F. S. Regs., Part II. and the Staff Manual respectively. Title pages will be prepared in manuscript.

34

Army Form C. 2118.

WAR DIARY or INTELLIGENCE SUMMARY.

6TH (S) Bn. THE CONNAUGHT RANGERS

(Erase heading not required.)

Place	Date	Hour	Summary of Events and Information	Remarks and references to Appendices
			POSEN ALLEY. 'A' COY occupied RESERVE TRENCH from POSEN ALLEY to VENDIN ALLEY. Much work was done during the night at repairing trenches. There were a few casualties during the night from Rifle Grenades.	
HULLUCH [RIGHT] SECTOR	7/4/16		Distribution same as previous day. Some slight activity on both sides with Rifle Grenades and artillery, otherwise a very quiet day.	
"	8/4/16		Much work done during previous night at cleaning up trenches, building shelters behind traverses, and revetting broken portions of parapet. Quiet day. Slight Rifle Grenade activity. CAPT TAMPLIN rejoined the BN, on conclusion of Artillery Course at AIRE.	
"	9/4/16		Slight intermittent hostile shelling throughout early portion of the day. Relieved by 6th ROYAL IRISH RGT. at 4 P.M. Proceeded to Billets in PHILOSOPHE. Draft of 30 all ranks joined.	
PHILOSOPHE	10/4/16		Inspections of Kit, trench Stores &c. Working and Carrying Parties at night. C.O. inspected draft.	
	11/4/16		CAPT TAMPLIN and 9 O.R. proceeded on Leave. Working and Carrying parties during the night.	

Army Form C. 2118.

Instructions regarding War Diaries and Intelligence Summaries are contained in F. S. Regs., Part II. and the Staff Manual respectively. Title pages will be prepared in manuscript.

WAR DIARY or ~~INTELLIGENCE SUMMARY.~~ 6TH (S) Bn THE CONNAUGHT RANGERS

(*Erase heading not required.*)

Place	Date	Hour	Summary of Events and Information	Remarks and references to Appendices
PHILOSOPHE	12/4/16		C.O. and Representatives from All Coys. proceeded to reconnoitre portion of line, which we are to take over from 7th LEINSTERS to-morrow. Supplied several Working + Carrying Parties during the night.	
HULLUCH SECTION [SUPPORT]	13/4/16		Moved up to SUPPORT Position in 10th AVENUE and relieved 7th LEINSTERS. 'C' COY in RESERVE TRENCH with their RIGHT on VENDIN ALLEY: 'D' Coy. in 10th AV. from STONE STREET to WINGSWAY: 'A' COY in 10th AV. from WINGSWAY to VENDIN ALLEY: 'B' COY. in 10th AV. from VENDIN ALLEY to POSEN ALLEY. Practically the whole Bn. was out on Working and Carrying Parties day and night.	
"	14/4/16		Trenches cleaned up during the day. Working and Carrying parties same as previous day. Draft of 46 O.R. joined from Base.	
"	15/4/16		Very quiet day. Working and carrying parties same as 13th inst.	
HULLUCH [RIGHT] SECTOR.	16/4/16		Relieved 6th ROYAL IRISH RGT. in HULLUCH [RIGHT] SECTOR. Distribution 'C' Coy in RESERVE TRENCH from VENDIN ALLEY to POSEN ALLEY. 'B', 'A' and 'D' Coys in front line finding their own supports. 'B' Coy. from POSEN ALLEY to TREE LANE: 'A' Coy. from TREE LANE to Point half way between	

T2134. Wt. W708–776. 500000. 4/15. Sir J. C. & S.

Army Form C. 2118.

Instructions regarding War Diaries and Intelligence Summaries are contained in F. S. Regs., Part II. and the Staff Manual respectively. Title pages will be prepared in manuscript.

WAR DIARY or INTELLIGENCE SUMMARY. 6TH (S) Bn. THE CONNAUGHT RANGERS

(Erase heading not required.)

Place	Date	Hour	Summary of Events and Information	Remarks and references to Appendices
			VENDIN ALLEY and QUEENSWAY: 'D' Coy. from HOLLY LANE to LEFT of 'A' COY. Afternoon and night quiet except for slight Rifle Grenade activity.	
HULLUCH [RIGHT]	17/4/16		Quiet day. Trenches slightly damaged after dusk by hostile shelling.	
SECTOR.	18/4/16		Slight Rifle Grenade and Artillery Activity on both sides throughout the day.	
		10 P.M.	Heavy bombardment on front line for half an hour. Enemy sent over many rifle grenades and aerial torpedoes. We retaliated effectively. CAPT. N. J. WICKHAM killed. CAPT TAMPLIN rejoined having been recalled from leave.	
	19/4/16		Fairly quiet day. Usual Rifle Grenade activity. A few casualties occurred.	
	20/4/16		Relieved by 7th INNISKILLING FUSILIERS about 1 p.m. Proceeded to Rest Billets in MAZINGARBE.	
MAZINGARBE	21/4/16		The battalion was billeted in huts in L 22. d. Sheet 36 B N.E.	

T2134. Wt. W708–776. 500000. 4/15. Sir J. C. & S.

Army Form C. 2118.

Instructions regarding War Diaries and Intelligence Summaries are contained in F. S. Regs., Part II. and the Staff Manual respectively. Title pages will be prepared in manuscript.

WAR DIARY of 6TH (S) Bn THE CONNAUGHT RANGERS INTELLIGENCE SUMMARY.

(Erase heading not required.)

Place	Date	Hour	Summary of Events and Information	Remarks and references to Appendices
MAZINGARBE	21/4/16		A party of 2 Officers and 80 O.R. were attached to R.E. 12TH DIVISION at VERMELLES. Special classes of snipers, bombers, wirers, and rifle grenades were formed and working parties to the number of about 100 men were sent daily for work in the support, reserve, and communication trenches.	
"	22/4/16		Special classes got in some useful instruction.	
"	23/4/16 to 26/4/16		Classes and working parties as on 21st and 22nd.	
"	27/4/16		At 5 A.M. the enemy lanched an attack accompanied by gas against the 48th and 49TH BRIGADES in the PUITS 14 BIS sector. The gas was very slightly felt by our men in huts. The enemy bombarded our huts from 5 A.M. to 7.30 AM and got some direct hits. Our casualties were 3 killed and 20 wounded (Appendix ~~No.~~ annexed). The battalion stood to arms all day but were not called on as the enemy was soon driven out and ~~our~~ line was held intact	Appendix No VI Casualties on 27/4/16
"	28/4/16		The relief orded for the 28/29th April had to be postponed	

T2134. Wt. W708—776. 500000. 4/15. Sir J. C. & S.

Instructions regarding War Diaries and Intelligence Summaries are contained in F. S. Regs., Part II. and the Staff Manual respectively. Title pages will be prepared in manuscript.

WAR DIARY
or
INTELLIGENCE SUMMARY.
(Erase heading not required.)

6TH (S) Bn THE CONNAUGHT RANGERS

Army Form C. 2118.

Place	Date	Hour	Summary of Events and Information	Remarks and references to Appendices
MAZINGARBE	28/4/16		on account of the attack on the 27th some of the communication trenches requiring repair. Advance parties to take over from the 9TH DUBLIN FUSILIERS ~~in~~ 10TH AVENUE PUITS 14 BIS sector proceeded to the trenches at 3 P.M.	
10TH AVENUE [illegible]	29/4/16		The Battalion relieved the 9TH ROYAL DUBLIN FUSILIERS in 10TH AVENUE PUITS 14 BIS SECTOR. in Brigade support. The 6TH ROYAL IRISH on our right in the front line trenches and the 8TH MUNSTERS on our left in the front line trenches. The enemy had released gas against our left ~~sub~~-section in the morning about 5 A.M. and many of the 8TH DUBLINS and the 8TH IRISH FUSILIERS were gassed. Some of our machine gunners were also caught in this gas attack and LIEUT E.E. BEATTY died from the effects of gas poisoning. Three of his machine gun section died, and five were gassed more or less seriously. The enemy were reported massing for an attack behind their lines but a sudden change	

39

Army Form C. 2118.

WAR DIARY 6TH S. Bn. The Connaught Rangers
or
~~INTELLIGENCE SUMMARY.~~
(Erase heading not required.)

Instructions regarding War Diaries and Intelligence Summaries are contained in F. S. Regs., Part II. and the Staff Manual respectively. Title pages will be prepared in manuscript.

Place	Date	Hour	Summary of Events and Information	Remarks and references to Appendices
10TH AVENUE	29/4/16.		in the wind sent the gas back on these troops which were seen to leave their trenches hurridly and were badly punished by our artillery in doing so. Their infantry attack was not made and to judge from the number of motor ambulances hastily sent forward their losses were serious.	
"	~~30/4/16~~		From enquiries made amongst casualties it appears certain that the P.H. Gas Helmets supplied to our troops were effective protection against the German Gas and that casualties occurred through carelessness in use or adjustment of the helmets.	
"	30/4/16		There were two gas alarms which proved false. The battalion supplied working and carrying parties for the 47TH INF BDE and the day was quiet. Lieut. Col LENOX CONYNGHAM proceeded on leave and MAJOR G F BROOKE assumed temporary command of the battalion	

G. F. Brooke Major
Commanding 6TH (S) Bn. The Connaught Rangers

2353 Wt. W2544/1454 700,000 5/15 D. D. & L. A.D.S.S./Forms/C. 2118.

APPENDIX No VI.

6TH (S) BN. THE CONNAUGHT RANGERS.

CASUALTIES 27-4-16.

KILLED.	1629	L/C.	Monk	J.	C. Coy.
	3421	Pte.	Duane	M.	B. "
	4259	"	Reynolds	D.	B. "
WOUNDED.	1092	Sgt.	Fitzharris	J.	B. Coy.
	1469	"	Charles	T.	D. "
	4392	Pte.	Doran	J.	B. "
	4326	"	McCann	J.	B. "
	6392	"	Murphy	W.	B. "
	2630	"	Sharkey	J.	B. "
	6117	"	Veale	D.	B. "
	5522	C.Q.M.S.	Poole	J.	B. "
	2024	Pte.	Gallagher	P.	A. "
	3630	"	McGowan	F.	A. "
	4436	"	Murphy	J.	C. "
	4142	"	Hayden	P.	C. "
	4606	"	Clarke	A.	C. "
	1457	"	Brogan	W.	D. "
	10686	"	Burke	W.	D. "
	2127	"	Dunne	P.	D. "
	6839	"	Fannon	J.	D. "
	6733	"	Tate	J.	D. "
	1586	"	Robertson	A.	D. "
	4123	"	Coyle	J.	D. "

E.F. Brooke Major

~~Lieut. Colonel.~~

Commdg. 6th (S) Bn. The Conn. Rangers.

28-4-16.

40.

Army Form C. 2118.

Instructions regarding War Diaries and Intelligence Summaries are contained in F. S. Regs., Part II, and the Staff Manual respectively. Title pages will be prepared in manuscript.

WAR DIARY

~~INTELLIGENCE SUMMARY~~ of 6th (S) Bn. THE CONNAUGHT RANGERS

(Erase heading not required.)

XVI Vol 5

Place	Date	Hour	Summary of Events and Information	Remarks and references to Appendices
10th AVENUE	1/5/16		Gas alarms, always false, and working parties to the front trenches continued to be the fashion during our stay in 10TH AVENUE. Deep latrines of the French type, from 10' to 15 feet deep were made for the summer months; it having been found that this type well covered in was not so popular with flies as the bucket system. The enemy was quiet on our front	
"	2/5/16 & 3/5/16		Trench maintenance and working parties supplied to front line trenches. A draft of 30 men joined on 2/5/16	
LOOS	4/5/16		On the night of the 3/4th the Battalion relieved the 6TH ROYAL IRISH REGIMENT in the right sub-section of the PUITS 14TH BIS sector. Our right on GORDON ALLEY or left just S of RAILWAY ALLEY. The Companies from Right to left in front line trench were A ~~B~~ D with ~~B~~ C in RESERVE TRENCH. The 8TH MUNSTERS were on our left and the 5TH NORTHANTS on our right. The enemy was very active during the four days we remained in	

41

Instructions regarding War Diaries and Intelligence Summaries are contained in F. S. Regs., Part II. and the Staff Manual respectively. Title pages will be prepared in manuscript.

WAR DIARY
or
INTELLIGENCE SUMMARY.
(Erase heading not required.)

Army Form C. 2118.

Place	Date	Hour	Summary of Events and Information	Remarks and references to Appendices
LOOS		4/5/16	this sub-sector. the right of our line in front of GORDON ALLEY and SCOTS ALLEY coming in for a lot of attention. Gas alarms still continued, and it was thought that the enemy had started some of our many false ones.	
"		5/5/16	Our companies in the front line trenches were almost fully occupied in keeping those very bad old trenches which were daily knocked about with Artillery in repair. LOOS received its daily shelling but little damage was done. GORDON CRATER a small crater midway between our lines and the GERMAN lines gave some anxiety but it was patrolled on the night of the 4/5TH and again on the night of the 5th 6th and found to be unoccupied by the enemy. It was too ~~far out~~ small and too ~~small~~ far out from our lines to make it worth while sapping out to it. The BOSH wired his side of it lightly and we patrolled it constantly, and so the matter ended	
"		6/5/16	The usual daily shelling continued. The enemy, showing a	

T2134. Wt. W708—776. 500000. 4/15. Sir J. C. & S.

42.

Army Form C. 2118.

Instructions regarding War Diaries and Intelligence Summaries are contained in F. S. Regs., Part II. and the Staff Manual respectively. Title pages will be prepared in manuscript.

WAR DIARY
or
INTELLIGENCE SUMMARY.
(Erase heading not required.)

Place	Date	Hour	Summary of Events and Information	Remarks and references to Appendices
LOOS		6/5/16	very decided readiness to use more shells than our artillery who were on short rations, had certainly the best of the argument in these exchanges with the result that trench mortar and rifle grenade enterprise on our behalf was not as enthusiastic as it might have been. the enemy being always ready to employ heavier ammunition than us.	
"	"	7/5/16	The wire on our front was very bad and we were making every effort to get up an effective obstacle in front of our trenches. bright moonlight and the nearness of the opposing lines being deterrent factors. Today some useful shooting with one of our Howitzers was done at an old house at ~~H~~ 31 D 5. 3½ where a machine gun gave some trouble. Our Medium Trench Mortar battery also began to justify its existence on this date	
"	"	[illegible]/5/16	On our left we had a lively exchange of rifle grenades, whizzbang shrapnel and trench mortars. Our casualties were very slight and we could with safty claim to have had the best of the show.	
			During these last four days the absolute	

8353 Wt. W2544/1454 700,000 5/15 D. D. & L. A.D.S.S./Forms/C. 2118.

43

Army Form C. 2118.

Instructions regarding War Diaries and Intelligence Summaries are contained in F. S. Regs., Part II. and the Staff Manual respectively. Title pages will be prepared in manuscript.

WAR DIARY
or
INTELLIGENCE SUMMARY.
(Erase heading not required.)

Place	Date	Hour	Summary of Events and Information	Remarks and references to Appendices
LOOS		7/3/16	necessity for a more thorough organisation of our work was very apparent. Continuity of work is often neglected and work started by one unit in the line is promptly treated with scorn by the unit taking over and allowed to remain in a half finished condition and sometimes undone. e.g. Our left company with much time and labour made a deep latrine but before it was properly covered over and seated a mining party filled it up again with evacuated sandbags from a listening post. Again the infantry without proper skilled supervision started deep dug-outs, and much time and material was wasted, as the next unit taking over had but little faith in the soundness of the work of their predecessors and refrained from continuing their labours.	
10TH AVENUE		8/3/16	We were relieved by the 6TH ROYAL IRISH. ~~The 8th Munsters~~ The relief was the smoothest and quickest yet experienced, taking only 2½ hours. 10TH AVENUE proved the haven of rest and peace	

2353 Wt. W2514/1454 700,000 5/15 D. D. & L. A.D.S.S./Forms/C. 2118.

44

Army Form C. 2118.

Instructions regarding War Diaries and Intelligence Summaries are contained in F. S. Regs., Part II. and the Staff Manual respectively. Title pages will be prepared in manuscript.

WAR DIARY
or
INTELLIGENCE SUMMARY.
(Erase heading not required.)

Place	Date	Hour	Summary of Events and Information	Remarks and references to Appendices
10TH AVENUE		8/3/16	it usually is. About 300 men for working and carrying parties for battalions in front line and for R.E. were supplied nightly	
		9/3/16 10/3/16 11/3/16	during the 9TH, 10TH and 11TH and the usual trench maintenance work continued during those days. A draft of 26 men joined on 10/5/16.	
LOOS		12/3/16	On the night of the 12th–13TH we relieved the 6TH ROYAL IRISH in the PUITS 14 BIS sector our dispositions being the same as on the 4TH except that B was in RESERVE TR and C in the centre of our line. On this date the enemy displayed unusual artillery activity which was spread along our front support and reserve trenches. Our artillery reply was feeble. the difference being that the enemy was lavish in his use of all types of ammunition from whizzbangs to 5.9s whereas we were parsimoneous in our use of 18 pounders and negligible	

8353 Wt. W2544/1454 700,000 5/15 D. D. & L. A.D.S.S./Forms/C. 2118.

Army Form C. 2118.

Instructions regarding War Diaries and Intelligence Summaries are contained in F. S. Regs., Part II. and the Staff Manual respectively. Title pages will be prepared in manuscript.

WAR DIARY
or
~~INTELLIGENCE SUMMARY.~~
(Erase heading not required.)

Place	Date	Hour	Summary of Events and Information	Remarks and references to Appendices
LOOS		12/5/16	in anything else. Our casualties were considering everything extremely slight. but it was demonstrated that without artillery support other arms of trench warfare, viz rifles, rifle grenades, hand grenades and trench mortars are of little use, or rather can be but little used.	
LOOS		13/5/16	A somewhat similar day to the 13TH our weak artillery reply crippling our efforts of maintaining an equal fight. The 7TH LEINSTERS are now on our left.	
		14/5/16	There was bright moonlight during the night of the 13/14TH but nevertheless every effort was made to get some wiring of our front done. The morning was normal but at 6 P.M in the evening the enemy begun shelling our front and support trenches. The bombardment increased in	

Army Form C. 2118.

Instructions regarding War Diaries and Intelligence Summaries are contained in F. S. Regs., Part II. and the Staff Manual respectively. Title pages will be prepared in manuscript.

WAR DIARY
or
INTELLIGENCE SUMMARY.
(Erase heading not required.)

Place	Date	Hour	Summary of Events and Information	Remarks and references to Appendices
LOOS		14/5/16	intensity until 8.50 P.M. when the bombardment on our right company might be described as intense. Our artillery reply on this occasion was slow in coming but was effective as guns of heavier calibre than the usual 18 pdrs were employed and the shooting was accurate, more accurate than that of the enemy, even though we had a more difficult target. which proves that with a plentiful supply of ammunition our artillery is as good as the best. Our Trench mortars were enabled to join in the straff and did some useful work. Our men expected the enemy to attack after this bombardment but they did not leave their trenches much to the disappointment of our men whose fighting spirit is now of the highest degree	
		15/5/16	Much useful wiring was done this night by our three companies in the front line trench. The day was quiet	

2353 Wt. W2544/1454 700,000 5/15 D. D. & L. A.D.S.S./Forms/C. 2118.

Army Form C. 2118.

Instructions regarding War Diaries and Intelligence Summaries are contained in F. S. Regs., Part II. and the Staff Manual respectively. Title pages will be prepared in manuscript.

WAR DIARY
or
~~INTELLIGENCE SUMMARY.~~
(Erase heading not required.)

Place	Date	Hour	Summary of Events and Information	Remarks and references to Appendices
LOOS		16/5/16	This day passed off quietly, comparatively speaking, we having a few casualties from rifle grenades. On the night of the 16TH - 17TH the 48TH INF BDE relieved the troops of the 47TH INF BDE north of ENGLISH ALLEY which now became the Brigade boundary. This liberated our D Coy and three platoons of B Coy who were relieved by B and A Companies respectively of the 7TH ROYAL IRISH RIFLES. Our relieved men proceeded to billets in NOEUX LES MINES	
		17/5/16	This also proved to be a comparatively quiet day and the remainder of the battalion viz C+A Coys and 1 platoon of D Coy were relieved and joined D Coy in NOEUX LES MINES. A draft of 29 men and one officer 2nd LIEUT. J. J. DILLON joined today	
NOEUX LES MINES		18/5/16	The day was spent in rest and cleaning up after	

2353 Wt. W2544/1454 700,000 5/15 D. D. & L. A.D.S.S./Forms/C. 2118.

48

Army Form C. 2118.

Instructions regarding War Diaries and Intelligence Summaries are contained in F. S. Regs., Part II. and the Staff Manual respectively. Title pages will be prepared in manuscript.

WAR DIARY
or
INTELLIGENCE SUMMARY.
(Erase heading not required.)

Place	Date	Hour	Summary of Events and Information	Remarks and references to Appendices
NOEUX LES MINES	18/5/16		eighteen days in the trenches. Special wiring, bombing, sniping, stretcher bearer and signalling classes were formed.	
do.	19/5/16		The musketry range near the Distillery was used by all companies and the men were practised in the new method of wearing and adjusting the gas helmets. The helmet being pinned to the shirt in such a position that it could immediately be slipped over the head without undoing the pins and at the same time when not required it was under the coat in its own waterproof covering and not exposed to the action of the air: — a great improvement on the old method of wearing it rolled up on the head during the "gas alert" period	
do.	20/5/16		Baths were arranged for the men; classes as on the 19/5/16	

2353 Wt. W2544/1454 700,000 5/15 D. D. & L. A.D.S.S./Forms/C. 2118.

4[?] Army Form C. 2118.

Instructions regarding War Diaries and Intelligence Summaries are contained in F. S. Regs., Part II. and the Staff Manual respectively. Title pages will be prepared in manuscript.

WAR DIARY
or
INTELLIGENCE SUMMARY.
(Erase heading not required.)

Place	Date	Hour	Summary of Events and Information	Remarks and references to Appendices
NOEUX LES MINES	20/5/16		A careful inspection of all equipment and stores was made by the Commanding Officer.	
"	21/5/16		Divine Service in the morning. In the afternoon there was a lecture and demonstration on Gas and in the use of incendiary and smoke bombs. NOEUX LES MINES was shelled by the enemy three shells bursting amongst the billets doing considerable damage, there being eleven casualties in the Battalion all wounded, some civilians were killed.	
do	22/5/16		A careful inspection of all rifles was made by the Divisional armourers. Classes were as usual.	
do	23/5/16		Two hundred men of the battalion attended a Gas demonstration at the Divisional Gas School VERQUIN. The usual classes were paraded also Company parades for arms drill and general smartening up.	

2353 Wt. W2514/1454 700,000 5/15 D. D. & L. A.D.S.S./Forms/C. 2118.

50

Instructions regarding War Diaries and Intelligence Summaries are contained in F. S. Regs., Part II. and the Staff Manual respectively. Title pages will be prepared in manuscript.

WAR DIARY
or
INTELLIGENCE SUMMARY.
(Erase heading not required.)

Army Form C. 2118.

Place	Date	Hour	Summary of Events and Information	Remarks and references to Appendices
NOEUX LES MINES	24/5/16.		Classes as usual. The weather is now warm and nearly all parades are in shirt sleeves. the men are very fit	
"	25/5/16		The 47TH INF BDE relieved the 48TH INF BDE in the PUITS 14 BIS SECTION on the night of the 25/26TH As this Battalion was going into BRIGADE Support into 10TH AVENUE it moved by daylight marching off at 8 30 A.M the move being complete by 2 P.M. A Coy was pushed forward into GUN TRENCH D Coy on the right in 10TH AVENUE holding 65 METRE POINT REDOUBT with one platoon the other three platoons along 10TH AVENUE to junction with NORTHERN UP. B Coy was in the centre to NORTHERN SAP REDOUBT holding that with one platoon also. C Coy on the left extending to VENDIN ALLEY. The relief passed off without incident Holding our front ~~on~~ the right was the 6TH ROYAL IRISH ~~on~~ the left the 8TH MUNSTERS. The 49TH BRIGADE was on our right in the LOOS SECTION. The boundaries of the 14 BIS SECTION now stand ~~RAILWAY~~ ENGLISH ALLEY on the SOUTH VENDIN ALLEY	

353 Wt. W2544/1454 700,000 5/15 D. D. & L. A.D.S.S./Forms/C. 2118.

51. Army Form C. 2118.

Instructions regarding War Diaries and Intelligence Summaries are contained in F. S. Regs., Part II. and the Staff Manual respectively. Title pages will be prepared in manuscript.

WAR DIARY
or
INTELLIGENCE SUMMARY.
(Erase heading not required.)

Place	Date	Hour	Summary of Events and Information	Remarks and references to Appendices
			on the North. being sub-divided into right and left sub-sections ~~Adj~~. Boyau 60. A draft of fourteen men joined today	
10TH AVENUE	26/5/16.		Working and carrying parties were supplied ~~to~~ the battalions in the front.	
do	27/5/16		As an attack by the enemy in force was anticipated C Coy was pushed forward to RESERVE TRENCH under the command of the 8TH ROYAL MUNSTER FUSILIERS and three platoons of D Coy into MEATH TRENCH under command of the 6TH ROYAL IRISH. their places being taken respectively by two companies of the 7TH LEINSTERS moved up from PHILOSOPHE. No attack came as anticipated	
"	28/5/16		A quiet day but the enemy was reported to be very active in transport behind their lines whether this was the withdrawal of troops or the moving up of troops was not clearly established but air reconnaisance reported the enemies trenches to be strongly held	
In the trenches	29/5/16		We relieved the 6TH ROYAL IRISH in the right sub sector, the	

Army Form C. 2118.

WAR DIARY
or
INTELLIGENCE SUMMARY.
(Erase heading not required.)

Instructions regarding War Diaries and Intelligence Summaries are contained in F. S. Regs., Part II. and the Staff Manual respectively. Title pages will be prepared in manuscript.

Place	Date	Hour	Summary of Events and Information	Remarks and references to Appendices
In the trenches	29/5/16		dispositions being A Coy in RESERVE TRENCH with one platoon in MEATH TRENCH and one platoon in FOREST TRENCH. D Coy on our right from RAILWAY ALLEY to BOYAU 51 B Coy from BOYAU 51 to BOYAU 54. C Coy from BOYAU 54 to BOYAU 60. 2nd LIEUT D MATTHEWS was killed by a heavy trench mortar. The enemy was doing much damage to our front and support lines with their minenwerfer three of whom were located. When we took over we found a sad mess, the ROYAL IRISH being unable to cope with the damage done to their trenches. We set to work and succeeded in clearing up to a certain extent on the night of the 29/30.	
	30/5/16		On this day the enemy renewed their bombardment with their heavy trench mortars which did great damage to our trenches but our casualties were slight as special sentries were placed to warn men of the approach of the slow moving but effectively powerful explosives. During the night of the 30/31st every available man was employed in repairing the damage with tolerable success. The communication trenches	

2353 Wt. W2544/1454 700,000 5/15 D. D. & L. A.D.S.S./Forms/C. 2118.

Instructions regarding War Diaries and Intelligence Summaries are contained in F. S. Regs., Part II. and the Staff Manual respectively. Title pages will be prepared in manuscript.

WAR DIARY
or
INTELLIGENCE SUMMARY.
(Erase heading not required.)

53 Army Form C. 2118.

Place	Date	Hour	Summary of Events and Information	Remarks and references to Appendices
In the trenches	30/5/16		POSEN ALLEY and CHALKPIT ALLEY were shelled and blocked in several places this damage was also repaired during the night. The close attention of our artillery had a subduing influence on the enemies activities	
"	31/5/16		Early in the morning of this day the battalion suffered a great loss in the death of LIEUT T K OBRIEN who was shot by a sniper. ~~His~~ intelligence and sniping officer he had rendered invaluable service since the arrival of the battalion at the front; ~~and~~ he was ever ready for any job however ~~risky~~ when duty called him. and it was a lucky bullet indeed for the enemy that cut short his exceedingly promising military career, and an unlucky one for us.	
			The day passed quietly and ~~extra~~ ammunition and a supply of trench emergency rations were draw and deposited in suitable stores along our lines, extra machine guns had been placed along the Reserve lines and we were quite ready for any attentions the enemy should choose to pay us He refrained from doing so, and showed his good sense	
			The feverish haste with which ammunition	

2353 Wt. W2544/1454 700,000 5/15 D. D. & L. A.D.S.S./Forms/C. 2118.

54 Army Form C. 2118.

Instructions regarding War Diaries and Intelligence Summaries are contained in F. S. Regs., Part II. and the Staff Manual respectively. Title pages will be prepared in manuscript.

WAR DIARY
or
INTELLIGENCE SUMMARY.
(Erase heading not required.)

Place	Date	Hour	Summary of Events and Information	Remarks and references to Appendices
In the trenches	31/5/16.		food and machine guns were thrown into the lines when an attack was anticipated would suggest that sufficient attention had not been paid to these details in normal times. Water was not supplied though it is the first necessity of life and if food is to be stored for emergencies in the trenches it is equally important that a supply of water should also be at hand if continued fighting is to be maintained when supplies are temporarily interfered with in the rear and prevented from being brought up in the daily regular fashion	
			Annexed is a list of casualties during month and	Appendix VII
			also of honours gained for conspicuous acts of courage	Appendix VIII

[signature]
Comdg. 6th (S) Bn. [illegible]

Appendix VII

6TH (S) BN. THE CONNAUGHT RANGERS.

****

CASUALTIES.

****

	No.	Rank & Name.		Initials	Coy.	Date.
KILLED.		Lieut.	O'Brien	T.K.		31-5-16.
		2/Lieut.	Matthews	D.		29-5-16.
	6/2341	Pte.	Healy	M.P.	B. Coy.	4-5-16.
	6/2368	"	Lyons	J.	B. "	4-5-16.
	6/4602	"	Hynes	P.	C. "	4-5-16.
	6/2759	"	Rush	J.	A. "	5-5-16.
	3/6191	"	Connor	B.	A. "	5-5-16.
	6/1349	"	Reilly	T.	D. "	8-5-16.
	6/4215	L/C.	Lyons	T.	A. "	13-5-16.
	6/4224	Pte.	Byrne	D.	C. "	13-5-16.
	6 4627	"	Naughton	J.	A. "	14-5-16.
	6 2813	"	Campbell	G.	B. "	15-5-16.
	4930	"	Handcock	J.	B. "	15-5-16.
	~~3/3959~~	~~"~~	~~Byrne~~	~~E.~~	~~A. "~~	~~15-5-16.~~
	6/2868	"	Hughes	E.	C. "	17-5-16.
	6/4442	"	O'Dowd	J.	C. "	17-5-16.
	4/5911	"	Williams	C.	D. "	30-5-16.
	6/2112	"	Cassidy	J.	D. "	30-5-16.
	6/3579	"	Steenson	A.	D. "	30-5-16.
	6/1564	"	Madden	P.	D. "	28-5-16.
DIED OF WOUNDS.	6 02	Pte.	McGoldrick	E.	C. Coy.	17-5-16.
		2/Lieut.	Smyth	P.J.		16-5-16.
WOUNDED.		2/Lieut.	Mathews	P.D.		6-5-16.
	1/9846	L/C.	Dolan	M.	B. Coy.	1/5-16.
	5/ 585	Pte.	McKenna	J.	B. "	1-5-16.
	6/2351	"	Ward	N.	B. "	4-5-16.
	5811	L/C.	Kavaney	P.	C. "	4-5-16.
	6/2358	Pte.	Alexander	S.	C. "	1-5-16.
	6/2806	"	Rogan	P.	C. "	4-5-16.
	6/4610	"	Lowans	J.	A. "	5-5-16.
	6/1212	"	Flynn	S.	B. "	5-5-16.
	6/1300	"	Murphy	J.	B. "	5-5-16.
	6/2860	C.S.M.	Rice	D.	B. "	6-5-16.
	6/2432	Pte.	McErlane	J.J.	B. "	6-5-16.
	4/5880	"	McCloskey	T.	B. "	6-5-16.
	6/1313	"	Barrett	J.F.	D. "	6-5-16.
	6/2201	"	Creen	R.	B. "	6-5-16.
	5932	"	Tracey	W.	D. "	7-5-16.
	6/1545	"	Healy	T.	D. "	7-5-16.
	4/5958	"	Walsh	S.	D. "	7-5-16.
	6/4514	"	Corrigan	P.	A. "	13-5-16.
	2/8345	"	Cosgrove	M.	A. "	13-5-16.
	6/3568	Cpl.	Donagh	P.A.	D. "	13-5-16.
	3/6074	Pte.	Farry	C.	A. "	13-5-16.

WOUNDED. (Continued)

	Rank & Name.			Coy.	Date.
1/9338	Pte.	Gresham	W.	A. Coy.	13-5-16.
6/4182	"	Kilgallon	J.	A. "	14-5-16.
6/2436	"	Prenter	J.	C. "	14-5-16.
3960	"	Garvey	M.	C. "	14-5-16.
6106	L/C.	Jordan	J.	B. "	14-5-16.
1/7937	Pte.	Sweeney	P.	D. "	14-5-16.
6/2492	"	Doherty	J.	C. "	14-5-16.
4/4193	"	McGrail	J.	C. "	14-5-16.
4/5802	"	Barrett	P.	A. "	15-5-16.
6/3835	L/C.	Parle	P.	C. "	15-5-16.
6/1496	Sgt.	Robinson	H.	D. "	15-5-16.
6/3553	Pte.	Lagan	D.	D. "	15-5-16.
6/4556	"	Lynch	J.	B. "	15-5-16.
2/6628	"	Mitchell	J.	A. "	15-5-16.
4/5916	"	Airlie	E.	A. "	15-5-16.
4/4561	"	Dolan	D.	A. "	15-5-16.
3/6529	"	Ralph	J.	A. "	15-5-16.
5/3030	"	Collin	T.	A. "	15-5-16.
~~3/3959~~	~~"~~	~~Byrne~~	~~E.~~	~~A. "~~	~~15-5-16.~~
6/2886	"	Lysaght	M.	C. "	15-5-16.
6/3551	Cpl.	Hennon	M.	C. "	16-5-16.
6/1633	Pte.	McMahon	T.	C. "	16-5-16.
5165	"	Morrell	J.	C. "	16-5-16.
6/2490	Sgt.	Shannon	P.	A. "	18-5-16.
4/4700	"	Melly	T.	A. "	18-5-16.
3/6356	Pte.	Doody	C.	A. "	18-5-16.
1/8760	"	Byrne	M.	C. "	18-5-16.
6/2229	L/Sgt.	McCann	J.	C. "	18-5-16.
5627	L/C.	Cartwright	T.	D. "	21-5-16.
6185	Pte.	Walsh	J.	D. "	21-5-16.
6/1330	"	Healy	M.	D. "	21-5-16.
6/1499	"	Madden	S.	D. "	21-5-16.
6/4567	"	O'Donnell	P.	D. "	21-5-16.
6/2802	"	Ferguson	M.	B. "	21-5-16.
6/4073	Cpl.	Atkinson	C.	C. "	21-5-16.
6555	Pte.	Tully	B.	C. "	21-5-16.
2/10870	"	Muldoon	T.	C. "	21-5-16.
6/4235	"	Duignan	T.	C. "	21-5-16.
6/1728	"	Richards	T.	B. "	21-5-16.
6/4159	"	Kelly	J.	D. "	26-5-16.
6/4370	"	McKenna	J.	B. "	26-5-16.
6/2166	"	Ward	E.	D. "	26-5-16.
6/4227	Cpl.	Kirkwood	S.	C. "	28-5-16.
6/1614	Pte.	Fleming	J.	C. "	28-5-16.
6/1542	"	Gavin	M.	D. "	28-5-16.
6/2502	"	McIlvenny	R.	B. "	28-5-16.
5468	"	McTigue	M.	B. "	28-5-16.
6/2633	"	Tierney	J.	B. "	28-5-16.
6/2844	Cpl.	McCambridge	J.	C. "	29-5-16.
6/2138	Pte.	Joyce	J.	D. "	30-5-16.
10340	"	Johnston	T.	D. "	30-5-16.
6024	"	Rooney	F.	D. "	30-5-16.

	Rank & Name.				Coy.	Date.
WOUNDED. (Continued).	6/4427	Pte.	O'Sullivan	W.	A. Coy.	30-5-16.
	6/4543	L/C.	Twohig	D.J.	A. "	30-5-16.
	6/4619	Pte.	Feeney	F.	D. "	31-5-16.
	6/4425	"	Simmons	P.	B. "	31-5-16.
	11038	"	Egan	B.	C. "	31-5-16.
	6730	"	Kelly	M.	C. "	31-5-16.
	4661	"	McMorrow	J.	C. "	31-5-16.

WOUNDED AT DUTY.	6/4330	Pte.	Benson	A.	B. Coy.	21-5-16.
ACCIDENTALLY WOUNDED.	6/4654	Pte.	Smith	J.	D. Coy.	30-5-16.
MISSING.	3100	L/C.	Swinburne	J.	D. Coy.	31-5-16.

[signature]

Lieut. Colonel.

Commdg. 6th (S) Bn. The Connaught Rangers.

4th June, 1916.

Appendix VIII

The following acts of conspicuous courage were performed by men of this Battalion during the month and were awarded as stated.

No 6/2847 Private D. LYNCH during the gas attack on the morning of the 29th April 1916 was one of a team of a LEWIS GUN in the front trench. Though the rest of his team were gassed and though suffering from the effects of gas himself he continued to use his gun with great effect against the attacking enemy when the company on his flank's had been practically wiped out. On this company being reinforced the by his good work stopped a fresh infantry attack on the reinforced line and knocked a gas cylinder the enemy were placing on their parapet back into their trenches before they had liberated the gas. He refused to leave his gun, though almost in a state of collapse from gas, until relieved some hours afterwards. He was awarded for this act the D.C.M. and the parchment certificate of the G.O.C. 16th DIVISION

No 6/6293 Private P. REILLY and No 3673 Private J. GAFFNEY were recommended for the D.C.M. and No 1326 L/Corp. D FALVEY and 6155 Pte J. REILLY for the parchment certificate for courage of the G.O.C 16th DIVISION. On the 7th May 1916 when some of their comrades were buried the two former worked in full view of the enemy and exposed to their fire for three quarters of an hour digging out their comrades. The latter two assisted them by working in the trench where they were only partly sheltered from the enemies fire

16 55 JUNE

Instructions regarding War Diaries and Intelligence Summaries are contained in F. S. Regs., Part II. and the Staff Manual respectively. Title pages will be prepared in manuscript.

WAR DIARY
of 6th (S) Bn. THE CONNAUGHT RANGERS
~~INTELLIGENCE SUMMARY.~~
(Erase heading not required.)

Army Form C. 2118.

June 1916
Vol 6

Place	Date	Hour	Summary of Events and Information	Remarks and references to Appendices
In the Trenches	1/6/16.		The Dispositions remained as on the 29/5/16 viz. A in Reserve with D, B and C holding front and Support lines as from the right. The enemy's heavy trench mortars which did such damage on the 28/5/16 and 29/5/16 did not again fire. They were either put out of action by our artillery fire or removed to another part of the line, probably the latter. This quietness enabled much trench work to be done. We also were busy with useful patrol work, their invariable report being that the enemy was doing much work in his front trench, probably also trench repair work by him necessitated by the attentions of our heavy Artillery. Grass cutting in front of our trenches had to be started, it continued nightly. A draft of 18 other ranks joined the Battalion this day.	
	2.6.16.		A quiet day except that the Battalion Hd. Qrs. at junction of GUN TRENCH and POSEN ALLEY was heavily shelled. On the	

T2134. Wt. W708–776. 500000. 4/15. Sir J. C. & S.

56

Instructions regarding War Diaries and Intelligence Summaries are contained in F. S. Regs., Part II. and the Staff Manual respectively. Title pages will be prepared in manuscript.

WAR DIARY
or
~~INTELLIGENCE~~ SUMMARY.

6th Bn Connaught Rangers

(*Erase heading not required.*)

Army Form C. 2118.

Place	Date	Hour	Summary of Events and Information	Remarks and references to Appendices
In the Trenches	2/6/16		night of the 2/3rd we were relieved by 6TH ROYAL IRISH REGT. and two companies A and B returned into Brigade Reserve in PHILOSOPHE and the remaining two companies C + D were attached to the 8TH ROYAL MUNSTER FUSILIERS in 10TH AVENUE.	
	3/6/16		The two Companies in PHILOSOPHE provided working parties for the 47TH BRIGADE and did some training in wiring CAPTAIN J. J. KAVANAGH, LIEUT. H. M. SWIFTE, 2ND LIEUTENANTS L. G. D'ARCY, J. F. B. O'SULLIVAN, C. W. B. FITZGERALD, M. J. B. DAVY and U. A. MOORE reported for duty with the Battalion today having been dispatched from the Base on the 31st May and 1st June	
	4/6/16 5/6/16		Working parties provided nightly from all four Companies for work in the trenches and under R. E. s	

T2134. Wt. W708–776. 500000. 4/15. Sir J. C. & S.

57

Instructions regarding War Diaries and Intelligence Summaries are contained in F. S. Regs., Part II. and the Staff Manual respectively. Title pages will be prepared in manuscript.

WAR DIARY
or
~~INTELLIGENCE~~ SUMMARY. 6th Bn. Connaught Rangers

(*Erase heading not required.*)

Army Form C. 2118.

Place	Date	Hour	Summary of Events and Information	Remarks and references to Appendices
PHILOSOPHE	6/6/16		The Battalion relieved the 6th ROYAL IRISH in the right sub-section PUITS 14 BIS section, A Coy. holding from ENGLISH ALLEY to BOYAU 57, B Coy from there to BOYAU 54. C Coy. BOYAU 54 to BOYAU 61. D Coy. 2 platoons in RESERVE TRENCH from CHALK PIT ALLEY ~~to~~ HUGO LANE, one platoon in FORREST TRENCH and one platoon in MEATH TRENCH. The 1ST. MUNSTERS were on our right and the 8TH MUNSTERS on our left. One company of the 7TH LEINSTERS in RESERVE TRENCH was also attached to our Battalion for duty. The trenches had been badly damaged by the enemy's fire when we took over and necessitated much work. The Battalion Hd. Qrs. was again in GUN TRENCH near its junction with POSEN ALLEY and again it daily received much attention from the enemy's artillery.	
In the Trenches	7/6/16		The enemy was comparatively quiet and gave us a good opportunity of repairing our trenches. Our Artillery	

T2134. Wt. W708–776. 500000. 4/15. Sir J. C. & S.

58.

Instructions regarding War Diaries and Intelligence Summaries are contained in F. S. Regs., Part II. and the Staff Manual respectively. Title pages will be prepared in manuscript.

WAR DIARY
or
~~INTELLIGENCE SUMMARY.~~
(Erase heading not required.)

Army Form C. 2118.

6th Bn Connaught Rangers.

Place	Date	Hour	Summary of Events and Information	Remarks and references to Appendices
In the Trenches	7/6/16		not being prepared to support our efforts in rifle grenade and trench mortar activity we were not as aggressive as otherwise we might have been but some very good work was done on our wire and much grass cut. Our patrols were also active and much valuable information as to the enemies wire and work collected.	
	8/6/16.		Our dispositions remained the same as on the 6th and 7th with the exception that the Company of the 7th LEINSTERS was withdrawn into Brigade Support and our D Coy. took over RESERVE TRENCH from ENGLISH ALLEY to HUGO LANE. Nothing of importance happened.	
	9/6/16.		The enemy shelled around Battalion Hd. Qrs. heavily this day and also did some damage to HUGO LANE where it cuts SUPPORT LINE. The damage was repaired. Lieut A. J. KEARNEY joined for duty today.	
	10/6/16.		We were relieved on the night of the 10th–11th by the 8TH ROYAL IRISH FUSILIERS and the Battalion returned to Billets in MAZINGARBE	

Instructions regarding War Diaries and Intelligence Summaries are contained in F. S. Regs., Part II. and the Staff Manual respectively. Title pages will be prepared in manuscript.

WAR DIARY
or
~~INTELLIGENCE SUMMARY.~~
(Erase heading not required.)

59

Rangers

Army Form C. 2118.

Place	Date	Hour	Summary of Events and Information	Remarks and references to Appendices
MAZINGARBE	11/6/16.		The day was spent in resting the men and the usual cleaning up of clothes and equipment and the checking of trench mobolization Stores. Working parties for the 1st CORPS and 47th INFANTRY BRIGADE were employed on the night 11/12th. Classes of instruction were formed for 12.6.16.	
	12/6/16 to 16/6/16		Large working parties from the Battalion being required daily but little training could be indulged in. Some work was however done in the instruction of wirers, grenade throwing and in the training of a special raiding party. A draft of 100 men joined the Battalion on the 15-6-16.	
	17.6.16.		The 47th. INF. BDE relieved the 48th INF. BDE in the LOOS Section. The Battalion relieving the 8th ROYAL DUBLIN FUSILIERS in Brigade Reserve in PHILOSOPHE. Special carrying parties, eleven parties of 1 Officer 2 N.C.Os and 40 men each, were sent.	

T2134. Wt. W708-776. 500000. 4/15. Sir J. C. & S.

Instructions regarding War Diaries and Intelligence Summaries are contained in F. S. Regs., Part II. and the Staff Manual respectively. Title pages will be prepared in manuscript.

WAR DIARY
or
~~INTELLIGENCE~~ SUMMARY.
(Erase heading not required.)

60

Army Form C. 2118.

6th Bn Connaught Rangers.

Place	Date	Hour	Summary of Events and Information	Remarks and references to Appendices
PHILOSOPHE	17/6/16. to 19/6/16.		sent immediately into the VILLAGE LINE and were engaged each night on 17TH, 18TH and 19TH in carrying gas cylinders into the front line trench along the PUITS 14 BIS frontage. These parties did excellent work and the officer in charge CAPT. KAVANAGH was specially thanked by the G.O.C. for the efficient way his men performed their arduous duties.	
			The remainder of the Battalion remained in PHILOSOPHE and furnished working and carrying parties to the Brigade. 2nd Lieut. P.L.N. GORDON-RALPH joined for duty on 19/6/16.	
	20/6/16.		Working parties supplied and some little training done of the remaining men.	
In the Trenches	21/6/16		The Battalion relieved the 6TH ROYAL IRISH REGIMENT in	

T2134. Wt. W708-776. 500000. 4/15. Sir J. C. & S.

61.

Army Form C. 2118.

Instructions regarding War Diaries and Intelligence Summaries are contained in F. S. Regs., Part II. and the Staff Manual respectively. Title pages will be prepared in manuscript.

WAR DIARY
or
~~INTELLIGENCE SUMMARY.~~

(Erase heading not required.)

6th Bn Connaught Rangers

Place	Date	Hour	Summary of Events and Information	Remarks and references to Appendices
In the Trenches	21/6/16		the left sub-section of the LOOS Section on the night of the 21/22nd June. D Coy. holding from LOOS CRASSIER to GORDON ALLEY. A Coy. from GORDON ALLEY to BOYAU 45. B Coy. from BOYAU 45 to ENGLISH ALLEY with C Coy. in reserve in RESERVE TRENCH. The 8th MUNSTERS were on our right and the 8th IRISH FUSILIERS on our left. The trenches were in a fair state of repair and the enemy was very quiet on our immediate front but we soon roused him into activity.	
	22/6/16.		The day passed quietly except for the usual exchange of rifle grenades and light Trench Mortars. We organised a bombardment of the enemy's two smaller craters on our front GORDON and CAMERON for the night of the 22/23 and this proved very effective, much damage being done	

T2134. Wt. W708–776. 500000. 4/15. Sir J. C. & S.

62

Army Form C. 2118.

Instructions regarding War Diaries and Intelligence Summaries are contained in F. S. Regs., Part II. and the Staff Manual respectively. Title pages will be prepared in manuscript.

WAR DIARY
or
~~INTELLIGENCE SUMMARY.~~
(Erase heading not required.)

6th Bn. Connaught Rangers

Place	Date	Hour	Summary of Events and Information	Remarks and references to Appendices
In the trenches	22/6/16.		and a large Bomb store in CAMERON CRATER being exploded. The enemy's casualties were considerable as they were caught in large working parties in the craters and also by our machine guns when retiring in confusion from the craters to their trenches across the open.	
	23/6/16.		In retaliation for our activities on the night of the 22/23rd the enemy heavily shelled our front support and reserve trenches from 7 p.m. to 9.30 p.m. on this date but our casualties three killed and five wounded were extremely light owing to the precautions taken by Company Commanders in getting their men under cover. Our trenches were badly damaged but this did not prevent us carrying out another bombardment with trench mortars and rifle grenades on him this night doing more damage to him than he had done to	

T2134. Wt. W708–776. 500000. 4/15. Sir J. C. & S.

Instructions regarding War Diaries and Intelligence Summaries are contained in F. S. Regs., Part II. and the Staff Manual respectively. Title pages will be prepared in manuscript.

WAR DIARY
or
~~INTELLIGENCE SUMMARY.~~
(Erase heading not required.)

63

Army Form C. 2118.

6th Connaught Rangers.

Place	Date	Hour	Summary of Events and Information	Remarks and references to Appendices
In-the-Trenches	23/6/16		us with the result that we reduced him to a state of quietness and meekness unusual to the Hun unless he is getting the worst of the exchanges.	
	24/6/16		A very quiet day except for some heavy trench mortar activity on behalf of the enemy in the evening which damaged CAMERON ALLEY and part of our centre Company front line. We were relieved on the night of the 24/25th and returned to Billets in PHILOSOPHE. the 6th ROYAL IRISH taking our place.	
PHILOSOPHE	25/6/16		The relief was carried out smoothly and a quiet morning was spent so as to allow the men to rest and clean themselves. In the evening carrying parties were provided and a special party of 2 Officers 6 N.C.O and	

T2134. Wt. W708-776. 500000. 4/15. Sir J. C. & S.

64

Army Form C. 2118.

Instructions regarding War Diaries and Intelligence Summaries are contained in F. S. Regs., Part II. and the Staff Manual respectively. Title pages will be prepared in manuscript.

WAR DIARY
or
~~INTELLIGENCE SUMMARY.~~
(Erase heading not required.)

6th Connaught Rangers.

Place	Date	Hour	Summary of Events and Information	Remarks and references to Appendices
PHILOSOPHE	25/6/16.		52 men. 2nd LIEUT. O'MALLEY and 2ND. LIEUT. SHERIDAN being in charge was sent up to the left of the LOOS sector to partake in a proposed gas attack on the enemy accompanied by a raid. The rôle of this party was to throw smoke bombs along a sector of our front whilst a raid was in progress. The conditions were not favourable and the enterprise for that night was abandoned.	
	26/6/16.		The special smoke bomb party under 2ND. Lieuts. O'MALLEY and SHERIDAN was again sent up to the front. Several carrying parties helped to draw bombs and R.E. stores to our right sub-section. Two special parties of 1 Officer 2 N.C.O.s and 52 men, one under 2nd. Lieut. J. F. B. O'SULLIVAN and the other under 2nd LIEUT. L. G. D'ARCY were detailed as consolidating parties to two craters which were blown up near the existing HARTS and HARRISONS Craters. This enterprise was entirely	

T2134. Wt. W708—776. 500000. 4/15. Sir J. C. & S.

Instructions regarding War Diaries and Intelligence Summaries are contained in F. S. Regs., Part II. and the Staff Manual respectively. Title pages will be prepared in manuscript.

WAR DIARY
or
~~INTELLIGENCE~~ SUMMARY.
(*Erase heading not required.*)

65

Army Form C. 2118.

6th Connaught Rangers.

Place	Date	Hour	Summary of Events and Information	Remarks and references to Appendices
PHILOSOPHE	26/6/16		Successful. The 7th LEINSTERS provided a raiding party who were to raid the enemy's front and support lines behind the new craters whilst the work of consolidation proceeded. Nearly 100 Germans were killed in the explosion of the mines and in the raid and the work of consolidation was ably done by our two special parties assisted by the Royal Engineers the work of course being done under intense artillery and machine gun fire. At dawn our parties withdrew the 7th LEINSTER Raiders having been in the enemy's trenches for 1¾ hours and our parties under 2nd LIEUT. O'SULLIVAN and 2nd LIEUT. D'ARCY had completed a bombers' post on the near lips of the craters and connected them with saps to our trenches and wired those saps	

T2134. Wt. W708–776. 500000. 4/15. Sir J. C. & S.

66

WAR DIARY
or
~~INTELLIGENCE SUMMARY.~~
(Erase heading not required.)

6th Bn. Connaught Rangers

Army Form C. 2118.

Instructions regarding War Diaries and Intelligence Summaries are contained in F. S. Regs., Part II. and the Staff Manual respectively. Title pages will be prepared in manuscript.

Place	Date	Hour	Summary of Events and Information	Remarks and references to Appendices
PHILOSOPHE	27/6/16.		The Special Smoke bomb party under 2/Lt. SHERIDAN + 2/Lt. O'MALLEY went up to the left subsector LOOS Section to assist the ROYAL IRISH REGT. in a smoke demonstration. The Smoke was let off with great success, and our Artillery shelled the enemy's trenches very effectively, their reply was not heavy or effective and our party suffered no casualties.	
PHILOSOPHE	28/6/16.		A quiet day. We supplied various working parties at night. The raiders were practised in night patrolling and work with Bangalore Torpedos.	
PHILOSOPHE	29/6/16.		More work with the Bangalore Torpedo for the Raiders. We relieved the ROYAL IRISH REGT. this night in the left sector of LOOS section. Relief was complete by 12 midnight. The centre Coy's (A Coy's) front trench had been practically obliterated by MINENWERFER for about 70 yds. between GORDON + CAMERON ALLEYS, work was started on this as soon as relief was complete. The transport was shelled on the way from MAZINGARBE to LOOS + in LOOS, but luckily we had no casualties – A wagon with bombs was hit and set on fire.	
In the Trenches	30/6/16.		A quiet day – LOOS was shelled intermittently all day with 5.9" + a few 8" – At 9.10 p.m. we made a demonstration to assist an attack by the 1st DIVISION. We opened rifle +	

T2134. Wt. W708–776. 500000. 4/15. Sir J. C. & S.

67

Army Form C. 2118.

Instructions regarding War Diaries and Intelligence Summaries are contained in F. S. Regs., Part II. and the Staff Manual respectively. Title pages will be prepared in manuscript.

WAR DIARY
or
~~INTELLIGENCE SUMMARY.~~

(Erase heading not required.)

6th Bn. Connaught Rangers

Place	Date	Hour	Summary of Events and Information	Remarks and references to Appendices
In the Trenches	30/6/16		rifle grenade fire for two minutes + our trench mortars + artillery kept up an intense bombardment for half an hour. The enemy's retaliation was poor and did very little damage – we had practically no casualties. Our trench mortars were active most of the night. Work on the front trench between GORDON + CAMERON ALLEYS was continued.	
			Capt. TAMPLIN + 2/Lt. SHERIDAN were authorised to assume the rank + badges of MAJOR + CAPT. respectively pending confirmation of rank.	
			[illegible] Lt. Col. Comdg. 6th (S) Connaught Rangers	

T2134. Wt. W708—776. 500000. 4/15. Sir J. C. & S.

W A R D I A R Y

6th (S) Bn The Connaught Rgrs

1st. July to 31st. July 1916.

VOLUME No. 8.

16 July
6 Connaughts
vol 7

8

Instructions regarding War Diaries and Intelligence Summaries are contained in F. S. Regs., Part II. and the Staff Manual respectively. Title pages will be prepared in manuscript.

WAR DIARY 6th (S) Bn THE CONNAUGHT RANGERS

~~or~~

~~INTELLIGENCE SUMMARY.~~

(*Erase heading not required.*)

Army Form C. 2118.

68

Place	Date	Hour	Summary of Events and Information	Remarks and references to Appendices
In the trenches	1/7/16		MAJOR R.J.A. TAMPLIN took over command of D Coy – LT J.J. MARTIN became A/Adjutant – A fairly quiet day – Our rifle grenades + STOKES guns were active against the craters + enemy's front line + reduced him to almost complete silence – A minenwerfer fired on our left coy (B Coy), blew in the trench in two or three places + started a gas cylinder leaking, LT COONEY + 8 men were slightly gassed – No 7815 Pte J. McKENDRY, No 7820 Pte J. COLLINS + No 7821 Pte H McEWAN distinguished themselves by working all night trying to get this cylinder out though the broken trench here was kept under machine gun fire all night by the enemy – About 6 P.M LT. SWITTE located where the minenwerfer was firing from + on our getting a howitzer to fire at the point indicated the firing ceased entirely –	
In the trenches	2/7/16		A quiet day – Our Stokes guns were active as usual + the enemy made hardly any reply – The minenwerfer started again in the afternoon but was silenced by our 4.5" howitzers – At 10 P.M. we, in cooperation with 48th Bde, had a smoke demonstration combined with a heavy bombardment by our artillery + T.Ms – The enemy's retaliation was heavy but inaccurate, his trench mortars did most of the damage – Our casualties were about 5 men slightly wounded –	

T2134. Wt. W708–776. 500000. 4/15. Sir J. C. & S.

Instructions regarding War Diaries and Intelligence Summaries are contained in F. S. Regs., Part II. and the Staff Manual respectively. Title pages will be prepared in manuscript.

WAR DIARY
or
INTELLIGENCE SUMMARY.
(Erase heading not required.)

6th Conn Rangers

69

Army Form C. 2118.

Place	Date	Hour	Summary of Events and Information	Remarks and references to Appendices
In the trenches	3/7/16		A quiet day – In the afternoon our left coy's (D Coy) line was damaged by medium trench mortars but was cleared by the evening – We were relieved this night by 8th INNISKILLING FUSILEERS – Relief complete by 12.30 A.M. – During the second half of our tour our artillery had been extremely active, cutting enemy's wire, firing on communicating trenches and O.Ps etc, we maintained a very vigourous offensive spirit & by the time we left him the HUN had been reduced to almost complete quiet, his guns fired less than usual & his heavy guns very rarely, his heavy trench mortar was the only thing that did us much damage – A Coy were working hard on the damaged front line between GORDON & CAMERON ALLEYS & had got into more or less reconstructed, they were congratulated by the Brigadier on the way they had tackled this job & the splendid progress they had made with it – On relief the battalion returned to NOEUX les MINES which was reached by 4.15 AM.	
NOEUX les MINES	4/7/16 to 10/7/16		Drill – Special classes in bombing & raiding – On night of 6th we found a working party of 80 men under Lt KEARNEY and 2/Lt ROUSSELL, to work in front of FOSSE 7, on arrival at the spot they were to work at they found the FOSSE being heavily bombarded with gas & tear shells, a party from another regiment considered it impossible to work and went back but our party, in spite of many men feeling the	

GB

T2134. Wt. W708–776. 500000. 4/15. Sir J. C. & S.

Instructions regarding War Diaries and Intelligence Summaries are contained in F. S. Regs., Part II. and the Staff Manual respectively. Title pages will be prepared in manuscript.

WAR DIARY
or
INTELLIGENCE SUMMARY.
(Erase heading not required.)

6th Connaught Rangers

Army Form C. 2118.

Place	Date	Hour	Summary of Events and Information	Remarks and references to Appendices
NOEUX les MINES			the effects of the gas & all of them weeping from the tear shells, stuck to their work, till the proper hour for them to knock off – On the nights of 8th & 9th parties were carrying empty gas cylinders out of the trenches.	
In the trenches	11/7/16		The battalion relieved the 9th DUBLIN FUSILEERS in 10th AVENUE as Brigade Support battalion.	
"	12/7/16 to 14/7/16		Found heavy working parties every night chiefly carrying timber for RE or T.M ammunition – MAJOR BROOKE left on 13th to take up command of a battalion & MAJOR R. J. A. TAMPLIN took his place as 2nd in command –	
"	15/7/16		The battalion relieved the 6th ROYAL IRISH REGIMENT in RIGHT SUBSECTOR 14BIS SECTION – Company's were distributed as follows, Right D Coy, Centre A Coy, Left C Coy, Reserve B Coy. – A mine was blown & a raid carried out by the battalion on our right & a certain amount of the artillery retaliation fell on our right coy, but little damage was done – Otherwise the night was quiet – The trenches round the CHALK PIT were in a very bad way, particularly the support line, which had ceased to exist as a fighting trench and gave very little cover as a communicating trench – 2/Lt BLAKE-OSULLIVAN took up	

T2134. Wt. W708–776. 500000. 4/15. Sir J. C. & S.

Instructions regarding War Diaries and Intelligence Summaries are contained in F. S. Regs., Part II. and the Staff Manual respectively. Title pages will be prepared in manuscript.

WAR DIARY
or
INTELLIGENCE SUMMARY.
(Erase heading not required.)

71

Army Form C. 2118.

6th Connaught Rangers

Place	Date	Hour	Summary of Events and Information	Remarks and references to Appendices
			the duties of INTELLIGENCE OFFICER.	
In the trenches	16/7/16		A quiet day. The usual rifle grenade & T.M activity, the activity was mostly on our part but between 3 P.M & 5 P.M an enemy Medium TRENCH MORTAR ~~got~~ started firing on our ~~right~~ left T.M emp & did a good deal of damage to the FIRE TRENCH – RESERVE TRENCH was shelled from 2.30 P.M to 3 P.M –	
In the trenches.	17/7/16		A very quiet morning – TRENCH MORTAR activity in afternoon all to our advantage – At 7 P.M all companys combined in a strafe with rifle grenades & the STOKES GUNS cooperated, over 200 grenades were sent over, enemy made no attempt at retaliation.	
In the trenches.	18/7/16		Lt H.R. MILES was killed by a shell this morning, he had quite recently been recommended for promotion to Captain, he is a great loss to the battalion – There was intermittent shelling all day doing little damage – We were very active with rifle grenades – At 12.30 AM in support to a raid by the MUNSTERS on the left of us opened a very heavy rifle grenade & T.M fire, the enemy's retaliation was feeble – In all we fired over 500 rifle grenades in the 24 hours – We had constructed a dummy Headquarters	

T2134. Wt. W708–776. 500000. 4/15. Sir J. C. & S.

Instructions regarding War Diaries and Intelligence Summaries are contained in F. S. Regs., Part II. and the Staff Manual respectively. Title pages will be prepared in manuscript.

WAR DIARY
or
INTELLIGENCE SUMMARY.
(Erase heading not required.)

Army Form C. 2118.

72

6th Connaught Rangers

Place	Date	Hour	Summary of Events and Information	Remarks and references to Appendices
			in an abandoned trench & this was most satisfactorily shelled this afternoon.	
In the trenches	19/7/16		A quiet morning – the battalion was relieved by the 6th ROYAL IRISH in the afternoon, the relief was complete by 5 P.M & the battalion returned to 10th AVENUE where the companies were disposed as follows; D Coy on right holding 69 METRE POINT REDOUBT, C Coy in centre & B Coy on left holding NORTHERN SAP REDOUBT, A Coy in JUN TRENCH.	
In the trenches	20/7/16 – 24/7/16		Battalion remained in Brigade support & furnished working parties nightly. The following officers joined the battalion on 19/7/16 – LT. D. H. COOKE (14th Bn) Lt. J. H. R. DICKSON (2nd Bn) – 2/Lt. B. T. UTLEY (2nd Bn) – 2/Lt S. B. MINCH (3 Bn) – 2/Lt J. T. LEONARD joined on 23rd.	
In the trenches	25/7/16		The battalion relieved the 6th ROYAL IRISH in Right subsection 14 B[illegible] this day. Relief was complete by 4.30 P.M. Several patrols went out during the night to examine the enemy's wire, one weak spot was found. A quiet night. Coys were in same order	

T2134. Wt. W708–776. 500000. 4/15. Sir J. C. & S.

Instructions regarding War Diaries and Intelligence Summaries are contained in F. S. Regs., Part II. and the Staff Manual respectively. Title pages will be prepared in manuscript.

WAR DIARY
or
INTELLIGENCE SUMMARY.
(Erase heading not required.)

Army Form C. 2118.

73

6th Connaught Rangers

Place	Date	Hour	Summary of Events and Information	Remarks and references to Appendices
			as last time in except that A was in Reserve & B Coy took their place in centre –	
In the trenches	26/7/16		Enemy's artillery was fairly active all day but did little damage – Our STOKES guns & rifle grenades were very active all day – Each coy sent out an officers patrol again – On right & centre there was nothing to report on left enemy was wiring his parapet between Saps Y12 & Y14, our Lewis guns got onto this party & claim at least 3 hits –	
In the trenches	27/7/16		Enemy was very active today, shelling both front & support lines at intervals. From 11.30 AM to 2 P.M he bombarded our left coy (C Coy) with Medium Trench Mortars & Aerial torpedoes & did considerable damage to our trenches & caused some casualties – Our STOKES guns & Medium T.M's replied but could not silence him – From 8 P.M to 9 P.M he did the same thing again & caused a good many casualties – 2/Lt J.T. LEONARD was wounded by premature explosion of a rifle grenade this morning & Lt O'MALLEY went down with shell shock in the afternoon.	
In the trenches	28/7/16		A quiet day – At 11 P.M we made an attempted raid on the enemy's trenches by PUITS 14 BIS (H 25 d 1.2.) where there was a weak spot in the enemies wire – There was to be no artillery preparation & the whole enterprise depended on surprise – A party of 11 men under 2/Lt HARFORD was to move out & lay mats over the enemy's wire, a second	

T2134. Wt. W708–776. 500000. 4/15. Sir J. C. & S.

Instructions regarding War Diaries and Intelligence Summaries are contained in F. S. Regs., Part II. and the Staff Manual respectively. Title pages will be prepared in manuscript.

WAR DIARY
or
INTELLIGENCE SUMMARY.
(Erase heading not required.)

Army Form C. 2118.

74

6th Connaught Rangers

Place	Date	Hour	Summary of Events and Information	Remarks and references to Appendices
			party under LT KEARNEY were to cross the mats & raid the trench to the right, capture a prisoner & return doing what damage they could, 2Lt HARBORD's party were to block the trench to the left & cover the withdrawal — 2Lt HARBORD's party found the gap all right & cut the first wire they met, keeping the mats for the low wire they expected to find on the parapet, however when through the first wire they found no more, the whole of 2Lt HARBORD's party got through without being spotted, there was some delay in getting LT KEARNEY's party through the gap in the wire & before they were up the enemy saw them, manned his parapet in strength & opened rifle fire & threw some bombs — As the surprise had failed & several men had been hit there was nothing for it but to withdraw, during the withdrawal L/Cpl LEARY was badly hit, SERGT PARLIN stayed behind with him & tried to bring him in after some time finding he could not do it alone & having been slightly hit himself he went back & report — MAJOR R.J.A. TAMPLIN & CAPT J.J. KAVANAGH went out guided by SERGT PARLIN to where LEARY lay in the GERMAN wire, & brought him in, they were fired on & some bombs were thrown at them whilst bringing him in — Our total losses in this affair were one man (L/Cpl LEARY) died of wounds & six men wounded, all fairly slightly — Our guns had been called on	

T2134. Wt. W708—776. 500000. 4/15. Sir J. C. & S.

Instructions regarding War Diaries and Intelligence Summaries are contained in F. S. Regs., Part II. and the Staff Manual respectively. Title pages will be prepared in manuscript.

WAR DIARY
or
INTELLIGENCE SUMMARY.
(Erase heading not required.)

Army Form C. 2118.

75

6th Connaught Rangers

Place	Date	Hour	Summary of Events and Information	Remarks and references to Appendices
			to cover the withdrawal & had fired very well, our STOKES guns & rifle grenades were very active – A draft of 15 N.C.O.s joined the battalion today.	
In the trenches	29/7/16		A fairly quiet day – At 11.20 P.M our STOKES guns & M.T.Ms opened on enemy's line in support of a raid by the MUNSTERS on our left – The enemy's retaliation was feeble & did not damage except for a T.M which blew in our line near C Coy's H.Q in three places – Lt KEARNEY was transferred to 1st R. MUNSTER FUS this day & 2/Lt P.J. SMYTH went to the ROYAL FLYING CORPS.	
In the trenches	30/7/16		A fairly quiet day, a little shelling of the head of RAILWAY ALLEY with 4.2s which our artillery retaliation soon silenced – ~~at 11.20 P.M we made a demonstration~~ – Hostile Trench Mortars did a little damage to C Coy's trenches but were easily silenced by our artillery & trench mortars – An exceptionally quiet night – Lt R.E BOWEN joined the battalion this day	
	31/7/16		A quiet morning – The battalion was relieved in the afternoon by 8th ROYAL IRISH FUSILIERS – At 6. P.M hostile Trench Mortars became active against our left coy (C Coy)	

T2134. Wt. W708–776. 500000. 4/15. Sir J. C. & S.

Instructions regarding War Diaries and Intelligence Summaries are contained in F. S. Regs., Part II. and the Staff Manual respectively. Title pages will be prepared in manuscript.

WAR DIARY
or
INTELLIGENCE SUMMARY.
(Erase heading not required.)

Army Form C. 2118.

76

6th Connaught Rangers

Place	Date	Hour	Summary of Events and Information	Remarks and references to Appendices
			& did some damage before they could be silenced – Relief was complete by 8.10 P.M. & the battalion returned to the S. HUTS MAZINGARBE –	
			J. Lenox Conyngham Lt Colonel	
			2 · 8 · 16 Comdg 6th (S) Connaught Rangers	

T2134. Wt. W708 – 776. 500000. 4/15. Sir J. C. & S.

Vol 8

WAR DIARY.

6th Connaught Rangers

MONTH OF AUGUST, 1916.

VOLUME:- 9

Instructions regarding War Diaries and Intelligence Summaries are contained in F. S. Regs., Part II. and the Staff Manual respectively. Title pages will be prepared in manuscript.

WAR DIARY
or
INTELLIGENCE SUMMARY.
(Erase heading not required.)

August 1916

Army Form C. 2118.

77

Place	Date	Hour	Summary of Events and Information 6th Bn Connaught Rangers	Remarks and references to Appendices
MAZINGARBE	1/8/16 to 2/8/16		On the nights of 1st & 2nd practically the whole battalion was out carrying up gas cylinders, this very heavy work coming on the top of 20 days in the trenches caused a good deal of sickness in the battalion for the next 10 days –	
MAZINGARBE	3/8/16 to 9/8/16		Steady drill & training in MAZINGARBE, there were very few working parties & we had a very quiet time –	
[illegible]	9/8/16		The Bn relieved coys of the following battalions in Brigade Support 19 H.L.I. 14 A&SH & 13th E. SURREY Regt of the 40th DIV in the LOOS SECTOR – Companies were as follows A & B in ENCLOSURE, LOOS – D Coy in DUKE STREET. C Coy in LENS ROAD REDOUBT, Hd Qrs in VILLAGE LINE near PREVITE PASSAGE.	
	10/8/16 to 12/8/16		We provided working parties for the Miners & for work on front line – The ENCLOSURE was occasionally shelled & A Coy had a couple of casualties –	
	13/8/16		The battalion relieved the 5th ROYAL IRISH REGT in the RIGHT SUB-SECTION LOOS on afternoon & evening – The coys were in the following order D Coy on right A in Centre B on Left & C in reserve in the ENCLOSURE – The trenches were very bad particularly the centre & left of the front line which was practically non existent – There was a certain amount of T.M. & artillery activity in the afternoon & evening on both sides	[signature]

T2134. Wt. W708–776. 500000. 4/15. Sir J. C. & S.

WAR DIARY
or
INTELLIGENCE SUMMARY.
(Erase heading not required.)

Army Form C. 2118.

Instructions regarding War Diaries and Intelligence Summaries are contained in F. S. Regs., Part II. and the Staff Manual respectively. Title pages will be prepared in manuscript.

78

Place	Date	Hour	Summary of Events and Information 6th Bn Connaught Rangers	Remarks and references to Appendices
			& a little damage done to our trenches – Enemy was very busy all night working on his trenches & saps	
In the trenches	14/8/16		A quiet morning except for our STOKES & rifle grenades to which the enemy did not reply till 6 P.M when he retaliated with Heavy Trench Mortars & some 4.2s our guns opened & our Medium T.M. & STOKES GUNS were very active & eventually the enemy was silenced at about 7 P.M. – though he had sent over a good deal the aim was poor & little damage was done to our trenches – A camouflet was blown by us E. of MAVNUNGS MOUND at 8 P.M smoke & flames were observed to issue out of a green mound S.W of HARTS CRATER after the blow – no surface alterations – Four officers patrols went out during the night the enemy was again working hard on his trenches –	
	15/8/16		A quiet morning – Our STOKES guns kept up their usual activity on the enemy's trenches & at 3.15 P.M he opened up in reply on our centre company with MINENWERFER and artillery our T.Ms replied vigorously & after about an hour the enemy was silenced – Our support line was damaged in 2 or 3 places but our casualties were light – At 1.30 AM the battalion on our left carried out a minor operation, in retaliation	[illegible] Major

Instructions regarding War Diaries and Intelligence Summaries are contained in F. S. Regs., Part II. and the Staff Manual respectively. Title pages will be prepared in manuscript.

WAR DIARY
or
INTELLIGENCE SUMMARY.
(Erase heading not required.)

Army Form C. 2118.

79

Place	Date	Hour	Summary of Events and Information 6th Bn Connaught-Rangers	Remarks and references to Appendices
			to this the enemy opened a severe but inaccurate fire along our whole front, our guns answered quickly & silenced him, no damage done to our trenches. 2 [illegible] officers patrols were out at night the enemy was still busy in his trenches & had covering parties out. it was found impossible to get really close to him on account of the bright moonlight.	
[illegible]	16/8/16		Our STOKES & T.M.s were busy all day drawing very little answer. At 4 P.M. our howitzers, field guns, T.M.s & some of the Corps heavies opened a 28 minute bombardment on four selected spots in the enemy's lines, the fire seemed very effective & must have caused a lot of damage. At 5 P.M. a 9 inch gun of ours fired 10 rounds on the enemy's front & support line most effectively. The enemy's retaliation was feeble & badly aimed & did no damage to our trenches or men. We started a sap to the mound S.W. of HARTS CRATER. The quietest night we have had yet in this sub section.	
	17/8/16		The battalion was relieved this evening by the 6th Royal IRISH REGT. The day	

T2134. Wt. W708—776. 500000. 4/15. Sir J. C. & S.

Instructions regarding War Diaries and Intelligence Summaries are contained in F. S. Regs., Part II. and the Staff Manual respectively. Title pages will be prepared in manuscript.

WAR DIARY
or
INTELLIGENCE SUMMARY.
(Erase heading not required.)

Army Form C. 2118.

80

Place	Date	Hour	Summary of Events and Information 6th Bn Connaught Rangers	Remarks and references to Appendices
	17/8/16		passed quietly except for the usual activity of our Trench Mortars. Our steady aggressiveness with STOKES GUNS + Medium T.M backed by our 18 prs. who open on the enemy the moment he starts to retaliate have had a very quietening effect on the enemy. A company from a pioneer battalion of the NORTHUMBERLAND FUSILIERS have been working in our lines + have done most excellent work in our front line. The RE have also been working at shelters + on the CRATERS. The relief by the ROYAL IRISH was complete by 10 P.M + the battalion returned to MAZINGARBE HUTS (S), the last company being in by 12 midnight.	
	18/8/16		spent the day resting	
	19/8/16		ditto much rain	
	20/8/16		ditto weather fine	
	21/8/16		about 3.30 PM left MAZINGARBE to relieve the 6th R.I. Regt in R.S. Section of LOOS – B Coy on the LEFT. beside the Cassier occupying HARTE'S Crater. A Coy Centre Coy occupying MANNINGS MOUND (by night only) and HARRISON'S Crater. C Coy on the Right holding DEADMANS SAP	

T.2134. Wt. W708—776. 500000. 4/15. Sir J. C. & S.

Instructions regarding War Diaries and Intelligence Summaries are contained in F. S. Regs., Part II. and the Staff Manual respectively. Title pages will be prepared in manuscript.

WAR DIARY
or
INTELLIGENCE SUMMARY.
(Erase heading not required.)

Army Form C. 2118.

81

Place	Date	Hour	Summary of Events and Information 6th Btn Connaught Rangers	Remarks and references to Appendices
	21/8/16		to HAYMARKET. The MUNSTERS (8th) on our left and a Battalion of the MIDDLESEX on our Right. D Coy occupied Enclosure Avenue & the reserve trench B Coy had 3 casualties in carrying out the Relief the night passed quietly	
	22/8/16		the usual T.M. activity on part of the Enemy was displayed through out the day – At 5 PM our artillery organised a strafe assisted by Heavy & medium T.M.s. No reply was made by the Enemy until about 11 PM when they bombarded LOOS But not heavily – otherwise the night passed quietly	
	23/8/16		day passed quietly & uneventfully.	
	24/8/16		About 4 AM our heavy T.M.s were active. But the Enemy only replied slightly. In the afternoon about 5 PM we were relieved by a Battalion of the WELSH Regt. ~~and~~ The relieving Battalion suffered some casualties in carrying out relief. The centre Coy was not relieved till after Dark	

T2134. Wt. W708–776. 500000. 4/15. Sir J. C. & S.

Instructions regarding War Diaries and Intelligence Summaries are contained in F. S. Regs., Part II. and the Staff Manual respectively. Title pages will be prepared in manuscript.

WAR DIARY
or
INTELLIGENCE SUMMARY.
(Erase heading not required.)

Army Form C. 2118.

82

Place	Date	Hour	Summary of Events and Information 6th Bn Connaught Rangers	Remarks and references to Appendices
	24/8/16		The Battalion arrived at LE BRÉBIS about 2 AM	
	25/8/16		We left LE BREBIS at 12 NOON and proceeded by march to MARLES MINES via MAZINGARBE and NOEUX LES MINES we arrived at our destination at 8 PM. on this date the Batt. was augmented by a draft of 96 men, the weather continued fine	
	26/8/16		marched from MAR LES MINES to BAS RIEUX arriving 1 PM	
	27/8/16		Rested	
	28/8/16		ditto	
	29/8/16		at 3 AM left BAS RIEUX and marched to CHOQUE where we Entrained at 7 AM for HEILLY arriving at 4 PM. we left here at 6 PM and marched to camp near MEAULTE where we Bivouac. the night turned very wet	
	30/8/16		Remained in camp & constructed Shelters. very wet day.	
	31/8/16		at 10 AM left camp & arrived at CITIDAL 1 PM. at 4 PM. left camp for the Trenches in rear of GUILLEMONT.	[illegible signature] Major

T2134. Wt. W708–776. 500000. 4/15. Sir J. C. & S.

Instructions regarding War Diaries and Intelligence Summaries are contained in F. S. Regs., Part II. and the Staff Manual respectively. Title pages will be prepared in manuscript.

WAR DIARY
or
INTELLIGENCE SUMMARY.
(Erase heading not required.)

Army Form C. 2118.

83

Summary of Events and Information 6th Bn Connaught Rangers

Place	Date	Hour	Summary of Events and Information	Remarks and references to Appendices
	31/8/16		C Coy occupied the Left of the front line and D Coy the Right opposite the QUARRIES. A Coy in the Support line, and B Coy in RESERVE. The 7th LEINSTER'S were on our Left, and a Battalion of the STAFFORDSHIRES on our Right	

[signature] Major

T2134. Wt. W708–776. 500000. 4/15. Sir J. C. & S.

47
16

WAR DIARY.

6th Connaught Rangers.

MONTH OF ~~AUGUST~~ SEPTEMBER. 1916.

VOLUME:- 10

Vol 9

10 11

Instructions regarding War Diaries and Intelligence Summaries are contained in F. S. Regs., Part II. and the Staff Manual respectively. Title pages will be prepared in manuscript.

WAR DIARY
or
~~INTELLIGENCE SUMMARY.~~
(Erase heading not required.)

6th (S) Bn. THE CONN. RANGERS

84

Army Form C. 2118.

Place	Date	Hour	Summary of Events and Information	Remarks and references to Appendices
	1/9/16		The Battalion spent the day + night improving trenches. no change in position of Companies from previous date	
	2/9/16		Further improvements were being made in the trenches. our reserve line was heavily shelled from 6 to 8 PM B Coy suffered severely 10 men killed + 30 wounded. We were informed during the afternoon, that we were to take part in the attack arranged for the next day in place of the Rifle Brigade 20th Division	
	3/9/16		at 5 AM the Battalion was drawn up in position for the attack the Battalion was to go over in (3) three waves. C Coy on the LEFT attack from RIM TRENCH, D Coy on the Right to attack through the QUARRY. The 2nd Wave consisted of 2 platoons of B Coy to assist C Coy. + 2 platoons of A Coy to assist D Coy. The 3rd Wave 2 platoons of B Coy on the left + 2 platoons of A Coy on the Right. About 8 AM. our Artillery commenced to shell German front line - unfortunately	

T2134. Wt. W708-776. 500000. 4/15. Sir J. C. & S.

Instructions regarding War Diaries and Intelligence Summaries are contained in F. S. Regs., Part II. and the Staff Manual respectively. Title pages will be prepared in manuscript.

WAR DIARY
or
INTELLIGENCE SUMMARY.
(Erase heading not required.)

Army Form C. 2118.

85

Place	Date	Hour	Summary of Events and Information	Remarks and references to Appendices
	3/9/16		several of our own H.T.M's fell short & landing in RIM TRENCH HUN ALLEY & Support trench. Up to 12 NOON our casualties numbered nearly 200. At 11-55 AM the two Coys making the 1st wave were so weakened ~~for~~ by casualties that the Commanding Officer fearing an attack by the Enemy ordered the ~~2~~ & Coys forming the 2nd & 3rd wave to reinforce the 1st wave in their assembly trenches. At 12 NOON our R.F.A opened an intense barrage on the Enemy's front & support trenches. At 12.3 the barrage lifted and C & D Coys commenced the attack followed by B & A Coys. Very little opposition was met with on the LEFT as the Enemy surrendered at once, though they experienced some casualties from M.G. fire coming from direction of the QUARRIES. Some opposition ~~was opposition~~ was experienced on the Right but was soon over come. They then devoted their attention to clearing the cellars in the QUARRIES. The 1st objective was obtained at 12-9 PM 2nd objective obtained 12-20 and the 3rd objective NORTH St. at 12-55 PM	

T2134. Wt. W708—776. 500000. 4/15. Sir J. C. & S.

Instructions regarding War Diaries and Intelligence Summaries are contained in F. S. Regs., Part II. and the Staff Manual respectively. Title pages will be prepared in manuscript.

WAR DIARY
or
INTELLIGENCE SUMMARY.
(Erase heading not required.)

Army Form C. 2118.

86

Place	Date	Hour	Summary of Events and Information	Remarks and references to Appendices
	3/8/16	12-55 PM	On reaching the 3rd objective the 8th Royal Munster Fusiliers and 6th Royal Irish Regiment, passed through us on their way towards Sunken Road, the final objective	
			About 140 of our men joined in the advance of the R. I. Regt + RMF, and remained with them till the final objective was reached. The remainder of the Battalion got in touch with Right flank of the 7th LEINSTER Regt, and occupied a trench which was dug by the R.E's, parallel to BROMPTON ROAD. While this trench was being dug, the enemy were very quiet. We were informed by Bde Hd Qrs that we were to be relieved that night, this did not come off. Very little shelling during that night, anxiety was caused by the counter attacks on the R.M.F. left flank. About 70 of our men rejoined the Batt. during the night making in all 120 to hold our position	

T2134. Wt. W708–776. 500000. 4/15. Sir J. C. & S.

Instructions regarding War Diaries and Intelligence Summaries are contained in F. S. Regs., Part II. and the Staff Manual respectively. Title pages will be prepared in manuscript.

WAR DIARY
or
INTELLIGENCE SUMMARY.
(Erase heading not required.)

Army Form C. 2118.

87

Place	Date	Hour	Summary of Events and Information	Remarks and references to Appendices
	4/9/16		The Enemy shelled us intermittently with 5-9's but inflicted little damage. about 11 AM we were again notified by the Bde that we would be relieved that afternoon, later the Relief was postponed till dark -	
	5/9/16		The Batt was relieved at 3-50 AM relief was complete by 4-15 AM. The Batt returned to CARNOY 124 strong - There we found about 70 men who had ~~being~~ been relieved when with R.I.R + RMF we were reinforced by a draft of 91 men from the Base.	
	6/9/16		Major R.C. Feilding 1st Coldstream Guards assumed Command of the Battalion about 3 PM.	
	7/9/16		At 5.50 pm. the Battalion, 200 strong with 11 Officers, 31 Lewis Gunners plus Signallers and Headquarters, marched from CARNOY, timing its arrival at BERNAFAY WOOD for 8.20 pm, when darkness would have set in. Here we were met by a guide and conducted to the JUNCTION of the SUNKEN ROAD and MOUNTSTREET which was reached about 10.30 p.m.	

T2134. Wt. W708–776. 500000. 4/15. Sir J. C. & S.

Instructions regarding War Diaries and Intelligence Summaries are contained in F. S. Regs., Part II. and the Staff Manual respectively. Title pages will be prepared in manuscript.

WAR DIARY
or
INTELLIGENCE SUMMARY.
(Erase heading not required.)

Army Form C. 2118.

88

Place	Date	Hour	Summary of Events and Information	Remarks and references to Appendices
	7/9/16	Contd.	Delay was caused opposite and after leaving GUILLEMONT by the enemy's shell fire. which was considerable, catching us while we were crossing the open. and wounding the guide as well as causing several casualties to the Battalion.	
			On reaching the Junction of the SUNKEN ROAD and MOUNTSTREET the Battalion was with some difficulty accommodated in the Assembly Trenches allotted to it for the coming attack. These trenches were found to be very primitive and shallow, and so irregular in form that it was only by distributing the Companies in scattered portions of trench that it was possible to fit them in at all. It took until the early morning to accomplish this.	
	8/9/16		Was occupied in preparing for the attack to take place the following day	
	9/9/16		The orders for the attack in so far as they affected the troops under my command, were briefly as follows:—	

Instructions regarding War Diaries and Intelligence Summaries are contained in F. S. Regs., Part II. and the Staff Manual respectively. Title pages will be prepared in manuscript.

WAR DIARY
or
INTELLIGENCE SUMMARY.
(Erase heading not required.)

Army Form C. 2118.

89

Place	Date	Hour	Summary of Events and Information	Remarks and references to Appendices
	9/9/16	cont^d	Objectives 47th Brigade First Objective T.20. b 4½. 3½ – point where trench crosses GINCHY LEUZE WOOD ROAD at T.14.C 3½. 1½ (inclusive) Second objective Trench junction at T.14. d. 8½. 4 (exclusive) – point where trench crosses road at T.14.C.5.4½ (inclusive) METHOD OF ATTACK (a) At Zero (4.45 pm) plus 2 minutes the 6th Royal Irish on right and 8th MUNSTERS on left to advance and clear the German trench from T.20 CENTRAL to T.20 a.1.6., and having cleared it to push on and take the first objective (b) The 6th (S) BATT CONNAUGHT RANGERS to move up as soon as the first line had cleared the German trench from T.20 CENTRAL to T.20 a.1.6., and to occupy the left portion of that trench. One company 7th BATT LEINSTER REGT and two companies 11th BATT HANTS (PIONEERS) to move up and occupy the right portion of the German trench. (c) The LEINSTERS and HANTS on the right and the CONNAUGHTS on the left to advance, so as to pass through the first objective at Zero plus 40 minutes	

T2134. Wt. W708–776. 500000. 4/15. Sir J. C. & S.

Instructions regarding War Diaries and Intelligence Summaries are contained in F. S. Regs., Part II. and the Staff Manual respectively. Title pages will be prepared in manuscript.

WAR DIARY
or
INTELLIGENCE SUMMARY.
(Erase heading not required.)

Army Form C. 2118.

90

Place	Date	Hour	Summary of Events and Information	Remarks and references to Appendices
	1916 Sept 9	cont'd	and to take the second objective, dig themselves in, linking up with the 168th Brigade on their right, and the 48th Brigade on their left.	
			(d) At Zero a final intensive bombardment to commence and to last for two minutes.	
			The preliminary bombardment by the BRITISH ARTILLERY commenced between 8 and 9 o'clock in the morning.	
			The disposition of the forces in my immediate vicinity before the attack is shown in the rough sketch attached.	
			The intention was that the MUNSTERS and R IRISH should advance in four waves, at distances of 50 paces, followed at 15 paces, first by a line composed from left to right as follows; 2 companies of CONNAUGHTS, ½ company 7th BATT LEINSTER REGT, 1 company HANTS; and secondly, again at 15 paces distance, by a second line composed as the first. Each company was to be accompanied by Lewis Guns.	
			The last two lines were under my command.	
			During the preliminary bombardment a good many of our shells fell	

T2134. Wt. W703–776. 500000. 4/15. Sir J. C. & S.

Instructions regarding War Diaries and Intelligence Summaries are contained in F. S. Regs., Part II. and the Staff Manual respectively. Title pages will be prepared in manuscript.

WAR DIARY
or
INTELLIGENCE SUMMARY.
(Erase heading not required.)

Army Form C. 2118.

91

Place	Date	Hour	Summary of Events and Information	Remarks and references to Appendices
	1916 Sept 9	contd.	short, in one case wounding four men of the Battalion under my command. A very large proportion of the shells aimed at the German trenches in front of us were blind. I reported both these facts at the time. The troops on my immediate left (the 1st MUNSTERS) moved forward at Zero, or 2 minutes before their allotted time. I cannot say whether this influenced our Artillery though it is a fact that the Germans in front seemed very little disturbed even by the final intensive bombardment, their snipers coolly continuing their operations up to the very moment when the first wave of 8th MUNSTERS and ROYAL IRISH crossed the parapet. The first wave was immediately mown down by a devastating fire from Machine Guns. I believe that the three remaining waves of ROYAL IRISH and part of the second wave of 8th MUNSTERS also attempted to advance but met with the same fate. The remainder of the 8th MUNSTERS did not leave their trenches, with the result that 'A' and 'B' Companies of the CONNAUGHTS, who it had been planned should occupy these trenches immediately the 8th MUNSTERS had left them, were unable to do so. 'C' and 'D' Companies of the	

Instructions regarding War Diaries and Intelligence Summaries are contained in F. S. Regs., Part II. and the Staff Manual respectively. Title pages will be prepared in manuscript.

WAR DIARY
or
INTELLIGENCE SUMMARY.
(Erase heading not required.)

Army Form C. 2118.

92

Place	Date	Hour	Summary of Events and Information	Remarks and references to Appendices
	1916 Sept 9	Cont^d	CONNAUGHTS, under Captains Stewart and Bain respectively, were not hampered in this manner, and noticing a pause, assumed that the four waves of 8th MUNSTERS and the first wave of the CONNAUGHTS had gone over. They therefore started themselves. They were able however, to advance only a few yards, both officers being wounded, the first seriously. Captain Stewart has since died. On the right, there being no suitable jumping off trench it had been arranged that the LEINSTERS and HANTS should cross the open to their starting point, but before they were able to reach it, all the HANTS officers but one had been hit, in addition to many of the rank and file. The Officer commanding the two HANTS Companies had already been wounded by a sniper earlier in the day. From my observation of the terrific fire which the leading Companies encountered on leaving their trench, directed not only from the German trench in front but from numerous shell holes, I do not believe it would have been possible to do more than they accomplished. Officers and non-commissioned officers who actually saw the German trench report that it had escaped our preliminary bombardment almost entirely and that it was thickly manned. This	

T2134. Wt. W708–776. 500000. 4/15. Sir J. C. & S.

Army Form C. 2118.

93

Instructions regarding War Diaries and Intelligence Summaries are contained in F. S. Regs., Part II. and the Staff Manual respectively. Title pages will be prepared in manuscript.

WAR DIARY
or
INTELLIGENCE SUMMARY.
(Erase heading not required.)

Place	Date	Hour	Summary of Events and Information	Remarks and references to Appendices
	Sept 9	Cont'd	report was confirmed later – so I have been informed by the O.C. 1st MUNSTERS by a map dropped from an aeroplane in the neighbourhood of GINCHY.	
			Heavy shelling continued during the rest of the day and the night, delaying our relief by the 4th BATT. GRENADIER GUARDS who did not reach us till about 4.40 the following morning.	
			The casualties incurred by the 6th BATTN CONNAUGHT RANGERS for the three days had then amounted to 9 officers and 83 other ranks killed, wounded and missing.	
			The Battalion was well served by its Medical Officer, Lieut KNIGHT, who was methodical and untiring throughout in his care of the wounded. All of the latter who had not already been removed, we took with us when we left the trenches.	
			All ranks behaved with the greatest gallantry throughout.	
	Sept 10		At 7.30 a.m. I reported at BRIGADE H.Q at the BRIQUETERIE, and thence marched with the Battalion to CARNOY CRATERS.	

T2134. Wt. W708–776. 500000. 4/15. Sir J. C. & S.

Instructions regarding War Diaries and Intelligence Summaries are contained in F. S. Regs., Part II. and the Staff Manual respectively. Title pages will be prepared in manuscript.

WAR DIARY
or
INTELLIGENCE SUMMARY.
(Erase heading not required.)

Army Form C. 2118.

94

Place	Date	Hour	Summary of Events and Information	Remarks and references to Appendices
	11/9/16		At 3.30 pm on 11/9/16 the Battalion marched to HAPPY VALLEY where it rested for the night and joined our 1st line Transport.	
	12/9/16		At 3.0 p.m. on 12/9/16 the Battalion left HAPPY VALLEY and marched to VAUX SUR SOMME where we arrived about 8 p.m. Officers and men were billetted.	
	13/9/16		The greater part of the day was spent in general cleaning up etc. Rifles were inspected in morning and a little steady drill was done in the afternoon. Under arrangements made by 47th I.B., ground for practice of the Assault, Rifle Range and Bombing ground was arranged. Companys were practised in the Assault & Musketry was carried out on Rifle Range. The Bombers under the Bomb[g] Officer were practised in throwing live grenades and the Lewis Gunners under the L.G. Officer were on Rifle Range.	
	14/9/16		The same as on 13/9/16	
	15/9/16		The same as on 13/9/16.	

T2134. Wt. W708—776. 500000. 4/15. Sir J. C. & S.

Instructions regarding War Diaries and Intelligence Summaries are contained in F. S. Regs., Part II. and the Staff Manual respectively. Title pages will be prepared in manuscript.

WAR DIARY
or
INTELLIGENCE SUMMARY.
(Erase heading not required.)

Army Form C. 2118.

95

Place	Date	Hour	Summary of Events and Information	Remarks and references to Appendices
	16/9/16		In the morning two Companies went on the Range, and two Companies practised assault. Two N.C.O. Instructors of the COLDSTREAM GUARDS joined the Battalion. In the afternoon a class of N.C.O's was formed for instruction in Drill, Handling of Arms etc. under Instructors.	
	17/9/16		Companys were instructed in Drill etc. under COLDSTREAM GUARDS Instructors.	
	18/9/16		The Battalion left VAUX SUR SOMME at 10.15 a.m and marched through CORBIE ~~...~~ The Battn was conveyed by French motor buses to HUPPY. We arrived at HUPPY about 7 p.m, where we were billeted.	
	19/9/16		It rained until about noon. The Battn. prepared for further move into 2nd Army Area. Move was postponed ~~...~~ till 21/9/16	
	20/9/16		The day was spent in cleaning up Billets previous to departure, and a little steady drill was done.	

Instructions regarding War Diaries and Intelligence Summaries are contained in F. S. Regs., Part II. and the Staff Manual respectively. Title pages will be prepared in manuscript.

WAR DIARY
or
INTELLIGENCE SUMMARY.
(Erase heading not required.)

Army Form C. 2118.

96

Place	Date	Hour	Summary of Events and Information	Remarks and references to Appendices
	21/9/16		The Battalion left HUPPY at 5.15 a.m. and marched to ABBEVILLE. We entrained at ABBEVILLE for BAILLEUL at 9.45 a.m. On arrival at ~~ABBEVILLE~~ BAILLEUL the Battalion marched through METEREN to FONTAINE HOUCK where we were billeted.	
	22/9/16		G.O.C. 47th Infantry Brigade inspected the Billets occupied by the Batt. today. The weather was very fine and some Steady Drill and Handling of Arms was done. A draft of 20 other ranks joined the Battalion on this date.	
	23/9/16		~~A draft of 20 other ranks joined the Battalion this day.~~ Weather still keeping very fine. Steady drill was carried out morning and afternoon. A draft of twelve Officers joined on this date. Orders were received that the Battalion would move on the following day into Divisional Reserve.	
	24/9/16		The Battalion marched at 8.45 a.m. through ST JEAN CAPPEL to LOCRE. We arrived about 11.30 a.m. The Battalion was encamped in Huts	

Instructions regarding War Diaries and Intelligence Summaries are contained in F. S. Regs., Part II. and the Staff Manual respectively. Title pages will be prepared in manuscript.

WAR DIARY
or
INTELLIGENCE SUMMARY.
(*Erase heading not required.*)

Army Form C. 2118.

97

Place	Date	Hour	Summary of Events and Information	Remarks and references to Appendices
	25/9/16		The Battalion was inspected this day by the Army Commander, at 11 a.m. and marched past in Column of route.	
			At 12 noon the Battn proceeded by Companies to the Baths at WESTOUTRE	
	26/9/16		The Battalion drilled by Companies in the morning. Inspections of clothing and necessaries were carried out and deficiencies made up.	
	27/9/16		In the morning Officers and N.C.O.s were lectured in the use of the new Box Respirator which had been issued but not taken into use	
			The Battalion prepared to move to the trenches. We moved by Companies to the trenches and relieved the 8th ROYAL DUBLIN FUSILIERS in the VIERSTRAAT SECTOR, Relief was complete about 11.0 p.m. and the Battalion was distributed as follows. Headquarters at ~~York House~~ YORK HOUSE, 'D' Company two platoons in front line, and two platoons in Support. 'B' Company, one platoon on the right of 'D' Coy in front line taken over from 7th ROYAL IRISH RIFLES, the remainder of 'B' Coy at S.P.13.	

T2134. Wt. W708–776. 500000. 4/15. Sir J. C. & S.

Instructions regarding War Diaries and Intelligence Summaries are contained in F. S. Regs., Part II. and the Staff Manual respectively. Title pages will be prepared in manuscript.

Army Form C. 2118.

98

WAR DIARY
or
INTELLIGENCE SUMMARY.
(Erase heading not required.)

Place	Date	Hour	Summary of Events and Information	Remarks and references to Appendices
	27/9/16	Contd	'A' Company occupied SANDBAG VILLA and 'C' Company were in reserve at IEGE FARM.	
	28/9/16		The Battalion found the quietness of the new sector a welcome change, and with the exception of some rifle and Machine Gun fire during the night and some Artillery activity during the day on our left there were no operations to report.) During the night much work was done in the front line in defilading the fire-trench and nightly working parties were supplied by the Companies in reserve and support.	
	29/9/16		The day passed quietly. A few rounds were fired at intervals by our Batteries. This provoked no enemy retaliation. During the night there was the usual Rifle and Machine Gun activity on both sides. A draft of one officer and 42 other ranks joined the Battalion on this date.	

Instructions regarding War Diaries and Intelligence Summaries are contained in F. S. Regs., Part II. and the Staff Manual respectively. Title pages will be prepared in manuscript.

WAR DIARY
or
INTELLIGENCE SUMMARY.
(Erase heading not required.)

Army Form C. 2118.

99

Place	Date	Hour	Summary of Events and Information	Remarks and references to Appendices
	30/9/16		The situation was very quiet to day and the weather fine. The same working parties for the front line were provided by the Companies in support and reserve, and much revetting work was done. During the night we received information that a raid was being made by the Australian Division on our left at 10 p.m. At that hour there was great Artillery activity on our left with which our Stokes Guns cooperated, firing on the enemy trenches on our left front. Ten of the enemy shells fell in our lines and we had only one casualty. This was the only casualty we suffered during our occupation of the line. Some of the shells that fell in our line while the raid was in progress smelt strongly of phosphorous, and one of our Officers complained of being slightly burned on the hand by what he believed was a piece of phosphorous.	
			The situation was again normal at 11.0 p.m.	
			A draft of one officer joined the Battalion on this date.	

[signature] LIEUT. COLONEL,
COMDG. 6th (S) Bn. THE CONNAUGHT RANGERS

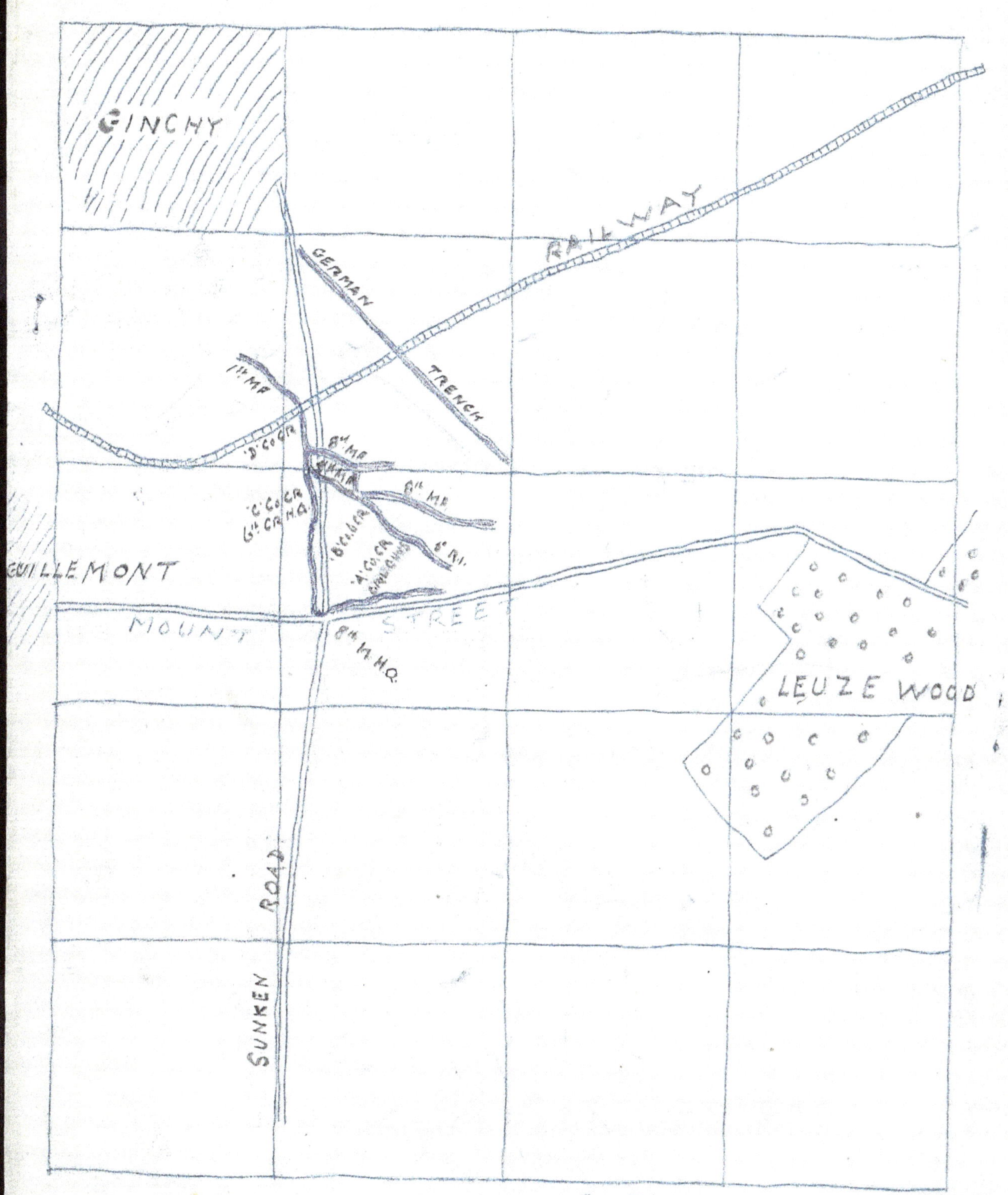

ROUGH SKETCH

SCALE

EACH SQUARE = 250 YDS x 250 YDS

W A R D I A R Y

MONTH OF OCTOBER, 1916.

VOLUME 11

6th Connaught Rangers.

Instructions regarding War Diaries and Intelligence Summaries are contained in F. S. Regs., Part II. and the Staff Manual respectively. Title pages will be prepared in manuscript.

WAR DIARY 6th (S) BN. THE CONNAUGHT RANGERS

or

~~INTELLIGENCE SUMMARY.~~

(Erase heading not required.)

Army Form C. 2118.

100

Place	Date	Hour	Summary of Events and Information	Remarks and references to Appendices
	1/10/16		The day passed quietly. Weather still very fine. On this date the dispositions were changed. At 6 a.m "C" Coy left SIEGE FARM and relieved the 1st BN. ROYAL MUNSTER FUSILIERS in the following strong Points :- S.P. 13 (old) and TURNER'S TOWN. "B" Coy extended our RIGHT front by putting another platoon into the front line, relieving 1st BN. ROYAL MUNSTER FUSILIERS. The remaining 2 platoons of B COY were in Support Line. 2 Platoons of A COY relieved B COY in S.P. 13 (new) The other 2 platoons remained at SANDBAG VILLA. The whole of D COY was in front Line. At 3 pm. "D" COY was relieved by 8th ROYAL MUNSTER FUSILIERS and proceeded to SIEGE FARM, B COY was next relieved (about 4.30 pm.) by same BATTALION and proceeded to KEMMEL. The 2 platoons of "A" COY occupying S.P. 13 (new) were also relieved by "C" Coy 6th CONNAUGHTS and proceeded to join the platoons in SANDBAG VILLA. The dispositions of "C" COY remained, with the foregoing exception, the same. BN. HD. QRS. moved on relief by 8th R.M.F. from YORK HOUSE to SIEGE FARM. Relief was complete about 10 pm.	
			A Draft of 32 Other Ranks joined the Battalion this day.	

633d

T2134. Wt. W708—776. 500000. 4/15. Sir J. C. & S.

Instructions regarding War Diaries and Intelligence Summaries are contained in F. S. Regs., Part II. and Staff Manual respectively. Title pages will be prepared in manuscript.

WAR DIARY

~~or~~

~~INTELLIGENCE SUMMARY.~~

(Erase heading not required.)

6th (S) Bn. CONNAUGHT RANGERS

Army Form C. 2118.

101

Place	Date	Hour	Summary of Events and Information	Remarks and references to Appendices
	2/10/16		It rained during the night, the whole day and it was still raining in the evening. There was no activity of any kind to report. During the day A, B, D Coy + Hd. Qrs. provided working parties who were engaged in making Dug-outs and Shelters at SIEGE FARM and repairing + strengthening those already in existence. Dispositions remained the same as yesterday except that ~~in the afternoon~~ 1 Officer and 20 other Ranks of A COY relieved 1st BN: R.M.F. in FORT HALIFAX about 9.30 p.m. The night passed quietly with the exception of some Rifle and Machine Gun Activity on both sides. A Draft of 21 other Ranks joined the Battalion this date. They mostly comprised returned casualties of 3rd and 9th SEPTEMBER.	
	3/10/16		It still rained this morning until midday when the weather cleared. A Wiring class of ~~4~~ Officers and 8 N.C.Os proceeded to Hd. Qrs. 47th INFANTRY BRIGADE for instruction. LIEUT. F. BOOTH took over command of C COY this day. The night passed quietly.	

634a

Instructions regarding War Diaries and Intelligence Summaries are contained in F. S. Regs., Part II. and Staff Manual respectively. Title pages will be prepared in manuscript.

WAR DIARY
or
~~INTELLIGENCE SUMMARY.~~
(Erase heading not required.)

6th (S) Bn. CONNAUGHT RANGERS

Army Form C. 2118.

102.

Place	Date	Hour	Summary of Events and Information	Remarks and references to Appendices
	4/10/16.		It began to rain early in the morning and with a few fine intervals rained all day. The same parties were provided and the same work done as on 2.10.16. 1 Officer and 20 Other ranks of "C" Coy relieved same personnel "A" COY in FORT HALIFAX, The latter proceeded to SANDBAG VILLA. CAPT. W.P. LAMBERT proceeded on leave and the personnel who proceeded on the WIRING COURSE returned tonight. The Battalion was required to supply working Parties to the R.E. and 11th HANTS REGT. (PIONEERS). About 8 pm, there was some TRENCH MORTAR activity on our RIGHT. Otherwise the night passed quietly.	
	5/10/16		The Battalion was relieved today as follows by 6th Royal IRISH REGT and 7th LEINSTER REGT. "A" Coy in SANDBAG VILLA was relieved by 7th LEINSTERS, "B" Coy in KEMMEL was relieved by 6th ROYAL IRISH REGT, 3 platoons of "C" Coy. in S.P. 13 (new), FORT HALIFAX and TURNERS TOWN were relieved by 6th ROYAL IRISH REGT., the remaining platoon of "C" Coy in S.P. 13 (old) was relieved by 7th LEINSTER REGT. "D" Coy and Hd. Qrs. in SIEGE FARM was relieved by 6th ROYAL IRISH REGT. Relief was complete about 8.30 pm.	675a

T2134. Wt. W708–776. 500000. 4/15. Sir J. C. & S.

Instructions regarding War Diaries and Intelligence Summaries are contained in F. S. Regs., Part II. and the Staff Manual respectively. Title pages will be prepared in manuscript.

WAR DIARY
or
INTELLIGENCE SUMMARY.
(*Erase heading not required.*)

6th (S) Bn. CONNAUGHT RANGERS

Army Form C. 2118.

103

Place	Date	Hour	Summary of Events and Information	Remarks and references to Appendices
	5/10/16		On Completion of relief the Battalion marched to LA CLYTTE CAMP taken over from 6th ROYAL IRISH REGT.	
	6/10/16.		The greater part of the day was spent in cleaning up the camp, which was taken over in a dirty condition and as it had rained for several days previously it was found difficult to keep the camp clean. ~~2~~ Lieut G. HAIRE rejoined the Battalion from Hospital this day.	
	7/10/16		It rained practically all day today so that little Drilling was done. Company inspections were held and lists of deficiencies made. A service for JEWISH officers and Other Ranks was held at 3 pm. in the Y.M.C.A. HUT. 14 boxes of cigars and cigarettes were received from RANGOON RED CROSS SOCIETY. They were distributed and very much appreciated.	
	8/10/16		With the exception of CHURCH PARADE at 8.15 am., the Battalion rested today. The Rifles and Bayonets of Headquarters were inspected by the Armourer Sergeant. It rained at intervals during the day.	
	9/10/16.		A ~~and~~ B and C COYS were fitted with the new box RESPIRATOR in the morning under the direction of the Medical Officer. In the afternoon the Coys. proceeded to the BATHS at WESTOUTRE. 2/Lieut. BALBI and one N.C.O.	

*353 Wt. W2544/1454 700,000 5/15 D. D. & L. A.D.S.S./Forms/C. 2118.

6th Bn. CONNAUGHT RANGERS

Army Form C. 2118.

104

Instructions regarding War Diaries and Intelligence Summaries are contained in F. S. Regs., Part II. and the Staff Manual respectively. Title pages will be prepared in manuscript.

WAR DIARY
or
INTELLIGENCE SUMMARY.
(*Erase heading not required.*)

Place	Date	Hour	Summary of Events and Information	Remarks and references to Appendices
	9/10/16		proceeded to TERDEGHEM on Grenade Course. One N.C.O. proceeded to same place on Stokes Gun Course. The following Officers joined this day:- Major W.A.H. GRIMSHAW, Major J.E. HARDEN, Captain T.H. CROFTON, Captain J. TASKER. Major GRIMSHAW took over the duties of Second in Command, Major HARDEN took over command of "D" COY, Captain J. TASKER temporary command of "A" Coy (during the absence of Capt LAMBERT) and Capt CROFTON was posted to B COY. At 6.30 pm. this evening a Concert was given by the Battalion in the Y.M.C.A. HUT, LA CLYTTE. The BRIGADIER was present and expressed great satisfaction with the nights entertainment. The G.O.C. 16th Division visited the Battalion today about 3 pm.	
	10/10/16		The weather was much drier today and a rather strong wind soon dried up the camp and made it look much cleaner. In the morning the remaining Coy was fitted with the new Box Respirators. In the afternoon the Coys. Drilled. 2/Lieut. P.L.N. GORDON-RALPH rejoined the Battalion from Hospital today. Notification was received that the Corps Commander XIV CORPS has awarded MILITARY MEDALS to the following No. 1630 Pte. F. McPARTLAND, No. 1739 Pte. A. CORRIGAN, No. 848 Sgt. J. DEVEREUX	637d

353 Wt. W2544/1454 700,000 5/15 D. D. & L. A.D.S.S./Forms/C. 2118.

6th (S) Bn CONNAUGHT RANGERS

Army Form C. 2118.

105

~~WAR DIARY~~

or

INTELLIGENCE SUMMARY.

(Erase heading not required.)

Instructions regarding War Diaries and Intelligence Summaries are contained in F. S. Regs., Part II. and the Staff Manual respectively. Title pages will be prepared in manuscript.

Place	Date	Hour	Summary of Events and Information	Remarks and references to Appendices
	11/10/16.		In the morning the Companies marched to Divisional Gas School where the new Box Respirators were tested in Lacrymatory Gas. The Respirators were found most effective. At 12 noon the Divisional commander lectured all the officers of the Battalion. 2/Lieut. W. E. CARNAGHAN 5th CONN. RANGERS reported for duty today. A Draft of 11 other Ranks, mostly returned Casualties was received. The Companies drilled in the afternoon.	
	12/10/16.		In the morning and afternoon Lewis Gunners were practised on the Range and the Bombers bombed. A foot inspection by the Medical Officer was held in the morning. In the afternoon companies were drilled in the use of the new Box Respirator under the Company Gas N.C.O.S.	
	13/10/16.		The Battalion relieved the 6th ROYAL IRISH REGT and part of the 7th LEINSTER REGT. today. Relief was carried out as follows: "B" COY relieved the 7th LEINSTER REGT in the following Strong Points: S.P. 13 (new), TURNER'S TOWN LEFT and FORT HALIFAX. "A" COY relieved 6th ROYAL IRISH REGT in fire and Support Trenches, "C" COY relieved 6th ROYAL IRISH REGT in YORK HOUSE and VAN KEEP. "D" COY relieved the garrison of SANDBAG VILLA. Headquarters relieved 6th ROYAL IRISH REGT. at YORK HOUSE. Relief was complete about 9 pm. The night passed very quietly and there was nothing to report.	

6/8a

8353 Wt. W2544/1454 700,000 5/15 D. D. & L. A.D.S.S./Forms/C. 2118.

Instructions regarding War Diaries and Intelligence Summaries are contained in F. S. Regs., Part II. and the Staff Manual respectively. Title pages will be prepared in manuscript.

WAR DIARY
or
~~INTELLIGENCE SUMMARY.~~
(Erase heading not required.)

6th (S) Bn. CONNAUGHT RANGERS

Army Form C. 2118.

106

Place	Date	Hour	Summary of Events and Information	Remarks and references to Appendices
	14/10/16.		The day passed very quietly with the exception of some slight Enemy Artillery about 2 p.m. when the trench at the junction of WATLING STREET and SUPPORT TRENCH was blown in. The night was quiet. Some rifle and Machine Gun fire on both sides. An Enemy Sniper was observed in NO MAN'S LAND and bombed. He is believed to have been killed. One Enemy Working Party was dispersed by our LEWIS GUNS.	
	15/10/16.		Enemy Artillery was rather unusually active about S.P.13 today. We had one casualty – CAPTAIN W.H. PARKE was killed. This Officer was one of the few of the original 6th BATTALION remaining and had served with the Battalion from its inception. He had commanded the Battalion after the capture of GUILLEMONT from 3.9.16 to 6.9.16.	
			Our Snipers claimed one direct hit today. 2 Enemy Machine Guns were observed firing at our Aeroplanes from UNNAMED WOOD and the BRICK STACK.	
			About 7.30 p.m. our artillery was very active on our left front. We had	639a

5353 Wt. W2544/1454 700,000 5/15 D. D. & L. A.D.S.S./Forms/C. 2118.

Instructions regarding War Diaries and Intelligence Summaries are contained in F. S. Regs., Part II. and the Staff Manual respectively. Title pages will be prepared in manuscript.

WAR DIARY
or
~~INTELLIGENCE SUMMARY.~~
(Erase heading not required.)

6th (S) CONNAUGHT RANGERS

Army Form C. 2118.

107

Place	Date	Hour	Summary of Events and Information	Remarks and references to Appendices
			previously received notification that a raid by the Australian Brigade on our left was intended. At 8 pm, the situation was again NORMAL. Nothing to relate during the night.	
	16/10/16		Enemy Artillery was rather active this morning between 8.30 am. and 10 am. on our left Coy. front. We suffered no casualties. Enemy sent over some rifle grenades at same place to which we retaliated in kind. Between 4.45 pm. and 6.30 pm. enemy MEDIUM TRENCH MORTARS strafed our front line. Some damage was done which was repaired during the night. About the same time there was considerable shelling about VAN KEEP and WATLING STREET. Little damage was done. We suffered two slight casualties.	
			A TEST GAS ~~ATTACK~~ ALARM was carried out today throughout the Division. The message "TEST GAS ALARM TRENCH" was received at Bn. Hd. Qrs. at 12.41 pm. Artillery fire was immediately requisitioned through LIAISON OFFICER and obtained at 12.44 pm. All Companies ~~and~~ the Brigade Pioneers, the Battalion Aid post and the 113th Field Ambulance were warned. All Officers, N.C.Os and men 'stood to' and small BOX RESPIRATORS were adjusted, and were worn for TEN MINUTES. Nothing to report during the night.	

2353 Wt. W2544/1454 700,000 5/15 D. D. & L. A.D.S.S./Forms/C. 2118.

640d

Instructions regarding War Diaries and Intelligence Summaries are contained in F. S. Regs., Part II. and the Staff Manual respectively. Title pages will be prepared in manuscript.

WAR DIARY
or
~~INTELLIGENCE SUMMARY.~~
(Erase heading not required.)

6th (S) Bn. CONNAUGHT RANGERS

Army Form C. 2118.

108

Place	Date	Hour	Summary of Events and Information	Remarks and references to Appendices
	17/10/16		The day passed quietly. Our snipers claimed one hit during the day. The Battalion was relieved this evening by the 8th ROYAL MUNSTER FUSILIERS. The relief was carried out as follows: A COY 6th CONN. RANGERS was relieved by A COY 8th ROYAL MUNSTER FUSILIERS. 2 platoons C COY and 1 platoon D COY 6th CONN. RANGERS in front line were relieved by B and D Coys 8th ROYAL MUNSTER FUSILIERS. 2 platoons of D Coy 6th CONN. RANGERS in Support line were relieved by 3 platoons of C COY 8th ROYAL MUNSTER FUSILIERS. The remaining platoon of D COY at SAND BAG VILLA was relieved by 1 platoon C COY, 8th ROYAL MUNSTER FUSILIERS. A COY proceeded on relief to SIEGE FARM, D COY and 2 platoons C COY to KEMMEL. Relief was complete about 9 pm. and the Dispositions of the Battalion were then as follows: HEADQUARTERS at SIEGE FARM, A COY SIEGE FARM, B COY TURNER'S. TOWN LEFT, FORT HALIFAX and S.P. 13, 2 Platoons "C" COY at VAN KEEP, 2 platoons "C" COY at KEMMEL and "D" COY at KEMMEL.	
			There was nothing to report during the night.	

641 a

#353 Wt. W2544/1454 700,000 5/15 D. D. & L. A.D.S.S./Forms/C. 2118.

Instructions regarding War Diaries and Intelligence Summaries are contained in F. S. Regs., Part II. and the Staff Manual respectively. Title pages will be prepared in manuscript.

WAR DIARY

or

~~INTELLIGENCE SUMMARY.~~

(Erase heading not required.)

6th (S) Bn. CONNAUGHT RANGERS

109

Army Form C. 2118.

Place	Date	Hour	Summary of Events and Information	Remarks and references to Appendices
		18/10/16	All the men in reserve were employed in finding working parties for the R.E. During the day some work was done by A Coy. in cleaning up and improving the Billets at SIEGE FARM. The weather was very wet and it was difficult to keep the Billets clean. Much work was done however in repairing the roofs of some of the Billets and sandbag foundations for 4 tents were begun. Work was continually interrupted owing to heavy rain. There was nothing to report during the night.	
		19/10/16	It still rained at intervals during the day. This prevented continuous work being done. During the dry periods the work of improving the Billets at SIEGE FARM and KEMMEL was carried on. The night passed without any occurrence.	
		20/10/16	The day was much finer than usual and a slight frost was experienced in the early morning. The work of improving the billets went on apace. One new SANDBAGGED TENT was finished and three others are nearing completion. The new billets at BUTTERFLY FARM were inspected. The night passed uneventfully.	642d

6th (S) Bn CONNAUGHT RANGERS

Army Form C. 2118.

11D

Instructions regarding War Diaries and Intelligence Summaries are contained in F. S. Regs., Part II. and the Staff Manual respectively. Title pages will be prepared in manuscript.

WAR DIARY
or
INTELLIGENCE SUMMARY.
(Erase heading not required.)

Place	Date	Hour	Summary of Events and Information	Remarks and references to Appendices
	21.10.16		The Battalion was relieved today by the 6th ROYAL IRISH REGT. and portion of the 7th LEINSTER REGT. 2 platoons of C COY. in VAN KEEP were relieved by "B" COY 7th LEINSTER REGT. B COY. in S.P. 13 was relieved by A COY. 6th ROYAL IRISH REGT. B COY. in TURNERS TOWN LEFT and FORT HALIFAX were relieved by B COY 6th ROYAL IRISH REGT. A COY. in SIEGE FARM was relieved by D COY. 6th ROYAL IRISH REGT. at 5.15 pm. D COY and 2 platoons of "C" COY. in NORTH KEMMEL were relieved by C COY. 6th ROYAL IRISH REGT at 5.45 pm.	
			On relief, the Battalion moved to BUTTERFLY FARM (N.14.d.7.4)	
			The Battalion was accommodated in tents.	
	22/10/16		Today (Sunday) CHURCH PARADE was at 9 am. There were no parades during the remainder of the day. It rained at intervals.	
	23/10/16		The majority of the Battalion was employed in Working Parties, about 100 men being found by the Battalion each day. The remainder of the Bn. paraded under Lieut T. BOOTH and were instructed in Coy. and platoon drill. In the afternoon a concert organised by 2/Lieut HOLLAWAY	64 Bde

#353 Wt. W2544/1454 700,000 5/15 D. D. & L. A.D.S.S./Forms/C. 2118.

6th (S) Bn. CONNAUGHT RANGERS

Instructions regarding War Diaries and Intelligence Summaries are contained in F. S. Regs., Part II. and the Staff Manual respectively. Title pages will be prepared in manuscript.

WAR DIARY
or
INTELLIGENCE SUMMARY.
(Erase heading not required.)

Army Form C. 2118.

111

Place	Date	Hour	Summary of Events and Information	Remarks and references to Appendices
	23/10/16.		was given for the benefit of the Battalion. The Brigadier and G.O.C. 16th Division attended and expressed themselves delighted with the evenings entertainment.	
	24/10/16.		Very little work could be done today as it rained heavily. It was very difficult to keep the Camp clean. The erection of a hut for a Canteen was begun today. A tent was used today as an extemporised Canteen and beer Tickets were issued to Coy. Commanders. The call was nobly responded to.	
	25/10/16		A Coy. provided Working Parties today and the rifles of B, C and D Coy. were inspected by the Armourer Sergeant. In the afternoon the Battalion not employed on Working parties were drilled under Lieut. BOOTH.	
	26/10/16.		Lieut. ~~Booth~~ THOMAS BOOTH took over acting ADJUTANT from 2nd Lieut FRANCIS WILLIAM SEYMOUR JOURDAIN today. The latter took over the Battalion Signalling Section. Working parties were found by companies in turn and the rifles of A. Coy and SPECIALISTS were examined by the armourer Sgt. today.	644d

8353 Wt. W2544/1454 700,000 5/15 D. D. & L. A.D.S.S./Forms/C. 2118.

6th (S) Bn. CONNAUGHT RANGERS

Army Form C. 2118.

112

Instructions regarding War Diaries and Intelligence Summaries are contained in F. S. Regs., Part II. and the Staff Manual respectively. Title pages will be prepared in manuscript.

WAR DIARY
or
~~INTELLIGENCE SUMMARY.~~
(Erase heading not required.)

Place	Date	Hour	Summary of Events and Information	Remarks and references to Appendices
	26/10/16		Captain STEPHEN LUCIUS GWYNNE, Lieut. CHARLES ANTHONY BRETT, Lieut. GEOFFREY CHARLES PATRICK RANDAL O'DONOGHUE and 2/Lieut. RICHARD HENRY FRENCH joined the Battalion for duty today. CAPT. GWYNN took over Command of B Coy from 2/Lieut. W. R. MAGUIRE. The Companies not on Working parties were drilled under 2/Lieut. T. BOOTH.	
	27/10/16		Parades were as yesterday. Weather very cold with heavy showers at intervals. The construction of the Hut for the Canteen was completed today.	
	28/10/16		Same parades as yesterday. Same working Parties found by Coys. in turn. Still raining.	
	29/10/16		The Battalion relieved the 6th ROYAL IRISH REGT and portion of the 7th LEINSTER REGT today. B Coy and 2 platoons of C Coy. 6th CONNAUGHTS relieved 6th ROYAL IRISH REGT in front Line. 2 platoons of 'C' Coy relieved 6th ROYAL IRISH REGT. in Support Line. 2 platoons of D Coy. relieved 6th ROYAL IRISH REGT. in VAN KEEP and 2 platoons of D COY. relieved 7th LEINSTERS in S.P. B. 2 platoons of 'A' Coy relieved 7th LEINSTERS in turners TOWN LEFT and FORT HALIFAX. 2 platoons of A Coy proceeded to SANDBAG VILLA.	6450

8353 Wt. W2544/1454 700,000 5/15 D. D. & L. A.D.S.S./Forms/C. 2118.

6th (S) Bn CONNAUGHT RANGERS

Instructions regarding War Diaries and Intelligence Summaries are contained in F. S. Regs., Part II. and the Staff Manual respectively. Title pages will be prepared in manuscript.

WAR DIARY
or
INTELLIGENCE SUMMARY.
(Erase heading not required.)

Army Form C. 2118.

113

Place	Date	Hour	Summary of Events and Information	Remarks and references to Appendices
	29/10/16		Relief was completed at 5 pm and the Dispositions of the Battalion were as follows: B Coy FRONT LINE. C COY. 2 platoons FRONT LINE 2 platoons SUPPORT LINE. D COY 2 platoons VAN KEEP, 2 platoons S.P. 13. A COY 1 platoon TURNERS TOWN LEFT, 1 platoon FORT HALIFAX, 2 platoons SANDBAG VILLA. The night passed quietly. Our Artillery was active between 5.45 pm and 7 pm during the demonstration in front of GRAND BOIS by 2 Battalions on our RIGHT FRONT. 2/Lieut BASIL TEMPLE UTLEY and 2/Lieut HAROLD PERCY PICKETT were accidentally wounded about 10.30 pm.	
	30/10/16		The day passed quietly. There were frequent heavy showers. Some draining of the front line was done by B Coy during the day. At 5.30 pm, a patrol of 1 officer 1 N.C.O. and 2 men left our lines and proceeded to examine the enemy's wire. Two rows of wire were found — a row of TRIP WIRE in front and a row of HIGH WIRE in front of the enemy parapet. The patrol remained out 2 hours.	646a

2353 Wt. W2544/1454 700,000 5/15 D. D. & L. A.D.S.S./Forms/C. 2118.

Instructions regarding War Diaries and Intelligence Summaries are contained in F. S. Regs., Part II. and the Staff Manual respectively. Title pages will be prepared in manuscript.

WAR DIARY
or
~~INTELLIGENCE SUMMARY.~~
(Erase heading not required.)

6th (S) Bn CONNAUGHT RANGERS

Army Form C. 2118.

114

Place	Date	Hour	Summary of Events and Information	Remarks and references to Appendices
	31/10/16		There was some enemy Trench Mortar Activity today on both our flanks. The LAITERIE was shelled but not hit. At 4 pm the junction of MAYO STREET and FRONT LINE was shelled with 4.2". One direct hit was obtained causing some damage. In the course of the day our Snipers claimed one hit. During the night there was the usual Machine Gun and sniping activity on both sides. We had 2 casualties.	

[signature]
LIEUT. COLONEL,
COMDG. 6th (S) Bn. THE CONNAUGHT RANGERS.

447a

2353 Wt. W2544/1454 700,000 5/15 D. D. & L. A.D.S.S./Forms/C. 2118.

W A R D I A R Y .

F O R

MONTH OF NOVEMBER, 1916.

VOLUME 12.

6th Connaught Rangers.

Instructions regarding War Diaries and Intelligence Summaries are contained in F. S. Regs., Part II. and the Staff Manual respectively. Title pages will be prepared in manuscript.

WAR DIARY
or
~~INTELLIGENCE SUMMARY.~~
(Erase heading not required.)

6th (S) Bn. The Connaught Rangers

Army Form C. 2118.

Place	Date	Hour	Summary of Events and Information	Remarks and references to Appendices
	1/11/16		The day passed quietly. At 6.15 pm. a patrol under 2/Lieut. C. L. McCARTHY consisting of 2 N.C.O.s and 1 man left our trenches at Bay No. 5 N.24.10. They met an enemy patrol which on seeing them retired and informed the Enemy who opened rapid fire and forced our patrol to retire. We had no casualties. The night passed uneventfully.	
	2/11/16		The day passed quietly and in the evening portion of the Battalion was relieved by the 8th Royal MUNSTER FUSILIERS. 2 platoons of C Coy in front line were relieved by C COY. 8th ROYAL MUNSTER FUSILIERS and 2 platoons of C COY in Support were relieved by 3 platoons D COY 8th ROYAL MUNSTER FUSILIERS. C COY on relief proceeded to KEMMEL. B COY in front line was relieved by A + B COYS 8th ROYAL MUNSTER FUSILIERS and proceeded on completion of relief to SIEGE FARM. 2 platoons of A COY in SANDBAG VILLA were relieved by 1 platoon D Coy. 8th ROYAL MUNSTER FUSILIERS and on relief proceeded to KEMMEL.	

2353 Wt. W2544/1454 700,000 5/15 D. D. & L. A.D.S.S./Forms/C. 2118.

Army Form C. 2118.

WAR DIARY

or

~~INTELLIGENCE SUMMARY.~~

(*Erase heading not required.*)

Instructions regarding War Diaries and Intelligence Summaries are contained in F. S. Regs., Part II. and the Staff Manual respectively. Title pages will be prepared in manuscript.

Place	Date	Hour	Summary of Events and Information	Remarks and references to Appendices
	2/11/16.		On completion of relief dispositions were as follows:- A COY : 2 platoons in KEMMEL, 1 platoon TURNERS TOWN LEFT, 1 platoon FORT HALIFAX. B COY in SIEGE FARM. C COY in KEMMEL. D COY 2 platoons in S.P. 13 and 2 platoons in VAN KEEP. Battalion HD. QRS. in SIEGE FARM.	
			Relief was complete about 8 pm.	
	3/11/16		The Companies in Brigade Support were required to find working Parties amounting to about 90 N.C.Os and men for the R.E. During the morning 3" heavy Trench Mortars fell in the neighbourhood of VAN KEEP. No damage was done. Otherwise the day passed quietly. During the night there was the usual Machine Gun and Sniping on both sides.	
	4/11/16		Between 10.30 and 11 am. today 4 of our own 18 pounders fell in the neighbourhood of VAN KEEP and 7 near S.P. 13. No damage was done. Between 3.15 pm + 3.30 pm our Artillery + Trench Mortars carried out an intense bombardment of the Enemy's lines. Retaliation was very slight and caused no damage.	
			The night passed quietly.	

8353 Wt. W2544/1454 700,000 5/15 D. D. & L. A.D.S.S./Forms/C. 2118.

Army Form C. 2118.

Instructions regarding War Diaries and Intelligence Summaries are contained in F. S. Regs., Part II. and the Staff Manual respectively. Title pages will be prepared in manuscript.

WAR DIARY
or
~~INTELLIGENCE SUMMARY.~~
(Erase heading not required.)

Place	Date	Hour	Summary of Events and Information	Remarks and references to Appendices
	5/11/16.		The day passed quietly. The Battalion was relieved tonight by 6th ROYAL IRISH REGT. and portion of 7th LEINSTER REGT. and proceeded on relief to the Huts at CURRAGH CAMP, LOCRE. 2 platoons of D Coy in VAN KEEP were relieved by C COY, 7th LEINSTER REGT. and 2 platoons of D COY. in S.P. 13 were relieved by 2 platoons of C COY. 6th ROYAL IRISH REGT. C COY and 2 platoons of A COY at KEMMEL were relieved by B COY 6th ROYAL IRISH REGT. 1 platoon of A COY in FORT HALIFAX and 1 platoon of A COY in TURNERS TOWN LEFT were each relieved by 1 platoon C COY 6th ROYAL IRISH REGT. B COY at SIEGE FARM were relieved by A + D COYS 6th ROYAL IRISH REGT. Relief was complete about 7.30 pm.	
	6/11/16.		The Huts at CURRAGH CAMP had only been completed a few days before the arrival of the BATTALION there and consequently there was much work to be done in the way of improvements. On arrival it was found that there were few, if any, benches or tables and the	

2353 Wt. W2544/1454 700,000 5/15 D. D. & L. A.D.S.S./Forms/C. 2118.

Instructions regarding War Diaries and Intelligence Summaries are contained in F. S. Regs., Part II. and the Staff Manual respectively. Title pages will be prepared in manuscript.

WAR DIARY
or
~~INTELLIGENCE SUMMARY.~~
(Erase heading not required.)

Army Form C. 2118.

Place	Date	Hour	Summary of Events and Information	Remarks and references to Appendices
			Battalion Pioneers were got busy on this at once. It was also found necessary to dig a shallow drain round the sides of each hut and to wire off the unoccupied spaces at the camp so as to prevent puddling.	
			Lewis Gunners and Bombers were practised today under the L.G.O. and Bombing Officer.	
			All Companies held a kit Inspection today and in the afternoon the Rifles were inspected by the Armourer Sgt. The Medical Officer also held a foot Inspection today.	
	7/11/16		A + B Coys Drilled for 3 hours today. A Coy. was inspected by the C.O. at 9.30 am. this morning. C and D Coys did 2 hours Drill and 1 hours Bayonet Fighting. The C.O. inspected A Coy. at 9.30 am. Lewis Gunners and Bombers were practised under their respective Officers today and inspected by the C.O.	

2353 Wt. W2544/1454 700,000 5/15 D. D. & L. A.D.S.S./Forms/C. 2118.

Army Form C. 2118.

Instructions regarding War Diaries and Intelligence Summaries are contained in F. S. Regs., Part II. and the Staff Manual respectively. Title pages will be prepared in manuscript.

WAR DIARY
or
~~INTELLIGENCE SUMMARY.~~
(Erase heading not required.)

Place	Date	Hour	Summary of Events and Information	Remarks and references to Appendices
	8/11/16		A + B Coys did 2 Hours Drill today and 1 hours Bayonet Fighting and physical training under 2/Lieuts WILLIAMSON and MONAN. C and D Coys did 3 hours drill under Coy Arrangements. Much work was done today in sandbagging the lower parts of the Huts under the Supervision of Lieut. T. HUGHES. Specialists were practised as yesterday	
	9/11/16.		Companies drilled as yesterday. There is nothing new to report. The work of improvement went on apace.	
	10/11/16		Baths at LOCRE were at the disposal of the Battalion and were allotted to Companies as follows:– A Coy: 8 am. to 9 am, B Coy. 9 am. to 10 am, C Coy. 10 am. to 11 am; D Coy 11 am. to 12 noon. Companies drilled in the afternoon under Coy. Arrangements.	
	11/11/16.		The C.O. inspected ~~the~~ B Coy. at 9.30 am today and the Transport at 12 noon. Companies were practised in the handling of arms and drilled for	

2353 Wt. W2544/1454 700,000 5/15 D. D. & L. A.D.S.S./Forms/C. 2118.

Army Form C. 2118.

Instructions regarding War Diaries and Intelligence Summaries are contained in F. S. Regs., Part II. and the Staff Manual respectively. Title pages will be prepared in manuscript.

WAR DIARY
or
~~INTELLIGENCE SUMMARY.~~
(Erase heading not required.)

Place	Date	Hour	Summary of Events and Information	Remarks and references to Appendices
			2 hours today.	
			There was a comparison of Company Conduct sheets with Report Books at 2.30 p.m. today.	
			2/Lieut. C.W.B. FITZGERALD was authorised to wear the Badges of CAPTAIN whilst commanding "C" Coy. under C.D.S. 384, Sec. III (7).	
			2/Lieut. J.Y. HADDEN was transferred from B to C Coy.	
	12/11/16		After DIVINE SERVICE today the C.O. inspected the Quartermaster's Staff. There was nothing else to report.	
	13/11/16.		In the morning Companies drilled under Coy. arrangements and Specialists were practised under Specialist Officers.	
			In the afternoon a concert, organized by 2/Lieut. S.A. HOLLOWAY, was held in the Cinema Theatre LOCRE. The DIVISIONAL GENERAL and BRIGADIER who were present expressed themselves very much pleased with the evening's entertainment.	

Instructions regarding War Diaries and Intelligence Summaries are contained in F. S. Regs., Part II. and the Staff Manual respectively. Title pages will be prepared in manuscript.

WAR DIARY
or
~~INTELLIGENCE SUMMARY.~~
(Erase heading not required.)

Army Form C. 2118.

Place	Date	Hour	Summary of Events and Information	Remarks and references to Appendices
	14/11/16		The early morning was spent in cleaning up the Huts and the area surrounding them. The Battalion relieved the 6th ROYAL IRISH REGT. and portion of 7th LEINSTER REGT. in FRONT and SUPPORT LINES and in the STRONG POINTS this evening. On completion of relief the Battalion was disposed as follows:- D Coy in FRONT LINE, A COY 2 platoons in FRONT LINE and 2 platoons in SUPPORT LINE. C COY 2 platoons in S.P.13 and 2 platoons in VAN KEEP. B COY 1 platoon TURNERS TOWN LEFT 1 platoon FORT HALIFAX and 2 platoons SANDBAG VILLA. Battalion HD. QRS were in YORK HOUSE. The night passed quietly and there was nothing to report	
	15/11/16.		There was some enemy Trench Mortar activity during the morning. Our retaliation was prompt and effective and for the remainder of the day Enemy Trench mortars were silent. There was much sniping activity on both sides during the day. Much work was done draining the front Line. 2/Lieut. D. J. LYONS was accidentally killed today.	

2353 Wt. W2541/1454 700,000 5/15 D. D. & L. A.D.S.S./Forms/C. 2118.

Army Form C. 2118.

WAR DIARY
or
~~INTELLIGENCE SUMMARY.~~
(*Erase heading not required.*)

Instructions regarding War Diaries and Intelligence Summaries are contained in F. S. Regs., Part II. and the Staff Manual respectively. Title pages will be prepared in manuscript.

Place	Date	Hour	Summary of Events and Information	Remarks and references to Appendices
	16/11/16		The night passed quietly with the exception of the usual Sniping and Machine Gun activity on both sides. Our Snipers claimed 3 hits during the day. About 5.30 pm a patrol went out on our left and examined the enemy's wire. It was found to be strong. The patrol returned about 7.45 pm. We had one slight casualty today.	
	17/11/16		The enemy strafed VAN KEEP today with aerial Torpedoes. We had no casualties. At 10.30 pm our artillery carried out a bombardment lasting about 10 minutes. The enemy did not retaliate. There was the usual Sniping and Machine gun activity on both Sides during the night. Otherwise nothing to report. We had no casualties today.	
	18/11/16		Nothing to report during the morning. At 3.15 pm Enemy Trench Mortars were active. Our artillery was informed and about 3.30 pm the situation was quiet. The usual work of drainage and repairing the parapet was carried out. A Draft of 4 other Ranks joined the Battalion today.	

2353 Wt. W2541/1454 700,000 5/15 D. D. & L. A.D.S.S./Forms/C. 2118.

Army Form C. 2118.

Instructions regarding War Diaries and Intelligence Summaries are contained in F. S. Regs., Part II. and the Staff Manual respectively. Title pages will be prepared in manuscript.

WAR DIARY
or
~~INTELLIGENCE SUMMARY.~~

(Erase heading not required.)

Place	Date	Hour	Summary of Events and Information	Remarks and references to Appendices
	19/11/16		The day passed quietly. Portion of the Battalion was relieved tonight by the 8th ROYAL MUNSTER FUSRS, in FRONT and SUPPORT LINES and in SANDBAG VILLA. Relief was complete about 7 pm and the Battalion was then disposed as follows:- A COY and 2 platoons B Coy in KEMMEL. 1 platoon B COY in FORT HALIFAX and 1 platoon B COY in TURNERS TOWN LEFT. 2 platoons COY in S.P. 13 and 2 platoons C COY in VAN KEEP. D COY and BATTALION HD. QRS in SIEGE FARM. There was nothing to report during the night. A draft of 30 Other Ranks joined the Battalion today.	
	20/11/16.		The Companies in Brigade Support were required to find the usual working parties for the R.E amounting to about 100 Other Ranks. During the day the men who were not on Working Parties were employed in cleaning up and improving the Billets in SIEGE FARM and in KEMMEL. A Draft of 4 Other Ranks (all returned casualties) joined the Battalion from 16th INFY. BASE. DEPOT today.	

2353 Wt. W2544/1454 700,000 5/15 D. D. & L. A.D.S.S./Forms/C. 2118.

Instructions regarding War Diaries and Intelligence Summaries are contained in F. S. Regs., Part II. and the Staff Manual respectively. Title pages will be prepared in manuscript.

WAR DIARY
or
~~INTELLIGENCE SUMMARY~~.
(*Erase heading not required.*)

Army Form C. 2118.

Place	Date	Hour	Summary of Events and Information	Remarks and references to Appendices
	21/11/16		The same working Parties as yesterday were found today. The weather was very bad and many Trench Boards had to be put down to provide clean passages at SIEGE FARM. Otherwise nothing to report.	
	22/11/16		Working Parties were again found today for the R.E. A wash-house was constructed today at SIEGE FARM and a drain dug to carry the water into the stream close by.	
	23/11/16		The Battalion was relieved tonight by the 6th ROYAL IRISH REGT and portion of the 7th LEINSTER REGT. A COY and 2 platoons of B COY in KEMMEL were relieved by 6th ROYAL IRISH REGT. 2 platoons C COY in S.P. 13 ~~and VAN KEEP~~ were relieved by 6th ROYAL IRISH REGT. and 2 platoons C COY in VAN KEEP were relieved by 7th LEINSTER REGT. 1 platoon B COY in FORT HALIFAX and 1 platoon B COY in TURNERS TOWN LEFT were each relieved by 6th ROYAL IRISH REGT. Relief was complete by 8 pm and on relief the Battalion proceeded to BUTTERFLY FARM.	

2353 Wt. W2544/1454 700,000 5/15 D. D. & L. A.D.S.S./Forms/C. 2118.

Army Form C. 2118.

Instructions regarding War Diaries and Intelligence Summaries are contained in F. S. Regs., Part II. and the Staff Manual respectively. Title pages will be prepared in manuscript.

WAR DIARY

or

~~INTELLIGENCE SUMMARY.~~

(Erase heading not required.)

Place	Date	Hour	Summary of Events and Information	Remarks and references to Appendices
	24/11/16.		Lieut. Colonel R.C. FEILDING proceeded on leave today and the command of the Battalion was assumed by Major W.A.H. GRIMSHAW. The work of Sandbagging all the tents at BUTTERFLY FARM was undertaken today but, as it was difficult to obtain the necessary material from the R.E the work was not begun until the afternoon.	
	25/11/16.		It rained all day today and very little work could be done to the tents. The Baths at LOCRE were at the disposal of the Battalion today and were used between the hours of 9 a.m. & 4 p.m. The day was too wet for any parades.	
	26/11/16.		The Battalion marched to the CHAPEL HOSPICE LOCRE for divine Service today. In the afternoon the Battalion moved into Brigade support. A and B Coys. relieved 1st ROYAL IRISH REGT. in KEMMEL. C COY and Battalion Hd. Qrs.	

2353 Wt. W2541/1454 700,000 5/15 D. D. & L. A.D.S.S./Forms/C. 2118.

Instructions regarding War Diaries and Intelligence Summaries are contained in F. S. Regs., Part II. and the Staff Manual respectively. Title pages will be prepared in manuscript.

WAR DIARY

or

~~INTELLIGENCE SUMMARY.~~

(Erase heading not required.)

Army Form C. 2118.

Place	Date	Hour	Summary of Events and Information	Remarks and references to Appendices
			relieved 6th ROYAL IRISH REGT. in SIEGE FARM. D COY relieved 6th ROYAL IRISH REGT. in S.P.B, TURNERS TOWN LEFT and FORT HALIFAX. Relief was complete about 7 p.m. and the Battalion was then disposed as follows A and B COYS KEMMEL, C COY and BATTN. HD.QRS, SIEGE FARM, D COY S.P.B, TURNERS TOWN LEFT and FORT HALIFAX, The night passed quietly.	
	27/11/16		The usual working parties for the Battalion in BRIGADE SUPPORT were provided today. A new Latrine was built at SIEGE FARM. The Sandbag wall of the COY. STORE at SIEGE FARM was rebuilt as the old one was falling out. No, casualties,	
	28/11/16.		A pit was sunk today in SIEGE FARM to provide water for the new wash-house and the drain leading to the stream was deepened. The duck boards were taken up, ~~and~~ cleaned and improved. The usual working Parties were formed. No casualties to report.	

2353 Wt. W2544/1454 700,000 5/15 D. D. & L. A.D.S.S./Forms/C. 2118.

Instructions regarding War Diaries and Intelligence Summaries are contained in F. S. Regs., Part II. and the Staff Manual respectively. Title pages will be prepared in manuscript.

WAR DIARY
or
~~INTELLIGENCE SUMMARY~~.
(Erase heading not required.)

Army Form C. 2118.

Place	Date	Hour	Summary of Events and Information	Remarks and references to Appendices
	29/11/16.		The work of making a Bath Room at SIEGE FARM was begun today. The Medical Inspection Room was whitewashed. 2/Lieut. C. E. CARNAGHAN was wounded whilst in charge of a working Party last night. We had no other casualties. A draft of 4 Other Ranks joined the Battalion today.	
	30/11/16.		The Battalion was relieved tonight by 7th LEINSTER REGT and portion of 1st ROYAL MUNSTER FUSRS. A + B COYS in KEMMEL and C COY. and BnHd. Qrs in SIEGE FARM were relieved by 7th LEINSTER REGT. 2 platoons D COY in S.P. 13 were relieved by 1st ROYAL MUNSTER FUSILIERS and 1 platoon D COY in FORT HALIFAX and 1 platoon D COY in TURNERS TOWN LEFT were relieved by 7th LEINSTER REGT. Relief was complete about 8 pm and on completion on relief the Battalion proceeded to BUTTERFLY FARM. There were No casualties.	

H Grimshaw Major ~~LIEUT. COLONEL~~,
COMDG. 6th (S) Bn. THE CONNAUGHT RANGERS.

#353 Wt. W2544/1454 700,000 5/15 D. D. & L. A.D.S.S./Forms/C. 2118.

WAR DIARY FOR MONTH OF DECEMBER, 1916.

VOLUME ~~13~~

6th Connaught Rangers

Vol 12

Instructions regarding War Diaries and Intelligence Summaries are contained in F. S. Regs., Part II. and the Staff Manual respectively. Title pages will be prepared in manuscript.

WAR DIARY
or
INTELLIGENCE SUMMARY.
(Erase heading not required.)

Army Form C. 2118.

6th Btn (S) The Connaught Rangers

M. Jourdain Lt Col Adjt. for Lt-Col Cmdg. 6. C.R.

Place	Date	Hour	Summary of Events and Information	Remarks and references to Appendices
	1/12/16		There was a rifle inspection by the Armourer Sergeant, and a considerable amount of work was done in cleaning and improving the camp.	
	2/12/16		Divine service was attended by Roman Catholics at Locre, Church of England in the Canteen, 1st Entrenching Battalion, Presbyterians & other Denomination at Mont Kemmel.	
	3/12/16		The Battalion proceeded to the Baths at Locre by companies, it was announced that Major Redmond The Royal Irish Regiment would carry out an inspection of all kitchens cookhouses and cooking arrangements throughout the division, with the object of discovering the unit in which the cooking attained the highest standard, and that prizes would be given to the three best units.	
	4/12/16		Companies were at the disposal of Company Commanders for three hours drill and inspections	
	5/12/16		The Battalion relieved the 10th Inniskilling Fusiliers, the 47th Infantry Brigade relieving the 109th Infantry Brigade in the SPANBROEK SECTION	

2353 Wt. W2541/1454 700,000 5/15 D. D. & L. A.D.S.S./Forms/C. 2118.

Instructions regarding War Diaries and Intelligence Summaries are contained in F. S. Regs., Part II. and the Staff Manual respectively. Title pages will be prepared in manuscript.

WAR DIARY
or
INTELLIGENCE SUMMARY.
(Erase heading not required.)

Army Form C. 2118.

Place	Date	Hour	Summary of Events and Information	Remarks and references to Appendices
	6/12/16.		Between 2 30 PM and 3-30 PM while the relief was taking place, the enemy bombarded our line with trench mortars, our artillery and stokes guns replied. At 6-55 AM this morning the enemy fired on Durham ROAD with aerial darts and at 11-30 AM they fired eight aerial darts. At 3 PM our stokes guns opened fire, and the enemy retaliated with heavy trench mortars on the left of our line. Our Howitzers, trench mortars, and field guns replied and silenced the enemy. The trenches that were blown in were repaired, and we had only one casualty. A number of the enemy were seen repairing their wire and our snipers claimed to have hit several of them.	
	7/12/16		At 11-45 last night a small enemy working party was dispersed by our Lewis guns. At 1-5 AM three of the enemy were observed near our parapet opposite KINGSWAY and were fired on by the Lewis guns. One man was hit and the other ~~two~~ put up their hands. All three were taken prisoners by 2nd Lt USSHER and a number of men. They stated that they were a patrolling party and the wounded man was the N.C.O in charge. He spoke	

Instructions regarding War Diaries and Intelligence Summaries are contained in F. S. Regs., Part II. and the Staff Manual respectively. Title pages will be prepared in manuscript.

WAR DIARY
or
INTELLIGENCE SUMMARY.
(Erase heading not required.)

Army Form C. 2118.

Place	Date	Hour	Summary of Events and Information	Remarks and references to Appendices
	7/12/16		English but was too badly wounded to give any real information, except that they were all Saxons. At 7-30 A M the brigade on our right opened fire with trench mortars, and the enemy retaliated on our line with heavy trench mortars, our stokes guns and artillery silenced the enemy. At 3-30 P M our stokes guns fired about 60 rounds, the enemy retaliated at 6-5 P M, but was silenced by our Artillery in a few minutes. We fired 90 rifle grenades in the last 24 hours. At stand to the enemy exposed themselves, attempting to repair the line, our sentries and snipers accounted for several of them.	
	8/12/16		Last night passed quietly, about 3-30 P M this evening, the enemy strafed with heavy trench mortars, of which only a few were on our front, and they fell between our front line and supports. SAMMY, SATAN and SIDNEY were active, until our Artillery opened fire.	
	9/12/16		Usual machine gun & rifle fire. About 5 P M SALLY was active, one of of our bays was blown in and we had six casualties. Retaliation was asked for and received. SALLY was silenced. A patrol left our line consisting of LT O H WICKHAM, 2LT C L MCARTHY and Sgt J. CASEY, about	

2353 Wt. W2544/1454 700,000 5/15 D. D. & L. A.D.S.S./Forms/C. 2118.

Instructions regarding War Diaries and Intelligence Summaries are contained in F. S. Regs., Part II. and the Staff Manual respectively. Title pages will be prepared in manuscript.

WAR DIARY
or
INTELLIGENCE SUMMARY.

(*Erase heading not required.*)

Army Form C. 2118.

Place	Date	Hour	Summary of Events and Information	Remarks and references to Appendices
	9/12/16		5-20 PM and remained out for an hour. They reported our own and the enemies wire to be low and bad, very few shell holes of any size or cover in No Mans Land they also observed an enemy working party, and when our patrol returned, they pointed out the position to our Lewis gunners who opened fire immediately.	
	10/12/16		Last night and this morning passed quietly. Our stokes guns and medium trench mortars opened fire at 3 PM. The enemy retaliated with about twenty Whizz bangs between the SOUTHERN MINE SHAFT and COOKERS FARM, no damage was done. The parapets of our trenches were repaired, and drainage work was continued. Our snipers and Lewis Gunners have compelled the enemy to cease in any way to expose himself.	
	11/12/16		At 11-45 AM several rum jars fell behind our line. At 3 PM one rum jar fell immediately behind our trench at N 36 [illegible] B 9 and blew the parados into the trench. At 4 PM two rum jars fell in our trench on the extreme right of the left company, damaging the	

2353 Wt. W2544/1454 700,000 5/15 D. D. & L. A.D.S.S./Forms/C. 2118.

WAR DIARY
or
INTELLIGENCE SUMMARY.
(Erase heading not required.)

Instructions regarding War Diaries and Intelligence Summaries are contained in F. S. Regs., Part II. and the Staff Manual respectively. Title pages will be prepared in manuscript.

Army Form C. 2118.

Place	Date	Hour	Summary of Events and Information	Remarks and references to Appendices
	11/12/16		the trench badly. The damaged portion of the trench was repaired and drainage work continued.	
	12/12/16		The Batallion was billeted at Canada Corner & paraded by Companies for baths at Locre, the usual inspections took place	
	13/12/16.		The Companies were at the disposal of Company Commanders for drill and the work of improving and cleaning the camp was continued	
	14/12/16.		The Companies were at the disposal of Company Commanders for drill and inspection both morning and afternoon. A working party paraded daily during the Batallion stay at Canada Corner to sand bag the spaces under the huts. The transport was inspected by the Commanding Officer.	
	15/12/16		There were the usual Parades under Company Commanders	
	16/12/16		Divine service was held for Roman Catholics at LOCRE at 11-45 AM Church of England at LOCRE other denominations at YMCA LOCRE	
	17/12/16		The band of the Royal Engineers played at Locre today at 2 PM	
	18/12/16.		The Batallion paraded as strong as possible for a route march.	

2353 Wt. W2544/1454 700,000 5/15 D. D. & L. A.D.S.S./Forms/C. 2118.

Instructions regarding War Diaries and Intelligence Summaries are contained in F. S. Regs., Part II. and the Staff Manual respectively. Title pages will be prepared in manuscript.

WAR DIARY
or
INTELLIGENCE SUMMARY.
(Erase heading not required.)

Army Form C. 2118.

Place	Date	Hour	Summary of Events and Information	Remarks and references to Appendices
	18/12/16		The Divisional and Brigade Commanders complimented the Battalion on the exceedingly smart and soldierly appearance of all ranks at Church Parade on 17/12/16, and also upon the March discipline. The Commanding Officer congratulated all Officers, N.C.O.s and Men, and thanked them for the manner in which all ranks co-operated for the credit of the battalion, stating that it had only been the constant and loyal co-operation of all ranks which had rendered possible the high state of efficiency of the battalion in the trying conditions under which they lived.	
	19/12/16		Usual parades under Company Commanders. 2/LIEUT S A HOLLOWAY was invalided to England and struck off the strength of the Battalion from 13/12/16.	
	20/12/16.		The Battalion relieved the 6th Royal Irish Regiment in the Right Subsection	
	21/12/16		The night and day passed quietly with no T.M. or Artillery activity, the trenches were very much damaged when handed over to our Battalion, and large working parties, night and day were essential to open up the trench sufficiently to pass along without being seen	

2353 Wt. W2544/1454 700,000 5/15 D. D. & L. A.D.S.S./Forms/C. 2118.

Instructions regarding War Diaries and Intelligence Summaries are contained in F. S. Regs., Part II. and the Staff Manual respectively. Title pages will be prepared in manuscript.

WAR DIARY
or
INTELLIGENCE SUMMARY.
(Erase heading not required.)

Army Form C. 2118.

Place	Date	Hour	Summary of Events and Information	Remarks and references to Appendices
	22/12/16		There was little TM or Artillery activity, large working parties were again busy during the day & night building up & revetting the front line trench.	
	23/12/16.		The night passed quietly. Very little Artillery or TM activity during the day. About 5 PM there was some enemy TM activity, a few whizz bangs were also sent over. Our Artillery and TMs replied and at 5.30 PM the situation was normal. A patrol went out about 5-30 PM and remained out for 1½ hours. Our Lewis guns fired on a working party of the German opposite W. 4. 36. 11 in the second line. They also fired on a German working party at 9 AM. The front & patrol trench were drained & trench boards raised and cleaned, the parapet was also built up in places. 50 yards of wire was put out in front of our line. A large searchlight was observed at 8 PM a long way to our right.	
	24/12/16		The night and day passed very quietly. Two enemy working parties were caught by our Lewis guns this morning, one to the right	

2353 Wt. W2544/1454 700,000 5/15 D. D. & L. A.D.S.S./Forms/C. 2118.

Army Form C. 2118.

WAR DIARY
or
INTELLIGENCE SUMMARY.
(Erase heading not required.)

Instructions regarding War Diaries and Intelligence Summaries are contained in F. S. Regs., Part II. and the Staff Manual respectively. Title pages will be prepared in manuscript.

Place	Date	Hour	Summary of Events and Information	Remarks and references to Appendices
	24/12/16		of the BULL RING at 7-30 AM, the other opposite STRETCHER LANE at 8 AM. Most of the second party fell to the ground. Both parties consisting of about 12 men.	
	25/12/16		During the night there was increased machine gun and rifle fire. An SOS test attack was carried out last night at 9-30 PM. A patrol having returned, the position of a German Patrol was indicated to our Lewis gunners, who immediately opened fire on the position indicated, the repairing of the damaged portion of our line has been continued	
	26/12/16		There was no TM activity on our front during the day or night. About 8 PM the enemy sent over a number of heavy shells, which fell a long way in the rear and to the right of our line. There was some artillery activity on both sides this afternoon between 4 and 5 PM	
	27/12/16.		At intervals between 10-30 PM and 3-30 AM last night the enemy sent over medium and heavy TMs, also Aerial Torpedoes. Our medium TMs replied and sounds of confusion were heard in the enemy front line	

WAR DIARY
or
INTELLIGENCE SUMMARY.
(Erase heading not required.)

Army Form C. 2118.

Instructions regarding War Diaries and Intelligence Summaries are contained in F. S. Regs., Part II. and the Staff Manual respectively. Title pages will be prepared in manuscript.

Place	Date	Hour	Summary of Events and Information	Remarks and references to Appendices
	27/12/16		An intense TM bombardment of the enemy line on our left took place this afternoon, there was very little retaliation on our front, and no damage of any kind was done. Three heavy TMs fell in the vicinity of advanced Battn HQ. A few apparently GAS SHELLS fell between our support line and BOOKER FARM. Our STOKES and medium TMs replied with apparently good effect. The enemy shelled S 86 in retaliation for TM activity, no damage was done except the cutting of two telephone wires. A patrol went out on our front last night. The parapet has been built up at N 36 9 8, the trenches have been cleaned and a dug out completed. The enemy could be plainly heard working and talking in their front line at 7.30 AM. Smoke could also be seen in their support trenches and also a long way behind	
	28/12/16		The Battalion was relieved by the 6th Royal Irish Regiment, the relief was carried out without any unusual incident, we proceeded on being relieved to Derry Huts, our day and night in the trenches having been very quiet	

Instructions regarding War Diaries and Intelligence Summaries are contained in F. S. Regs., Part II. and the Staff Manual respectively. Title pages will be prepared in manuscript.

WAR DIARY
or
INTELLIGENCE SUMMARY.
(Erase heading not required.)

Army Form C. 2118.

Place	Date	Hour	Summary of Events and Information	Remarks and references to Appendices
	29/12/16.		The usual inspections were held, five working parties with Officers were sent to different portions of the line. The cleaning of the Camp was begun, and various improvements were carried out.	
	30/12/16		As the Batallion was in the trenches for Xmas day, today was kept as Xmas day. There was a very large voluntary Church Parade at DRANOUTRE. The request of the Commanding Officer that the men should be relieved from fatigues and working parties was granted. Dinner was provided consisting of roast turkey & plum pudding. The following Officers joined the Batallion Capt. J H GARVEY, Capt. N S B HUDSON [?] 2nd Lieuts. G E MAGUIRE, J J BARRY, A H E RUSSELL and W KEEGAN.	
	31/12/16.		The usual Church Parades were held, and a number of working parties provided. 2nd Lieuts. C J W PAYNE and H E TAGGART joined the Batallion.	

2353 Wt. W2544/1454 70,000 5/15 D. D. & L. A.D.S.S./Forms/C. 2118.

47/16 14E

WAR DIARY for month of JANUARY, 1917.

VOLUME 14

6th Bn The Connaught Rangers

Vol 13

Confidential

Instructions regarding War Diaries and Intelligence Summaries are contained in F. S. Regs., Part II. and the Staff Manual respectively. Title Pages will be prepared in manuscript.

January 1917

WAR DIARY *or* INTELLIGENCE SUMMARY

(Erase heading not required.)

Army Form C. 2118.

Sheet I

Place	Date	Hour	Summary of Events and Information	Remarks and references to Appendices
In the Field	Jany.	1st.	Voluntary Church parade for R.C's at DRANOUTRE at 9.0 a.m. Parade at 10.30 am for Battn 1st. Class Bombers 3 men trained in Lewis Guns not attached to L.G. Section.	
		2nd.	Parade of 1st. Class bombers and Lewis gunners at 9.30 am. All men who had not had their Box Respirators tested in gas proceeded to Divl. Anti-Gas School at 9.30 am. Major R.J.A. Tamplin D.S.O rejoined the Battn. and assumed tempy. command of 'D' Coy.	
		3rd.	Parades as on 2nd. inst. Following New Year's Honours announced:— Capt. & Adjt. J.J. MARTIN awarded MILITARY CROSS; 3640 C.S.M. J. STANTON " D.C.M; 4348 Sergt. J.T. COX " D.C.M.	
		4th	Parade of bombers & Lewis Gunners at 9.30 am. Brigade & Divisional Commanders visited batt.	
		5th.	Battalion relieved 6th. Bn. Ryl. Irish Regt. in the line: the battalion disposed as follows— 3 platoons of 'D' Coy. and 1 of 'C' Coy. in front line; 3 platoons of 'C' Coy. 1 of 'D', and 2 of 'A' Coy. in S.P. 6; 'B' Coy in SHAMUS DUG-OUTS; 2 platoons of 'A' Coy. in GALWAY DUG-OUTS. Front line reinforced at night by 1 platoon of 'C' Coy.	Appendix I
		6th.	Hostile T.M's active from 11 pm. to 1 am and 11. a.m. to 1 pm. Our Stokes guns fired 280 rounds in retaliation doing good shooting. Neighbourhood of SHAMUS FARM & BURNT FARM shelled with field guns at 2 pm.	
		7th.	At 4 am. enemy opened intense bombardment on our line N.36.7–9. At 4.30 am. he attempted to enter our trenches at N.36.7, but was ejected at once. Day passed quietly. About 4.15 pm. some 20 shells fell in neighbourhood of S.P. 6	

2449 Wt. W14957/M90 750,000 1/16 J.B.C. & A. Forms/C.2118/12.

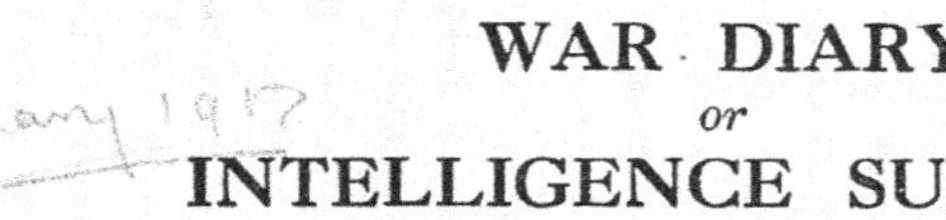

Confidential

Instructions regarding War Diaries and Intelligence Summaries are contained in F. S. Regs., Part II. and the Staff Manual respectively. Title Pages will be prepared in manuscript.

January 1917

WAR DIARY *or* INTELLIGENCE SUMMARY

(Erase heading not required.)

Army Form C. 2118.

Sheet II

Place	Date	Hour	Summary of Events and Information	Remarks and references to Appendices
In the field	Jany.	8th.	Night quiet except for abnormal hostile sniping. BAYWAY DUG-OUTS shelled with "whizz-bangs" at 10. am and 12 noon. At 10.30 am. Right Coy. H.Q in front line shelled with 4.2 gun. Afternoon quiet.	
		9th.	At 7.30 a.m. retaliation for our Stokes' activity blew in our trench at N. 36. 2. and Bay 11 N.36.9. Promiscuous shelling throughout the day, particularly on front line at N.36.10, SHAMUS FARM and S.P.6. The following reliefs took place:- 'B' Coy. relieved 3 platoons of 'D' Coy and 1 of 'C' Coy. in the front line. The platoon of 'C' Coy. moved into S.P.6 and the 3 platoons of 'D' Coy. to SHAMUS FARM Dug-outs.	Appendix II
		10th.	Night quiet. Enemy's artillery less active than usual by day. Slight hostile T.M. activity at 10 a.m. and 2 p.m. No damage done.	
		11th.	Night quiet. Day exceptionally quiet, except for slight hostile T.M. & artillery activity at 2.0 p.m. All quiet by 3.30 pm. Weather bad; snow & mist.	
		12th.	Night quiet. Slight T.M. activity on centre of our line and DURHAM ROAD at 2 pm. Some whizz-bangs and 4.2's between SHAMUS DUG-OUTS and CORNER FARM at 3.15 pm. Strong enemy retaliation to 49th. Bde. bombardment at 7.30 and 9.30 pm. on S.P.6. and SHAMUS FARM. At 11.40 pm. enemy sent up 3 red lights and his artillery put a fierce barrage on our front line & S.P.6 – SHAMUS FARM. Our trench damaged in 3 places & KINGSWAY blown in opposite S.P.6. Our casualties 3 O.R. killed, 1 O.R. wounded.	
		13th.	No activity except for a few harmless whizz-bangs at 9.15 a.m. The battalion was relieved by 6th. Ryl. Irish and moved into Divisional Reserve at CURRAGH CAMP	Appendix III

2449 Wt. W14957/M90 750,000 1/16 J.B.C. & A. Forms/C.2118/12.

Confidential

Instructions regarding War Diaries and Intelligence Summaries are contained in F. S. Regs., Part II. and the Staff Manual respectively. Title Pages will be prepared in manuscript.

January 1917

WAR DIARY
or
INTELLIGENCE SUMMARY

(Erase heading not required.)

Army Form C. 2118.

Sheet III.

Place	Date	Hour	Summary of Events and Information	Remarks and references to Appendices
In the field	14th.	Jany.	Church-parade for R.C.'s at 8.45 a.m. Kit inspection 1.30 pm.	
	15th.		Companies at disposal of Coy. Commanders. Army Commander was to have visited the camp, but did not come. Baths for men in afternoon cancelled.	
	16th.		Companies at disposal of Coy. Commanders. 'B' Coy. had their Box Respirators tested at Anti-gas School. 4 Officers & 6 N.C.O's attended lecture on Machine Guns at LOCRE 11. a.m. Draft of 57 O.R. arrived about 6.0 a.m.	
	17th.		Companies used Divisional Baths in morning. Coys. at disposal of Coy. Commanders in afternoon. S.O.S. Rocket tested 6.0 pm.	
	18th.		Comparison of Conduct Sheets and Coy. Report Books by the Adjt. 10 am. Baths for all men who had not baths the previous day. Coys. at disposal of Os. C. Coys. in afternoon. Capt. T.H. CROFTON rejoined from tempy. duty with 47th. T.M. Battery.	
	19th.		Companies at disposal of Coy. commanders all day.	
	20th.		Parades at 9 a.m. and 2 p.m. Divisional Commander visited Battn. H.Q.	
	21st.		Battn. paraded for Divine Service (R.C.) at 10.45 a.m. for 11.15 am. at LOCRE Church. C. of E. parade at 10.30 am. for 11 am. at Y.M.C.A. Hut LOCRE. Battn. relieved 6th. Ryl. Irish Regt. in the line, first platoon at DAYLIGHT CORNER at 4 pm. Battn. disposed as follows:– 'A' Coy. LURGAN CAMP (M.35. b. 7.0.), 'B' Coy. S.P. 6.; 2 platoons 'C' Coy. GALWAY DUG-OUTS and 2 in LEFT FRONT LINE; 2 platoons 'D' Coy. SHAMUS DUG-OUTS and 2 platoons RIGHT FRONT LINE. 1 platoon 'B' Coy. reinforcing front line at night.	Appendix IV

2449 Wt. W14957/M90 750,000 1/16 J.B.C. & A. Forms/C.2118/12.

Confidential

Instructions regarding War Diaries and Intelligence Summaries are contained in F. S. Regs., Part II. and the Staff Manual respectively. Title Pages will be prepared in manuscript.

January 1917

WAR DIARY
or
INTELLIGENCE SUMMARY

(Erase heading not required.)

Army Form C. 2118.

Sheet IV

Place	Date	Hour	Summary of Events and Information	Remarks and references to Appendices
In the field	Jany.	22nd.	Hostile patrols active between 5.30 & 6.0 am. 12.45 pm our T.M's opened fire; enemy's retaliation effected no damage.	
		23rd.	Enemy snipers active at dawn, our snipers claim 3 hits. Hostile retaliation to our Medium T.M. fire at 2.0 pm was severe, but did no damage. All quiet by 3 pm.	
		24th.	Enemy artillery active throughout day. Our artillery fired a Bde. shoot at 3. pm in punishment.	
		25th.	Unusually quiet night and day. Enemy working very hard during the night. Working-party dispersed by Lewis Guns opposite N.36.11. Bay 2. Hostile aircraft active 11 am. - 12 noon and 3 - 4 pm. 'B' Coy relieved 2 platoons of 'C' Coy. and 2 platoons of 'D' Coy. in front line.	Appendix V
		26th.	Nothing to report, except hostile aircraft activity in morning. Battn. was relieved by 6th Royal Irish Regt. at 2 pm. and moved into Brigade Reserve at DERRY HUTS.	Appendix VI
		27th.	Following inspections held under Coy. arrangements:- Clothing, Boots, necessaries and Identity Discs; by arrangement with M.O., feet, box respirators and P.H. Gas Helmets. Also rifle inspection by Armourer Sergt. Court of Enquiry held at Battn. H.Q. at 11 am.	
		28th.	Divine Service as follows:- R.C.'s parade at 8.15 a.m. for 9 a.m. at DRANOUTRE church. C of E. parade at 8.30 am. for 9.15 am at YMCA Hut, DRANOUTRE. Coy. Commanders reconnoitred new Bde. front.	
		29th.	Battn. relieved 8th R. Inniskilling Fusilrs. and 7/8th R. Irish Fusilrs. in line, commencing at 11 am. Coys. disposed as follows:- 'A' Coy. Right front line; 'B' Coy. Right support, 3 platoons in REGENT DUG-OUTS & 1 platoon S.P. 9; 'C' Coy. Left front line; 'D' Coy. Left support, 3 platoons S.P. 11 & 1 platoon S.P. 10.	App. VII
		30th.	Night quiet. 3 a.m. enemy bombed his own wire for 4 mins. Enemy artillery active throughout the day, particularly on S.P. 10. Our artillery wire cutting at 3 pm.	

2449 Wt. W14957/M90 750,000 1/16 J.B.C. & A. Forms/C.2118/12.

Confidential

Instructions regarding War Diaries and Intelligence Summaries are contained in F. S. Regs., Part II. and the Staff Manual respectively. Title Pages will be prepared in manuscript.

January 1917

WAR DIARY
or
INTELLIGENCE SUMMARY
(Erase heading not required.)

Army Form C. 2118.

Sheet V

Place	Date	Hour	Summary of Events and Information	Remarks and references to Appendices
In the field	Jany	31st.	At 8.30 a.m. enemy field-guns shelled N.29 2 and 3 obtaining direct hit on signal-office. 3.15 p.m. enemy T.M's very active, supplemented by Hows. One of our Stokes guns knocked out. 'D' Coy. relieved 'C' Coy. in the left front line, 'C' Coy. returning to the Strong Points held by 'D' Coy. Remainder of battalion disposed as before. Bde. conference at Battn. H.Q. 11.30 a.m.	Appendix VIII

/ A Booth Lt
a/ADJUTANT 6TH (S) BN. THE CONNAUGHT RANGERS.

2449 Wt. W14957/M90 750,000 1/16 J.B.C. & A. Forms/C.2118/12.

Appendix III

6th (S) Bn The Conn Rangers

SECRET OPERATION ORDERS COPY No

[illegible] Battalion will be relieved tomorrow by the 6th ROYAL IRISH REGT and on completion of relief will proceed to CURRAGH CAMP

Relief will be carried out in the following order –

1st platoon of C Coy. 6th R. I. Regt [illegible] at DAYLIGHT CORNER at 8 pm

B. B Coy. 6th C. R. will be relieved by C Coy. 6th R. I. Regt in F. C. Right and by D. Coy 6th R. I. Regt in F. C. Left

D Coy 6th C. R. will be relieved by 2 platoons A. Coy. 6th R. I. Regt in Right CHAMUS DUGOUTS, and by Headquarters Section 6th R. I. Regt in left CHAMUS DUGOUTS

C Coy and 2 platoons A. Coy. 6th C. R. will be relieved by B Coy. 6th R. I. Regt in S. P. 6

SNIPERS 6th C. R. in GALWAY DUGOUTS will be relieved by 2 platoons A Coy. 6th R. I. Regt

[illegible] will be relieved in daylight. Arrangements to be made [illegible] Officers concerned.

[illegible] Outgoing companies will proceed via KINGSWAY to DAYLIGHT ~~[illegible]~~ CORNER ~~[illegible]~~ Movement E of DAYLIGHT CORNER will [illegible] WEST of DAYLIGHT CORNER [illegible] will be by platoons at 300 yards interval

5 Gum BOOTS will be handed over on relief and a receipt taken on attached form

6 Company Commanders will ensure that trenches and Supporting Points are handed over in a clean condition

7 [illegible] Sergts will meet the Adjutant at CURRAGH CAMP at [illegible] to arrange accommodation for their companies

[illegible] will meet companies as they arrive at CURRAGH CAMP and conduct them to their huts

9 Completion of [illegible] will be reported by RUNNER to Battn Headquarters

[illegible] Transport Officer will make arrangements for removal of Cooking [illegible] Kit from CHAMUS DUGOUTS and COOKER FARM as soon after dark as possible

Copies of [illegible] Receipts will be handed into Orderly Room by [illegible]

— —

(Sd) F. W. S. [illegible], Lieut

12-1-17 Act Adjt. 6th (S) Bn The Conn Rangers

Appendix IV

6th (S) Bn. THE CONN. RANGERS.

SECRET. **OPERATION ORDERS.** COPY NO.

(1) The Battalion will relieve the 6th ROYAL IRISH REGT. in the Right Sub-section tomorrow.

(2) On completion of relief the companies will be disposed as under:-

A. Coy.	LURGAN CAMP (M.35. b. 7.0.)	– – –	3-5 ~~[illegible]~~ p.m.
B. "	S.P. 6	– – –	2-50 ~~[illegible]~~ p.m.
2 platoons C. Coy.	GALWAY DUG-OUTS	– – –	2-20 ~~[illegible]~~ p.m.
2 " C. "	LEFT FRONT LINE	– – –	2 p.m. ~~[illegible]~~
2 " D. "	SHAMUS DUG-OUTS	– – –	2-40 ~~[illegible]~~ p.m.
2 " D "	RIGHT FRONT LINE	– – –	2-10 ~~[illegible]~~ p.m.

(3) 1 Platoon of "B" Coy at S.P. 6. will reinforce Front line each night.

(4) Battalion Bombers will be at Battn. H.Q.

(5) Lewis Guns will be relieved in daylight, and will use SHAMUS DUG-OUTS. All arrangements to be made between Officers concerned.

(6) Movement E. of DRANOUTRE – LOCRE Road to be by platoons at 300 yards distance.

(7) Minimum Garrison of Front Line by night 100 men, 6 Lewis Guns.
" " " " " " day 80 ", 6 " "
" " S.P. 6. 3 platoons.

(8) Troops occupying GALWAY DUG-OUTS must not walk about outside in daylight.

(9) Completion of relief to be reported in Code to Battn. Hd. Qrs.

(10) Copies of Trench Store receipts will be handed into Orderly Room by 11 a.m. 22nd Jany. 1917.

(11) Gum Boots will be taken over, they must be carefully checked and attached receipt forms completed and handed in with Trench Store receipts.

(12) Coy. Commanders will render clean billet certificates to Orderly Room half-an-hour before departure.

(13) Officers Kits, mens packs, and musical instruments will be stacked by Guard Room by Companies ready for removal by Transport by ~~[illegible]~~ 2 p.m.

(14) Coy. Commanders, L.G.O., & Bombing Officer will see that every man under their command has rubbed his feet with Whale Oil before leaving for the trenches. Also that a daily issue of Whale Oil and clean socks is made during the time the Battalion is in the trenches.

———— " ————

(Sd) T. BOOTH, Lieut.

20-1-17. of Adjt. 6th (S) Bn. THE CONN. RANGERS.

No. 1. C.O.
" 2. 6th Royal Irish Regt.
" 3. O.C. "A" Coy.
" 4. O.C. "B" "
" 5. O.C. "C" "
" 6. O.C. "D" "
" 7. L.G.O.
" 8. Bombing Officer.
" 9. ~~Transport Officer.~~ Qr. Mr.
" 10. Transport Officer.
" 11. 2nd in Command & M.O.
" 12.

Appendix V

Secret

Copy No. 8

Operation Orders
6th (S) Bn CONNAUGHT RANGERS.

I The following reliefs will take place tomorrow the 25th inst commencing at 5-15 p.m.

II B Coy will relieve C & D Coys in the Front line.

III 1 Platoon of A & D Coys will reinforce Front line at night.

IV Movement along DURHAM. ROAD must never be of more than 5 at a time.

V 'C' Coy will garrison S.P. 6.

VI D. Coy will remain in SHAMUS. DUGOUTS and O.C. D Coy. has for his Coys use GALWAY. DUGOUTS.

VII Relief complete will be reported to Bn H.Q. in code. Code word. TRAC

VIII Care should be taken when handing over, or taking over gum boots, as there is always trouble over the matter when this Bn is being relieved or relieving.

24-1-17

[signature] Capt & Adjt 6 CR

Appendix VII

6th (S) Bn. THE CONN. RANGERS.

OPERATION ORDERS.

I. The Battalion will relieve a portion of the 7/8th Royal Irish Fus. and a portion of the 8th Royal Innis. Fus. tomorrow in the Sector now held by the 49th Brigade.

II. A. Coy. will relieve two companies of the 8th Royal Innis. Fus. in the Right Sub-section of the Front Line. Guides to be at entrance to REGENT ST. at 10 a.m.

C. Coy. will relieve A. Coy. and a portion of B. Coy. of the 7/8th Royal Irish Fus. in the Left Sub-section of the Front Line. Guides to be at DOCTOR'S HOUSE, KEMMEL at 11 a.m.

III. 3 Platoons of B. Coy. will relieve 3 platoons of the Royal Innis. Fus. in REGENT ST. DUG-OUTS.

1 Platoon of B. Coy. will relieve 1 platoon of the Royal Innis. Fus. in S.P. 9. Guides to be at entrance to REGENT ST. at 11 a.m. for all B. Company.

3 Platoons of D. Coy. will relieve 3 platoons of C. Coy. 7/8th Royal Irish Fus. in S.P. 11. Guides to be at DOCTOR'S HOUSE, KEMMEL at 11-30 a.m.

1 Platoon of D. Coy. will relieve 1 platoon of the 8th Royal Innis. Fus. in S.P. 10. Guides to be at entrance to REGENT ST. at 11 a.m.

IV. The L.G.O. will be responsible that all Lewis Gun positions at present being used are maintained, i.e. each gun at present in the line will be relieved by another gun. All arrangements to be made by Officers concerned.

V. Movements will be by platoons at 300 yards distance, along the routes already reconnoitred.

DOCTOR'S HOUSE, KEMMEL is at N.21. d. 7.7.

VI. Advance Parties will be at DOCTOR'S HOUSE and REGENT ST. one hour before companies arrive.

VII. Trench Store and Gum Boot receipts will be handed into Orderly Room by 10 a.m. 30th instant.

VIII. Completion of relief will be reported in Code to Battn. Headquarters at FORT VICTORIA N.28. c. 5. 3.

IX. Coy. Commanders will render a Clean Billet Certificate to Orderly Room half-an-hour before leaving.

X. Officers Kits, men's packs and drums will be stacked outside the Guard Room by 9 a.m. for removal by Transport.

XI. Quartermaster will notify the Adjutant regarding the dumping of rations.

28-1-17.

(Sd) T. BOOTH, Lieut.
a/Adjt. 6th (S) Bn. THE CONN. RANGERS.

Secret Appendix VIII

Operation Orders No. 1..
6th (S) Bn Conn: Rangers

File

War Diary

(1). The following relief will take place to-morrow 31st inst Commencing at 2 pm.

(II) D Coy will relieve "C" Coy in the Left Sub Section. "C" Coy will take over Strong Points now held by "D" Coy.

III On completion of relief the Bn will be disposed as follows;-

Front Line "A" Coy Right Sub-Sectn
- DO - "D" Coy Left Sub Section
"B" Coy Regent St Dug-outs & S.P.9
"C" Coy S.P.10. & S.P.11. Hd. Qrs, at "Fort Victoria"

IV Completion of relief will be reported in Code to Bn H.Q.

V Trench Stores & Gum: Boots receipts will be handed in to O.Room by 9am 1st Feb., 1917.

VI D Coy will handover their Blankets to "C" Coy..

30/1/17

(Sd) T. Booth LIEUT.
A/Adjt 6th (S) Bn Conn! Rangers

O P E R A T I O N   O R D E R   No.16.

by

LIEUT COLONEL R.C. FEILDING D.S.O.

COMMANDING 6TH BN THE CONNAUGHT RANGERS:

30th Jany.1918.

1. The following inter-coy reliefs will take place today,30th Inst. commencing at 4-30pm.

2. "A" Coy will relieve "C" COY in Right Front Line.
"B" Coy .. .. "D" Left Front Lin .

3. On relief "C" & "D" Coy's will proceed to the positions vacated by "A" & "B" Coy's,respectively.

4. "A" & "B" Coy's will hand over their Blankets to "C" & "D" Coy's

5. "C" & "D" Coy's will take over all working parties from 6pm., today onwards. Table attached for those concerned.

6. Trench Stores (particularly Gum Boots) and work in progress will be carefully handed over and trench store receipts sent to Bn.Hd.Qrs. by 9 am 31st Inst.

7. "C" & "D" COY's will send out a protective patrol of 1 Officer and 10 O.R.,each immediately after dark. These Patrols will withdraw at 6pm.

8. Completion of relief will be wired to Bn Hd Qrs,Code word "VERTICAL"

(sd) F.T. CHAMIER LIEUT.
A.ADJUTANT 6TH BN THE CONNAUGHT RANGERS.

15E

W A R   D I A R Y .

FOR MONTH OF FEBRUARY, 1917.

VOLUME 15

UNIT:- 6th Connaught Rangers.

Vol 14

Confidential

February 1917.

WAR DIARY
or
INTELLIGENCE SUMMARY.
(Erase heading not required.)

Army Form C. 2118.

Instructions regarding War Diaries and Intelligence Summaries are contained in F. S. Regs., Part II. and the Staff Manual respectively. Title pages will be prepared in manuscript.

Sheet I

Place	Date	Hour	Summary of Events and Information	Remarks and references to Appendices
In the field.	Feby.	1st.	At 5.15am the enemy opened a sudden & fierce artillery and T.M. bombardment along Right Coy. front, particularly at junction of N.29.2 & 3. After 20 mins. he sent up a rocket bursting into 2 green lights, whereupon his fire lifted to a line about 70 yds. behind our front trench. A few minutes later a party of the enemy, dressed in white and in close formation, advanced towards the gap cut in our wire by their artillery, but were dispersed by rifle fire from our trench. While recrossing NO MAN'S LAND, they were caught by the fire of 3 Lewis Guns and left at least 9 dead. Our casualties were 4 wounded, of whom 3 remained at duty. Prominent during the operation were CAPT. I.H. GARVEY, Comdg. 'A' Coy., LIEUT. A.G.F. SIMMS, Lewis Gun Officer, and 2LIEUT. W.H. ODBERT the officer on duty at the time. The first & last named have since been awarded the MILITARY CROSS. At 5.25 am., in response to our S.O.S., our field artillery, heavy artillery and T.M's opened a vigorous fire, the first named alone firing over 1500 rounds. The situation was normal by 6.30 am. Telephone communication with the right coy. was interrupted from 5.30 – 7.0 am. About 9.30 am. hostile T.M's opened another severe bombardment, searching our line near top of KETCHEN AVENUE and obtaining some direct hits on VIA BELLIA. Our retaliation was vigorous and by 10.15 am. the enemy was	

2353 Wt. W2544/1454 700,000 5/15 D. D. & L. A.D.S.S./Forms/C. 2118.

Confidential

Instructions regarding War Diaries and Intelligence Summaries are contained in F. S. Regs., Part II. and the Staff Manual respectively. Title pages will be prepared in manuscript.

February 1917.

WAR DIARY
or
INTELLIGENCE SUMMARY.

(Erase heading not required.)

Army Form C. 2118.

Sheet II

Place	Date	Hour	Summary of Events and Information	Remarks and references to Appendices
In the field	Feby.	1st.	silenced. The situation was normal throughout the day until 9.0pm. when the enemy started another sudden and intense T.M. bombardment on the same part of our line. Our artillery re-taliated and all was quiet by 9.30pm.	
		2nd.	Night & morning passed quietly. The battalion was relieved by the 6th. Royal Irish Regt. & moved into Bde. Reserve with H.Q. and 'A' & 'C' Coys. at DERRY HUTS and 'B' & 'D' Coys. at KEMMEL CHATEAU.	Appendix I.
		3rd.	A patrol went out & recovered one of the bodies (left behind by the enemy on the 1st) at 4 am. Identifications normal. Enemy aircraft very active during morning. DAYLIGHT CORNER and battery position nearby shelled by 5.9" Hows. throughout forenoon. About 12 5.9's fell some 400 yds. West of camp between 11 am. & 12 noon, killing an A.S.C. driver and a civilian. Coys. at disposal of their commanders all day.	
		4th.	Church parades as follows:— R.C.'s 8.15 am. for 9am. at DRANOUTRE CHURCH for H.Q. and 'A' & 'C' Coys. and 10 am. for 10.15 am. at KEMMEL CHATEAU for "B" & "D" Coys. C. of E. 8.45 am. for 9.30 am. at YMCA Hut, DRANOUTRE for H.Q., 'A' & 'C' Coys. and 11am. for 11.35am at BEAVER FARM for 'B' & 'D' Coys. Coys. at disposal of Coy. Commanders in afternoon. C.O. left to attend course at 2nd. Army School & Major W.A.H. GRIMSHAW	

2353 Wt. W2544/1454 700,000 5/15 D. D. & L. A.D.S.S./Forms/C. 2118.

Confidential

Instructions regarding War Diaries and Intelligence Summaries are contained in F. S. Regs., Part II. and the Staff Manual respectively. Title pages will be prepared in manuscript.

February 1917

WAR DIARY
or
INTELLIGENCE SUMMARY.
(Erase heading not required.)

Army Form C. 2118.

Sheet II

Place	Date	Hour	Summary of Events and Information	Remarks and references to Appendices
Wakefield.	Feby.	4th.	assumed temporary command of the battalion.	
		5th.	Patrol went out at 4 am. and recovered second German body. Coys. at disposal of Commanders all day. Q.M. & 4 C.Q.M.S. met a/Adjutant at KEMMEL SHELTERS at 3 pm. for purpose of allotting huts to coys.	
		6th.	G.O.C. Division visited battalion in morning and congratulated Capt. L.H. GARVEY on the behaviour of his coy. on 1st inst. Battn. relieved by 8th R. Inniskilling Fusiliers & proceeded into Divl. Reserve at KEMMEL SHELTERS.	Appendix II
		7th.	Following inspections held:– Kits, Clothing and Necessaries under Coy. arrangements; Feet, Box Respirators & P.H. Helmets by M.O.; Rifles by Armourer-Sergt. Officers reconnoitred TORONTO, WINNIPEG and VANCOUVER Sections of KEMMEL HILL DEFENCES, the roads leading to them & lines of advance thence towards any portion of front line.	
		8th.	At 10.30 am. enemy opened with 5.9" Hows. on huts occupied by 'A & B' Coys & portion of 'C' Coy. at N.20.c.0.3. 'A' & 'B' Coys., being on parade, were able to evacuate the camp quickly and in good order, but an unfortunate hit ~~[illegible]~~ was scored on the hut occupied by 'C' Coy. before the men could leave it & it was here that most of the	

2353 Wt. W2544/1454 700,000 5/15 D. D. & L. A.D.S.S./Forms/C. 2118.

Confidential

Instructions regarding War Diaries and Intelligence Summaries are contained in F. S. Regs., Part II. and the Staff Manual respectively. Title pages will be prepared in manuscript.

February 1917

WAR DIARY
or
INTELLIGENCE SUMMARY.
(Erase heading not required.)

Army Form C. 2118.

Sheet IV

Place	Date	Hour	Summary of Events and Information	Remarks and references to Appendices
In the field	Feby	8th.	casualties occurred. Steps were also taken to evacuate the remainder of the camp. After a while, the enemy's range lengthened as if to catch the men as they left the huts. Soon after noon it was possible to re-occupy the huts on the northern side of the LOCRE–KEMMEL Road, but the remainder were too damaged to use. The casualties were 3 O.R. killed and 11 O.R. wounded, of whom one died later, and a good deal of damage was done to rifles, kit, etc. At 2.35 pm the enemy started another bombardment, this time on the northern side of the Road at about N.19.d.3.6. & the camp was again evacuated for safety's sake; it was found possible to return after an hour. No casualties or damage was sustained. 'A' & 'B' Coys. were later accommodated in DONCASTER HUTS and BIRR BARRACKS respectively. During the afternoon the G.O.C. Division visited the camp.	
		9th.	During the morning 'D' Coy. went for a route-march, the other 3 Coys. being employed in refitting after the previous day's bombardment. A number of men from each Coy., not exceeding 12, entered on a 3 days' course in bombing under 2Lt. C. L. McCARTHY. In the afternoon baths were allotted to the battalion at WESTOUTRE for the purpose of exchanging clothing. About 2.30pm the G.O.C. 47th Inf. Bde. visited	

Confidential

Instructions regarding War Diaries and Intelligence Summaries are contained in F. S. Regs., Part II. and the Staff Manual respectively. Title pages will be prepared in manuscript.

February 1917

WAR DIARY
or
INTELLIGENCE SUMMARY.

(Erase heading not required.)

Army Form C. 2118.

Sheet V.

Place	Date	Hour	Summary of Events and Information	Remarks and references to Appendices
[illegible]	Feby.	9th.	the camp to inspect damage.	
		10th.	'C' Coy. went for route-march in morning, while 'A' & 'B' & 'D' Coys. carried out training with following directions:- Physical Training, Rifle Exercises, Lectures to Junior N.C.O's on Discipline, & Practising firing from the hip while advancing. The rifles of H.Q. and the rifles & guns of the Lewis Gun Section were inspected by the Armourer-Sergt. Hair-cutting parade was held under coy. arrangements, H.Q. being inspected by the Adjt. at 10 am. Major W.A.H. GRIMSHAW proceeded on leave and Major R.J.A. TAMPLIN D.S.O. assumed temporary command of the battalion. In the evening Lieut. Col. R.C. FEILDING rejoined after his course at the 2nd. Army School & re-assumed command of the batn.	
		11th.	Church parades as follows:- R.C's 11am, at HOSPICE, LOCRE; C. of E. 11am at YMCA Hut, LOCRE. Coys. at disposal of Coy. Commanders in afternoon. A thaw at last, but freezing again in evening.	
		12th	Coys. at disposal of Coy. Commanders. Recruits paraded at 9 am. & 2 pm. for drill under the Adjutant. Signallers paraded for station work (visual signalling). Bombing Officer's class concluded with live throwing. Unfortunate accident with rifle grenade	

2353 Wt. W2544/1454 700,000 5/15 D. D. & L. A.D.S.S./Forms/C. 2118.

Confidential

February 1917

Instructions regarding War Diaries and Intelligence Summaries are contained in F. S. Regs., Part II. and the Staff Manual respectively. Title pages will be prepared in manuscript.

WAR DIARY
or
INTELLIGENCE SUMMARY.
(Erase heading not required.)

Army Form C. 2118.

Sheet VI

Place	Date	Hour	Summary of Events and Information	Remarks and references to Appendices
In the field.	Feby.	12th.	resulted in Sgt. CASEY being wounded in the back. C.O. interviewed officers of 'A' & 'B' Coys. at DONCASTER HUTS. The assistant-adjutant represented the C.O. at a reconnaissance of back areas of 41st. Division.	
		13th.	Parades as on 12th. Box Respirators of H.Q. and Lewis Gunners inspected by M.O. in morning. C.O. held conference of officers of 'C' & 'D' Coys., Lewis Gun officers and H.Q. at 5.30 pm.	
		14th.	Coys. at disposal of commanders in morning. Battn. relieved 8th. R. Inniskilling Fusiliers in Left Sub-section at 4 pm. The battn. disposed as follows:— 'A' Coy. Right Front line; 'B' Coy. REGENT ST. DUG-OUTS (less 1 platoon in S.P. 9); 'C' Coy. Left Front Line; 'D' Coy. S.P. 11 (less 1 platoon in S.P. 10).	Appendix III
		15th.	At 6.30 pm. a German ran across NO MAN'S LAND towards our line with his hands up, but was shot by his own men on reaching our wire. A patrol fetched in his body after dark. Identifications normal. A quiet day.	
		16th.	Much movement heard during night on trench tramway behind PECKHAM, also hammering & talking opposite left coy. front. Morning quiet. At 2 pm. IX Corps H.A. bombarded enemy's support trench from N. 31. d. 08. 50 to N. 30 b. 8. 3., also engaging hostile batteries. Enemy's	

2353 Wt. W2544/1454 700,000 5/15 D. D. & L. A.D.S.S./Forms/C. 2118.

Confidential

February 1917

Instructions regarding War Diaries and Intelligence Summaries are contained in F. S. Regs., Part II. and the Staff Manual respectively. Title pages will be prepared in manuscript.

WAR DIARY
or
INTELLIGENCE SUMMARY.

(Erase heading not required.)

Army Form C. 2118.

Sheet VII

Place	Date	Hour	Summary of Events and Information	Remarks and references to Appendices
In the field.	Feby.	16th.	retaliation was slight, only a few T.M's & Rifle Grenades behind the front line & some 4.2's & 5.9's in the vicinity of S.P's 10 & 11 and REGENT ST. DUG-OUTS.	
		17th.	Our artillery very active throughout the day with organized strafes. Enemy's artillery retaliation was feeble, but his T.M's replied vigorously, in answer to which our 18 pdrs opened up. Conference for operation on 19th. held at Bn. H.Q. at 2 pm. G.O.C. 16th Divn. [illegible] visited Bn. H.Q. 3 pm.	
		18th.	Battalion relieved in left sub-section by 6th Royal Irish Regt. & moved into Bde. Support with H.Q. at DOCTOR'S HOUSE, KEMMEL. Battn. disposed as follows: 'A' Coy. FAIRWAY DUG-OUTS, COOKER FARM (H.Q.) & BEEHIVE DUG-OUTS; 'B' Coy. YONGE ST. DUG-OUT (H.Q. & 2 platoons) and FORT REGINA (2 platoons); 'C' Coy. FORT EDWARD (2 platoons), LA [illegible] (H.Q. & 1 platoon) and FORT SASKATCHEWAN (1 platoon). 'D' Coy. FORT EDWARD (2 platoons) & LA POLKA (H.Q. and 2 platoons). Our Lewis Guns (6) took over 25 yds. of the front line (Right Sub-section) from 1st. R. Munster Fusiliers, southern boundary at [illegible] ROAD. Stores of 'P' Bombs etc. made in front line.	[illegible] VI
		19th.	At 7.15 am. 3 parties from the battalion, comprising 9 officers and 190 O.R., attempted to enter the enemy's trenches at N.36.d.20.78, N.36.b.05.10 and N.36.a.80.30.,	

2353 Wt. W2544/1454 700,000 5/15 D. D. & L. A.D.S.S./Forms/C. 2118.

Confidential

Instructions regarding War Diaries and Intelligence Summaries are contained in F. S. Regs., Part II. and the Staff Manual respectively. Title pages will be prepared in manuscript.

February 1917

WAR DIARY
or
INTELLIGENCE SUMMARY.
(Erase heading not required.)

Army Form C. 2118.

Sheet VIII

Place	Date	Hour	Summary of Events and Information	Remarks and references to Appendices
Whitefield	Feby.	19th	during a dense fog. The centre party reached the enemy's wire, but evidently missed the gap previously cut by T.M. fire. 2Lt. E.B.B. WILLIAMSON, second-in-command of the party, was killed here & 2Lt. J.A.V. KENT, commanding the party was wounded in the right arm, but continued to fire his revolver at the enemy, while 6123 Pte. J. WHITE was conspicuous in standing up & bombing the German trench. The party then fell back. The right party also reached the hostile wire & here 2Lt. W.R. BRADSHAW, second-in-command of the party, was wounded & fell back towards our line, but was killed on the way. 2Lt. H.P. CARDWELL, commanding the party, was severely wounded. Having thrown all the bombs they were carrying, the party withdrew. The left party met with considerable opposition & though splendidly led by 2Lt P.R. CUMMINS, began to falter. Capt. I.H. GARVEY, O.C. Assault, & Lt. T. HUGHES, O.C. Left Support, ran across to rally them, assisted by 4217 Pte. J. COLLINS, who had previously acted with the greatest gallantry during the assault. Capt. GARVEY fell wounded & was subsequently brought in by Lt. HUGHES, 2Lt. CUMMINS, 3916 Pte. P. KING & 7342 Pte. M. HEALY, but died later. When the parties had returned, Pte. COLLINS persistently went out into NO MAN'S LAND under heavy fire & brought in dead & wounded. About 9.15 am. the enemy offered an armistice to collect the wounded and our	

Confidential

Instructions regarding War Diaries and Intelligence Summaries are contained in F. S. Regs., Part II. and the Staff Manual respectively. Title pages will be prepared in manuscript.

February 1917

WAR DIARY
or
INTELLIGENCE SUMMARY.
(Erase heading not required.)

Army Form C. 2118.

Sheet IX

Place	Date	Hour	Summary of Events and Information	Remarks and references to Appendices
[illegible]	Feby.	19th.	men went out for this purpose. When all had been collected & the dead also brought in, both sides withdrew to their trenches. Although the enemy had stipulated that our men should not be armed, 2Lt. R.E.M. GORDON-RALPH, [illegible] officers, went out with his revolver & was taken prisoner. Our casualties were:—	

	Killed	Died of wounds	Wounded	Missing (believed prisoners)	Totals
Officers – 6th. Conn. Rangers.	2	1	2	1	6
O.R. " " "	6	2	~~7~~ 16	~~[illegible]~~ 5	30
" 47th. M.G. Coy.	1	–	–	–	1
" 47th. T.M. Batt.	6		1	1	8
Totals	~~17~~ 18		~~20~~ 19	~~3~~ 7	44

Remainder of day passed quietly. About 6.45pm. an explosion, as of a mine, was felt.

Place	Date	Hour	Summary of Events and Information	Remarks and references to Appendices
		20th.	A similar explosion to that recorded on 19th. was felt about 5am. 16th. Div'l. Arty. & IX Corps Heavy Arty. carried out a bombardment at 1.15pm. C.O. attended Brigade Conference at FORT VICTORIA at 2.30pm. Raining all day.	

Confidential

Instructions regarding War Diaries and Intelligence Summaries are contained in F. S. Regs., Part II. and the Staff Manual respectively. Title pages will be prepared in manuscript.

February 1917

WAR DIARY
or
INTELLIGENCE SUMMARY.
(Erase heading not required.)

Army Form C. 2118.

Sheet X

Place	Date	Hour	Summary of Events and Information	Remarks and references to Appendices
[illegible]	Feby.	21st.	Foggy all day, so practically no activity by either side. Battn. occupied with working-parties as usual.	
		22nd.	Battn. relieved by 2nd. R. Irish Regt. at 2.30 pm. and moved into Divl. Reserve at CURRAGH CAMP. Very foggy again all day.	Appendix V.
		23rd.	Inspection of Kits, Clothing and necessaries under Coy. arrangements; Box Respirators & Feet by M.O.; Rifles by Armourer-Sergt. Battalion paraded at 1.30 pm. in clean fatigue dress & was addressed briefly by C.O. on the operations of 19th.	
		24th.	'A' Coy. occupied for baths 9 – 10.45 a.m., 'B' Coy. 10.45 am. – 12.30 pm., 'C' Coy. 1.30 – 3.0 pm., 'D' Coy. 3 – 4.30 pm. 'A' & 'B' Coys. paraded at 2.30 pm. and 'C' & 'D' Coy. at 10 am. for inspection by C.O. in new formation. Divisional Commander inspected camp at 11 am. C.O. held conference of officers at 6 pm.	
		25th.	Church parades as follows:– C. of E. 9.0 am. for 9.30 am. at YMCA Hut, SCHERPEN-BERG; Presbyterians & Non-conformists 9.30 am. for 10.0 am. at YMCA Hut, LOCRE; R.C.'s 10.30 am. for 11.15 am. at LOCRE CHURCH. This parade was played back from the Church by the 16th. Divisional Band. Coys. at disposal of commanders for afternoon.	

2353 Wt. W2544/1454 700,000 5/15 D. D. & L. A.D.S.S./Forms/C. 2118.

Confidential

Instructions regarding War Diaries and Intelligence Summaries are contained in F. S. Regs., Part II. and the Staff Manual respectively. Title pages will be prepared in manuscript.

February 1917

WAR DIARY
or
INTELLIGENCE SUMMARY.

(Erase heading not required.)

Army Form C. 2118.

Sheet XI

Place	Date	Hour	Summary of Events and Information	Remarks and references to Appendices
In the field.	Feby.	26th	Coys. paraded for drill at 9.0 am. 6 men per coy. began a two days' course of instruction in bombing under Battn. Bombing Officer. Battn. was inspected in new formation in full marching order by C.O. at 2.35pm. C.O. interviewed all Sergeants in Canteen at 5pm.	
		27th	Battn. inspected in new organization by Bde. Commander at 10.30 am., after which the battn. marched past in column of route. Coys. paraded at 2.30 pm. for drill under the adjutant; bombing & Lewis Gun classes continued under their respective officers.	
		28th.	Coys. paraded for drill under the adjt at 9.30 am. Coys. at disposal of commanders in afternoon. Bombing class finished with live throwing at LURGAN CAMP in the afternoon. Lewis Gun class continued under Lieut. A. G. F. SIMMS. Officers reconnoitred KEMMEL DEFENCES, approaches thereto, and lines of advance to any portion of the front line. Lecture for all available officers & senior N.C.Os at 5pm. in YMCA Hut, LOCRE, by G.O.C. 16th Divl. Arty.	

[signature]
Lieut. Col.
COMDG. 6th (S) Bn. THE CONNAUGHT RANGERS

2353 Wt. W2544/1454 700,000 5/15 D. D. & L. A.D.S.S./Forms/C. 2118.

Appendix I.

6th (S) Battn. The Connaught Rangers File.

SECRET. OPERATION ORDERS. COPY NO. [illegible]

I. The Battalion will be relieved by the 6th ROYAL IRISH REGT. in the left sub-section tomorrow, commencing at 2.30 p.m.

II. On completion of relief the Battalion will be disposed as follows:-

"A" COY	-	DERRY HUTS.
"B" "	-	KEMMEL CHATEAU.
"C" "	-	DERRY. HUTS.
"D" "	-	KEMMEL CHATEAU.
LEWIS GUNNERS	-	DERRY HUTS
HEADQUARTERS	-	DERRY HUTS.

III. Completion of relief will be reported in code to Battn Headquarters

IV. 1 Guide per platoon from "C" & "D" Coys will be at DOCTORS HOUSE, KEMMEL at 2 pm.

V. Movement will be by platoons at 300 yds distance.

VI. Copies of Trench Stores & Gum Boot receipts will be handed into Orderly Room by 9 a.m. 3rd inst.

VII. Blankets will be carried on the man.

(Sd.) J. Booth. Lieut.
a/Adjt. 6th (S) Battn. The Conn. Rangers

1.2.17.

Appendix II

6th (S) Bn. THE CONN. RANGERS

SECRET

OPERATION ORDERS

0.0625

COPY. NO.

Ref. TRENCH. MAP, BELGIUM & FRANCE
Sheet 28. S. W. 6d, 3. D. Scale. 1/20,000

I The Battalion will be relieved to-morrow in DERRY. HUTS and KEMMEL CHATEAU by the 8th Bn. ROYAL. INNISKILLING. FUSILIERS Relief to commence at 1-30. p. m.

II On completion of relief the Battalion will move to KEMMEL SHELTERS. (N. 19. d.) where billets have already been allotted Coy. Qr. Mr. Sergts. Headquarters will be in farm at N. 19. C. 9. 1.

III Movement will be by platoons at 300 yards distance

IV The routes to be taken are as follows. A. C. Coys. and Lewis Gunners. W. along DAYLIGHT. CORNER - DRANOUTRE ROAD to N. 31. C. 9. 0., thence by new road (not shown on map) to road junction. N. 19. C. 8. 0. "B" & D. Coys. Road junctions at N. 21. C. 95. 60. and N. 21. C. 65. 60. thence along main KEMMEL - LOCRE. ROAD

V O. C. A. & C. Coys. and L. G. O. will hand in clean billet certificates to Orderly Room. by 1 p. m. O. C. Detachment, KEMMEL will be responsible that the billets there are left in a clean and Sanitary condition.

VI Copies of billet and Camp store receipts (if any) will be rendered to Orderly Room. by 10. a. m. 7th inst

VII Completion of relief and arrival in KEMMEL SHELTERS. will be reported by runner to Orderly Room. in that Camp

VIII One limber per Company. will be at the disposal of Company Commanders. for the removal of Kit. The mess cart will be at DERRY. HUTS at 2 p. m. One limber will be at disposal of ~~Headq~~ Headquarters all Kits to be ready for removal by Transport by 10. A. M.

IX Strict attention will be paid to the maintenance of March Discipline

X Before taking over the huts at KEMMEL. SHELTERS. Company Commanders and L. G. O. will inspect them and render a report on their condition to Orderly Room. by 6. p. m.

XI The first two days in Divisional Reserve will be spent in cleaning and refitting the men — .. — (Sd) T. BOOTH Lieut

5-2-17

a/Adj 6th (S) Bn. THE. CONN. RANGERS

Appendix III

6th (S) BN. THE CONN. RANGERS.

.SECRET.

OPERATION ORDERS.

COPY NO.

I The Battalion will relieve the 8th ROYAL INNISKILLING FUS. in the Left Sub-section of the SPANBROEK Section tomorrow, commencing at 4 p.m.

II On completion of relief the Battalion will be disposed as follows:-

"A" Coy. 1 Bay N. of PICCADILLY to End of Trench N.29.4.
"C" Coy. N.29.5 to BROADWAY (exclusive)
"D" " S.P's. 10 & 11.
"B" " REGENT ST. DUG-OUTS. S.P.9.
HD. QRS. FORT VICTORIA.

III Relief will be carried out as follows:-

"A" Coy. 6 C.R. will relieve "A" & "B" Coys. 8th R. INNIS. FUS. on Left of Front Line.
"C" " " " " "C" & "D" " " " " on Right of Front Line.
"B" " " " " in REGENT St. DUG-OUTS.
"D" " " " " in S.P's. 10 & 11.

IV Lewis Guns will relieve by daylight, all Lewis Gun positions at present in use to be maintained. Details of relief to be arranged between officers concerned.

V Movements will be by platoons at 300 yards distance on all roads, and by sections at 5 minutes interval in trenches.

VI Trench Store and Gum Boot receipts will be handed into Orderly Room by 11 a.m. 15th inst. Care must be taken to ensure that these are correct.

VII Completion of relief will be notified in B.A.B. Code to Battn. Headquarters.

VIII Company Commanders will render Clean Billet Certificates to Orderly Room at KEMMEL SHELTERS before leaving.

IX All Surplus Kit will be stacked outside DONCASTER HUTS, BIRR BARRACKS and outside Orderly Room at KEMMEL SHELTERS by 12 noon tomorrow, for removal by Transport under arrangements to be made by the Transport Officer.

X Company Commanders and L.G.O. will render a certificate that every N.C.O. & man under their commands, have rubbed their feet with Whale Oil before going into the trenches, and that all arrangements have been made for the necessary clean socks.

13-2-17. (Sd) T. BOOTH, Lieut.

a/Adjt. 6th (S) BN. THE CONN. RANGERS.

Appendix IV

6TH (S) BN. THE CONN. RANGERS.

SECRET.

OPERATION ORDERS.

COPY NO.

I. The Battalion will be relieved by the 6TH ROYAL IRISH REGT. tomorrow 18th inst. commencing at 10 a.m. and will proceed to Brigade Support.

II. "B" Coy. 6 C.R. will be relieved by B. Coy. 6th R.I. Regt. in Right Front Line.

"D" Coy. 6 C.R. will be relieved by A. Coy. 6th R.I. Regt. in Left Front Line.

"A" Coy. 6 C.R. will be relieved by D. Coy. 6th R.I. Regt. in Regent St. Dug-outs and S.P. 9.

"C" Coy. 6 C.R. will be relieved by C. Coy. 6th R.I. Regt. in S. P's. 10 + 11.

III. The Lewis Gun Teams and Advance Parties of the 6TH R.I. Regt. will arrive about 8 a.m.

IV. On completion of relief the Battalion will be disposed as follows:- HD. QRS. - DOCTOR'S HOUSE.

A. Coy. Hd. Qrs. + 1 platoon at COOKER FARM.
2 platoons at GALWAY DUG-OUTS.
1 platoon at BEEHIVE DUG-OUTS.

B. Coy. HD. Qrs. + 3 platoons at YONGE ST. DUG-OUTS.
1 platoon at FORT REGINA and 1 Lewis Gun.

C. Coy. HD. Qrs. + 2 platoons at FORT EDWARD.
1 platoon at FORT SASKATCHEWAN.
1 platoon at LA POLKA.

D. Coy. HD. Qrs. + 2 platoons at LA POLKA.
2 platoons at FORT EDWARD.

V. All Lewis Gunners will rejoin their companies.

VI. Rations for "A" Coy. will be dumped at COOKER FARM.
" " FORT EDWARD will be dumped at FORT VICTORIA.
" " YONGE ST. + FORT REGINA will be dumped at FORT VICTORIA.
" " LA POLKA will be dumped at DOCTOR'S HOUSE.
" " Headquarters will be dumped at DOCTOR'S HOUSE.

VII. Advance parties should arrive at their various destinations at 8-30 a.m. An Officer will accompany each party if possible.

VIII. Copies of Trench Store and Gum Boot receipts to be handed into Orderly Room by 8 p.m. 18th inst. Care should be taken to fill in all receipts in a correct manner, if this is not done it causes unnecessary trouble.

IX. "A" + "C" Coys. will hand blankets back to "B" + "D" Coys. respectively.

X. Completion of relief will be reported in code to Battn. HD. Qrs. Doctor's House.

—— " ——

14-2-17. (Sd) T. BOOTH, Lieut.

for Adjt. 6TH (S) BN. THE CONN. RANGERS.

Appendix V

6th (S) Bn. The Connaught Rangers.

OPERATION ORDERS

SECRET.

COPY NO.

21st. February 1917.

I. The 49th Inf Bde will relieve the 47th Inf Bde in the Spanbroek Section tomorrow 22nd inst.

II The 47th Inf Bde on relief will become the Brigade in Divisional Reserve, as will be disposed as follows.

Brigade H.Q.	LOCRE	
1st R. Munster Fus.	WAKEFIELD CAMP.	
6th R. Irish Regt.	DONCASTER HUTS.	
6th Conn. Rangers.	CURRAGH CAMP.	
7th Leinster Regt.	KEMMEL SHELTERS	H.Q + 2 Coys
	DONCASTER HUTS	1 Coy
	CURRAGH CAMP.	1 Coy.

III The Battalion will be relieved by 2ND R. IRISH. REGT in Brigade support commencing at 2.30pm. On relief the companies will proceed to CURRAGH CAMP.

IV Movement E of LOCRE — LA CLYTTE road will be by platoons at 300 yards distance

V Completion of relief will be reported in Code to F.I.Z. the code word being "Armed Civilian"

VI Lewis Gunners will be relieved during the morning if possible. all arrangements to be made between those concerned.

VII C.Q.M. Sergts. will meet the Quartermaster at CURRAGH CAMP at 10am. to arrange the accomodation.

VIII. REMOVAL OF KITS.

Mess Cart will be at Kemmel Chateau at 2pm. 3 Limbers will be at KEMMEL by 2pm. for the use of Hd. Qrs. 'B' Company and the garrison of LA POLKA and FORT SASKETCHEWAN. 1 Limber will be at DAYLIGHT CORNER for the use of 'A' COY and the garrison of FORT EDWARD at 2pm.

(Sd) T. BOOTH. Lieut.

A/ADJT. 6th (S) Bn. THE. CONN. RANGERS

16E

W A R D I A R Y

FOR MONTH OF MARCH, 1917.

VOLUME 16

UNIT :- 6th Btn Connaught Rangers

Vol 15

Confidential

WAR DIARY
or
INTELLIGENCE SUMMARY
(Erase heading not required.)

Army Form C. 2118.

Instructions regarding War Diaries and Intelligence Summaries are contained in F. S. Regs., Part II. and the Staff Manual respectively. Title Pages will be prepared in manuscript.

March 1917

Sheet I

Place	Date	Hour	Summary of Events and Information	Remarks and references to Appendices
LOCRE. (CURRAGH CAMP)	1/3/17		Coys paraded for drill under the Adjutant at 9am. Lewis Gun. Class under Lieut A.G.F. Simms continued. 2 officers per Coy paraded under Lieut SIMMS for instruction in Lewis Gun. There were no parades in the afternoon as the Bn. played the 1ST. R.M.F in a game of Hurley, that match resulting in a draw. Hostile Aeroplanes displayed great activity between 3pm & 4pm. Lieut. D.D. BECKETT and 18 OR's joined the Bn. for duty today. Lieut Beckett was posted to D. COY. The weather was fine and clear, visibility being excellent.	
BDE. RESERVE	2/3/17		The 47th Inf Bde relieved the 49th Inf and was disposed as follows. Right-Subsection. 1st. R.M.F. Left Subsection 6th R.I. REGT. Bde Support 7th LEINSTERS. Bde Reserve 6th CONN. RANGERS. The Bn. relieved the 7th R.I. Fus. in Bde Reserve at DERRY HUTS and KEMMEL CHATEAU commencing at 1-30 pm. The Bn was then disposed as follows. Hd. Qrs. A + B. COY. DERRY HUTS. + C + D COYS at KEMMEL CHATEAU. Dispositions made and trenches and dugouts alloted to men in case of hostile shelling.	Appendix I
BDE RESERVE	3/3/17		Coys were at the disposal of Coy. Commanders as far as the exigencies of Working parties allowed. The C.O. attended at Bde. H.Q. at 11 am. to meet Army Commander. He interviewed newly joined Officers at 3pm	

2449 Wt. W14957/M90 750,000 1/16 J.B.C. & A. Forms/C.2118/12.

Confidential

March 1917

Instructions regarding War Diaries and Intelligence Summaries are contained in F. S. Regs., Part II. and the Staff Manual respectively. Title Pages will be prepared in manuscript.

WAR DIARY
or
INTELLIGENCE SUMMARY

(Erase heading not required.)

Army Form C. 2118.

Sheet II

Place	Date	Hour	Summary of Events and Information	Remarks and references to Appendices
Bde Reserve	3/3/17	(Contd)	and all officers of HdQrs. A & B Coys at 3pm. Among other work done one of the dugouts near the farm was drained of water and rendered serviceable. The heating apparatus of the officers bath was taken down and erected inside the shelter and fresh slats were nailed on duck-boards where required.	
Bde. Reserve	4/3/17		Lieut.-Col. R. C. Feilding proceeded on 21 days leave of absence & Major W.A.X. Grimshaw assumed temporary command of the Bn. 16th Divl Artillery and IX Corps. H.A. carried out a bombardment of SPANBROEKMOLEN at 3.8 pm for about 1½ hours. One Officer from this Bn. was selected to watch the rolling barrage from an Artillery O.P.	
Bde Reserve	5/3/17.		16th Divl Artillery and IX Corps H.A. bombarded enemy trenches for about 1½ hours at 7-18 am. Rest of day passed quietly, snowed early, but soon thawed, Evening foggy.	
Left Subsection (SPANBROEK. SGT)	6/3/17		Bn. relieved the 6th R. I. REGT. in the left-subsection commencing at 2.30pm and was disposed as follows. A COY. Right front line. B. COY Right Support (HQ and 3 platoons REGENT ST. D.O. 1 platoon S.P.9) C. COY. Left front line. D. COY. Left Support (HQ and 3 platoons S.P11. 1 platoon S.P 10.) Remainder of Bde disposed as follows. 6th R. I. REGT in Bde Reserve. 7th LEINSTERS in Right Subsection and 1st R.M.F in Bde support. Lieut. A.E. MALE Transport Officer was	Appendix II

2449 Wt. W14957/M90 750,000 1/16 J.B.C. & A. Forms/C.2118/12.

Confidential

March 1917 — Sheet III

Army Form C. 2118.

WAR DIARY
or
INTELLIGENCE SUMMARY

(Erase heading not required.)

Instructions regarding War Diaries and Intelligence Summaries are contained in F. S. Regs., Part II. and the Staff Manual respectively. Title Pages will be prepared in manuscript.

Place	Date	Hour	Summary of Events and Information	Remarks and references to Appendices
Left Sub Section	6/3/17		admitted to Hospital and Lieut F. N. S. JOURDAIN temporarily assumed the duties of Transport Officer and Quartermaster (Lieut. J. P. Praeger being on leave)	
Lt Sub-Section	7/3/17		At 6.45am enemy seen dribbling through gap at N.30 A.5.8. and were engaged with rifle and L.G. Fire. At 7-30am a party of the enemy was observed apparently advancing across the open at N.30 B.0.3. they were dispersed by Lewis Guns. Enemy were quiet during the night. A Patrol was sent out by each Coy in the line but nothing was seen or heard of the enemy except that work was going on at N.30.3. Between 1-30pm and 2pm. SP 11 was shelled with 5.9's a dugout was blown in a 5 casualties inflicted. From 3.30pm to 5pm a few Whizz-bangs fell near the top of VIA GELLIA but no damage was done. Our Snipers claim 3 hits. A high wind prevailed all day.	
Left S.S.	8/3/17		The day passed quietly until 3-30pm when intense Artillery & T.M. fire was opened on our front line and supports. At about 4.40pm two parties of the enemy effected an entry into the trenches of the Brigade on our left. C & D Coys at once formed a defensive flank along VIA GELLIA and despatched bombing parties to the left, who assisted in driving the enemy out, when he was caught by Enfilade ~~fire~~ from C. Coy Lewis Guns. The enemy also tried to raid this Battn but was driven off before he could reach our trenches. The situation was normal by 6-30pm. Considerable damage was done to our trenches by the bombardment. About 100 yards of the front line at the GLORY HOLE was	Appendix III

2449 Wt. W14957/M90 750,000 1/16 J.B.C. & A. Forms/C.2118/12.

Confidential

Instructions regarding War Diaries and Intelligence Summaries are contained in F. S. Regs., Part II. and the Staff Manual respectively. Title Pages will be prepared in manuscript.

March 1917.

WAR DIARY
or
INTELLIGENCE SUMMARY
(Erase heading not required.)

Army Form C. 2118.

Sheet IV

Place	Date	Hour	Summary of Events and Information	Remarks and references to Appendices
L.S.S	8/3/17	(Contd)	rendered impassable and the trench was blocked again near the top of KETCHEN AVENUE. 4 direct hits were obtained on VIA GELLIA between Coy. H.Q. and the front line and S.P.11 was considerably damaged. At 9pm B. COY relieved A COY in the Right front line and D COY relieved C COY in Left front line. A+C coys proceeded to the positions vacated by B+D coys. respectively, this relief was to have taken place at 4pm but was stopped by hostile bombardment. The following awards were announced. 2/Lieut. H.F CARDWELL + 2/Lt J.A.V. KENT. MILITARY CROSS and No 5332 PTE. P. COLLINS. D.C.M.	Appendix
L.S.S.	9/3/17		At intervals throughout the night the enemy whizz-banged our front line and put T.M's into the GLORY HOLE but did no damage. At 4 am he started another intense bombardment along the entire front line and on S.P.11. About 4.30 am he raided the Left Coy at N.30.A.3.9. and after he had retired 10 men and 1 Lewis Gun were found to be missing. Some German bombs were found in the trench. More damage was done to the front line, VIA GELLIA and S.P.11. The total casualties for the two raids were.	

	KILLED.	DIED OF WOUNDS.	WOUNDED.	MISSING.	TOTAL
OFFR.	–	–	–	–	–
O.R.	8	1	42.	10.	61

The remainder of the day passed quietly. Our Snipers claim two hits.

2449 Wt. W14957/M90 750,000 1/16 J.B.C. & A. Forms/C.2118/12.

Confidential

Instructions regarding War Diaries and Intelligence Summaries are contained in F. S. Regs., Part II. and the Staff Manual respectively. Title Pages will be prepared in manuscript.

March 1917

WAR DIARY
or
INTELLIGENCE SUMMARY

(Erase heading not required.)

Army Form C. 2118.

Sheet V

Place	Date	Hour	Summary of Events and Information	Remarks and references to Appendices
Left S.S.	10/3/17		The day passed quietly except for a few T.M.s on the left Coy about 9 am which did no damage. The Bn. was relieved by the 6th ROYAL I. REGT. and proceeded into Bde. Support with HQ at the DOCTORS HOUSE KEMMEL. The Bn was disposed as follows A Coy HQ + 2 Platoons COOKER FARM. 2 platoons GALWAY D.O. B Coy HQ and 1 Platoon BEEHIVE D.O. 3 platoons FORT EDWARD. C Coy HQ + 2 Platoons YONGE ST D.O. 2 platoons FORT REGINA. D Coy HQ and 2 platoons LA POLKA, 2 PLATOONS FORT SASKATCHEWAN. The Remainder of the Bde was disposed as follows. 6th R.I.R. left front line. 7th LEINSTERS Bde Reserve 1st MUNSTERS Right front line. The following officers reported arrival and were posted to Coys as under. MAJOR C. F. UNDERHILL-FAITHORNE A. COY. CAPT. H. R. GOODE. B COY. LIEUT. P. MCBRIDE B. COY 2/LIEUT. S. W. O'COFFEY A. COY. 2/LIEUT. R. B. PHILLIPSON D. COY 2/LIEUT. T. F. GILMORE. C. COY. MAJOR H. F. N. JOURDAIN C.M.G. joined the Bn this day and assumed temporary command.	Appendix IV
Bde Support.	11/3/17		Kemmel was shelled at intervals during the day, otherwise the situation remained normal. A meeting of the Bde Sports Committee was held at Bde H.Q. at 2-30pm	

Confidential

March 1917.

WAR DIARY
or
INTELLIGENCE SUMMARY
(Erase heading not required.)

Army Form C. 2118.

Sheet VI

Instructions regarding War Diaries and Intelligence Summaries are contained in F. S. Regs., Part II. and the Staff Manual respectively. Title Pages will be prepared in manuscript.

Place	Date	Hour	Summary of Events and Information	Remarks and references to Appendices
Bde Support	12/3/17		A portion of the 47th Inf Bde was relieved by a portion of the 107th Inf Bde 36th (Ulster) DIV. The Bn was relieved by the 10th BN ROYAL I. RIFLES and proceeded to the BERTHEN area (R.22 etc) The relief commenced at 2-30pm and was completed by 5-30pm and the Bn was settled in billets by 11pm. The Battn billeting area was as follows – Q 24 R 15 c+d 16 c+D, 19 20 21 + 21 A+C as far as the BOESCHEPE — BERTHEN — SCHAEXKEN road and 26 a+b, 27 a+b. The Bn was distributed amongst the following farms HQ round cross roads R.19.D.6.5. A COY R.19 D 3.7 B. COY R.19.B.2.7. C.COY. R.19.A.7.4 D.COY R.20.C.3.5. The 7th LEINSTER REGT was relieved the same day and were billeted further South with HQ at R.31.D.4.3 Bde HQ remained at LITTLE KEMMEL	Appendix V
Berthen.	13/3/17.		Coys were at the disposal of Coy Commanders all day. The C.O. inspected billets in the morning and the Armourer Sgt inspected the rifles of HdQrs. B+C Coys. Lieut. D J. McSherry reported for duty today and was posted to C Coy.	
"	14/3/17		Coys at the disposal of Coy Commanders in the morning. Armourer completed the inspection of the Battn's rifles. HdQrs played A Coy at Soccer Football and beat them by 6 goals to 1. Bde HdQrs moved to THIEUSOUCK (Q.35.)	
"	15/3/17		Coys were at the disposal of Coy Commanders in morning. Afternoon devoted to Coy football, sports etc. HdQrs beat B COY at Soccer by 2 goals to nil.	

2449 Wt. W14957/M90 750,000 1/16 J.B.C. & A. Forms/C.2118/12.

Confidential March 1917

Instructions regarding War Diaries and Intelligence Summaries are contained in F. S. Regs., Part II. and the Staff Manual respectively. Title Pages will be prepared in manuscript.

WAR DIARY
or
INTELLIGENCE SUMMARY
(Erase heading not required.)

Sheet VII

Army Form C. 2118.

Place	Date	Hour	Summary of Events and Information	Remarks and references to Appendices
Berthen	16/3/17		The Bn was inspected and addressed by the Brigadier. The C.O. saw all officers in the H.Q. Mess at 12 noon. D. COY beat C. COY at soccer by 5 goals to nil	
"	17/3/17		The Bn paraded by Coys and marched to mass at MONT DES CATS Monastery at 10 A.M. Regimental sports were held in the afternoon from 2.15 pm.	
"	18/3/17		The R.Cs attended Divine Service at MONT DES CATS Monastery at 11 am and other denominations at PIEBROUCK. A cross-country race postponed from yesterday was run off and won by D. COY. 2/Lt F. T. CHAMIER reported to Bde for duty. 2/Lt J. J. Pope joined the Bn and was posted to C. COY. The day was fine after a dull morning.	
"	19/3/17		A large and varied training programme was carried out. A + B Coys made use of the Rifle Range at Q.29.D.95.75 and C+D Coys attended the Baths at WESTOUTRE. The Bn beat the 111th F.A. at Football 4 goals to 2. All officers attended a conference at Bn. H.Q. Major R.J.A TAMPLIN D.S.O. was admitted to Hospital	
"	20/3/17		During the morning the Coys paraded for training but the unpleasant weather caused most of the work to be done in billets. During the afternoon the Bn attended the Brigade Sports in BERTHEN, where in spite of the poor weather a pleasant evening was spent. The Bn was represented amongst the prize winners in almost every event.	

2449 Wt. W14957/M90 750,000 1/16 J.B.C. & A. Forms/C.2118/12.

Confidential

Instructions regarding War Diaries and Intelligence Summaries are contained in F. S. Regs., Part II. and the Staff Manual respectively. Title Pages will be prepared in manuscript.

March 1917.

WAR DIARY
or
INTELLIGENCE SUMMARY

(Erase heading not required.)

Sheet VIII

Army Form C. 2118.

Place	Date	Hour	Summary of Events and Information	Remarks and references to Appendices
Berthen	20/3/17	(Contd)	after tea they were lectured by the Coy Commanders. C.S.M. NORMAN was granted a commission as Lieut and was heartily congratulated by all ranks	
"	21/3/17		A very interesting programme of training was again carried out and the Baths at BAILLEUL were attended by A & B Coys. Several fields were at the disposal of Coys for recreational purposes and several interesting sporting contests were brought off. H.Qrs beat D. Coy by 1 goal to 0.	
"	22/3/17		The Bn was today inspected by the Army Commander and it was apparent to all ranks that he was very pleased with the parade. The evening being wet it was spent in billets, Musketry & Lectures being the order. Lieut. J.Y. HADDEN rejoined from Hospital today.	
"	23/3/17		A fine spring day enabled us to get through a lot of outdoor work. The Baths at WESTOUTRE were at the disposal of A & B Coys. Lieut. B.M. BALBI departed today enroute for England where he is taking up duty with the M.G.C. H.Qrs played a drawn game of Football with C. Coy. Several interesting lectures were given by platoon Commanders and the keen interest shown by the men was an instance of the good feeling and spirit of comradeship which exists between all ranks in the Bn.	

2449 Wt. W14957/M90 750,000 1/16 J.B.C. & A. Forms/C.2118/12.

Confidential

March 1917

WAR DIARY
or
INTELLIGENCE SUMMARY
(Erase heading not required.)

Army Form C. 2118.

Sheet IV

Instructions regarding War Diaries and Intelligence Summaries are contained in F. S. Regs., Part II. and the Staff Manual respectively. Title Pages will be prepared in manuscript.

Place	Date	Hour	Summary of Events and Information	Remarks and references to Appendices
Berthen.	24/3/17		Another fine day enabled training to proceed apace, practising the attack being the chief item. The afternoon was spent in Recreation and Physical training. Coys carrying out interplatoon football matches. The Cooking arrangements of the Bn. were inspected by Capt Clements, Inspector of Catering, 2nd Army. The following awards were notified and the recipients warmly congratulated. NO 1619. L/C. J. JOHNSTON. NO 4437 L/C G. BOND and NO 7761 PTE P. THOMPSON. MILITARY MEDALS.	
"	25/3/17		Summer time was in force today and the change was plainly noticable. Divine Service for RC at MONT DES CATS Monastery and other denominations at PIE BROUCK were attended. After dinner some very interesting training was carried out and in a game of Football the Bn beat the R.G.A by 7 goals to 2. 2/Lt Beckett rejoined today from a Course	
	26/3/17		Inclement weather made the march to WESTOUTRE for Baths rather disagreeable and on arrival there only a change of clothes were obtained. During the evening the men paraded in billets for rifle inspection by the Armourer Sgt and this together with Musketry + Lectures filled in the afternoon. Lt Gilmore and a Working Party of 35 other Ranks were despatched to BAILLEUL. they will remain away 7 to 10 days.	

2449 Wt. W14957/M90 750,000 1/16 J.B.C. & A. Forms/C.2118/12.

Confidential

Instructions regarding War Diaries and Intelligence Summaries are contained in F. S. Regs., Part II. and the Staff Manual respectively. Title Pages will be prepared in manuscript.

March 1917

WAR DIARY
or
INTELLIGENCE SUMMARY
(Erase heading not required.)

Sheet X

Army Form C. 2118.

Place	Date	Hour	Summary of Events and Information	Remarks and references to Appendices
Berthen	27/3/17		Training was again carried out in ideal weather and the baths at WESTOUTRE were very much appreciated. The Corps Commander paid a visit and watched some of the Coys at work. Capt T. H. CROFTON and CSM. NO 4093 J. BYRNE were awarded the MILITARY CROSS and D.C.M. respectively and on this honour were heartily congratulated. Lieut-Col R. C. FEILDING returned from leave and resumed command of the Bn.	
"	28/3/17		Training. Inspections of feet + Gas Helmets + Lectures were the programme. The C. O. saw all Officers at H.Q. Mess. Lieut R.B. PHILLIPSON rejoined from a Course	
	29/3/17		A Contact scheme was arranged but had to be postponed owing to inclement weather. The Corps Commander presented Medal Ribbons + parchments to some Offrs + Other Ranks who had not received them. Indoor work, Musketry with Dummy Cartridges etc. finished the day	
	30/3/17		Various forms of training in the morning and Recreation during the afternoon made a pleasant day. The Bn was beaten in a Game of Hurley by the 1st R.M.F. and the H.Q. football team suffered their first defeat, B Coy beating them by 3 goals to 2. 2/Lt A.C. HALL was attached to 47th T.M.B. today.	

2449 Wt. W14957/M90 750,000 1/16 J.B.C. & A. Forms/C.2118/12.

Confidential

Instructions regarding War Diaries and Intelligence Summaries are contained in F. S. Regs., Part II. and the Staff Manual respectively. Title Pages will be prepared in manuscript.

March 1917

WAR DIARY
or
INTELLIGENCE SUMMARY

(Erase heading not required.)

Army Form C. 2118.

Sheet XI

Place	Date	Hour	Summary of Events and Information	Remarks and references to Appendices
LOCRE.	31/3/17	—	The 47th Inf Bde relieved the 48th Inf Bde in the LOCRE area and the Battalion was billeted at DONCASTER HUTS before noon. The C.O. inspected the Camp and saw that all ranks were comfortable. The afternoon was spent in resting and the evening closed in wet & Cold. Bde H.Q. were at SCHERTENBERG. and the remainder of the Bde disposed as follows. 6th R.I. REGT. KEMMEL SHELTERS. 1st. R.M. Fus. BIRR BARRACKS. and the 7th LEINSTE REGT at CLARE CAMP.	Appendix VI

ORDERLY ROOM
1 – APR. 1917
6th SER. Bn. CONN. RANGERS

[signature]
LIEUT. COLONEL,
COMDG 6th (S) Bn. THE CONNAUGHT RANGERS.

2449 Wt. W14957/M90 750,000 1/16 J.B.C. & A. Forms/C.2118/12.

Appendix I

6TH (S) BN. THE CONN. RANGERS. COPY NO. 13

SECRET. OPERATION ORDERS. 1ST MARCH. 1917.

I. The 47th Inf. Bde will relieve the 49th Inf Bde in the SPANBROEK Section on the 2nd. March. 1917.

II On completion of relief the 47th Inf Bde will be disposed as follows

BDE. HD. QRS.	LITTLE KEMMEL
RIGHT. SUB. SECTION.	1ST ROYAL MUN. FUS.
LEFT. "	6th ROYAL IRISH REGT.
BDE. SUPPORT."	7th LEINSTERS
BDE. RESERVE.	6th CONN. RANGERS.

III. The battalion will relieve the 7th ROYAL: INNS FUS. in Bde Reserve commencing at 1-30 pm.

IV Hd. Qrs. 'A' and 'B' COYS. will relieve a portion of the 7th ROYAL INNS. FUS. at DERRY HUTS.

'C' and 'D' COYS will relieve a portion of 7th ROYAL INNS. FUS. at CHATEAU. KEMMEL.

V. Movement E. of the LOCRE-DRANOUTRE roads will be by platoons at 300 yards distance.

VI Completion of relief will be reported by runner to BN. HD.Q.R.S.

VII. Trench Store and Gum Boot receipts will be handed into Orderly Room by 6pm, 2nd inst.

VIII Advance parties will be sent from each company to take over.

X Clean billet certificates will be handed into Orderly Room half an hour before Companies march off.

X. All Officers kits ~~and ... packs~~ will be stacked outside the Guard Room by 10.am. ready for removal by transport

XI One limber will be alloted to each Company to take two Blankets per man to their respective billets. One limber will be alloted to Hd. Qrs. for removal of Orderly Room kit. ect. Mess Cart will be ready at 1-30pm

(Sd) T. BOOTH. Lieut

A/ADJT. 6TH (S) BN. THE. CONN RANGERS.

Appendix II. 6th (S) Bn. THE CONN. RANGERS
SECRET
OPERATION ORDERS
COPY No. 12.
5. MAR 1917

1. The Battalion will relieve the 6th. ROYAL IRISH REGT. in the LEFT SUB-SECTION tomorrow 6th inst commencing 2-30 pm.

2. A. Coy. 6 C.R. will relieve D Coy. 6 R.I.R. in the RIGHT. FRONT LINE
C " " C " LEFT. FRONT LINE
B " " A " REGENT ST. D.O. & S.P. 9.
D " " B " SP 10 & SP 11.

3. A & C Coys. will move off in time to reach front line by 2-30 pm. B & D Coys will follow.

4. All movement on ROADS to be by PLATOONS at 300 yards distance and in the TRENCHES by SECTIONS at 100 yards distance.

5. Completion of relief to be reported to Bn H.Q. by wire. Code Word – Company Commanders name e.g. TUITE.

6. B & D Coys. will carry one blanket per man. Remainder of A & C Coys will be returned to store.

7. The Transport Officer will arrange for one limber per company to be at KEMMEL CHATEAU and DERRY HUTS. at 11 am. for removal of surplus kit etc. and one limber to be at Orderly Room at DERRY HUTS at 2 pm. The mess cart will be at Hd. Qrs. DERRY HUTS at 2 pm.

8. The following Working Parties will NOT be found by this unit on the 6th inst.
"H" "J" "K" "L" "M" "N" (day) (7-5pm) "O" "P" "Q" "R" "S"
The following working parties WILL be found as usual.
"F" "G" "N" (night) and "T"

The following carrying party will be found NIGHTLY by the garrison of S.P. 11

STRENGTH	1. N.C.O. & 25 MEN.
TIME	7 P.M.
RENDEZVOUS	ENGINE HOUSE S.P. 11.
GUIDE.	OFFICER. 250th TUNNELLING COY. R.E.

Trench Store & Gum Boot receipts will be handed into Orderly Room by 10 AM. 7th inst.

Clean billet certificates will be handed into Orderly Room 11. DERRY HUTS by 1-30 pm. 6th inst.

(Sd) T. BOOTH Lieut
A/ADJT. 6th (S) Bn The Conn. Rangers

Appendix III

Secret. Operation Orders. Copy No.

I The following reliefs will take place tomorrow the 8th inst. commencing at 4 pm.

II B. COY will relieve A COY in Right Front Line
D " " " C " " Left " "

III B & D Coys will hand over the blankets to A & C Coys respectively

IV C: Coy will take over the Working Party found at S.P. 11.

V Care must be taken in handing over and receipts sent to Bn. HQ. by 9 am 9th inst.

7. 3. 17.

(Sd) T. BOOTH. Lieut
A/ADJT. 6th Bn. THE CORN RGT.

Appendix IV. 6th (S) Battn. The Connaught Rangers.

OPERATION ORDERS

SECRET. COPY. No. 10.

9th MARCH 1917

1. The Battalion will be relieved in the left Sub-section by the 6th ROYAL IRISH REGT. tomorrow, 10th inst, commencing at 2.30 p.m. and will move into Brigade Support.

2. On ~~relief~~ completion of relief the Battalion will be disposed as follows:-

"A" COMPANY. 2 platoons GALWAY DUGOUTS / 1 " BEEHIVE DUGOUTS / COY H.Q. & 1 platoon COOKER FARM } Rations will be dumped at COOKER FARM.

"B" COMPANY FORT EDWARD - Rations FORT EDWARD

"C" COMPANY. HDQRS & 2 platoons - YONGE STREET DUGOUTS / 2 platoons - FORT REGINA } (Rations will be dumped at DOCTORS HOUSE)

"D" COMPANY HDQRS & 2 platoons - LA POLKA / 2 platoons - FORT SASKATCHEWAN } Rations will be dumped at DOCTORS Ho.

Battalion HQRS. DOCTORS HOUSE, KEMMEL - Rations DOCTORS HOUSE.

3. Lewis Guns will be relieved about 11 a.m

4. Completion of relief will be reported to Battn H.QRS FORT VICTORIA by wire. Code word: Coy Commanders name - e.g. CROFTON

5. "A" & "C" Coys will arrange to hand back to "B" & "D" Coys respectively, the blankets now in their possession. Coy Quartermasters of "A" & "C" Coys will arrange that one blanket per man for their Coys is brought up with rations tomorrow night.

6. Every care must be taken in handing over. Trench Stores & Gum Boot Receipts, carefully checked, will be handed into Orderly Room by 10 a.m on 11th inst.

7. The Water Cart will be left, and refilled each night at FORT EDWARD and DOCTORS HOUSE

8. Working parties will be taken over. Working party chits will be issued to Company Commanders early tomorrow

9. All movement in Trenches will be by Sections at 100 yds distance. This order must be carefully observed

(Signed) J. Booth Lieut

A/Adjt. 6th (S) Battn. The Connaught Rangers

Appendix V

6th (S) Bn. THE CONN. RANGERS
OPERATION ORDERS.

COPY. NO 11.

SECRET.

11th MARCH 19[illegible]

1. The 108th Inf. Bde. 36th Division will relieve the 47th Inf Bde in the SPANBROEK SECTOR, tomorrow 12th inst.

2. The Battalion will be relieved by the 10th Bn. Royal Irish Rifs in Bde. Support, commencing at 2-30pm and will proceed to BERTHEN area on relief.

3. One guide per PLATOON will be at DAYLIGHT CORNER at 2pm and will be met there by LIEUT. SIMMS who will arrange the distribution

4. Completion of relief will be reported to BN. H.Q. F12 by wire, the Code word being BAGHDAD

5. A + B COYS will arrange to pick up their LEWIS GUN HANDCARTS at LINDENHOEK CROSS-ROADS.
C + D COY. will arrange to pick up their LEWIS GUN HANDCARTS at KEMMEL CHATEAU

6. All movement in the Trenches will be by SECTIONS at 100 yards distance, and on roads by platoons at 300 yds distance. which distance will be maintained to BERTHEN.
Route – CANADA CORNER – WESTOUTRE – BERTHEN

7. Special care must be taken in handing over. All TRENCH STORES, MAPS, and AIR PHOTOGRAPHS will be handed over and receipts obtained. Any paper giving details of Intelligence or information concerning the SECTOR should also be handed over. Trench Store and Gum Boot Receipts will be handed into Orderly Room by 9am on 13th inst.
The Trench Store + Gum Boot receipts for Stores taken over on 10th March are returned to Companys to assist in correctness in handing over.

8. One limber each for A+B COYS will be at DAYLIGHT CORNER at 3pm. All Offrs. kits. mens blankets, etc should be dumped there by 2pm
One limber each for C+D COYS will be at KEMMEL CHATEAU at 3pm. All Offrs kits, mens blankets, etc should be dumped there by 2pm.
Two limbers for HD. QR. OFFRS kits, mens blankets and Orderly Room kit, etc will be at KEMMEL CHATEAU at 3pm.
The Mess Cart will be at KEMMEL CHATEAU at 3pm.

9. 2/Lieut. F.W.S. JOURDAIN and the N.C.O per coy. already detailed, will meet the STAFF CAPT. 47th INF. BDE. at SCHAEXKEN at 9am.

10 PLATOON COMMANDERS marching in rear of their platoons will see that every attention is paid to MARCH DISCIPLINE en route. S.D. caps will NOT be worn. GREATCOATS are to be rolled inside the GROUND SHEET and NOT worn. Should it rain, GROUNDSHEETS will be worn across the shoulders, and not the GREATCOAT.

(Sd) T. BOOTH. Lieut
ADJT. 6th (S) Bn. THE CONN. RANGERS.

SECRET

Appendix VI
Mar XI

OPERATION ORDERS.
6TH (S) BN. THE CONN. RANGERS.

COPY NO 10

30. MARCH 1917.

1. The 47th Inf Bde will relieve the 48th Inf Bde in the LOCRE area tomorrow 31st inst.

2. The Battalion will proceed to DONCASTER HUTS at LOCRE

3. Coys will parade in Column of route in the following order. Hd. Qrs. DRUMS D. C. B. & A. Cy. head of the column to be at LE ROSSIGNOL ESTAMINET ready to move off at 9-30 am

4. Dress Marching Order. Steel Helmets on packs

5. ROUTE. SCHAEXKEN — LE LEVETTE — MONT NOIR — MONT. ROUGE to DONCASTER HUTS. The Bn will be clear of the SCHAEXKEN CROSS ROADS by 10-40 am.

6. 1ST & 2ND line Transport will accompany the Bn.

7. All Kits, blankets etc. will be stacked ready for removal by 8-30 AM.

8. The Transport Officer will arrange the allotment of G.S. & Limber Wagons

9. Orders re advance & taking over parties have been issued to all concerned.

10. Completion of relief will be reported to Bn H.Q. by runner.

(Sd) T. BOOTH. Lieut.

A/ADJT. 6TH (S) BN. THE CONN RANGERS

17E

WAR DIARY FOR MONTH OF APRIL, 1917.

VOLUME:- 17

UNIT:- 6th Connaught Rangers.

916

Confidential

April 1917

Instructions regarding War Diaries and Intelligence Summaries are contained in F. S. Regs., Part II. and the Staff Manual respectively. Title Pages will be prepared in manuscript.

WAR DIARY

~~or~~

~~INTELLIGENCE SUMMARY~~

(Erase heading not required.)

Army Form C. 2118.

Sheet I.

Place	Date	Hour	Summary of Events and Information	Remarks and references to Appendices
In the field	April	1st.	The 47th. Inf. Bde. relieved the 49th. Inf. Bde. in the VIERSTRAAT Sector. The battalion moved from DONCASTER HUTS with Brigade Reserve at BUTTERFLY FARM (N.19.a) in relief of 7/8th. R. Irish Fusilrs. Remainder of the Bde. disposed as follows:– 6th. R. Irish Regt. in Right Subsection, 7th Leinsters in Bde. Support and 1st. R. Munster Fusilrs. in Left Subsection, less 1 coy. accomodated in huts at BUTTERFLY FARM. G.O.C. Division (Maj-Gen. W.B. Hickie C.B.) visited the camp in the afternoon.	Appendix I.
—				
Ref. map SHEET 28.S.W. Ed. 5A. 1/20,000.		2nd. to 4th. (incl.)	The battalion was chiefly occupied with working-parties, 8 officers and 250 O.R. being engaged every 24 hours. During this period all officers reconnoitred the line to be occupied by the battalion. The weather was very bad, and snow fell every day.	
—		5th.	A voluntary Mass was held in camp at 8 am. At 8.45 pm. the 6th. R. Irish Regt. carried out a successful raid in the neighbourhood of MAEDELSTEDE FARM (N.24.c.), taking 21 prisoners of the 4th. Grenadier Regt (Prussians). This identification was not normal. The battalion relieved 6th R. Irish Regt. in the Right Sub-section (N.24.a.3.8. to N.24.c.2.4.), commencing at 10.30 pm. & 6th. R. Irish Regt. became battalion in Bde. Reserve. The 7th. Leinster Regt. occupied the left subsection, having relieved the 1st. R. Munster Fusilrs. on 4th. The battalion was disposed as follows – 'A' Coy. Right front Line; 'B' Coy. Right Support; 'C' Coy. Left front Line; 'D' Coy. Left Support.	Appendix II.
		6th.	The enemy's artillery fired bursts of 8-12 rounds at intervals in the neighbourhood of battalion H.Q. (N.23.b.3.8.). There was very little activity of any sort during the day.	
		7th.	The usual hostile activity continued during the night. Between 9 and 11 am. the enemy was sniping vigorously at trench N.24.6. From 11 – 11.35 am. the left company's trenches were shelled promiscuously with 77 mms. & 105 cms., but only 2 hits were effected.	

2449 Wt. W14957/M90 750,000 1/16 J.B.C. & A. Forms/C.2118/12.

Confidential

Instructions regarding War Diaries and Intelligence Summaries are contained in F. S. Regs., Part II. and the Staff Manual respectively. Title Pages will be prepared in manuscript.

April 1917.

WAR DIARY
or
~~INTELLIGENCE SUMMARY~~

(Erase heading not required.)

Army Form C. 2118.

Sheet II.

Place	Date	Hour	Summary of Events and Information	Remarks and references to Appendices
In the field	April	7th.	'B' & 'D' Coys. relieved 'A' & 'C' Coys. in the front line, the latter proceeding to the positions of Right & Left Support respectively. At 10.7 pm. a mine was felt to go up a long distance off. Between 10.37 and 10.50 pm. chains of white lights went up from the direction of SPANBROEKMOLEN and a red light was exposed in our back areas. No action followed. Aircraft was passing over at the time, going towards WYTSCHAETE.	Appendix III
Ref. Map Sheet 28.S.W. Ed. 5A. 1/20,000		8th.	During the night sounds were heard of transport near WYTSCHAETE, trollies in PETIT BOIS and an engine near MAEDEZSTEDE FARM. During the day there was considerable activity in the air on both sides, but not in any other direction. At 8.45 pm. two patrols were sent out; both reported the enemy to be working hard, but no information of importance was obtained.	
		9th.	Except for a few hostile rifle grenades & 3 or 4 "rum-jars", there was no activity during the 24 hours.	
		10th.	The battalion was relieved by the 6th. R. Irish Regt. and proceeded to Bde. Support in relief of 1st. R. Munster Fusiliers. On relief the battalion was disposed as follows — H.Q. and 'B' Coy. in ROSSIGNOL ESTAMINET (N.22.a.); 'A' Coy. LA PEZKA FARM (N.22.c.) and DOCTOR'S HOUSE, KEMMEL (N.21.d.) with one Lewis Gun in FORT SASKATCHEWAN (N.22.d.); 'C' Coy. H.Q. & 2 platoons at SIEGE FARM (N.16.c.) and 2 platoons SANDBAG VILLA (N.16.b.); 'D' Coy. at SIEGE FARM. 1st. R. Munster Fusiliers took over Left Sub-section from 7th. Leinsters, who proceeded to Bde. Reserve.	Appendix IV
		11th. to 14th.	Nothing unusual happened during this period. The battalion was occupied with working-parties every day. On 11th. the C.O. received a note from the Brigadier, complimenting him on the good work done by the battalion whilst in the line. All officers reconnoitred the VIERSTRAAT SWITCH from about N.11.c.3.0. to LA PEZKA FARM. The weather was bad, being mostly wet.	

2449 Wt. W14957/M90 750,000 1/16 J.B.C. & A. Forms/C.2118/12.

Confidential

Instructions regarding War Diaries and Intelligence Summaries are contained in F. S. Regs., Part II. and the Staff Manual respectively. Title Pages will be prepared in manuscript.

April 1917

WAR DIARY ~~or~~ ~~INTELLIGENCE SUMMARY~~

(Erase heading not required.)

Army Form C. 2118.

Sheet III

Place	Date	Hour	Summary of Events and Information	Remarks and references to Appendices
In the field Ref. map Sheet 28.SW. 1/20,000 Ed. 5A	April	15th.	Divine Service was held under difficulties, but by holding 3 separate services in the morning and one in the afternoon it was possible for the whole battalion to attend. Our heavy artillery carried out a bombardment of the enemy's lines from 9 a.m. till 3 p.m. About 1 p.m. the enemy shelled ROSSIGNOL WOOD in retaliation with 5.9's, necessitating the temporary evacuation of 'B' Coys. billets. Commencing at 6 p.m. the battalion relieved the 6th. R. Irish Regt in the Right Sub-section. On relief the battalion was disposed as on 5th. inst. Remainder of Bde. disposed as follows:- 7th. Leinsters in Left Sub-section, 6th. R. Irish in Bde. Support, 1st. R. Munster Fusiliers in Bde. Reserve.	Appendix V.
		16th.	The day (16th) passed unusually quietly. Our artillery carried out two brief bombardments of MAEDELSTEDE at 11.30 a.m. and 9.30 p.m. to interrupt the work that was going on there. An exchange of 1 runner per company and 1 from H.Q. was made for 3 days with the battalion on our right (a battalion of the 109th. Bde.). A patrol was	
		& 17th.	sent out from each company shortly before midnight & found the enemy's front line occupied, though his Very lights went up from his support line; no work was heard. About 2.15 a.m. a hostile patrol, 2 strong, was caught between our two patrols and being forced close up to a Lewis gun, surrendered. They belonged to the 4th. Grenadier Regt. (Prussians). (normal). The day of the 17th. passed normally, except for a burst of fire on the left coy. about 5 p.m. Owing to movements of the enemy observed and information obtained from the 2 prisoners captured, a hostile raid was anticipated on the night of 17th./18th., and, had the enemy come over, he would have undoubtedly been driven back with very heavy casualties. However, he did not come. The two prisoners captured gave very useful information.	

Confidential

Instructions regarding War Diaries and Intelligence Summaries are contained in F. S. Regs., Part II. and the Staff Manual respectively. Title Pages will be prepared in manuscript.

April 1917

WAR DIARY
or
~~INTELLIGENCE SUMMARY~~
(Erase heading not required.)

Army Form C. 2118.

Sheet IV

Place	Date	Hour	Summary of Events and Information	Remarks and references to Appendices
Wakefield	April	18th.	Snow & rain fell all day, rendering activity of any kind impossible.	
Ref. map Sheet 28.SW. Ed. 5A. 1/20,000		19th.	The weather continued bad. About 2 am. the enemy bombed his own wire in N.24.b. The 47th. Inf. Bde. was relieved by the 48th. Inf. Bde. and became the Brigade in Divisional Reserve. The battalion was relieved by the 7th. R. Irish Rifles, commencing at 2 pm., and on relief proceeded to BIRR BARRACKS, LOCRE, (M.29.a). The remainder of the Bde. was disposed as follows:- 6th. R. Irish Regt. in KEMMEL SHELTERS (N.19.d.), 7th. Leinster Regt. in DONCASTER HUTS, LOCRE, (M.23.c.), and 1st. R. Munster Fusilrs. in TALLY-HO! CAMP (M.5.c.), CLARE CAMP (M.33.a.) and (1 coy.) DONCASTER HUTS.	Appendix VI.
		20th.	The day was devoted to baths, general cleaning-up and paying. The Brigadier (Brig. Gen. G.E. PEREIRA, C.B., C.M.G., D.S.O.) visited the camp in the afternoon.	
		21st. to 30th.	This period was devoted as much as possible to the training of men for the attack. This was to some extent hindered by the number of working-parties to be found by the battalion, some 5 officers and 200 men being out daily. The coy. in waiting each day practised the attack, the remainder of the battalion available being trained in drill, bayonet fighting, physical training, respirator drill, etc. Reserve bombers, rifle bombers and Lewis Gun teams were trained under the supervision of the Battn. Bombing Officer & L.G.O. A rifle range was also available occasionally. Full advantage was taken of a model, on a scale of 1/50, of the WYTSCHAETE RIDGE on view at M.17.a.7.9., and frequent visits were paid to it by all ranks, and particularly by the battalion observers, of whom 10 were trained during the period.	

2449 Wt. W14957/M90 750,000 1/16 J.B.C. & A. Forms/C.2118/12.

Confidential

April 1917

Army Form C. 2118.

Instructions regarding War Diaries and Intelligence Summaries are contained in F. S. Regs., Part II. and the Staff Manual respectively. Title Pages will be prepared in manuscript.

WAR DIARY

~~or~~

~~INTELLIGENCE SUMMARY~~

(Erase heading not required.)

Sheet V

Place	Date	Hour	Summary of Events and Information	Remarks and references to Appendices
Kilterfield Ref. Map Sheet 28.SW. 93.5A 1/20,000	April	21st to 30th.	On 28th and 29th a composite company performed the attack on the Bde. Training Ground, in conjunction with 2 sections of Stokes Guns. On the first occasion the Brigadier was present and on the second the Divisional Commander. On the 27th the Divisional Commander addressed the officers of the battalion and afterwards inspected the lines. He expressed himself pleased with what he saw. From 25th onwards Major H.F.N. JOURDAIN, C.M.G., Second-in-command of the battalion, held a class for platoon-commanders of the 4 battalions in the Brigade. The athletic side of the training was not forgotten. Amongst others (important) 3 football matches were played with the following results:— v. 9th R. Irish Fusrs. Lost 2-0; v. 7th Leinsters Won 2-0; v. 9th R. Irish Fusrs. Lost 2-0. At the end of the month the battalion was 49 officers and 1083 O.R. strong, as compared with 50 officers and 1003 O.R. at the beginning of the month. Of these only 31 officers and 734 O.R. were actually with the battalion at the end of the month and 30 officers and 791 O.R. at the beginning.	

[signature]

LIEUT. COLONEL,

COMDG. 6th (S) Bn. THE CONNAUGHT RANGERS

2449 Wt. W14957/M90 750,000 1/16 J.B.C. & A. Forms/C.2118/12.

Appendix I.

6th (S) Bn THE CONN RANGERS.

OPERATION ORDERS.

SECRET.

COPY NO II

[illegible] MARCH 1917

1. The 47th Inf. Bde will relieve the 49th Inf Bde in the [illegible] [illegible]

2. [illegible] FARM. [illegible]

3. [illegible] BUTTERFLY [illegible]

4. [illegible] Coys. [illegible] distance in the following order, HQ.OFS. A.B.C. & D COYS.

5. [illegible] A.H.F. SIMMONS will [illegible] Orderly Room at [illegible] to take over. Sgt. KILLICKEY will take over for HQ OFS.

6. All kits [illegible] [illegible] day.

7. [illegible] by 10.30am.

[illegible]

8. Trench Stores will be taken over and Receipts handed into Orderly Room by 6pm.

9. The Transport Officer will arrange for transport of Kits blankets etc.

10. Completion of relief will be reported by runner to Bn. HQ.Ors. at BUTTERFLY FARM.

11. Two Officers per Coy will reconnoitre the trenches to be taken over during the day.

(Sd) T. BOOTH Lieut.

A/ADJT. 6th (S) Bn THE CONN RANGERS

Appendix II

6th (S) Bn The Conn Rangers
OPERATION ORDERS

COPY No 8

SECRET

4th Apl 1917

1 The Battalion will relieve the 6th Royal I Regt on the RIGHT SUB SECTION VIERSTRAAT SECTOR tomorrow 5th inst commencing at 10-30pm

2 On completion of relief the Bn will be disposed of as follows:-

RIGHT FRONT LINE (KETCHEN AVE to N 24 b)	A Coy 6CR	relieve C Coy 6RIR
LEFT FRONT LINE (N24 to LARK CORNER)	C Coy 6CR	" D " 6RIR
RIGHT SUPPORT (SP11 and ALBERTA DUGOUTS)	B Coy 6CR	" A " 6RIR
LEFT SUPPORT (SP12 and TURNERSTOWN RIGHT)	D Coy 6CR	" B " 6RIR
BATTALION HQRS HARLEY HOUSE		

3. 1 Guide per platoon for A Coy will be at DOCTORS HOUSE KEMMEL at 10-30pm
1 " " " C " " entrance ROSSIGNOL ROAD at 10-30pm
1 " " " B " " DOCTORS HOUSE KEMMEL at 11pm
1 " " " D " " entrance ROSSIGNOL ROAD at 11pm

4 All movement by road to KEMMEL will be by platoons at 300 yards distance and in communication trenches by parties of not more than 6 at 100 yards distance. C Coy will move off first followed by A D & B Coys as soon as platoon distance allows

5 Receipts for Trench Stores & Gum Boots taken over will be handed into Orderly Room by 10 am on 6th inst

6 Before moving off Coy Commanders will render a certificate to Orderly Room that all men of their Coys have had their feet rubbed with Whale Oil

7 Completion of relief will be reported to HQ by wire. Code word being Coy Commanders name e g CROFTON

8 Rations will be dumped as follows
A & B COYS at DOCTORS HOUSE KEMMEL
Bn HQ C & D COYS at YORK HOUSE (N 16 c 9 3)

9 B & D Coys will carry one blanket per man

10 Officers Kits blankets and all material for Transport will be stacked ready for removal by 3pm

11 Advance parties detailed under Coy arrangements will move off in time to reach their respective destinations by 10pm tomorrow 5th inst

(Sd) T. BOOTH Lieut

Adjt 6th (S) Bn The Conn Rangers

SECRET

Appendix VII Operation Orders Copy No. 12

BY

Lieut. Col R. C. Feilding

Commanding 6th (S) Bn Connaught Rangers.

18. 4. 17.

---

1 The 48th Inf Bde will relieve the 49th Inf Bde in the VIERSTRAAT section to-morrow 19th inst.

2 The Bn will be relieved in the Right Subsection to-morrow by the 7th Bn R. Irish Rifles commencing at 2pm.

3 On completion of relief the Bn will proceed to BIRR BARRACKS (M.29.a.8.8.).

4 Lewis Guns will be relieved by 1pm. One guide per gun from A & B Coys will be at the DOCTORS HOUSE, & from C & D at the entrance to ROSSIGNOL ROAD at 10-30am.

5 Aeroplane photographs, trench maps &c, taken over from the 49th Inf Bde, will be handed over to the 48th I. Bde. All those received since that date will be retained.

6 All standing working parties will be handed over.

7 Movement in the trenches will be by parties of not more than SIX at 200yds distance, and on the roads by Platoons at 300yds distance.

8 A & C Coys will hand over the blankets in their possession to B & D Coys on arrival at BIRR BARRACKS.

9 Officers Kits will be stacked at the CHATEAU KEMMEL ready for removal by 2pm.

10 The 4 C.Q.M.Ss & 1 Man per Coy. will meet Major Grimshaw at BIRR BARRACKS at 1pm to arrange accommodation.

11 Copies of trench store receipts will be handed in to O.Room by 9am 20th inst. The greatest care will be exercised in compiling these lists.

12 Completion of relief will be reported to Bn. H.Q. in B.A.B code, and arrival in camp by runner to O.Room there.

(Sd) T. Booth Lieut.,
A/Adjt 6th (S) Bn Conn: Rangers

Appendix IV.

[illegible] Order [illegible] SECRET

[illegible] 6th [illegible] Connaught Rangers. Copy No. [illegible]

I The following reliefs will take place tonight the 7th inst commencing at 10.30 pm.

II B Coy will relieve A Coy in R. front line.
D " " " C " " L. front line & [illegible] line.

III The L.G.O will make necessary arrangements for the relief of Lewis Gunners.

IV B and D Coys will hand over their [illegible] to A and C Coys respectively.

V Trench stores and [illegible] to be [illegible] on relief.

VI Relief completed to be reported to Bn HQ by code word "AMERICA".

VII Movement to be in parties of not more than five at 200x distance.

[illegible] Lt & Adjt

6-6-17 6th (S) Bn Connaught Rangers

Appendix IV.

Secret

Operation Orders No 10
By
Lieut Colonel R C Feilding
Commanding 6th (S) Bn Conn: Rangers

9-4-17

1 The Bn will be relieved by the 6/R. I Regt to-morrow the 10th inst commencing at 6 Pm, & move into Bde Res

2 On completion of relief the Bn will be disposed as follows

Bn H Qrs Rossignol Estaminet

"A" Coy H Qrs Doctors House 3 Platoons + 2 Sections at La Polka 2 Sections 1 L Gun Fort Saskatchewan

"B" Coy + H Qrs at Rossignol Estaminet

"C" Coy H Qrs + 2 Platoons Siege Farm, 2 Platoons at Sandbag Villa

"D" Coy + H Qrs at Siege Farm

3 All movement will be in small parties at usual distance

4 Copy of Trench Store receipts to be in O Room by 9am 11th

5 Rations for A Coy will be dumped at Doctors House
" " B " " " Rossignol Estaminet
" " C&D " " " Siege Farm

6 The O Room will be moved from Transport Lines to Bn H Qrs

(Sd) T. Booth Lieut
A Adjt 6th Conn Rangers

Appendix V

OPERATION ORDERS.
BY.
LIEUT–COL. R. C. FEILDING.
COMMDG. THE CONN. RANGERS.

COPY NO. [illegible]

SECRET.
IN THE FIELD.

14th APRIL 1917.

1. The Battalion will relieve 'B' THE ROYAL IRISH REGT. in the RIGHT SUB-SECTION, tomorrow, 15th inst. commencing at 6pm.

2. On relief, the Battalion will be disposed as follows:–
'A' COMPANY – – – – – – – RIGHT FRONT LINE.
'B' " – – – – – – RIGHT SUPPORT.
'C' " – – – – – – LEFT FRONT LINE.
'D' " – – – – – – LEFT SUPPORT.

3. Lewis Guns will relieve, one hour in advance of the Battalion under arrangements to be made by the Lewis Gun officer

4. An advance party from each Company, under an Officer, and one from H.Q. under an N.C.O. to be detailed by the R.S.M. will take over at 4pm.

5. Completion of relief to be reported in B.A.B. CODE.

6 'B' and 'D' COYS will take one blanket per man

7. Kits to be left under a guard, ready for removal by 6pm.

8. Rations will be dumped for 'A' and B COYS at SUICIDE CORNER. and for H.Q. and 'C' and 'D' COYS at end of ROSSIGNOL ROAD.

9. Movement will be by parties of not more 6. at the usual distances

10. Copies of Trench Store and Gum Boot Receipts to reach BATTN. H.Q. by 9am. 16th inst.

(Sd) T. BOOTH. Lieut.
A/ADJT. THE CONN. RANGERS.

[illegible] Appendix VI . Order No 5.

Operation Orders
6th [illegible] Bn Connaught Rangers

I The following reliefs will take place tomorrow 17th inst commencing 6 PM.

II B Coy will relieve A Coy in RIGHT FRONT LINE
D " " " C " LEFT

III On completion of relief the Bn will be disposed as follows:
A Coy RIGHT SUPPORT
B " " FRONT LINE
C " LEFT SUPPORT
D " " FRONT LINE.

IV Lewis Guns will be relieved in an arrangements to be made by L G O.

V B + D Coys will hand over their blankets to A and C Coys respectively.

VI Copies of Trench Store receipts must reach Bn H Q by 9 am the 18th inst

VII Movement will be in parties of not more than 6 at the usual intervals.

VIII Completion of relief to be reported in B A B code.

Signed T. BOOTH Lt A/Adjt
16-4-17 6th Connaught Rangers

18E

W A R   D I A R Y :

---ooo---

VOLUME:- 18

FOR MONTH OF MAY, 1917.

U N I T :- 6th. Connaught Rangers.

Vol 17

Confidential

Instructions regarding War Diaries and Intelligence Summaries are contained in F. S. Regs., Part II. and the Staff Manual respectively. Title Pages will be prepared in manuscript.

May 1917

WAR DIARY
or
INTELLIGENCE SUMMARY
(Erase heading not required.)

Army Form C. 2118.

Sheet 1.

Place	Date	Hour	Summary of Events and Information	Remarks and references to Appendices
In the field	May	1st. to 4th.	During this period the battalion was at BIRR BARRACKS (M.29.a), employed principally with working-parties. As far as possible, the usual training was carried out, principally in the attack, and on the 1st. a composite company carried out the attack on the Brigade Training Ground (M.21.d.) in conjunction with 2 sections of Stokes Guns of the 47th. T.M. Battery, in the presence of the Corps Commander.	
Ref. Sheet 28. S.W. 1/20,000. HAZEBROUCK 5A. 1/100,000		5th.	47th Inf. Bde. relieved 48th Inf. Bde. in the line (VIERSTRAAT SECTOR from N.18.a.75.80. to N.24.c.2.2.) Battalion relieved 2nd. R. Dub. Fus. in Bde. Reserve at BUTTERFLY FARM (M.25.a). Remainder of Brigade disposed as follows – 1st. R. Mun. Fus. – Left Subsection, 7th. Leinster Regt. – Right Subsection, 6th. R. Irish – Bde. Support.	Appendix
		6th.	Church Parades were held in the morning. No Working-Parties were required today.	
		7th.	Inspections of Kit, etc., & Inspections by M.O. carried out during the day. 2 five-minute bombardments, 8.45 – 8.50 pm. & 11.0 – 11.5 pm. were carried out by every gun & how. (except 12 in How.) at intense rate of fire along entire enemy front, in order to stop promiscuous shelling of back areas by enemy at night. This proved very effective.	
		8th.	Nothing to record.	
		9th.	At 6.0 am. the enemy started a heavy bombardment of the farm, his target probably being the 12" How. at M.19.a.4.7. The camp was successfully evacuated	

2449 Wt. W14957/M90 750,000 1/16 J.B.C. & A. Forms/C.2118/12.

Confidential.

Instructions regarding War Diaries and Intelligence Summaries are contained in F. S. Regs., Part II. and the Staff Manual respectively. Title Pages will be prepared in manuscript.

May 1917

WAR DIARY
or
INTELLIGENCE SUMMARY

(Erase heading not required.)

Army Form C. 2118.

Sheet 2

Place	Date	Hour	Summary of Events and Information	Remarks and references to Appendices
In the Field.	May	9th.	In an orderly manner without casualties. Only minor damage was done to the camp.	
Ref. Sheet 28 S.W. 1/20,000.		10th.	The 47th. Inf. Bde. was relieved by 49th Inf. Bde. Battalion was relieved by 7/8th R. Irish Fus. & proceeded to WESTON CAMP (M. 17. d. central).	Appendix II
HAZEBROUCK 5A 1/100,000		11th to 16th.	On 11th. the battalion proceeded to KEMMEL SHELTERS (M. 19. d.) in relief of 2 coys. 7th. R. Irish Rifles, while the remainder of the Brigade proceeded by march route to the CAESTRE AREA. During the period the battalion was employed in burying cables near the camp and also in N. 15, 16 & 22, about 12 offs. and 450 O.R. being employed every day, under O.C. 16th. Divl. Signal Coy., who afterwards wrote a letter of appreciation.	Appendix III
		17th.	Brigade marched to ST. OMER area and battalion arrived there, proceeding by train from BAILLEUL. Battalion billeted in ARQUES, where it was joined by the transport which had left KEMMEL SHELTERS the previous day.	Appendices IV & V
		18th.	Brigade marched to BAYENGHEM-LES-SENINGHEM area. Battalion billeted as follows:- H.Q., Q.M. Stores & 2 Coys. at COULOMBY; 2 coys. and Transport at SENINGHEM.	Appendix VI
		19th to 28th.	This period was taken up almost exclusively in practising the attack. The Bde. Training Ground was laid out to represent the GERMAN trenches immediately West of WYTSCHAETE (O.19.) & was used daily by battalions. 24th, 25th & 26th were Bde. Training Days. On the 26th a "dress rehearsal" was carried out in the	

Confidential. May 1917

Instructions regarding War Diaries and Intelligence Summaries are contained in F. S. Regs., Part II. and the Staff Manual respectively. Title Pages will be prepared in manuscript.

WAR DIARY
or
INTELLIGENCE SUMMARY

(Erase heading not required.)

Army Form C. 2118.

Sheet 3

Place	Date	Hour	Summary of Events and Information	Remarks and references to Appendices
In the field. Ref Sheet 28 S.W. 1/20,000. HAZEBROUCK 5A 1/100,000	May	26th.	presence of the following – G.O.C. 2nd Army, G.O.C. IXth Corps, G.O.C. 16th Division, G.O.C. 16th Div. Arty., G.O.C. 47th & 49th Bdes. & a number of others. A contact aeroplane attended. The battalion found parties for carrying, mopping-up, etc. All officers attended a conference afterwards.	Appendix VII
		27th.	Open-air Church Parades were held in morning & in the afternoon a very successful sports meeting was held by the battalion.	
		28th.	Day devoted to inspections, cleaning up etc. before leaving the area.	
		29th. to 31st.	Battn. proceeded by march-route to the forward area, by the following stages:– 29th – To ARQUES. Weather cool & dull, ideal for marching. 30th – To STAPLE. A conference of all officers was held at 3 pm. 31st. – To CLARE CAMP (M.33.c). A rather trying march as the weather was hot & dusty. Movement was carried out in accordance with the attached Operation orders.	Appendices VIII, IX & X

2.6.17.

[signature] Lt Col.
Comdg. 6th (S) Bn. The Connaught Rangers

2449 Wt. W14957/M90 750,000 1/16 J.B.C. & A. Forms/C.2118/12.

APPENDIX I

COPY No 10

OPERATION ORDERS
BY
LIEUT-COL R G FEILDING
COMMANDING THE CONN RANGERS

SECRET

4th MAY 1917

1. The 47th Inf Bde will relieve the 48th Inf Bde in the VIERSTRAAT SECTOR on May 5th

2. The Bn will relieve B Bn R. Dublin Fus in Bde Reserve at BUTTERFLY FARM commencing at 5.30pm

3. Coys will move off in the following order at the times stated -

D Coy 5.0pm
C Coy 5.15pm
B Coy 5.30pm
A Coy 5.45pm

4. Movement will be by Platoons at 200 yards distance

5. Kits and blankets will be stacked ready for removal by 3pm

6. 1 Limber per Coy and 2 for H.Q. together with the Mess Cart and Maltese Cart will be at the Camp at 4pm

7. H.Q. & Coy Q.M.S. and 1 man per Coy will meet the Quartermaster at BUTTERFLY FARM at 3.30 pm to arrange accommodation

8. Departure from Camp will be reported by runner to Orderly room here and arrival at BUTTERFLY FARM by runner to Orderly Room there

9. The Quartermaster will arrange to take over the Camp Stores at BUTTERFLY FARM and hand into Orderly Room receipts obtained by 9am on 6th inst

(Sd) T. Bush Lieut
A/Adjt The Conn Rangers

APPENDIX II OPERATION ORDERS BY LIEUT-COL R. C. FEILDING COPY No 8.

COMMANDING 6th (S) Bn THE CONN RANGERS

SECRET

REF SHEET 28 S W 1/20000 EDITION 5A. 9th MAY 1917

1. The 47th Inf Bde will be relieved by the 49th Inf Bde on May 10th & night of May 10/11th 1917.

2. The Battalion will be relieved by 7/8 Bn R. IRISH FUS on May 10th commencing at 11am.

3. On completion of relief the Bn will proceed to KEMMEL SHELTERS (M.19.d.3.3) ~~[illegible] (M.[illegible])~~

4. Advanced parties from the relieving Bn will report at BUTTERFLY FARM at 8am. The 2nd in Command will hand over the camp to the incoming unit.

5. The L. C. Q. M. S. and 1 man per Coy + 1 NCO from Bn HQ will meet the Quartermaster at KEMMEL SHELTERS ~~[illegible]~~ at 10am to arrange accomodation.

6. (a) Kits will be stacked ready for removal by 9am.

(b) 1 limber per Coy and 2 for HQ together with the Mess Cart and Maltese Cart will be at BUTTERFLY FARM at 9-30am.

7. (a) All aeroplane photographs maps etc will be returned except those taken over from 48th Inf Bde.

(b) Copies of trench stores receipts and clean billets certificates will be handed into Orderly Room by 6pm on 10th inst.

8. Coy Commanders will take particular care that the quarters occupied by their Coys and the surrounding ground are handed over in a scrupulously clean and sanitary condition.

9. All working parties will be carried on as usual up till 8pm from and including which hour they will be taken over by the relieving battalion.

10. All movement EAST of a N-S line through LOCRE will be by platoons at 300 yards distance.

11. Completion of relief will be reported by runner to Orderly Room here and arrival at KEMMEL SHELTERS ~~[illegible]~~ will be reported by runner to Orderly Room there.

12. ~~The Battalion will proceed to the CAESTRE area on May 11th Starting about 8-30 am Detail will be issued in Operation Orders tomorrow 10th inst.~~

Cancelled
[illegible]

(Sd) T BOOTH Lieut
A/ADJT 6th (S) Bn. THE CONN RANGERS

APPENDIX III OPERATION ORDERS Copy No. 9.

BY

LIEUTENANT [illegible] R. [illegible] FELDING

Commanding [illegible] Bn THE (Conn) RANGERS

[illegible]

[illegible]

1. [illegible] Battalion will [illegible] [illegible] R. Rifles [illegible] Kemmel Shelters [illegible] 11th inst.

2. Movement of platoons will [illegible] distance as follows: 1st Platoon [illegible] followed by B, C & D Coys [illegible] platoon distance between.

3. [illegible] CQMS and 1 man per Coy & 1 NCO from HQ will meet the Quartermaster at Kemmel Shelters at 10am to arrange accommodation.

4. The Transport Officer will arrange for the removal of Kits etc which will be stacked by 11am [illegible] for the removal of 450 [illegible] and 250 [illegible] to Kemmel Shelters.

5. Lines will be cleaned ready for inspection by 11am.

6. The usual certificates will be rendered by 6pm on 11th inst.

(Sd) A. BOOTH Lieut.

A/Adjt.

APPENDIX IV

OPERATION ORDERS.
BY
LIEUT-COL. R.C. FEILDING.
COMMANDING 6TH (S) BN. THE CONN. RANGERS

COPY No. 4

SECRET.

15th MAY 1917.

1. The 1st and 2nd line Transport of the Battalion will march to BAYENGHEM LES SENINGHEM by road, under orders of the Transport Offr. as follows:-

Date.	From	To	Remarks.
MAY 16th	LOCRE	— HONDEGHEM	
MAY 17th	HONDEGHEM —	ARQUES.	
MAY 18th.	ARQUES	— BAYENGHEM-LES-SENINGHEM	Join Battalion under orders of 47th Inf Bde.

2. Rations for Transport personnell and horses for 17th + 18th inst will be carried.

3. Rations for 17th inst will be delivered to the Battalion on the 16th inst before the Transport moves.

4. 6th (S) Bn. The Conn Rangers (less Transport) will entrain at HAEGEDOORNE at 12 noon 17th inst arriving at ST OMER about 2-30 pm. After detraining the Bn. will march to billets at ARQUES. Details will be issued in Operation Orders tomorrow 16th inst.

(Sd) T. BOOTH Lieut

A/ADJT. 6th (S) Bn. THE CONN RANGERS

APPENDIX V

[illegible]
BY
LIEUT. COL. R. C. FEILDING.
COMMANDING 6TH (S) BN. THE CONN. RANGERS.

COPY NO (?)

SECRET.

15TH MAY 1917

REF. SHEET 28. S.W. S.A. 1/20,000
REF. HAZEBROUCK. S.A. 1/100,000.

1. The Battalion will rejoin the 47th Inf. Bde tomorrow 17th May 1917.
2. The Battalion will entrain at HAEGEDOORNE (S. 9. a) at 12noon for St OMER and on arrival will march to billets at ARQUES.
~~3. The Battalion will march in the following order:- DRUMS. C Coy. D Coy. B Coy. A Coy. the leading platoon of C Coy to pass BRULOOZE CROSS ROADS at 10-30 am. Dress - Marching Order with blankets and steel helmet on back of packs.~~ CANCELLED
3. The platoons will march independently at not less than 300 yards distance, and will rendezvous on the LOCRE-BAILLEUL road, with the head of the column (in threes) ready to pass the 12 KILOMETRE STONE (M. 28. b. 8.4) at 10-30 am in the following order. H.Q. DRUMS. A. B. C. & D COYS. Dress — Marching order with blankets and steel helmets on back of packs.
4. All Coys. will render a certificate by 9 am that the huts have been cleaned and evacuated ~~by 9 am~~.
5. The Pioneer Cpl will be responsible that the H.Q. Billets are handed over clean, and the Sanitary Sgt that all Latrines are handed over clean.
6. 2 lorries are at the disposal of the Bn. for the move and are allotted as follows:- 1 between A+B Coys and 1 for H.Q. Cos. C+D Coys. They will report shortly after 7 am and if necessary may do two journeys, but this should be avoided if possible. When the lorry allotted to A+B Coys is loaded it should be instructed to proceed to KEMMEL SHELTERS. A baggage Guard of one man per Coy. will accompany the lorries. If any baggage is left behind for a second journey a guard will be left with it.
7. All Officers Kits, etc should be ready for removal by ~~9 am~~ 8-30 am
8. Each Coy will hand in a marching-out state to Orderly Room by 9 am.
9. ~~Clean billet certificates~~ Camp Store Receipts will be handed in on arrival at ARQUES.
10. On the 18th inst. the Bn. will march to the BAYENGHEM-LES-SENINGHEM area. Details will be issued in Operation Orders tomorrow 17th inst.

(Sd) T. BOOTH Lieut

A/ADJT. THE CONN. RANGERS

APPENDIX VI

OPERATION ORDERS. COPY No.
BY
LT-COL. R. C. FEILDING
COMMDG. 6th (S) Bn. THE CONN. RGS.

SECRET. 17th MAY 1917.

1. The Bn. will proceed to BAYENGHEM-LES-SENINGHEM tomorrow 18th inst.

2. Parade on the Square at 9.30am in same dress as today.

3. 4 CQMS will meet Lt. J. J. Chamier at BAYENGHEM-LES-SENINGHEM at 9am. Bicycles can be had at the Qr Mr. Stores.

4. Clean billet certificates will be handed to the adjutant by 9am

5 Dinners will be eaten during the midday halt, between 12.50 pm and 2pm.

6. All kits etc will be loaded by 9am.

(Sd) ? BOOTH A? Lt

A/ADJT. 6th (S) Bn. THE CONN RGS

APPENDIX VII

OPERATION ORDERS
BY
LIEUT-COL. R. G. FEILDING.
COMMANDING. THE CONN. RANGERS.

SECRET.

COPY NO

REF. SHEET. HAZEBROUCK 5A EDITION E. 23rd MAY 1917.

1. The 47th Inf Bde will carry out an attack on the Brigade Area on May 24th 25th & 26th.

2. The Battalion will provide the following parties with a proportion of officers to be detailed by the Coys stated against each:-

100 OR MOPPERS UP for 1st R.M.F. 'B' COY } The same men will be detailed
50 OR MOPPERS UP for 7th LEINSTERS 'A' COY } as have already been performing these duties.
80 OR. BDE. CARRYING PARTIES 'C' COY
50 OR CARRYING PARTY for 47th T.M.B. 'A' COY
40 OR CARRYING PARTY for 47th M.G.C. 'C' COY.

Lewis Gunners should not be taken for any of the above parties.

3. ZERO HOUR will be 10 am

4. The Battalion less 'D' COY will parade at 8.15 am in fighting order. Mess tins to be carried. 'D' COY will wear Forage Caps instead of Steel Helmets. Field Kitchens will attend for dinners

5. At 9.30 am the Bn. less 'D' COY will be disposed as follows:-

BN. HD. QRS. ROSSIGNOL WOOD.

BATTN (less parties detailed for special duties) CHINESE WALL.

6. The 6th ROYAL IRISH REGT and 7th ~~LEINSTER REGT~~ will each attack on a frontage of 400 yards and will capture the RED and BLUE LINES. The Mopping-up party detailed by O.C. 'A' COY will follow the leading wave of the 7th LEINSTERS and mop-up NANCY SWITCH and NANCY TRENCH as far as the RIGHT boundary of the 7th LEINSTERS (NANCY AVENUE exclusive) Dugouts will not be destroyed.

7. The 1st R.M.F. will capture the GREEN and BLACK LINES. The Mopping-up party, detailed by O.C. 'B' COY will accompany the leading wave of the SUPPORT COYS and mop-up WYTSCHAETE which will at once be put in a state of defence.

8. The following COMMUNICATION TRENCHES will be kept open and used as one-way trenches only.

NAP DRIVE —— UP
OCCASION ALLEY —— UP
NANCY AVE —— DOWN.
NANCY ST. —— UP
NANCY DRIVE —— UP
OCCASION DRIVE —— DOWN.

9. The BDE FORWARD STN will be established in the vicinity of the junction of NANCY AVE with the RED LINE, on the capture of the BLACK LINE it will move to the vicinity of WYTSCHAETE CHURCH, if possible to a point immediately N.W. of it.

10. All carrying parties will report at Advanced BDE. HQ. at 9.30 am where they will be met by the BDE. B.O. and representatives of the M.G. COY and T.M. BATTERY, respectively.

11. All watches will be synchronized at Advanced BDE. HQ. at 9 am.

(Sd) T. BOOTH. Lieut.
ADJT. THE CONN. RANGERS.

APPENDIX VIII

OPERATION ORDERS
BY
LIEUT-COL. R. C. FEILDING

SECRET

COPY NO.

COMMANDING 1ST (6) BN. THE CONN RANGERS.

REVEILLE 5am
BREAKFAST 5-30am
BKR PARADE B & C COYS 6-30am
— DO — A & D COYS 6am

28TH MAY 1917

1. The Battalion will parade tomorrow 29th inst in marching order, head of column at SENINGHEM CHURCH ready to move off at 7am in the following order: Bn. HQ. Bn. Drums D.A.B & C coys

2. Blankets of B & C coys will be rolled in tens and taken to QR MR. STORES by 6am. Those of A & D COYS will be stacked at SENINGHEM CHURCH by 6am. All officers kits and mess kits to be ready for removal by 6am.

3. Clean billet certificates will be handed to the Adjutant by 7am.

4. Billeting party of Coy Q.M. SERGTS. under 2/Lt T. F. GIBSON will meet at VAN DE PUTTE ST MARIE, ARQUES at 9am. For Bn. HQ. SGT. HADFIELD.

5. Transport will march with the Battalion.

(Sd) T. BOOTH Lieut.
ADJUT. THE CONN RANGERS.

APPENDIX IX

OPERATION ORDERS
BY
LIEUT. COL. R. G. FEILDING
COMMANDING THE CONN RANGERS.

29th Aug 1917

1 Tomorrow the 30th inst the Battalion will proceed to billets in STAPLE.

2. The Bn will parade in mass, on the Square, ready to move off at 8-30 am. in the following order:-
HD QRS. DRUMS. A B C D COYS Same as today.

3 The transport will accompany the Bn. An interval of 20 yards will be kept between every 6th vehicle. Water carts to be filled and kept full until arrival at STAPLE.

4. The same billetting party as today will meet M. CHAPPE at the Church, STAPLE at 9 am.

5 All kits blankets etc to be ready for removal at 7-30 am

6. Coy Commanders will report personally to the Adjutant on parade that all billets have been left in a clean condition.

7. Reports re Stragglers Casualties etc to be handed into Orderly Room immediately on arrival in billets

(Sd) T. BOOTH Lieut
ADJT. THE CONN RANGERS

APPENDIX X

Operation Orders
By
Lieut. Col. R.C. Feilding
Commanding The Conn Rangers.

30th May 1917

Reveille 4.30am
Breakfast 5.30 am
Sick Parade 5.30 am
Coy in Waiting B COY

1 The Bn will proceed to CLARE CAMP tomorrow 31st inst

2. Parade on the main St. through town with head of column at the Church ready to move off at 7am in the following order. HQ. Drums B. C. D. A. Coys. Dress as today

3. All Offrs Kits, Coy Stores etc will be ready for Removal by 6am.

4 The same billeting party as today will proceed in advance to CLARE CAMP

5. Transport will accompany the Bn. 20 yards distance between every 6th vehicle

6 Coy Commanders will report to Adjt on the parade ground that all billets were left clean.

(Sd) T. BOOTH Lt
A/Adjt The Conn Rs.

JL 7J Chamei

19 E

47/76

WAR DIARY.

FOR MONTH OF JUNE, 1917.

VOLUME:- 19

UNIT:- 6th Connaught Rangers

Vol 18

Confidential

6th (S) Bn Connaught Rangers Army Form C. 2118.

Sheet I

Instructions regarding War Diaries and Intelligence Summaries are contained in F. S. Regs., Part II. and the Staff Manual respectively. Title pages will be prepared in manuscript.

WAR DIARY ~~or~~ ~~INTELLIGENCE SUMMARY.~~

(Erase heading not required.)

JUNE 1917.

Place	Date	Hour	Summary of Events and Information	Remarks and references to Appendices
In the Field	1/6/17	—	The day was devoted to Baths, Inspections of all sorts and Resting. Camp was evacuated at night as there had been hostile shelling in the vicinity on previous nights. Lt J. J. POPE was notified that he had been awarded the Military Cross, for his services at REFARM during the shelling on the night of May 6th 1917.	
"	2/6/17	—	Church parades (voluntary) held for R.C. at 6-30 am and C of E at 8am. Coys were at the disposal of Coy Commanders, the following conferences were held:– 2nd in Commands and Adjutants at Bde HQ at 10 am in addition to one held at 9am at the same place at which the following attended CO 2nd in Commands. Adjutants, Coy Commanders, Coy 2nd in Commands and Specialist officers were seen by the C.O at 3pm. CO attended Bde HQ at 5pm to meet the Divl. Commander. In the evening the 47th and 49th Inf Bdes relieved the 48th Inf Bde in the VIERSTRAAT SECTOR. The Battn relieved the 2nd Bn. ROYAL DUBLIN FUS in the RIGHT FRONT LINE in accordance with attached operation order, in which all particulars are given. On completion of relief the 47th Inf Bde was disposed as follows. FRONT LINE 6th CONN RANGERS — SUPPORTING POINTS 1st ROYAL MUNSTER FUS. — BIRR BARRACKS 7th LEINSTER REGT — RENMORE LINES. 6th ROYAL IRISH REGT. Our Heavy Artillery bombarded WYTSCHAETE with Gas Shells from 10pm onwards, the enemy retaliated on KETAAL in kind and on S.P.12 with 5.9. H.E.	Appendix I

2353 Wt. W2544/1454 700,000 5/15 D. D. & L. A.D.S.S./Forms/C. 2118.

Confidential

Instructions regarding War Diaries and Intelligence Summaries are contained in F. S. Regs., Part II. and the Staff Manual respectively. Title Pages will be prepared in manuscript.

June 1917

WAR DIARY
or
INTELLIGENCE SUMMARY
(Erase heading not required.)

Sheet II

Army Form C. 2118.

Place	Date	Hour	Summary of Events and Information	Remarks and references to Appendices
In the field	3/6/17	—	Our artillery fired continuously throughout the day being intense at 11am and 3pm. The enemy fired intermittently chiefly on S.P. 12, they exploded a dump of T.M. ammunition at the junction of TIT ROAD and ROSSIGNOL ROAD. At about 3.30pm several of the enemy were seen running about the remains of the front line near MAEDELSTEDE bombing indiscriminately	
"	4/6/17	—	The enemys artillery sub-normal and our artillery has never ceased. At 10-30 pm the Bn carried out a successful raid on the enemy trenches immediately SOUTH of PETIT BOIS in which we took 4 prisoners, a detailed account is given in Operation Orders attached X.	Appendice II
"	5/6/17		Enemys artillery activity abnormal. S.P. 12 and HONG KONG were continuously shelled at a slow rate with 5.9" and 8" shells from 3-45 am to 11-30 am, particularly at the junction of TIT ROAD and ROSSIGNOL ROAD. HARLEY HOUSE and the BIRDCAGE received direct hits from 8" shells and about 300 yds of ROSSIGNOL ROAD EAST of TIT ROAD was blown in but casualties were surprisingly light. The enemys artillery fired intermittently during the afternoon. Under cover of a 10 minutes barrage of the 2nd Army front at 3pm, 1 off. and 20 other ranks of 1st R. Ir. Fus entered the enemys front line in PETIT BOIS nothing was found but two dead germans and the party returned after 10 mins without suffering any casualties, at the same time a similar party from the 49th Inf Bde visited the NORTH FACE of PETIT BOIS salient with exactly the same result. At 10-20 pm the 49th Inf Bde carried out a raid NORTH of PETIT BOIS, 4 prisoners were taken, for 10 mins from ZERO a dummy raid was made on the scene of the raid made by this Bn the previous night.	

2449 Wt. W14957/M90 750,000 1/16 J.B.C. & A. Forms/C.2118/12.

Confidential

Instructions regarding War Diaries and Intelligence Summaries are contained in F. S. Regs., Part II. and the Staff Manual respectively. Title pages will be prepared in manuscript.

WAR DIARY
~~or~~
~~INTELLIGENCE SUMMARY.~~

(*Erase heading not required.*)

June 1917 Sheet III

Army Form C. 2118.

Place	Date	Hour	Summary of Events and Information	Remarks and references to Appendices
In the Field	6/6/17	—	At 1am B+D Coys in the front line were relieved by 2 Coys each of the 6th R. IRISH REGT. and 7th LEINSTERS respectively and proceeded to open positions behind the CHINESE WALL. Bn HQ moved to IRISH HOUSE. In the evening the battalion moved to positions of assembly preparatory to the assault viz 'A' COY (less 3 platoons) + all Lewis Guns, except 6 to an open position behind CHINESE WALL 'B' COY (less L.G^{s}) to CHINESE WALL and assembly trench in front with 1st ROYAL MUNSTER FUS. for whom they were Mopping up. C COY (less L.G^{s}) divided into 2 carrying parties of 50 for 47th T.M.B. and 40 for 47th M.G.C. to various positions with these units to which they were temporarily attached. D COY (less L.G^{s}) to ROSSIGNOL WOOD for BDE Carrying parties. The 4 LEWIS GUNS of B COY and 2 from C COY held the front line from ZERO onwards. Bn HQ moved to KNOLL DUGOUTS	appendix III
"	7/6/17	—	At 3-10 am the 47th Inf Bde attacked with great success all objectives being taken, and numerous prisoners captured, while the casualties were light. The attack was opened at ZERO by the explosions of large mines all along the 2nd Army front, at ZERO + 15 SECS the first wave left our trench under cover of a creeping barrage	

2353 Wt. W2544/1454 700,000 5/15 D. D. & L. A.D.S.S./Forms/C. 2118.

Confidential

Instructions regarding War Diaries and Intelligence Summaries are contained in F. S. Regs., Part II. and the Staff Manual respectively. Title pages will be prepared in manuscript.

WAR DIARY
or
INTELLIGENCE SUMMARY.
(*Erase heading not required.*)

June 1917 — Sheet IV

Army Form C. 2118.

Place	Date	Hour	Summary of Events and Information	Remarks and references to Appendices
In the Field	7/6/17	(contd)	75% of the Guns on the army front being used for this barrage. the other 25% opened an intense fire on the enemy's battery positions. While all ranks worked with great credit to themselves a special mention should be made of the work done by our Artillery. The attack as far as it concerned this Battalion is set out in a separate appendice (A.T.I) attached.	Appendix A.T.I
"	8/6/17	–	The day was spent in consolidating the positions captured. the Bn (less parties on special duties) was withdrawn to ROSSIGNOL WOOD. The day passed very quietly, there being practically no hostile shelling, our Artillery kept up a steady fire as the guns were moved forward to advanced positions. Everyone was in excellent spirits the success of the attack could be plainly seen on the smiling faces of all ranks.	
"	9/6/17	–	The 47th Inf Bde was relieved and moved to the LOCRE AREA. The Bn was accomodated partly at KEMMEL SHELTERS (BnHQ A+B COYS) and partly at the old Transport lines of the 47th M.G.C (C+D COYS) owing to the scarcity of accomodation it was some time before the men were settled down and able to get to rest	Appendice IV

2353 Wt. W2544/1454 700,000 5/15 D. D. & L. A.D.S.S./Forms/C. 2118.

Confidential

Instructions regarding War Diaries and Intelligence Summaries are contained in F. S. Regs., Part II. and the Staff Manual respectively. Title pages will be prepared in manuscript.

June 1917

WAR DIARY
or
~~INTELLIGENCE SUMMARY.~~

(Erase heading not required.)

SHEET. VII

Army Form C. 2118.

Place	Date	Hour	Summary of Events and Information	Remarks and references to Appendices
In the Field	10/6/17	—	Divine Service was attended by R.C at FAIRY HOUSE and on return the Bn was addressed by the Brigadier who congratulated all ranks for their magnificent behaviour during the attack. The remainder of the day was spent in cleaning + resting	
"	11/6/17	—	Coys were at the disposal of Coy Commanders. The Bn was paid and Inspections of Kits, accoutrements etc were held. The following were notified they had been awarded the Military Medal No 2611 L/SGT J. KEARNS No 6410 L/C P. COYNE + NO 3624 PTE FLYNN P	
	12/6/17		The Bn was called on to find a Working party of 16 offrs. + 500 OR for road making near WYTSCHAETE the work was done in four, 6 hours reliefs. 2/Lt H.S. KIRKWOOD joined for duty and CAPT. AR GOODE and 2nd/LT F.T. CHAMIER proceeded on leave	
	13/6/17	—	The 47th Inf Bde moved to the MERRIS area. The Bn was billetted between OUTTERSTEENE and METEREN. Bde HQ being at OUTTERSTEENE The day being very hot the march was most exhausting. B COY were carried in Motor lorries as they had been working during the preceeding night	appendix V

2353 Wt. W2514/1454 700,000 5/15 D. D. & L. A.D.S.S./Forms/C. 2118.

Confidential

Instructions regarding War Diaries and Intelligence Summaries are contained in F. S. Regs., Part II. and the Staff Manual respectively. Title pages will be prepared in manuscript.

June 1917

WAR DIARY
or
~~INTELLIGENCE SUMMARY.~~
(Erase heading not required.)

Sheet VI

Army Form C. 2118.

Place	Date	Hour	Summary of Events and Information	Remarks and references to Appendices
In the Field	14/6/17	—	Training of Lewis Gunners & Bombers under specialist officers and Drill under the Adjutant was carried out during the day, lectures for all junior officers by Major Jourdain and all Corporals by the C.O were given. The weather was fine and good work was carried out. Major J.E. HARDED proceeded to take over the duties of Adjt of 27th LABOUR GROUP	
"	15/6/17	—	Parades as yesterday, except where interrupted by coys proceeding to BATHS at OUTTERSTENE between 2pm & 6pm. Capt. R.T. ROUSELL joined for duty.	
"	16/6/17	—	Parades as usual in splendid weather if somewhat hot. During the evening orders were received that the 15th Durham would move to the LOCRE area tomorrow and on 18th June the 47th Bde would relieve 58th Inf Bde, in Bde Reserve of the sector now held by the 19th DIVISION. 2/Lt J.S. DRYDEN rejoined from 156th Coy RE.	
"	17/7/17	—	The Bn paraded at 5-35am, packs & Lewis being carried on Motor Lorries, and marched in shirt sleeves to WESTON CAMP LOCRE, by 12 NOON everyone was settled in camp and dinners had been served. The evening was spent resting. The following Offrs joined for duty. 2/Lt H.L. PALMER, " H.E. FLINN, " C.M. STEPHENSON, " J.R. FORBES.	appendix VI

2353 Wt. W2514/1454 700,000 5/15 D. D. & L. A.D.S.S./Forms/C. 2118.

Confidential

Instructions regarding War Diaries and Intelligence Summaries are contained in F. S. Regs., Part II. and the Staff Manual respectively. Title pages will be prepared in manuscript.

Army Form C. 2118.

WAR DIARY
or
~~INTELLIGENCE~~ SUMMARY.

(Erase heading not required.)

June 1917 — Sheet VII

Place	Date	Hour	Summary of Events and Information	Remarks and references to Appendices
In the Field	18/6/17	—	At 2 am orders were received that the 47th Inf Bde would return to the MERRIS AREA at 8 am this morning each Bn resuming occupation of their old billets. The evening was spent in rest after the march a slight break in the weather make things a little unpleasant. 2/Lt. W. J. WALSH proceeded to R.F.C. on probation.	appendice No VII
"	19/6/17	—	Training was carried out, special attention being given to handling of arms. Lewis Gunners & Bombers carried on under their own instructions. The Adjutant took the Bn at drill both in the morning and afternoon. 2/Lts. J. J. BARRY and D. D. BECKETT rejoined from 156th Coy. R.E.	
"	20/6/17	—	The Bn paraded at 5.30 am and proceeded to EECKE area packs being carried by motor lorry. Billets about 1½ KILOMETRES from EECKE were reached about 11 am. The remainder of the day was spent in rest, billets were good if somewhat scattered. LT. THOS TUITE was awarded the Military Cross	appendice VIII
"	21/6/17		The Bn carried on with training during and carried out short route marches by Coys in the afternoon. A lecture for Jnr Offrs by Major Jourdain and Drill by the Adjutant completed the day's work.	

Confidential

Instructions regarding War Diaries and Intelligence Summaries are contained in F. S. Regs., Part II. and the Staff Manual respectively. Title pages will be prepared in manuscript.

June 1917

WAR DIARY
or
INTELLIGENCE SUMMARY.

(Erase heading not required.)

Army Form C. 2118.

Sheet VIII

Place	Date	Hour	Summary of Events and Information	Remarks and references to Appendices
In the field	22/6/17		The Bn paraded at 5am and marched to ERINGHEM area, packs being carried by lorry. The march took place in a steady downpour of rain and on arrival in the area it was some time before billets were arranged, as they were very scarce. Officers in some cases using barns. The Bn was established by 3pm and spent the evening in drying clothes where possible.	Appendix IX
"	23/6/17	—	During the morning Coy were at the disposal of Coy Commanders and in the afternoon Specialist parades were carried out, the remainder of the Bn being engaged at Drill, Physical Training & Bayonet Fighting and Musketry. 2/Lt R.H. FRENCH rejoined from 16th I.B.D.	
	24/6/17		R.C. attended Divine Service at 10.30am and other denominations at 9.45am both services being held in the open. After dinner training was carried out, work being somewhat hampered by lack of fields. After the Bn. was paid. The day was fine & clear.	
"	25/6/17	—	The C.O. inspected the Bn by Coys. HQ parading separately carried out a march past and ceremonial drill. The Divl Commander paid a surprise visit to "B" Coy and expressed himself highly pleased with all he saw. Afternoon devoted to cleaning up for inspection by Corps Commander. Fine until 6pm, wet afterwards.	

2353 Wt. W2544/1454 700,000 5/15 D. D. & L. A.D.S.S./Forms/C. 2118.

Confidential

Instructions regarding War Diaries and Intelligence Summaries are contained in F. S. Regs., Part II. and the Staff Manual respectively. Title pages will be prepared in manuscript.

June 1917

WAR DIARY

or

~~INTELLIGENCE~~ SUMMARY.

(Erase heading not required.)

Sheet IX

Army Form C. 2118.

Place	Date	Hour	Summary of Events and Information	Remarks and references to Appendices
In the field	26/6/17	–	The morning was devoted to the usual training and the afternoon spent in cleaning equipment etc. The photographs of Offrs & Sergeants were taken at Bn. HQ.	
"	27/6/17		The Bn marched past the Corps Commander on the roadside near ZEGGERS CAPPEL. The 47th Bde marching past in column of route. During the afternoon Coys were at the disposal of Coy Commanders for training etc.	
"	28/6/17		The usual training was carried out. A Coy had a short route march, in the afternoon lectures on Interior Economy, Discipline etc were given. MAJOR HFN JOURDAIN proceeded to take over command of the 16th Bn R. WELSH FNS. LT T. BOOTH proceeded on leave	
"	29/6/17	–	The Baths near BOLZEELE were at the disposal of the Bn all day. Training in the morning and Inspections of Kits etc in the afternoon completed a good days work. RC attended Divine Service at 7-30 am. Specialists paraded as usual.	
"	30/6/17		Training in the morning and Short Route marches in the afternoon together with lectures on the work done during the month for which all ranks were heartily congratulated. The weather was good	

[signature] LIEUT. COLONEL, COMDG. 6th (S) Bn. THE CONNAUGHT RANGERS.

2353 Wt. W2544/1454 700,000 5/15 D. D. & L. A.D.S.S./Forms/C. 2118.

APPENDIX I

OPERATION ORDERS
BY
LIEUT. COL. R. C. FEILDING
COMMDG. 6th (S) BN. THE CONN RANGERS

COPY NO 10

SECRET.

1st JUNE 17

1. The 48th INF BDE will be relieved in the line by the 47th and 49th INF BDES on the night of JUNE 2/3 1917.

2. The 47th INF BDE will take over from N. 24. C. 2. 2. to LARK CORNER inclusive.

3. The 49th INF BDE will take over from LARK CORNER exclusive to VIERSTRAAT-WYTSCHAETE ROAD, exclusive N. 18. a. 70. 80.

4. On completion of relief the 47th INF BDE will be disposed as follows.

FRONT SYSTEM.	6th Bn. CONN RANGERS	HQ. S.P.12
SUPPORTING POSITIONS.	1st ROYAL MUNSTER FUS.	HQ. KNOLL DUGOUTS
BIRR BARRACKS.	7th LEINSTER REGT.	
KEMMEL LINES.	6th ROYAL IRISH. REGT.	

5. The Bn will, on completion of relief be disposed as follows.

A COY . . . RIGHT. FRONT LINE
C COY . . . LEFT. FRONT LINE
B COY . . . RIGHT SUPPORT
D COY . . . LEFT SUPPORT.
BN. HD. QRS. S.P. 12.

6. A COY will enter track "A" at CLARE CAMP at 9.15pm and will move by track "A" and routes C + D as far as the trench system. "C" "B" + "D" COYS will follow with 10 minutes interval between companys. Movement East of N. NORTH and SOUTH line through LOCRE, to be by platoons at 2 minutes interval.

7. Head of "A" COY must not cross junction of A TRACK [illegible] HUT ROAD before 10.30 pm.

8. The present 47th INF BDE Defence Scheme will hold good as far as it affects the old Right . Subsection

9. Completion of relief to be reported [illegible] B.H.Q. [illegible].

10. Copies of Trench Store Receipts will be handed into Bn HQ. by 6pm on 3rd inst

11. Rations will be dumped as follows:-
A + B COYS. DOCTORS HOUSE.
HD QRS. C + D COYS. At Entrance to ROSSIGNOL ROAD.

12. Advance parties of 1 Off [illegible] 1 NCO per platoon from each Coy to arrive in the line by 4pm. [illegible] S.M. DEMPSEY and 1 NCO to be detailed by the R.S.M. will take over for Bn. HQ. at [illegible] time.

13. The Bn will relieve the [illegible] Bn. [illegible]

14. All Kits, packs etc for removal to Transport Lines will be stacked by 2pm.

15 Ref para 12. No 1 of each Lewis Gun team will accompany advance party

(Sd) T. BOOTH Lieut
A/ADJT. 6th (S) BN. THE CONN. RANGERS

APPENDIX II

OPERATION ORDERS
BY
LIEUT-COL. R. C. FEILDING.
COMMANDING THE CONNAUGHT RANGERS

COPY No 6

SECRET.

4th JUNE 191

B.E.F. TRENCH MAP 28 S.W. 2. EDITION 5.A

THE CONNAUGHT RANGERS will raid the enemys trenches on 4-6-17. ZERO hour being 10-30 pm

(1) INTENTION.

To kill Germans, take prisoners, destroy the enemys defences capture machine guns, etc.

(2) OBJECTIVES

1ST. NANCY SWITCH from N.24. b. 3. 4. to N. 24. b. 32. 73.
2ND. NANCY SUPPORT. from N. 24. b. 6.4. to N. 24. b. 60. 74.

(3) TROOPS EMPLOYED.

INFANTRY:– 3 Coys, less 2 platoons (C + D COYS and 2 platoons of A COY)

(4) DISPOSITIONS AND TIME TABLE.

2 Coys will attack in 2 WAVES, the 1ST WAVE seizing the 2ND OBJECTIVE and the 2ND WAVE the 1ST OBJECTIVE MOPPERS UP for the 1ST OBJECTIVE will follow the 1ST WAVE a platoon on either flank of the 1ST WAVE will move forward in ARTILLERY FORMATION, and will be responsible for the protection of the assaulting troops from flank attack, and also for the establishment of blocks in the 2ND OBJECTIVE when reached.
The 1ST WAVE will be responsible for its own front.
The 2ND WAVE will be responsible for the protection of its own flanks, once it has reached its objective.
Arrangements will be made to cover the flanks of the assaulting troops during their return.

ZERO	1ST. WAVE leaves our trench.
ZERO + 8	1ST. OBJECTIVE seized.
ZERO + 12	2ND. OBJECTIVE seized
ZERO + 32.	WITHDRAW from 2ND. OBJECTIVE
ZERO + 45	All troops must be back in our lines

Upon withdrawal the 1ST WAVE will pass through the 2ND WAVE, rearguards being told off to cover each party.
To Guide the parties on their return, some or all, of the following methods will be adopted:–

(a) a bonfire will be lighted in front of ROSSIGNOL WOOD
(b) a succession of GOLD + SILVER RAIN ROCKETS will be fired from LUNETTE DUGOUTS.
(c) An OIL DRUM – to be carried by the raiders – will be left burning at each extremity of the 2ND OBJECTIVE.

(5) SMOKE BARRAGE

If the wind is favourable a smoke screen will be provided to the EAST of the 2ND OBJECTIVE.

(6) ARTILLERY TRENCH MORTAR AND MACHINE GUN CO-OPERATION.

as shown by attached programme. (T.M. Programme only available. Details of artillery programme attached) RC

(7) RAID HEADQUARTERS.

~~LUNETTE DUGOUTS~~ S.P.12. RC

(8) O.C. ASSAULT. COY.

LIEUT T. M. H S. THITE, CONN. RANGERS will command the assault. He will establish his headquarters in the neighbourhood of the JUNCTION of NANCY SWITCH and NANCY STREET.

(9) PRISONERS.

Prisoners, machine guns, etc will be immediately evacuated through O.C. ASSAULT to ~~LUNETTE DUGOUTS~~. S.P.12 RC

(10) DRESS.

Musketry Order, with Steel Helmets P.H. Helmet and Box Respirator, the latter at the alert.
Each Rifleman will carry 170 rounds of S.A.A.
Each Bomber, rifle and hand, will carry 12 bombs.
No identification marks will be worn, and no maps or papers containing information, or pay books will be carried.

(11) CASUALTIES

To facilitate the checking of casualties every officer, NCO or man will carry a piece of paper, with his name (and number) upon it. He will hand this in immediately upon his return.

(12) DUMMY RAIDS.

Feints will be made ~~attacks~~ on each flank. ~~as shown by programme~~ RC

(13) TIME OF ASSEMBLY

The assaulting troops will assemble in the front line at ZERO ~~-20~~ -45. RC

(14) BLACKENED FACES

All ranks participating in the enterprise will have their faces blackened.

(Sd) R.C. FEILDING. Lt. Col.

COMMDG. THE CONN. RANGERS.

SECRET

OPERATION ORDERS
BY
LIEUT.-COL. R. C. FEILDING
COMMANDING THE CONN. RANGERS.

COPY No.

4th JUNE 191[illegible]

1. Order No. T.B. 26 issued from this Office is cancelled and the following substituted.

2. Assaulting troops will be in their place in the assembly trench by 0-45.

3. PROTECTION OF FRONT LINE DURING ENTERPRISE.

The left subsection will be defended by 4 Lewis Guns, 2 to be detailed by 'C' Coy. and 2 by 'D' Coy.

The right subsection will be defended by:-

(a) 2 platoons, to be detailed by 'A' Coy.

(b) 4 Lewis Guns { 2 to be detailed by 'A' Coy
2 to be detailed by R.M.Fus.

B. Coy will detail {
1 platoon and 1 Lewis Gun for S.P.12
1 platoon and 1 Lewis Gun for S.P.11
1 platoon and 1 Lewis Gun for LUNETTE.
1 platoon and 1 Lewis Gun for PARK AVENUE

R.M.F. (4 Lewis Guns) to be detailed thus { 2 Lewis Guns in Right Subsection as above
2 Lewis Guns in BROADWAY

4. GARRISONING OF FRONT LINE AFTER ENTERPRISE.

Left Subsection — As at present.

D Coy will relieve 'C' Coy by parties of not more than 5 at 5 minute intervals before 10 am on 5.6.17.

Right Subsection

B Coy will relieve 'A' Coy as soon as the position becomes normal after the enterprise. Upon Completion of relief O.C. 'B' Coy will send back the 4 Lewis Gun teams of the R.M.Fus. to their unit.

After relief the line will be held as follows.

LEFT.

D Coy { Front line 2 platoons and 4 Lewis Guns
Park Avenue 2 platoons

C Coy { S.P.12 4 platoons + 3 Lewis Guns
LARK LANE 1 Lewis Gun.

RIGHT

B Coy and 2 L.G. of A Coy { Front line 3 platoons + 4 Lewis Guns
BROADWAY 1 platoon + 2 Lewis Guns.

A Coy less 2 Lewis Guns { S.P.11 3 platoons + 1 Lewis Gun.
LUNETTE 1 platoon + 1 Lewis Gun

Lieut. C.A. BRETT will be in command of the front line and BROADWAY during the enterprise.

(Sd). R. C. FEILDING. Lt Col.
Comdg. The Conn Rangers.

Details of Artillery Programme

18-pdrs. barraged as follows:–

At Zero – N.18.c.93.00. – N.24.b.10.00. Then lifting 100 yds. every 2 minutes till Zero + 12, when a box barrage was formed with sides along NAME DRIVE and NANCY AVENUE and back from O.13.d.00.00 to O.19.a.05.10. A standing barrage was put up along German front line on both sides of box barrage.

4.5" Hows. partook in creeping barrage and also, in conjunction with 6" Hows. bombarded selected points in the vicinity.

Fire was continued until "Cease fire" ordered.

5.6.17

F. J. Chamier Lt.
Int. Off. [illegible]

STOKES MORTAR PROGRAMME.

FOR ENTERPRISE OF

CONNAUGHT RANGERS ON NIGHT OF 4th JUNE 1917.

(1) 47th T.M. Batt. will barrage German Front line from MAEDELSTEDE to junction of NANCY AVE and Front line. 400 rounds in all will be fired, distributed as follows:-

(a) ZERO to +5	Intense	150	400
(b) ZERO +5 to +32	Intermittent	100	
(c) ZERO +32 to +37	Intense	150	

(2) 49th T.M. BATT. will bombard German front line from mine crater in PETIT BOIS Salient to about N.18.d.20.30 firing 400 rounds in same manner as above.

4/6/17

(Sd) JAS P. ROCHE Capt.

47th T.M.B

SECRET. 47th Inf. Bde. No. G. 3336.

RAID BY 6th CONNAUGHT RANGERS
NIGHT of 4/5th JUNE, 1917.

1. Strength of raiding party about 11 Officers and 280 other ranks with 5 Lewis Guns. Enterprise Commander Lieut. TUITT.

2. Zero hour at 10.30 p.m. under a creeping artillery barrage, supported by heavy howitzers on selected points.

3. Attack in 2 waves, the 1st wave seizing the second objective, and the 2nd wave the first objective.

4. To guide parties back some or all of the following were used:-
   (a) bonfire East of ROSSIGNOL WOOD.
   (b) gold and silver rain rockets fired from vicinity of LUNETTE DUGOUTS.
   (c) oil barrels to be fired at each extremity of second objective. N.B. – (b) only was used.

5. 1st Munsters sent 4 Lewis guns with teams as reinforcement for holding the line.

6. Lieut. Col. FEILDING, D.S.O., Commdg. 6th Connaught Rangers acted as O.C. Enterprise with H.Q. at ~~LUNETTE dugouts~~ S.P. 12.

7. The place for the raid was the S. side of the PETIT BOIS, NANCY SWITCH was the 1st objective and NANCY SUPPORT the 2nd objective.

8. The enterprise was very successful, both the waves reaching their objectives. A few Germans were found in NANCY SWITCH, where a German acting Officer, wearing an Iron cross, was surprised and taken with some of his men. He stated his platoon was 16 strong, composed of young soldiers, who surrendered without fighting.
NANCY SUPPORT was held fairly strongly. Here the resistance was greater.
Every German encountered was either killed or captured.
A machine gun, which opened fire from NANCY SWITCH was destroyed, as well as the emplacement.

9. The wire on the S. side of PETIT BOIS in front of NANCY SWITCH is still uncut in places, and proved an obstacle. Some of the wire in front of NANCY SUPPORT also requires cutting. This trench has been badly damaged, and is scarcely recognizable, though a few good dugouts remain.

10. <u>Enemy's Casualties:-</u>

Prisoners (including Acting Officer with iron cross)	7
Killed (estimated a minimum of)	60
Total	67.

11, Our Casualties:-

	Officers.	Other ranks.	Total.
Killed.	1	2	3
Wounded.	1	34	35
Missing.	1	5	6
Total	3	41	44

2/Lieut. McSHERRY was killed.
2/Lieut. FITZPATRICK-ROBERTSON wounded.
2/Lieut. HAMILTON missing.

G. Pereira
Brigadier General,
Commanding 47th Infantry Brigade.

5-6-17.

APPENDIX No A-T-I

H.Q.
47th Inf Bde

Herewith my report on the part taken by the battalion under my command in the operations of June 7th against the WYTSCHAETE RIDGE.

In preparation for the attack the battalion was broken up and distributed as follows.

PARTY			Offrs	OR
	(1)	attached to R.E and employed on the construction of Strong Points	3 offs	100 Other Ranks
"	(2)	attached to 1st R.MUN.FUS. to mop up WYTSCHAETE VILLAGE.	4 offrs	100 OR.
"	(3)	attached to 47th M.G.C. to carry ammunition	2 offrs.	40. OR.
"	(4)	attached to 47th T.M.B. to carry ammunition	2 offrs.	50 OR
"	(5)	attached to 47th INF BDE to carry rations, ammunition + supplies	5 offrs	90 OR
	(6)	Garrison for Strong Points	3 offrs.	60 OR
			19 offrs	440 OR.

In addition to the above I manned the front line after the assaulting Infantry had vacated it, from KETCHEN AVE to LARK CORNER with Six Lewis Guns. The remainder of the battalion with ten Lewis Guns was held in reserve behind CHINESE WALL three of the Lewis Guns being subsequently sent to reinforce the Strong Points as soon as the latter had been completed.

During the night - previous to the attack - the parties were assembled as follows.

(1) With 156th Coy R E

(2) A hundred yards in front of ALBERTA DUGOUTS. This party had to dig itself in, in the open, under shell fire.

(3) With 47th M.G. COY

(4) LEEMING LANE and ROSSIGNOL ROAD

(5) ROSSIGNOL WOOD

(6) In the vicinity of BEAVER HAT.

The Reserve Company under Lieut. C.A. BRETT. dug in behind the hedges WEST of S.P.R. They experienced some shell fire and suffered casualties.

All Ranks displayed the greatest devotion carrying out the duties assigned to them unflinching and untiringly.

The Moppers Up, under Lieut. R.E. BOWEN, advanced behind the first wave of the 1st Bn. R. Munster Fus. Just before reaching the village of WYTSCHAETE they encountered an enemy Strong Point, This opposition however they rapidly overcame, and in the village itself, they captured and passed back 98 prisoners including an Officer, They also found two Machine Guns in the dug-outs, which they brought up and left on the parapet for the 1st R.M.F. to collect, the Officer commanding the Mopping Up party considering that as a wave of "Munsters" had gone over first these guns should go to that regiment.

We suffered the following Casualties.

	OFFRS	OTHER RANKS
KILLED	0	4
WOUNDED	2	32
MISSING	0	2
TOTAL	2	38

9-6-17

(Sd) R. C. FEILDING. Lt Col.
Commanding 6th (S) Bn The Conn Rangers

APPENDIX III
SECRET

OPERATION ORDERS
by
LIEUT-COL R C FEILDING
COMDG THE CONN RANGERS

COPY NO 6
5 June 17.

The following reliefs will take place on the night of 5/6th June 1917.
B Coy & C Coy will be relieved in the RIGHT front line by a Coy of the 6th R. IRISH R.
D Coy will be relieved in the LEFT front line by a Coy of the 7th LEINSTER REGT.

2. Relief commences about 1-30am

3. On completion of relief B & D Coys will move to an open position in rear of CHINESE WALL. These Coys will send an offr to Bn HQ at 5 pm today to reconnoitre the position.

4 Bn HQ will move to IRISH HOUSE on completion of front line relief.

5 Trench Store Receipts will be handed into Bn HQ by 2pm on 6th inst.

6

6. A & C Coys will remain in their present positions

7. Completion of relief will be reported by runner

Advanced parties & N.C.O. of Lewis Guns will [illegible] at 6pm today

(Sd) T BOOTH Lt
Adjt. 6th Conn Rgs

Secret OPERATION ORDERS BY LT-COL. R.C. FEILDING. DSO COMMANDING. 6th Bn THE CONN. RANGERS.

COPY No 6

APPENDIX 'IV'

9th JUNE 1917

1. The Bn will be relieved today relief commences about 12-30pm.

2. On completion of relief HQ. A+B Coys will proceed to KEMMEL SHELTERS and C+D Coys to KLONDYKE FARM

3 Evacuation of trenches + arrival in camp to be reported by runner

4. The usual distances between parties in the trenches and on the roads will be observed.

5. The transport offr will arrange for the removal of any Orderly Room + Coy mess kit, which will be stacked at ROSSIGNOL ROAD.

(Sd) T. BOOTH Lt.
A/ADJT. 6th CONN. RANGERS

15

1. The Battalion will move to the [illegible]

2. [illegible]

3. [illegible]

4. Head of column [illegible] starting point [illegible] CARRÉ – SEMPERSIN [illegible] – ST. JANS [illegible] will be [illegible]

5. [illegible]

OULTERSTEENE

6. [illegible]

7. The [illegible]

8. O.C. A Coy will detail one platoon to march in rear of Bn

9. [illegible]

10. The transport will not accompany the Bn

11. [illegible]

12. [illegible]

13. [illegible]

(Bn) [illegible]

APPENDIX VI

555

to be carried.

COPY No 10

APPENDIX VII

OPERATION ORDERS

BY

LT-COL. R.C. FEILDING D.S.O.

COMMDG. 6th (S) BN THE CONN. RANGERS.

SECRET

18th June 1918

1 Bn will proceed to MERRIS area today and occupy billets vacated yesterday

2. Parade at 8 am in the following order, H.Q. DRUMS. A B C + D Coys. Dress as today

3. Packs to be stacked by 7.20 am

4 Billetting party as yesterday

5 Transport will accompany the Bn.

6. Evacuation, clean billet and arrival certificates to be rendered by runner

7. Route of march will be, pass starting point 8.25 am and proceed by Coys at 30 yds distance via SCHAEXKEN — METEREN to Billets

(Sd) T BOOTH Lt.

A/ADJT 6th CONN. RANGERS.

APPENDIX VIII

OPERATION ORDERS
BY
LIEUT-COL. R. L. FEILDING D.S.O.
COMMANDING 6th (S) Bn. THE CONN RANGERS.

SECRET.

19th JUNE 1917

1. The Bn will move to the EECKE area tomorrow 20th inst.

2. The Bn will parade, in Marching Order, head of column at crossroads 1 KILOMETRE S.E. of METEREN CHURCH, ready to move off at 5-30am in the following order:- HD. QRS. B Coy. DRUMS. C Coy. D Coy and A Coy

3. The Bn will pass the starting point, road junction FLETRE at 6-20am and move via FLETRE and THEISHOUK to RAILWAY CROSSING G.22.C. where guides will be met.

4. Transport will accompany the Bn. No extra Transport is being allowed.

5. Billetting party of 1 O.R. per Coy and SGT W. HARFORD under Lieut T.F. GILMORE will meet M. [illegible] at EECKE CHURCH at 4-30am

6. All kits etc to be stacked by 4-30am

7. The usual certificates will be rendered before moving off and on arrival

Reveille 3am Breakfast 4am.

(Sd) T. BOOTH Lieut.
A/ADJT. 6th (S) Bn THE CONN. RANGERS

Copy to Co

8th Operation Orders [illegible] Copy No 10

[illegible] by [illegible]

Officer Commanding 6th (S) Bn The Conn Rangers 21 [illegible] 17

1 The 47th Inf Bde Group will march on [illegible] from LOCRINGHEM area route STEENVOORDE – WORMHOUDT – ESQUELBECQ. 500 yards distance between units

2 The Bn will parade with head of column at road junction 1 kilometre N.W of Bn HD.QRS. ready to move off at 5am in the following order HDQRS C COY D COY DRUMS A COY B COY

3 The Bn will pass starting point (road junction W of STEENVOORDE) at 5-40 am.

4 Billeting party of CQMS & 2/Lt J Gilmore will [illegible] forward in advance. Instructions will be issued

5 Officers kits mess packs etc to be stacked by Coys near the roads for removal by Motor transport by 4 am

6 The usual certificates will be rendered by Coys before departure and on arrival

7 Transport will accompany the Bn

8 Reveille 3am Breakfast 3-45am [illegible] C Coy

Sd T. BOOTH Lieut
A/ADJT. 6th Bn. THE CONN. RGS

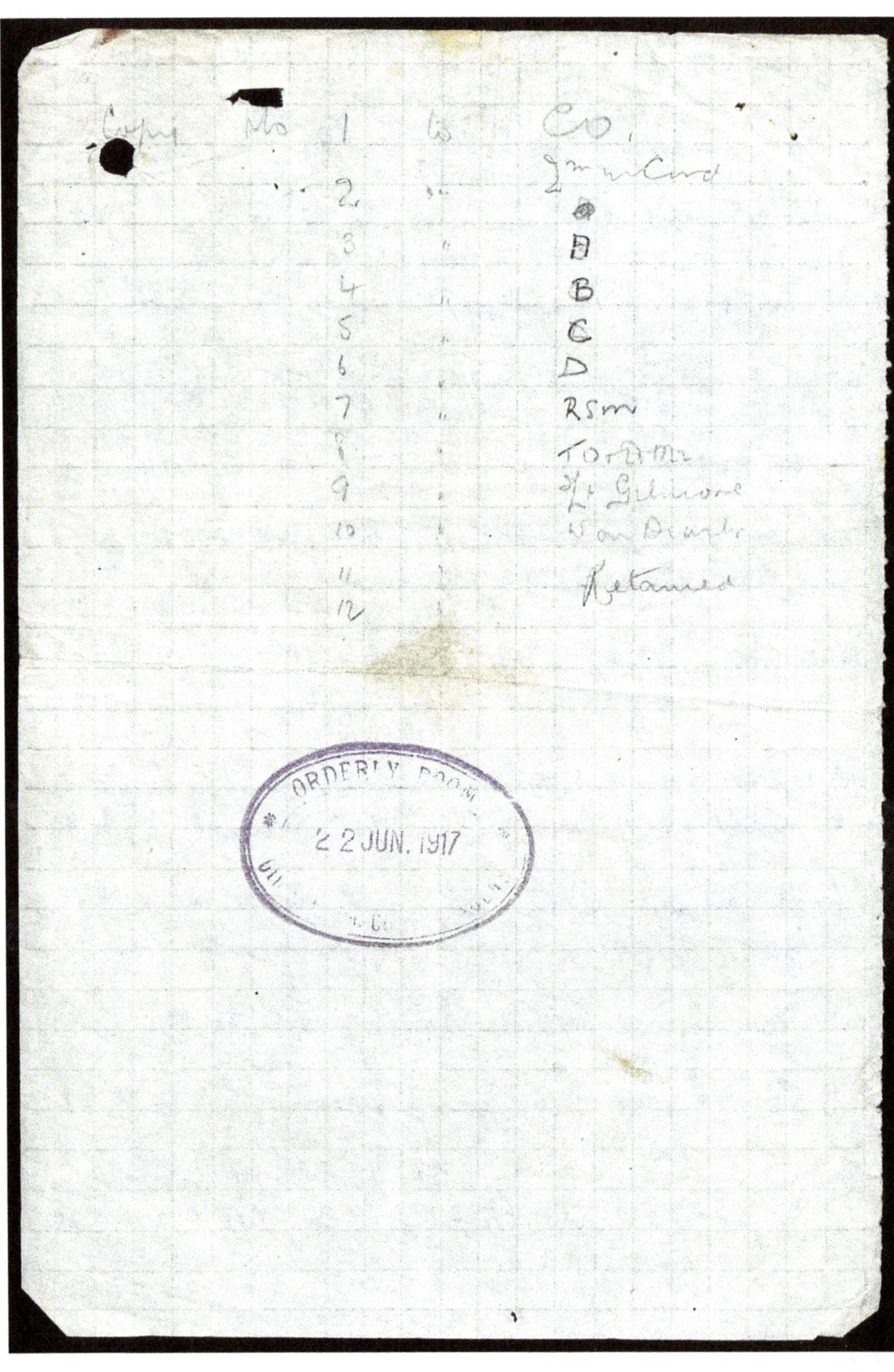

Copy No 1 to CO.
2nd in Cmd
2 " A
3 " A
4 " B
5 " C
6 " D
7 " RSM
8 " TO & QM
9 " Lt Gilmore
10 " War Diary
11 " Retained
12

ORDERLY ROOM
22 JUN. 1917

W 20

WAR DIARY.

FOR MONTH OF JULY, 1917.

VOLUME :- 20

UNIT :- 6th Connaught Rangers.

Confidential

Instructions regarding War Diaries and Intelligence Summaries are contained in F. S. Regs., Part II. and the Staff Manual respectively. Title pages will be prepared in manuscript.

July 1917

WAR DIARY
or
~~INTELLIGENCE SUMMARY.~~
(Erase heading not required.)

6th (S) Bn. The Connaughs Rangers Army Form C. 2118.

Sheet I

Place	Date	Hour	Summary of Events and Information	Remarks and references to Appendices
In the Field	1/7/17	—	The R. C. attended Divine Service at 10-30am in a field at A.10. 6 8.4 and other Denominations at ERINGHEM, the remainder of the day was devoted to cleaning of equipment etc	
"	2/7/17	—	Training on a large scale was carried between 7am and 4-30pm. Sports were held by the 1st Royal Munster Fus in which some of the officers and other Ranks of the Bn took part. While taking part in an officers jumping Competition, Lt-Col. R. C. FEILDING D.S.O. O.C. 6th Conn. Rangers, was thrown from his horse and was taken to Hospital suffering from the effects the Command of the Bn devolved upon Capt T. H CROFTON. M.C. Capt T. A. DILLON, acting 2nd in Command. 2/Lt. F.R. CUMMINS rejoined from Infantry Rest Camp and 2/Lt. M.P. O CONNOR from leave. The Bn was paid (5 francs) and work on the construction of Rifle Range and Bombing ground was continued.	
"	3/7/17	—	The Bn paraded at 8am and took part in a Route March returning to Billets about 1pm for dinners, Lewis Gunners & Bombers carried out training as usual. The morning was devoted to Foot + Rifle Inspections. Lieut. A.E. MALE died on his way to Hospital today from injuries sustained by being thrown from his horse the previous night. Lt. J. P. MONAN proceeded on leave.	

2353 Wt. W2544/1454 700,000 5/15 D. D. & L. A.D.S.S./Forms/C. 2118.

Confidential

Instructions regarding War Diaries and Intelligence Summaries are contained in F. S. Regs., Part II. and the Staff Manual respectively. Title pages will be prepared in manuscript.

WAR DIARY
or
~~INTELLIGENCE SUMMARY.~~

(Erase heading not required.)

July 1917

Sheet II

Army Form C. 2118.

Place	Date	Hour	Summary of Events and Information	Remarks and references to Appendices
In the Field	4/7/17	—	Training as usual, a Guard mounting Competition was organised. The evening was devoted to cleaning of equipment in preparation for inspection by the G.O.C. 16th DIV. Tomorrow. Lieut. R.E. BOWEN assumed Command of "D" Coy and Lieut HATHUNT took over the duties of Transport Officer. No .SGT. J. FISHER was awarded the Military Medal.	
"	5/7/17		The inspection by G.O.C. was cancelled and training was carried out as usual. 3 Officers per Coy attended a TANK demonstration at MERCKEGHEM at 9am.	
"	6/7/17		Training in usual subjects was carried out between 7am and 4pm. A TANK demonstration was held at MERCKEGHEM, 2 Offrs and 4 NCOs per Coy attended and interesting and instructive display. The judging of the Guard Mounting Competition was carried out by the C.O. and "B" COY were declared the winners.	
"	7/7/17		Training as usual. Kit inspections and inoculation of some men of "A" COY. 2/Lts J.P. RONAN and A.H.E. RUSSELL proceeded on leave. The evening was devoted to lectures on Discipline & Interior Economy. The weather was poor.	

A5834 Wt. W4973/M687 750,000 8/16 D. D. & L. Ltd. Forms/C.2118/13.

Confidential

Instructions regarding War Diaries and Intelligence Summaries are contained in F. S. Regs., Part II. and the Staff Manual respectively. Title pages will be prepared in manuscript.

July 1917

WAR DIARY
or
~~INTELLIGENCE SUMMARY.~~

(Erase heading not required.)

Sheet IIIA

Army Form C. 2118.

Place	Date	Hour	Summary of Events and Information	Remarks and references to Appendices
In the Field	8/7/17	—	RC's attended Divine Service at 10.30 am and Other Denominations at 8.30 am. The morning was very wet and on return from Divine Service the men were informed that the 47th Inf Bde Sports which were to have been held this evening, were cancelled. There were no parades during the evening owing to the weather.	
"	9/7/17	—	The Baths at L'ERKELSBRUGGE were at the disposal of the Bn all day and Coys when not engaged bathing were at the disposal of Company Commanders. The Bn was paid (5 francs) Lieut. T. BOOTH returned from leave this evening. Major J.D. RATHER arrived and took over Command of the Bn. assuming the rank of T/Lt. Col.	
"	10/7/17	—	The Bn was inspected by C.O. in their billets. Usual training and Specialist classes were carried out. The Bn was to have been inspected by the G.O.C. 16th Div. but this was cancelled.	
	11/7/17		Lectures, Musketry (fire control & fire orders) Physical Training and Bayonet Fighting were the order of the day. Some of the junior officers were taken at Drill, etc. by the Adjt. The men who were unable to attend the Baths on the 9th attended at 4pm to-day.	

A5834 Wt. W4973/M687 750,000 8/16 D. D. & L. Ltd. Forms/C.2118/13.

Confidential

Instructions regarding War Diaries and Intelligence Summaries are contained in F. S. Regs., Part II. and the Staff Manual respectively. Title pages will be prepared in manuscript.

July 1917

WAR DIARY
or
~~INTELLIGENCE SUMMARY.~~
(Erase heading not required.)

Army Form C. 2118.

Sheet IV

Place	Date	Hour	Summary of Events and Information	Remarks and references to Appendices
12/7/17	In the Field		Training was carried out during the morning there were no parades in the afternoon all ranks being free to attend the 47th Inf Bde SPORTS at LEGGATRS CAPPEL. A motor Disinfecting Lorry arrived and disinfected the clothes of H.Q. during the morning The G.O.C. 16th DIV. Inspected the men in billets during the morning and expressed himself highly pleased with the result.	
13/7/17.			Training was carried on as far as possible. The Disinfecting Lorry completed the Bn during the day. The Bde Interplatoon Competition was held at B.14.d.1.7 the Bn doing exceedingly well, Winning the "Best Platoon" and only being beaten by 1 point in the "Best Guard" Lieut. W.A. Farndon returned from 2nd Army School of Instruction.	
14/7/17			Training as usual. The C.O. inspected the two platoons which had done so well in the Bde Competition yesterday and congratulated them on their display. A large number of NCO paraded under SGT. WEBB. A.G.S for instruction in Bayonet Fighting and Physical Training, special attention being paid to the recreational side of the training.	

A5834 Wt. W4973/M687 750,000 8/16 D. D. & L. Ltd. Forms/C.2118/13.

Confidential

Instructions regarding War Diaries and Intelligence Summaries are contained in F. S. Regs., Part II, and the Staff Manual respectively. Title Pages will be prepared in manuscript.

July 1917.

WAR DIARY
or
~~INTELLIGENCE~~ SUMMARY

(Erase heading not required.)

Sheet V

Army Form C. 2118.

Place	Date	Hour	Summary of Events and Information	Remarks and references to Appendices
In the Field	15/7/17	—	The Bn paraded in mass formation at 10am and were addressed by the CO prior to Divine Service, which took place at 10.30am. 3 officers & 3 NCO per Coy attended an Infantry Field Practice at TILQUES area. The Prize platoon attended Divine Service at ST. OMER and gave a Demonstration before the 48th Inf Bde. There were no parades in the afternoon.	
Sheet 27 SE	16/7/17	—	The Bn paraded at 5am in French Order and marched to the TATINGHEM area, where they took over the billets of the 7th Bn. ROYAL IRISH RIFLES. Bn HQ. & A COY were billetted in CORMETTE and B C & D COYS at AUDENTHUN. The Remainder of the 47th Bde was disposed as follows. 47th Bde HQ TATENGHEM. 1st ROYAL MUN. FUS. & 7th LEINSTERS TATINGHEM. 6th ROYAL I. REGT LOULINGHEM. The evening was spent in rest. 2/Lt. French R.H. proceeded on leave. 2/Lt. J.P. ROHAN returned off leave	
	17/7/17	—	The Bn paraded on "A" RANGE (Q.14.b) at 6am and carried out various firing practises until midday. 2/Lt. J.D. BARRON assumed the duties of Intelligence Off & 2/Lt. H.S. KIRKWOOD of L.G. officer. Lt. J.J. BARRY proceeded on leave. The following awards were notified. MILITARY MEDALS. 1/9846 L/C DOLAN and 6/2272 Pte DEVLIN. The Bn was paid in the afternoon and some training was done.	

2449 Wt. W14957/M90 750,000 1/16 J.B.C. & A. Forms/C.2118/12.

Confidential

Instructions regarding War Diaries and Intelligence Summaries are contained in F. S. Regs., Part II. and the Staff Manual respectively. Title pages will be prepared in manuscript.

July 1917

WAR DIARY
or
INTELLIGENCE SUMMARY.
(Erase heading not required.)

Sheet VI

Army Form C. 2118.

Place	Date	Hour	Summary of Events and Information	Remarks and references to Appendices
Cormette Ref Sheet France 27A S.E	18.7.17		The battalion devoted the morning to musketry in billets owing to heavy rain which prevented companies practising the attack. In the afternoon the battalion paraded in musketry order and assembled at 3 p.m in the valley S.E. of CORMETTE. and advanced in artillery formation to the frontage of 600 yards, allotted to it in Brigade Operations, on the 'Green line' ie. from W.4.b.7.7 to Q.35.c.7.1. The battalion advanced on a 2 company frontage in 4 waves behind a 'barrage' of flags to the 'Red line' a distance of 900 yards & occupied the line from W.5.c.4.0 to W.5.d.4.5. C and D companies were in the front line - C on the right - with A and B in support. Zero hour at which the first wave left the 'Green line' was 4.30 p.m. The 'Red line' was reached at Z+40.	
			It was notified that Lt R.E. Bowen was awarded the Military Cross	
			Various awards were presented by Major General W.B. Hickie, C.B. at 12 noon	
	19.7.17		The 47th Brigade carried out an attack practice. Zero hour - 8 a.m. The Battalion paraded in fighting Order & played the same part as on the previous day. The 6th Royal Irish was on our right and a skeleton battalion on our left. The 1st Munsters (on the left) and 7th Leinsters were in support. They went through the Red line at Z+80 and took the Blue line at Z+152. All officers were afterwards addressed by the Brigadier.	

A5834 Wt. W4973/M687 750,000 8/16 D. D. & L. Ltd. Forms/C.2118/13.

Confidential

Instructions regarding War Diaries and Intelligence Summaries are contained in F. S. Regs., Part II. and the Staff Manual respectively. Title Pages will be prepared in manuscript.

July '17

WAR DIARY
or
INTELLIGENCE SUMMARY

(Erase heading not required.)

Sheet VII

Army Form C. 2118.

Place	Date	Hour	Summary of Events and Information	Remarks and references to Appendices
Cornette Ref Sheet France 27^A S.E.	19.7.17	(cont)	In the afternoon a large number of N.C.Os paraded under Sgt Hidden, A.G.S. for instruction in Bayonet fighting. In the evening the battalion practised compass marching by night by companies. Lt Bowen, M.C. took over command of C. Coy. The following awards were announced:- Legion of Honour - CAPT. S.L. GWYNN.; Medailles Militaires - 10623 Sgt J Sheehan and 3862 L/Cpl P. Conroy (att^d 47th T.M.B.)	
	20.7.17		2nd Lieut A.H.E. Russell returned from leave. The same scheme of Brigade attack-practice was carried out as on the previous day, with the exception that the Battalion occupied a frontage of 500 yards. Zero hour - 2 p.m. Major General W.B. Hickie, C.B., was present as well as the Brigadier. At the conference of officers afterwards, which was addressed by the Divisional & Brigade Commanders, there was ~~a~~ a successful exhibition given of the new message-rocket. Lt T. HUGHES and 2.LT. E.C. NORMAN left the battalion to join the 19th CORPS REINFORCEMENT DEPOT at MERCKEGHEM.	
	21.7.17		The Brigade attack-practice scheme was carried out as on the previous day. Zero hour - 8.0 a.m. The officers were afterwards addressed by the Brigadier and by Major Carter M.G.C. (heavy) on the subject of 'Tanks'. An exhibition of message rockets was given to all ranks. CAPT. T.H. CROFTON left the Battalion & proceeded to MERCHEGHEM as Musketry Instructor to the 19th Corps Reinforcement Depot	

2449 Wt. W14957/M90 750,000 1/16 J.B.C. & A. Forms/C.2118/12.

Confidential

Army Form C. 2118.

WAR DIARY
or
INTELLIGENCE SUMMARY
(Erase heading not required.)

Instructions regarding War Diaries and Intelligence Summaries are contained in F. S. Regs., Part II. and the Staff Manual respectively. Title Pages will be prepared in manuscript.

July 1917 Sheet VIII

Place	Date	Hour	Summary of Events and Information	Remarks and references to Appendices
Cornette Ref Sheet 27A SE	22.7.17		R.C.s paraded in the valley S of Cornettes at 9.30 a.m and other denominations at Royal Irish HQ at LEULINE at 8.30a.m. 2nd LIEUT T.F. GILMORE went home on leave. Transport proceeded to the Winnezeele Area (see Appendix 1)	
Winnezeele Ref Sheet 27.	23.7.17		The battalion proceeded by road and train to the Winnezeele Area arriving at billets at 6.30 a.m (see Appendix). The battalion were billeted under canvas at BRIEL (D.10.b.2.0) 1100x N.W of WINNEZEELE	Appendix 1. Operation Orders No 23.
	24.7.17		Company training was proceeded with. Gas helmets were inspected by gas N.C.O.s 2nd LIEUT S.W. O'COFFEY went to Poperinghe to inspect the model of the German trenches on the 19th Army Corps front	
WATOU K.12. b. 4. 9 Sheet 27.	25.7.17		Company training was proceeded with. The battalion paraded at 6.45 p.m and proceed by route march in heavy marching order to the WATOU district where they arrived at billets at 10 p.m at VALLEY CAMP (K.12. b. 4. 9.) See Appendix 2nd LIEUT R.E. ATWELL rejoined the battalion from hospital.	Appendix 2. Operation Orders No 24.
	26.7.17		Company training including a short practice route march in heavy marching order was the day's programme. The C.O, the Adjutant and 3 company officers went to East of YPRES on a preliminary survey of the Corps frontage. ~~2nd~~ LIEUT D.H. WICKHAM returned to the battalion from the 47th T.M.B., 2nd LIEUT M.P. O'CONNOR taking his place. LIEUT R.H. FRENCH returned from leave a day early.	

2449 Wt. W14957/M90 750,000 1/16 J.B.C. & A. Forms/C.2118/12.

Confidential

Instructions regarding War Diaries and Intelligence Summaries are contained in F. S. Regs., Part II. and the Staff Manual respectively. Title Pages will be prepared in manuscript.

July 1917

WAR DIARY
or
INTELLIGENCE SUMMARY
(Erase heading not required.)

Army Form C. 2118.

Sheet IX

Place	Date	Hour	Summary of Events and Information	Remarks and references to Appendices
Waton Ref Sheet 27	27.7.17		The battalion paraded at 6.15 a.m for an attack practice in the ~~St~~ STEENVORDE training area. Zero hour was 8 a.m. The general scheme and the line of battle were the same as at CORMETTE a week previously. The CONNAUGHT RANGERS started from the RED LINE (K.22.c.3.0 to K 21.d.0.0.) captured the BROWN LINE and consolidated it after which the 1st R.M.F went through and took the YELLOW LINE. MAJOR GENERAL HICKIE, C.B., and BRIG. GENERAL PEREIRA, C.B., C.M.G., D.S.O. were present and addressed a conference of officers. 2ND LT. E.C. LIEBURNE was admitted to hospital with inflammation of the knee.	
	28.7.17		In the morning all N.C.O's were instructed by their Platoon officers in the art of using a compass. The battalion paraded under the adjutant for drill. There was an inspection of gas helmets in the afternoon. The battalion paraded in fighting order at 7.45 p.m for night operations, returning to camp at 11.45 p.m (see Appendix 3.) 2ND LIEUT G.E. MAGUIRE went on leave. 2ND LIEUT E.A.W. SMITH returned from a Coy Corps course. 2ND LIEUT J.J. BARRY returned from leave and 2ND LIEUT E.C. NORMAN from the Corps Reinforcement Depot. 2ND LIEUT J.J. CONLON left for a Lewis Gun Coy Com's course.	Appendix 3 Night Operations 28.7.1917
	29.7.17		Church parades were cancelled on account of heavy rain. The brigadier addressed all officers of the battalion in the afternoon.	

2449 Wt. W14957/M90 750,000 1/16 J.B.C. & A. Forms/C.2118/12.

Confidential

Instructions regarding War Diaries and Intelligence Summaries are contained in F. S. Regs., Part II. and the Staff Manual respectively. Title Pages will be prepared in manuscript.

July 1917

WAR DIARY
or
INTELLIGENCE SUMMARY
(Erase heading not required.)

Sheet X

Army Form C. 2118.

Place	Date	Hour	Summary of Events and Information	Remarks and references to Appendices
BRANDHOEK Area Ref Sheet Belgium 28.N.W.	30.7.17		Companies proceeded with training paying special attention to gas helmet drill. The battalion paraded at 6.45 in H.M.O. and marched to the Brandhoek area arriving at billets, G 15. a.0.1, at 10 p.m. (See Appendix 4)	Appendix 4 Operation Order No 25.
	31.7.17		The great attack started on a large front the battalion remained in reserve in the above billets.	

T A Dillon Captain
for LIEUT. COLONEL
[illegible] 6th (S) Bn. THE CONNAUGHT RANGERS

2449 Wt. W14957/M90 750,000 1/16 J.B.C. & A. Forms/C.2118/12.

Appendix 1.

OPERATION ORDER No. 33
~~OPERATION ORDER~~

BY

LIEUT-COLONEL J.D. MATHER
COMMANDING 6TH BN THE CONNAUGHT RANGERS.

Copy No. ..9...

21st July 1917.

Reference Sheet 27.
Sheet 27A S.E.

---

1. The Battalion will move by train on the 23rd. It will pass the Starting Point Q.35.d.2.4. at 8.15 am.

2. An advance party of 1 Sergeant and 1 men per company, 1 Sergeant from H.Q., 1 N.C.O. from the Q.M. Stores and 1 N.C.O. from the Transport, under 2/Lt T.F. GILMORE, will leave by ordinary train at 2.50 pm on the 22nd. and report to the Area Commandant for billets, afterwards meeting omnibus train and Battalion train to provide guides to camp.

3. Officers' kits and messes will be carried on a lorry on 23rd, to be loaded by 9 am 23rd. One N.C.O. per company and the Quarter--master will proceed with it.

4. The Battalion Transport (less vehicles mentioned in para 5) will be brigaded and proceed by road on the 22nd. A March-Table has been issued to the Transport Officer.

5. The omnibus train will leave ST. OMER with the following trans--port at 0 am 23rd, transport to be at station at 5.55 am on that date.

   4 Cookers, with horses and drivers.
   2 Water-carts " " " "
   1 Mess-Cart " " " "
   4 Chargers, i.e. C.O's two horses and groom, Second-in-Command's horse and groom, Adjutant's horse and groom.
   Medical Officer, Maltese Cart and driver, 2 O.R. medical personnel.

6. There will be two distributions of rations on the 21st inst., i.e. for consumption on 22nd and 23rd inst. Rations for consump--tion by train portion on 23rd will be delivered to Quarter--masters on the 21st inst, the proportion of rations required for road portions being retained on the Supply wagons.
On the 23rd rations for consumption on the 24th will be dumped in the 47th Brigade Area, WINNEZEELE, and delivered to units.

(sd) T. BOOTH, LIEUTENANT,
A/ADJUTANT 6TH BN THE CONNAUGHT RANGERS.

Copy No. 1. Commanding Officer.
.. .. 2. O.C. "A" Coy.
.. .. 3. O.C. "B" Coy.
.. .. 4. O.C. "C" Coy.
.. .. 5. O.C. "D" Coy.

Copy No. 6. Transport Officer & Quartermaster.
.. .. 7. Medical Officer.
.. .. 8. R.S.M.
.. .. 9. War Diary.

Copy No. 10. Retained.

****

Appendix 2

OPERATION ORDER NO. 24.
BY
LIEUT-COLONEL J.D.MATHER
COMMANDING 6TH BN THE CONNAUGHT RANGERS.

Copy No. ......

In the Field.
24.7.17.

1. The 47th Infantry Brigade will move by march route from the WINNEZEELE Area to the WATOU No. 3 Area on July 25th.

2. The Battalion will parade in mass formation in the field in which the camp is situated at 6.45 pm to-morrow and will move off in the following order:- H.Q.,"D" Coy., "A" Coy., Drums, "B" Coy., "C" Coy., Transport.

3. The head of the column will pass the starting-point (J.17. 00.70.) at 7.15 pm; the tail will clear by 7.25 pm.

4. Advance Parties, consisting of 1 N.C.O. and 1 man per company and 1 N.C.O. each from H.Q., Q.M. Stores and the Transport, under 2/Lieut. H.S. KIRKWOOD, will parade outside Orderly Room at 8 am to-morrow. They will receive their instructions from the Adjutant on parade.

5. Strict march discipline will be enforced during the move, in accordance with the Divisional Commander's instructions, circulated round companies to-day.

6. All kits will be stacked at O. Room by 4 pm.

(sd) T. BOOTH, LIEUTENANT,
A/ADJUTANT, 6TH BN THE CONNAUGHT RANGERS.

Copy No. 1. Commanding Officer.
... 2. Second-in-Command.
... 3. O.C. "A" Coy.
... 4. O.C. "B" Coy.
... 5. O.C. "C" Coy.
... 6. O.C."D" Coy.
... 7. Medical Officer.
... 8. Quartermaster and Transport Officer.
... 9. R.S.M.
... 10. All C.S.Ms.
... 11. War Diary.
... 12. Retained.

Appendix 3

NIGHT OPERATIONS

28-7-1917.

REFERENCE STEENVOORDE TRAINING AREA MAP.

GENERAL IDEA.

The RED & BROWN LINE have been occupied by our troops.

SPECIAL IDEA.

The 47th Infantry Brigade (Divisional Reserve) is ordered to advance and seize a line with right resting on 3 roads K.16.d. 3.3. - left on farm K.16.d.8.8.

For the purpose of this exercise the battalion will be the right battalion.

1.The battalion in column of route reaches 3 roads K.28(see under 22)b.3.7., this is point R.at 9 pm.

2.At 9-15 pm the battalion divides into two columns C & A, D" & B Coys, which move by nearly parallel tracks called F & C (marked at places by men of drums) on a bearing of 304 & 280 deg.(T.B.) until the RED LINE (representing our original front line) and which is called A, this point should be reached at 9-35pm.

3.At 9-45pm the battalion will continue its advance on a bearing of ZERO (T.B.) in platoon columns at suitable intervals & distances reaching BROWN LINE at 10-15 pm, this is called "V" point

The battalion will here be deployed for attack as per usual in four waves, and will move on at 10-45 pm to BLUE LINE which is called point "G", bearing still being ZERO(T.B.).

The Intelligence Officer will be responsible for direction of right column, the O.C. "C" Coy, for the proper objective being reached.

A Subaltern detailed by the O.C."D" Coy., for direction of No. 2 Column, the O.C."D" Coy for the proper objective being reached.

The Intelligence Officer will have one Sergeant and 2 Runners attached to him.

Bn Hd Qrs will be with "C" Coy until the BROWN LINE is reached when it will be at K. 16.d.6.5. (Road)

The Map to which the above map references refer can be seen at the O.Room by Coy Comdrs.

PARADE.

Parade for this Exercise will be at 7-45pm - Dress Fighting Order.

(Sd) T.BOOTH LIEUTENANT.
ADJUTANT 6TH BN THE CONNAUGHT RANGERS.

S E C R E T. *Appendix IV.* Copy No. 12.

OPERATION ORDERS NO. 25.
BY
LIEUT-COLONEL J.D.[illegible]
COMMANDING 6TH BN THE CONNAUGHT RANGERS.

In the Field, 30th July 1917

Reference Sheet 27.
.. 28.

1. The Battalion will move to the BRANDHOEK No. 3 Area to-morrow.
Parade at 6.45 pm in H.M.O. and move off in the foll-owing order:- H.Q., "A", "B", Drums, "C", "D".
The head of the column will pass the starting-point (L.14.central) at 8 pm and the tail will clear by 8.15 pm.

2. Advance Parties, consisting of one N.C.O. and one man per company, 1 N.C.O. each from H.Q., the Q.M. Stores and the Transport, under 2/Lt. H.S. KIRKWOOD, will parade in H.M.O. outside Orderly Room at 8.30 am. They will receive their in-structions from the Adjutant on parade.

3. A. and B. Echelon of the Transport will be formed up on the farm road at L.7.a.central, reddy to move with the battalion.

4. All Officers' Kits will be stacked at the Q.M. Stores by 2 pm.
All Mess Kit, etc., will be loaded on the motor-lorry at the road junction at L.7.a.central by 5.45 pm.

5. Rations for the 1st prox. will be delivered in the new area.

(sd) T. BOOTH, LIEUTENANT,
A/ADJUTANT, 6TH BN THE CONNAUGHT RANGERS.

Copy No. 1. Commanding Officer.
.. .. 2. Second-in-command.
.. .. 3. O.C. "A" Coy.
.. .. 4. O.C. "B" Coy.
.. .. 5. O.C. "C" Coy.
.. .. 6. O.C. "D" Coy.
.. .. 7. Medical Officer.
.. .. 8. Quartermaster.
.. .. 9. Transport Officer.
.. .. 10. All C.S.Ms.
.. .. 11. R.S.M.
.. .. 12.)
.. .. 13.) War Diary.
.. .. 14. Retained.

WAR DIARY.

FOR MONTH OF AUGUST, 1917.

VOLUME 21..........

UNIT 6th Connaught Rangers

August 1917 Sheet 1.

WAR DIARY ~~or~~ ~~INTELLIGENCE~~ SUMMARY.

6th Battn, The Connaught Rangers

Confidential

Army Form C. 2118.

Instructions regarding War Diaries and Intelligence Summaries are contained in F. S. Regs., Part II. and the Staff Manual respectively. Title pages will be prepared in manuscript.

(*Erase heading not required.*)

Place	Date	Hour	Summary of Events and Information	Remarks and references to Appendices
The Line N.E. of YPRES Ref Sheets Belgium 28 N.W and N.E.	1.8.17		The battalion received an hour's notice to depart for the line at 5.0 p.m. They proceeded by train as far as Goldfish Chateau and thence marched via YPRES and the MENIN GATE to the old British reserve line on the left sector of the Corps front where it relieved the 2nd R.D.F. three companies occupying the trenches on the left of the ST JEAN – WIELTJE Road and D Coy on the right. Battalion HQ were at the VINERY (I.4.a.5.8). In this line they remained for the night Aug 1-2 and the rain poured incessantly. The trenches like all those to follow were in a terrible condition.	
	2.8.17		A stretcher bearing party of 200 men (50 from each coy) under 2nd Lt J.J. POPE was out working for the 55th Divn from 2 a.m. to 11 a.m. searching for and bringing in wounded from the area covered by the Old German front system in C.29 b & d. Their task was very arduous and under the most trying conditions and the way in which it was carried out was acknowledged in the attached letters from the G.O.Cs 16th & 55th Divns (Appendices 1 & 2). At 11 a.m. the battalion was relieved by the 15th R.I. RIFLES and moved from the 55th Divn into reserve to 15th Divn and occupied	Appendix 1. letter from G.O.C 55th Divn to G.O.C 16th Divn. Appendix 2. letter from G.O.C 16th Divn to G.O.C 47th Bde

D. D. & L., London, E.C. (A7883) Wt. W3o3/M1672 350,000 4/17 Sch. 52a Forms C/2118/14

August 1917. Sheet 2.

Instructions regarding War Diaries and Intelligence Summaries are contained in F. S. Regs., Part II, and the Staff Manual respectively. Title pages will be prepared in manuscript.

WAR DIARY ~~or~~ ~~INTELLIGENCE SUMMARY.~~

(*Erase heading not required.*)

Confidential

Army Form C. 2118.

Place	Date	Hour	Summary of Events and Information	Remarks and references to Appendices
The Line	2.8.17		the old British front system on the right sector of the Corps front. C & D Coys	
N.E. of YPRES	(cont)		were in the front line and A & B in support and Battn HQ in	
Ref Sheets			CAMBRIDGE TRENCH. Hostile shelling until this time had not been	
Belgium 28 N.W			too heavy but a great change was to come. At 8 p.m. the battalion	
& N.E			proceeded up the POTIJZE Road to the BLUE LINE – the first objective of	
			the attack of July 31 – in close support of the 6th ROYAL IRISH REGIMENT	
			whom we relieved and who moved to the front – the BLACK – line. Two	
			lines were occupied by us on either side of the road C & D being	
			in front and A & B in support about 150 yards behind. Battalion HQ	
			were situated in a German dug out at C.29.d 72.67 in CAMERON RESERVE.	
			A, B & C Coys were on the reverse slope of FREZENBERG RIDGE but D were	
			on the forward slope and in full view of the enemy. The advance	
			up the road and the actual relief took place under a heavy	
			bombardment which continued throughout the night on both lines and	
			on Battn HQ. Immediate connection was established with the R.I. RIFLES	
			on our left and next morning with the 6th R. IRISH REGT in the Black Line	

D. D. & L., London, E.C. (A7883) Wt. W803/M1672 350,000 4/17 Sch. 52a Forms/C/2118/14

August 1917 Sheet 3

Instructions regarding War Diaries and Intelligence Summaries are contained in F. S. Regs., Part II. and the Staff Manual respectively. Title pages will be prepared in manuscript.

WAR DIARY
or
~~INTELLIGENCE SUMMARY.~~
(Erase heading not required.)

Confidential.

Army Form C. 2118.

Place	Date	Hour	Summary of Events and Information	Remarks and references to Appendices
The Line N.E. of YPRES Ref Sheets Belgium 28 N.W and N.E	3.8.17		Shelling was considerable throughout the day and it was impossible to do much work on the lines which were in a terrible condition nearly all portions of trench which had been dug being under water. Casualties were heavy the Lewis gunners of A Coy being particularly unlucky. Batt'n H.Q were changed to I.6.a.16.81 in Iberia Reserve which received particular attention from the enemy's field guns and heavier calibre throughout the night. Heavy rain continued to fall as on the previous days.	
	4.8.17		Day broke under slightly improved conditions as there were occasional periods of sunshine and hostile artillery was not so active, though never negligible. B Coy and 1 platoon from each of A and D Coys were withdrawn at 8 p.m. to CAMERON SUPPORT. In the afternoon E.A. were very active, 14 planes being observed over our lines at one time. At 4 p.m. heavy shelling was reported on our front line occupied by the 6th ROYAL IRISH and D Coy prepared to reinforce but the intended attack was broken up by our barrage. During the night shelling was again heavy and the battalion had its first experience of the new mustard gas employed by the enemy the shells being cleverly mixed with whizz-bangs	

D. D. & L., London, E.C. (A7893) Wt. W5o9/M1672 350,000 4/17 Sch. 52a Forms/C/2118/14

August 1917 Sheet 4

Confidential

Army Form C. 2118.

WAR DIARY
or
~~INTELLIGENCE SUMMARY~~.
(*Erase heading not required.*)

Instructions regarding War Diaries and Intelligence Summaries are contained in F. S. Regs., Part II, and the Staff Manual respectively. Title pages will be prepared in manuscript.

Place	Date	Hour	Summary of Events and Information	Remarks and references to Appendices
The Line N.E. of YPRES Ref Sheets Belgium 28 N.W. & N.E.	5.8.17		Two E.A. flew very low over our front line and this was followed by heavy and accurate shelling at noon but casualties sustained were comparatively small. Very heavy shell fire was again experienced between 9 and 11 p.m. and during our relief by the 2nd ROYAL IRISH at midnight. The battalion proceeded to the railway line W of YPRES where the	
	6.8.17		brigade entrained being taken down in two journeys. The RANGERS were billeted in very comfortable huts in S^t. LAWRENCE'S CAMP (G. 11. c.) BRANDHOEK AREA. No 2. where they were issued with tea, rum and hot food on their arrival. (See also Appendix 3.)	Appendix 3
			Thus ended a very arduous and trying tour in which the conditions had been as adverse as could be imagined. The weather was execrable and the ground a sea of mud. 'Trench foot' was common. The men were almost continuously under fire without any opportunity of giving anything in exchange. But through all and in spite of all the spirit of the men was excellent and their behaviour could not have been better; the only grouse heard being	Letter from O.C. R.A.M.C. & O.C. 6 C.R.

D. D. & L., London, E.C. (A7883) Wt. W803/M1672 350,000 4/17 Sch. 52a Forms/C/2118/14

August 1917 Sheet 5.

WAR DIARY
or
~~INTELLIGENCE SUMMARY~~.
(Erase heading not required.)

Confidential

Army Form C. 2118.

Instructions regarding War Diaries and Intelligence Summaries are contained in F. S. Regs., Part II, and the Staff Manual respectively. Title pages will be prepared in manuscript.

Place	Date	Hour	Summary of Events and Information	Remarks and references to Appendices
	6.8.17 cont		that they were not allowed to go right through and continue the attack of July 31. Special mention perhaps should be made of the work of the runners. They were working day and night over awful country and under almost continuous fire but never was there the slightest hesitation and all messages were carried speedily. Nor should the transport be forgotten. Rations and ammunition were brought up regularly and punctually though every journey made was through shell fire of varying intensity.	
			On the 3rd 2Lt C.A. STEVENSON was wounded and admitted to hospital. 2nd Lt T.F. GILMOUR returned from leave. On the 4th 2nd Lt W.A. FARNDON (sick) and on the 5th Lt T.M.H.S. TUITE, M.C (wounded) and 2nd Lts J.P. MONAN (gassed) R.E. ATWELL and P. BROWNE (sick) were admitted to hospital.	
St LAWRENCE'S CAMP. BRANDHOEK G.11.c. Ref Sheet Belgium 28 N.W.	Aug 6.7.8.		Very little serious work was done the men being busily employed resting. Kits and equipment were cleaned and various inspections took place. On the 7th 2nd Lt S.W. O'COFFEY left for a course of wireless.	

D. D. & L., London, E.C. (A7833) Wt. W803/M1672 350,000 4/17 Sch. 52a Forms/C/2118/14

August 1917. Sheet 8.

Army Form C. 2118.

WAR DIARY
or
~~INTELLIGENCE SUMMARY.~~
(Erase heading not required.)

Confidential

Instructions regarding War Diaries and Intelligence Summaries are contained in F. S. Regs., Part II, and the Staff Manual respectively. Title pages will be prepared in manuscript.

Place	Date	Hour	Summary of Events and Information	Remarks and references to Appendices
ST. LAWRENCE'S CAMP. BRANDHOEK	9.8.17		2ND LT J.J. CONLON returned from a Coy Com's L.G. course at LE TOUQUET. LT McDONNELL and 2nd LTS J.P. HAMILTON, R.J. CAREY and J.P. CAFFERKEY joined the battalion. A pack convoy of 20 mules each from the 6th CONN RANGERS and 156 Coy R.E. carried various R.E. stores to FREZENBERG RIDGE under 2nd LT H.A. HUNT. They were out from 9 p.m to 4.30 a.m and experienced the usual shelling on the POTIJZE Road.	
	10.8.17		A party of 50 men under 2nd LT J. DRYDEN left the battalion to be attached to the R.Es. 200 men and 4 officers under LT R.E. BOWEN proceeded to the line by train and relieved the 9th R.D.F. in close support Right Subsector at about 8.30 p.m. They occupied the BLUE LINE and were formed in 2 lines in WILDE WOOD with the right resting on the YPRES-ROULERS railway. Conditions for their 2 days' tour were slightly better than on the previous occasion but still by no means good. FREZENBERG RIDGE received the usual attention from all calibres. Casualties were 1 killed and 14 wounded. The battalion supplied the same convoy as on the previous night - on this occasion under 2nd LT E.C. NORMAN.	

D. D. & L., London, E.C.
(A7883) Wt. W603/M1672 350,000 4/17 Sch. 52a Forms/C/2118/14

August 1917 Sheet 7

WAR DIARY
or
INTELLIGENCE SUMMARY.
(*Erase heading not required.*)

Confidential

Army Form C. 2118.

Instructions regarding War Diaries and Intelligence Summaries are contained in F. S. Regs., Part II. and the Staff Manual respectively. Title pages will be prepared in manuscript.

Place	Date	Hour	Summary of Events and Information	Remarks and references to Appendices
St LAWRENCE'S CAMP G. 11. C. Ref Sheet Belgium 28 N.W.	11.8.17		The remainder of the battalion still in camp went for a short practice route march from 9.30 a.m to 12 noon. 2nd Lt F.K. CUMMINS returned from a veterinary course at St OMER.	
	12.8.17		Church parades were held by Roman Catholics Church of England and Other Denominations. The R E pack convoy was out all night under 2nd Lt H.A. HUNT. The party of 200 men returned from the line being relieved by the 7th LEINSTERS.	
	13.8.17		A route march was held in the morning from 9.30 a.m to 12 noon The usual convoy was commanded by 2nd Lt J.P. HAMILTON. In the afternoon a party of 90 men and 3 officers under 2nd Lt E.C. NORMAN practised wiring under the 156th Coy R.E. 2nd Lt W.A. FARNDON was discharged from hospital and rejoined the battalion.	
	14.8.17		There was a Commanding Officer's inspection at 9.30 a.m. The R.E party paraded morning and afternoon for further instruction in wiring. 2nd Lt E. HAWORTH left on leave.	

D. D. & L., London, E.C. (A7833) Wt. W809/M1672 350,000 4/17 Sch. 52a Forms C/2118/14

August 1917. Sheet 8.

Instructions regarding War Diaries and Intelligence Summaries are contained in F. S. Regs., Part II. and the Staff Manual respectively. Title pages will be prepared in manuscript.

WAR DIARY
or
~~INTELLIGENCE SUMMARY~~.
(*Erase heading not required.*)

Confidential

Army Form C. 2118.

Place	Date	Hour	Summary of Events and Information	Remarks and references to Appendices
VLAMERTINGHE AREA No 3. Ref Sheet Belgium 28 N.W.	15.8.17		A reconnoitring officer of 5 officers and 7 runners explored tracks from YPRES to FREZENBERG RIDGE. In the evening the battalion moved to the VLAMERTINGHE AREA No 3 arriving at 11 p.m. The wiring party joined the R.E.s and moved to trenches near WILDE WOOD. 2nd LT G. E. MAGUIRE returned from leave.	
	16.8.17		At 9.45 a.m. the battalion moved up to HALF MOON TRENCH, HQ at L'ECOLE. All positions were occupied by ~~noon~~ 12.30 p.m. At 3.~~30~~55 p.m. it proceeded to close support in the BLUE LINE and occupied the same positions as from Aug 2–5 with HQ in IBERIA RESERVE as before. Shelling was considerable especially on C Coy's position. The companies were re-inforced by the wiring party of 30 men. At 9 p.m. the battalion moved up to the relief of the 2nd ROYAL IRISH who held the whole 49th brigade frontage in the front line. The HQ Coy were caught in a very heavy barrage on its way through to SQUARE FARM and suffered casualties. The companies were more fortunate in this particular but owing to the difficult conditions the guides supplied were of little use to them	

D. D. & L., London, E.C. (A7883) Wt. W789/M1672 350,000 4/17 Sch. 52a Forms/C/2118/14

August 1917 Sheet 9.

Instructions regarding War Diaries and Intelligence Summaries are contained in F. S. Regs., Part II, and the Staff Manual respectively. Title pages will be prepared in manuscript.

WAR DIARY
or
~~INTELLIGENCE~~ SUMMARY.
(Erase heading not required.)

Confidential

Army Form C. 2118.

Place	Date	Hour	Summary of Events and Information	Remarks and references to Appendices
BLACK LINE Ref Sheets Belgium 28 N.W & N.E	17.8.17 cont		in finding the way and the relief was not reported complete till 3:30 a.m. The line finally occupied ran from in front of FROST HOUSE through LOW FARM & a ~~pt~~ point 100 yards W. of BECK HOUSE and so to the valley of the STEENBEEK. It was held from right to left by A Coy, 1 Platoon B Coy, C & D Coys. B Coy (less 1 Platoon) remained in support in the BLUE LINE. On arrival there were found to be several wounded in LOW FARM and some twenty in SQUARE FARM. The work of evacuating these was immediately begun & was completed by 10 a.m. Recognition is due to the part the stretcher bearers played in this work as the carry from the two points to BAVARIA HOUSE was in full view of the enemy till the FREZENBERG RIDGE, which received its usual attention from all calibres, was crossed. Wounded, chiefly of the R. INNIS. FUS. who had attacked on the previous morning, were being continuously brought in from 'No Man's Land' and these also were taken back immediately after being treated by the Doctor	

August 1917. Sheet 10.

WAR DIARY
or
~~INTELLIGENCE SUMMARY.~~
(Erase heading not required.)

Confidential.

Army Form C. 2118.

Instructions regarding War Diaries and Intelligence Summaries are contained in F. S. Regs., Part II. and the Staff Manual respectively. Title pages will be prepared in manuscript.

Place	Date	Hour	Summary of Events and Information	Remarks and references to Appendices
17.8	17.8.17 (cont)		SQUARE FARM was bombarded throughout the day receiving several direct hits which however had no effect. At 9 p.m a patrol went out to reconnoitre BECK HOUSE and found it to be occupied by the enemy with machine guns. At the same time another patrol occupied the house at D.25.a.75.30. At 10 p.m the 10/11 H.L.I arrived to relieve the RANGERS. The move was carried out with much greater success than on the previous night and by 3 a.m the battalion marched into its billets in VLAMERTINGHE No3 AREA. During the two days tour the transport carried out its work with the same success as on the previous occasions and in particular it might be noted that the water cart was stationed throughout the tour at a point on the POTIJZE Road 50 yards E. of BAVARIA HOUSE. The night Aug 17-18 marked the end of the active part played by the battalion in the third battle of YPRES. Total casualties during the whole period July 31 - Aug 18 were 21 men killed and 9 missing, 4 officers and 205 other ranks wounded. (Appendix 4). (Appendix 5).	Appendix 4 Summary of Casualties
			2nd Lt F.H.S SEARIGHT rejoined the battalion from the divisional Intelligence Company.	
			2nd Lt J.J. CONLON and R.J. CAREY were admitted to hospital, wounded.	Appendix 5. Table of moves

August 1917 Sheet 11

Instructions regarding War Diaries and Intelligence Summaries are contained in F. S. Regs., Part II, and the Staff Manual respectively. Title pages will be prepared in manuscript.

WAR DIARY
or
~~INTELLIGENCE SUMMARY~~.
(*Erase heading not required.*)

Confidential

Army Form C. 2118.

Place	Date	Hour	Summary of Events and Information	Remarks and references to Appendices
VLAMERTINGHE No 3 AREA	18·8·17		The battalion remained in billets resting. 2nd Lt F.K. CUMMINS proceeded on leave. 2nd Lt J.P. HAMILTON was admitted to hospital	
WATOU Ref Sheet Belgium 28 N.W. & 27	19·8·17		The battalion moved to the WATOU B. AREA leaving billets at 6 a.m proceeding by train to POPERINGHE and arriving in camp at L.8.c.3.5 at 10 a.m. 2 Lt F.T. CHAMIER was admitted to hospital	
STEENVORDE	20·8·17		The battalion paraded in H.M.O at 2·30 p.m and marched to camp in the STEENVORDE Area arriving at 5·30 p.m. Lt T.M.H.S. TUITE was discharged from hospital and rejoined the battalion.	
STEENVORDE	21·8·17		A special performance was given by the PIERROTS of the 25th Division to the RANGERS at 3·15 p.m and was highly appreciated by those who attended about 300 in all. 2nd Lt J.J. POPE returned from leave.	
	22·8·17		The battalion paraded at 3·15 p.m and marched to CAESTRE Station where it entrained at 6 P.M. arriving at BAPAUME at 2 a.m	
	23·8·17		Tea was issued to the men at the Y.M.C.A and they then marched to CARLTON HILL CAMP at GOMIECOURT where there was more tea. CAPT T.H. CROFT and Lt T. HUGHES returned to the battn from the Reinforcement Depot	

August 1917 Sheet 72 Confidential

Army Form C. 2118.

WAR DIARY
or
INTELLIGENCE SUMMARY.
(Erase heading not required.)

Instructions regarding War Diaries and Intelligence Summaries are contained in F. S. Regs., Part II. and the Staff Manual respectively. Title pages will be prepared in manuscript.

Place	Date	Hour	Summary of Events and Information	Remarks and references to Appendices
GOMIECOURT Ref Sheet France 51C.	24-8-17		A conference of all officers of the 47th Bde was held at the CHATEAU, GOMIECOURT at 5 p.m. and was addressed by MAJ GEN W.B. HICKIE, C.M.G. on past & future events.	
ERVILLERS	25-8-17		The battalion paraded at 11 a.m. and moved to camp at Ervillers taking over from the 8th LEICESTERS. 2/LT E. HAWORTH returned from leave 2 LTS F.S. DRYDEN and F.G. WOODS went on leave	
	26-8-17		There were Church Parades for all denominations in the morning	
The Line Ref Sheet BULLECOURT 51B S.W.4			In the evening the 16th Division relieved the 21st Division in the right sector of the 6th Army Corps front. On completion the line was occupied in the following manner. The 47th Bde held the ~~left~~ right sub sector with the 6th R. IRISH REGT (right) and 6th CONN RANGERS (left) in the front line and the 1ST MUNSTERS in support and the 7th LEINSTERS in reserve. The RANGERS took over from the EAST YORKSHIRES and held the line from U.14.c.50.35 to U.7.d.0.5, the front line being held from right to left by A, B & D Coys with C Coy in support in LINCOLN TRENCH. Battalion HQ were situated at T.B.24.d.8.3.	
			2 LT F.H.S. SEARIGHT was admitted to hospital.	

D. D. & L., London, E.C. (A7883) Wt. W803/M1672 350,000 4/17 Sch. 52a Forms/C/2118/14

August 1917. Sheet 13. Confidential Army Form C. 2118.

WAR DIARY
or
INTELLIGENCE SUMMARY.
(Erase heading not required.)

Instructions regarding War Diaries and Intelligence Summaries are contained in F. S. Regs., Part II. and the Staff Manual respectively. Title pages will be prepared in manuscript.

Place	Date	Hour	Summary of Events and Information	Remarks and references to Appendices
The Line Ref Sheet. BULLECOURT 57B S.W.4	27.8.17		The day in the line was quiet and was spent largely in improving the trenches. At night a patrol went out under 2nd Lt J.M. FORBES	
	28.8.17		2/Lt J.J. CONLON was discharged from hospital & returned to the battalion. In the evening two patrols were out - one of 1 cpl & 1 private and one under 2nd Lt H.S. KIRKWOOD with 3 other ranks. A good deal of information concerning the enemy's trenches and his method of holding the front line was obtained. A party of 20 men worked under the R.Es under 2nd Lt R.H. FRENCH from 1.45 p.m to 12 midnight	
	~~29.8.17~~ 29.8.17		The same R.E. party went out on this and the following days under 2nd Lt J.J. CONLON and were employed chiefly in building dug-outs. 2nd Lt H.S. KIRKWOOD and 2 other ranks were out on patrol in the evening.	
	30.8.17		Our T.M.Bs and guns of all calibres indulged in a 'strafe' from 3 to 4 p.m. There was only slight retaliation from the enemy's medium T.M.Bs. 2nd Lt P.L. PALMER and 3 other ranks were out on patrol. C Coy relieved A Coy in BEAUMAN'S TRENCH. Lt J.P. PRAEGER went on leave and 2/Lt S.W. O'COFFEY returned from a wireless course	
	31.8.17		A quiet day.	

J. D. Mathey. Lt. Col
Comdg 6th Connaught Rangers

(A7883) Wt. W893/M1672 350,000 4/17 D. D. & L., London, E.C. Sch. 52a Forms/C/2118/14

Appendix 2.

G.O.C.

47th INFANTRY BRIGADE.

I send a copy of a letter I received this morning from the Division Commander 55th Division.

I need not say how pleased I am that the services of our Gallant CONNAUGHTS have been so well appreciated.

I am sending the original letter home for the 16th Divisional Book.

(sd) W.B. HICKIE. MAJOR GENERAL.

August, 6th 17.

Appendix 1a.

H.Q. 55th Division.

6-8-17

Dear Hickie,

We are very much indebted to you for the brave and devoted work of 150 men of the 6th CONNAUGHT RANGERS who were lent to us as stretcher bearers.

They had about the hardest task that any stretcher bearers have had in this war - a very long carry under severe fire over ground which was difficult beyond description. From all I hear they performed their task most gallantly - not I am afraid without severe casualties to themselves.

I should be very grateful if you could convey the thanks of all ranks of the 55th Division to their C.O. and to the men themselves, and tell them how much their services are appreciated.

Yours Sincerely,

(sd) H.S. JEUDWINE. MAJOR GENERAL.

Appendix 3.

O.C.,
6th BATTALION THE CONNAUGHT RANGERS.

5th August.1917.

The assistance rendered by men of your Battalion to the R.A.M.C. in bringing back wounded during the recent fighting is very much appreciated, and I thank you very much for their invaluable services.

Both Officers and men of the R.A.M.C. speak very highly of them for they worked splendidly and showed great self sacrifice and devotion to duty.

(sd) H. THURSTON COLONEL.
R. A. M. C.

August 1917.

Instructions regarding War Diaries and Intelligence Summaries are contained in F. S. Regs., Part II, and the Staff Manual respectively. Title pages will be prepared in manuscript.

Appendix 4. **WAR DIARY** . Summary of Casualties Army Form C. 2118.

or

~~INTELLIGENCE SUMMARY~~. 3rd Battle of YPRES

(*Erase heading not required.*)

Place	Date	Hour	Offrs. Wounded	Other Ranks Killed	Wounded	Missing	Total	Summary of Events and Information	Remarks and references to Appendices
	2.8.17		[illegible]	2	28	–	30		
	3.8.17		1	11	58	2	71		
	4.8.17		–	–	61	–	61		
	5.8.17		2	1	21	–	22	Missing corrected to date 30/8/17.	
	10.8.17		–	–	15	–	15		
	11.8.17		–	1	3	–	4		
	12.8.17		–	–	2	–	2		
	16.8.17		–	6	27	–	33		
	17.8.17		1	–	11	–	11		
	TOTAL		4	21	226	2	249		

D. D. & L., London, E.C. (A7883) Wt. W803/M1672 350,000 4/17 Sch. 52a Forms/C/2118/14

Appendix 5.

Table of moves of 47th INF.BDE.

29-7-17. 100men composed of 6th Royal Irish Regt., 7th Leinster Regt.and 1st Rl.Munster Fusrs.sent to 156th Field Coy. R.E.for work during course of operations.

30-7-17. 47th Inf.Bde.from WATOU (C) Area to BRANDHOEK No.3 Area.

31-7-17. 4 a.m.700 1st Rl.Munster Fusrs.and 500 7th Leinster Regt. under Lt.Col.Buckley,D.S.O.from POPERINGHE to GOLDFISH CHATEAU by train. Work on buried cable under XIX Corps Signals.

1-8-17. 1st Rl.Munster Fusrs.from GOLDFISH CHATEAU,6th CONNAUGHT RANGERS from BRANDHOEK No.3 Area moved into support and came under orders of 55th Divn.7th Leinster Regt.from GOLDFISH CHATEAU and 6th Royal Irish Regt.from BRANDHOEK No.3 moved into support of,and came under orders of 15th Divn.

2-8-17. 4 a.m.6th Royal Irish Regt.moved into close support of, and came under orders of 45th Inf.Bde. 5 a.m.Bde.H.Q. 47th Inf.Bde.to MILL COTT. 12 noon 7th Leinster Regt. moved to close support of,and came under orders of 44th Inf.Bde. 6th Connaught Rangers and 1st Rl.Munster Fusrs. from 55th Divn.into reserve to 15th Division and came under orders of 47th Inf.Bde.
At night 6th Royal Irish Regt.to front line in relief of 45th and 46th Inf.Bdes. 6th Connaught Rangers to close support of 6th Royal Irish Regt. 47th Inf.Bde.took over command left sector under 15th Divn.with 1st Rl.Munster Fusrs. in Cambridge Road reserve to 15th Divn.

3-8-17. At night 7th Leinster Regt.to front line in relief of 44th Inf.Bde. 1st Rl.Munster Fusrs.to close support of 7th Leinster Regt.
Divisional front then came under 47th Inf.Bde.

4-8-17. 10 a.m. Command passed from 15th to 16th Division.

5-8-17. At night 47th Inf.Bde. relieved by 48th Inf.Bde.on right and 49th Inf.Bde.on left and moved to BRANDHOEK No.2 Area.

10-8-17. Afternoon 50 6th Connaught Rangers sent to 157th Fd.Coy. R.E.for work during remainder of operations.
Afternoon 200 6th Connaught Rangers moved up into close support Right Subsector and came under orders of 48th Inf.Bde.

11-8-17. At night 1st Rl. Munster Fusrs. moved up and took over front line in Right Subsection and came under orders of 48th Inf.Bde.
At night 6th Royal Irish Regt.moved up and took over front line in Left Subsector and came under orders of 49th Inf.Bde.

Appendix 5. cont

12-8-17. 47th Inf.Bde.H.Q.to MILL COTT.and took over command of Left Subsector,with 1Battn.49th Inf.Bde.in close support to 6th Royal Irish Regt. 4p.m.18 O Rs from 6th Connaught Rangers to 113th Fd.Amb.as stretcher bearers . At night 200 7th Leinster Regt.relieved 200 6th Connaught Rangers in support. Right Subsector 6th Connaught Rangers returned to BRANDHOEK No.2 Area.

14-8-17. Night,200 7th Leinsters Regt.from support Right Subsector rejoined their Battn.in BRANDHOEK No.2 Area. 6th Royal Irish Regt.on relief by 2 Battns.49th Inf.Bde. from front line Left Subsector to VLAMERTINGHE No.3 arriving morning of 15th. 1st Rl.Munster Fusrs.from front line Right Subsector after relief by 2 Battns . 47th Inf.Bde.to ECOLE in reserve to 48yh Inf.Bde.

15-8-17 . 10.30 a.m. 47th Inf.Bde.handed over command of Left Sector to 49th Inf.Bde.and moved to VLAMERTINGHE No.3 Area. 9 p.m.47th T.M.Battery,7th Leinster Regt.and 6th Connaught Rangers moved from BRANDHOEK No.2 Area to VLAMERTINGHE No.3 Area arriving about 11 p.m. On arrival 6th Connaught Rangers replaced 6th Royal Irish Regt.in reserve to 49th Inf.Bde.and came under orders of 49th Inf.Bde. 90 6th Connaught Rangers and 70 7th Leinster Regt. joined R.E.and moved to trenches near WILDE WOOD. At night Bde.Major,47th Inf.Bde.went to 49th Inf.Bde. At night 1st Rl.Munster Fusrs.moved from ECOLE into Old German trenchesin Right Subsector.

16-8-17. 9.45 a.m.6th Connaught Rangers moved up to HALF MOON TRENCHES East of BAVARIA HOUSE. At night to front line in relief of 2 Battns 49th Inf. Bde.,all under orders of 49th Inf.Bde. 11.40 a.m.7th Leinster Regt.moved up to the line and came under orders of the 48th Inf.Bde. 6.45p.m.6th Royal Irish Regt.moved up to close support of 6th Connaught Rangers and came under orders of 49th Inf.Bde. 90 6th Connaught Rangers and 90 7th Leinster Regt.under R.E.moved to rejoin their units.in the line. At night 7th Leinster Regt to BLACK LINE Right Subsector. 1st Rl.Munster Fusrs.to close support of 7th Leinster Regt.

17-8-17. Night,All battalions to VLAMERTINGHE No.3 Area when they again came under orders of the 47th Inf.Bde.

19-8-17. 47th Inf.Bde.from VLANERTINGHE No.3 Area to WATOU (B). Area.

LB 22E

WAR DIARY.

FOR MONTH OF ~~AUGUST~~ September, 1917.

VOLUME 22

UNIT 6th Connaught Rangers.

Vol 21

September 1917 Sheet 1

6th Connaught Rangers

Confidential

Army Form C. 2118.

WAR DIARY
or
INTELLIGENCE SUMMARY.
(Erase heading not required.)

Instructions regarding War Diaries and Intelligence Summaries are contained in F. S. Regs., Part II. and the Staff Manual respectively. Title pages will be prepared in manuscript.

Place	Date	Hour	Summary of Events and Information	Remarks and references to Appendices
Supp The Line	1.9.17		The first two days of the month were quiet as before and on the night Sept 2-3 there was a readjustment of	
Ref Sheet BULLECOURT 51B S.W.4			the Divisional front and the battalion was relieved in the front line and proceeded to the reserve camp at ERVILLERS (B.13.b) (see Appendix 1). Hot tea was served on arrival in camp.	Appendix 1 Operation Order 2.9.17
ERVILLERS	3.9.17		Resting. Anniversary of 'GUILLEMONT'. See appendix 2.	Appendix 2 Letter of Brigadier 2.9.17
Ref Sheet France 57C.N.W.	4.9.17		Training was carried out by companies. Officers and N.C.Os. attended instruction in rapid wiring by the C.O who expounded a French method.	
			On the 1st inst 2/LTS J.A.V.KENT, U.MOORE, B.S.F.PICKARD and C.J.WAITES and on the 2nd A.F.ELLIOTT joined the battalion.	
	5.9.17		Baths parades and company training. The 16th Division method of rapid wiring was practised by officers and N.C.Os under CAPT. CROFTON. 2ND LTS H.McCULLOUGH and T.S.JENNINGS joined the battalion. 2ND LTS F.C.WOODS and J.S.DRYDEN returned from leave and 2ND LTS S.W.O'COFFEY and J.J.CONLON left on leave.	

September 1917. Sheet 2. Confidential

Army Form C. 2118.

WAR DIARY
or
INTELLIGENCE SUMMARY.
(*Erase heading not required.*)

Instructions regarding War Diaries and Intelligence Summaries are contained in F. S. Regs., Part II. and the Staff Manual respectively. Title pages will be prepared in manuscript.

Place	Date	Hour	Summary of Events and Information	Remarks and references to Appendices
ERVILLERS Ref Sheet France 57c N.W.	6.9.17		Company training. A football match in the evening against the 9th R.D.F. resulted in a win 4-0. 2nd Lt G.E. MAGUIRE left on a transport course.	
	7-8.9.17		Company training	
	9.9.17		Church parades for all denominations.	
	10.9.17		Companies practised a new formation in the attack. In the afternoon there was a cross-country race in which all ranks (and all costumes) took part. D Coy were the winners. Lt I.P. PRAEGER returned from ~~left on~~ and 2nd Lt W.F. FARNDON left on leave.	
	11.9.17		The battalion undertook a small field operation in the morning. A and B Coys attacked over ground in the area B.14.c,d & b. C and D Coys were the opposition and formed strong points and other nuisances and launched a counter attack - a very spectacular display. The battalion was addressed by the C.O. at the finish and the chief faults pointed out. A lecture on pigeons as message carriers and an exhibition of flying was attended by all officers	Appendix 3. 'Practice Attack'

D. D. & L., London, E.C. (A7883) Wt. W507/M1672 350,000 4/17 Sch. 52a Forms/C/2118/14

September 1917. Sheet 3.

Confidential

Army Form C. 2118.

WAR DIARY
or
INTELLIGENCE SUMMARY.
(Erase heading not required.)

Instructions regarding War Diaries and Intelligence Summaries are contained in F. S. Regs., Part II. and the Staff Manual respectively. Title pages will be prepared in manuscript.

Place	Date	Hour	Summary of Events and Information	Remarks and references to Appendices
ERVILLERS Ref Sheet. 57C N.W.	11.9.17 (Cont)		N.C.Os, signallers and observers. A football match against the 6th R IRISH REGT was won by us 2-1. 2ND LT D.D. BECKETT returned from a course	
	12.9.17		The companies paraded for baths in the morning. There was a rapid wiring competition which was won by D Coy, who excelled in method and silence, though B Coy's time was a trifle less. At 11am there was a conference of Intelligence Officers at which much was displayed.	
	13.9.17		An attack scheme on the same lines as that of the 11th inst was carried out in which parts played by the companies were reversed. A football match between the officers of the RANGERS and the ROYAL IRISH REGT was won by us 4-1.	
	14.9.17		Company training and inspections. The 9th R.D.F were defeated in a football match 6-0.	
	15.9.17		The morning was spent in cleaning up Camp and general preparations for the evacuation of the Camp. In the evening, after dusk, the Bn relieved the 7th Bn. LEINSTERS	

D. D. & L., London, E.C. (A7883) Wt. W803/M672 350,000 4/17 Sch. 52a. Forms/C/2118/14

September 1917 Sheet 4

Confidential

Army Form C. 2118.

Instructions regarding War Diaries and Intelligence Summaries are contained in F. S. Regs., Part II. and the Staff Manual respectively. Title pages will be prepared in manuscript.

WAR DIARY
or
INTELLIGENCE SUMMARY.

(Erase heading not required.)

Place	Date	Hour	Summary of Events and Information	Remarks and references to Appendices
			Regt in Bde Support and 6th Royal Irish Regt relieved 1st R. M. F. in the front line. On completion of relief the Batn was disposed as follows: 'A' Coy and 2 platoons of 'D' Coy were in the extreme right of RAILWAY RESERVE 'B' & 'C' Coys + 2 platoons of 'D' Coy were on the left of RAILWAY RESERVE. Headquarters [illegible] in RAILWAY RESERVE. Lt R.E. BOWEN and 2Lt [illegible] BECKETT went on leave.	
	16-9-17		The day was spent in supplying working parties for the front and support lines. 2Lt S.W. O'COFFEY returned from leave	
	17-9-17		The usual working parties were supplied. In the evening the two platoons of 'D' Coy on the right of RAILWAY RESERVE moved to [illegible] SUPPORT.	
	18-9-17		The usual working parties were supplied.	
	19-9-17		Working parties as usual. In the evening Lt Col R.C. FEILDING D.S.O. arrived at the Transport Lines where he spent the night.	
	20-9-17		Continuing working parties. In the morning Lt Col R.C. FEILDING D.S.O. joined the Battn in the line and took over command. Lt Col J.R. MATHER and Lt G.R. BARROW returned to the Transport Lines, and after dining at the Corps Club proceeded on leave to the U.K.	

D. D. & L., London, E.C.
(A7883) Wt. W801/M1672 350,000 4/17 Sch. 52a Forms/C/2118/14

September 1917 Sheet 5   Confidential   Army Form C. 2118.

Instructions regarding War Diaries and Intelligence Summaries are contained in F. S. Regs., Part II. and the Staff Manual respectively. Title pages will be prepared in manuscript.

WAR DIARY
or
INTELLIGENCE SUMMARY.
(Erase heading not required.)

Place	Date	Hour	Summary of Events and Information	Remarks and references to Appendices
	4-9-17		Nothing but working parties.	
	22-9-17		During the night a Task Attack was practised. The Battn stood to in most excellent time.	
	23-9-17		The Battn relieved 6th Royal Irish Regt in the Front Line, the latter on being relieved taking up the position we had just vacated. On completion of relief the Battn was disposed as follows. 'A' Coy right of Front Line. 'C' Coy centre of Front Line 'B' Coy left of Front Line 'D' Coy was in support in STRAY SUPPORT. Battn H.Q. was in RAILWAY RESERVE. The relief was carried out successfully without casualties. 2Lt E.A.W. SMITH proceeded on leave. The 7th R.I Rifles 48th Bde were on our left, the W. Yorks, 62nd Div on our right	
	24-9-17		Situation normal. Casualties nil. 2Lt A.F. ELLIOT proceeded to join R.F.C.	
	25-9-17		The day passed quietly. 1 Cpl HARRINGTON 'A' Coy was wounded in the arm by a piece of shrapnel. Capt E.C. HARMAN proceeded on leave.	
	26-9-17		There was a very considerable increase in the ~~[illegible]~~ hostile artillery activity. This resulted in 3 casualties, none of which were serious. 2Lt D.D. BECKETT returned off leave. The following officers proceeded on courses. 2Lt J.A.V. KENT, 2Lt C.S.F. RICHARDSON 2Lt I.S. JENNINGS	

D. D. & L., London, E.C.
(A7883) Wt. W809/M1672 350,000 4/17 Sch. 52a Forms C/2118/14

September 1917 Sheet 6 — Confidential.

Army Form C. 2118.

WAR DIARY
or
INTELLIGENCE SUMMARY.
(Erase heading not required.)

Instructions regarding War Diaries and Intelligence Summaries are contained in F. S. Regs., Part II. and the Staff Manual respectively. Title pages will be prepared in manuscript.

Place	Date	Hour	Summary of Events and Information	Remarks and references to Appendices
	27-9-17		At [illegible] am the [illegible] line was bombarded by our artillery and T.M.s. [illegible] During the course of this bombardment 2/Lt [illegible] was wounded in the eye by a piece of rifle grenade. Capt [illegible] proceeded on leave to the U.K. 2/Lt D.H. WICKHAM who had hitherto been in the transport lines as [illegible] took over the duties of Intelligence Officer.	
	28-9-17		The day passed quietly, nothing of importance occurring.	
	29-9-17		Lt E.K. CUMMINS executed a most interesting patrol, the report of which is [illegible] written in the Book of Patrols of the 6th Connaught Rangers. Later in the day he [illegible] a [illegible] together 2/Lt A.H.E. RUSSEL. The day passed as quietly as usual. In the afternoon Capt. R.T. RUSSELL and 2/Lt H.R. MOORE reported for duty and were posted as under. Capt RUSSELL Batt L.G.O., [illegible] to "C" Coy. Capt R.E. BOWEN returned from leave and reassumed command of "D" Coy. 2/Lt E.T. [illegible] rejoined from hospital [illegible] remained at the transport lines. 2/Lt A.E. FLYNN and 2/Lt W.A. FARNDON rejoined their companies. At about 9 p.m. an enemy aeroplane dropped two bombs in the neighbourhood of Batt. H.Q. but did no damage.	

D. D. & L., London, E.C. (A7853) Wt. W803/M1672 350,000 4/17 Sch. 52a Forms C/2118/14

September 1917 Sheet 7

Confidential.

Army Form C. 2118.

WAR DIARY
or
INTELLIGENCE SUMMARY.
(Erase heading not required.)

Instructions regarding War Diaries and Intelligence Summaries are contained in F. S. Regs., Part II. and the Staff Manual respectively. Title pages will be prepared in manuscript.

Place	Date	Hour	Summary of Events and Information	Remarks and references to Appendices
	30-9-17		The morning passed peacefully. During the afternoon Capt C A BRETT and 2Lt F T CHAMIER reported to Orderly Room for duty. The former reassumed command of "A" Coy; the latter appeared greatly refreshed after his stay in DIEPPE and will no doubt be able to carry out his military duties with renewed energy and vigour. At about 6 45 p m an enemy aeroplane again dropped bombs in the neighbourhood of Battn H.Q., thereby creating considerable alarm and despondency. Towards the end of dinner, however, the situation became once more pacific.	

[illegible] Lt Col.
Comdg 1/Camb Regt

D. D. & L., London, E.C. (A7883) Wt. W803/M1672 350,000 4/17 Sch. 52a Forms/C2118/14

23E

WAR DIARY

FOR MONTH OF OCTOBER, 1917.

UNIT 6th Connaught Rangers.

VOLUME NUMBER 23

October 1917 Sheet 7. 6th The Connaught Rangers Confidential

Army Form C. 2118.

WAR DIARY

~~or~~

~~INTELLIGENCE SUMMARY.~~

(Erase heading not required.)

Instructions regarding War Diaries and Intelligence Summaries are contained in F. S. Regs., Part II, and the Staff Manual respectively. Title pages will be prepared in manuscript.

Place	Date	Hour	Summary of Events and Information	Remarks and references to Appendices
Front Line	1.10.17		The 6th CONNAUGHT RANGERS in front line and the 6th R. IRISH REGT in support	
Ref Map.			were relieved by the 7th LEINSTER REGT and the 1st R. MUNSTER FUSILIERS respectively	
BULLECOURT			The 6th C.R. proceeded to INNISKILLING CAMP, ERVILLERS Lt T. HUGHES proceeded on	
57B S.W.4			leave.	
ERVILLERS	2.10.17		The battalion moved to DYSART CAMP (B.14.C.5.1.) 2nd Lt G.D. BARRON	
Ref Sheet			returned from leave	
57C N.W.	3.10.17		Baths parades occupied the whole day. At 6pm Major General W.B. HICKIE	
			C.B. presented the Military Medals earned at YPRES.	
	4.10.17		Company training commenced. In the afternoon the rifles of the battalion	
			were inspected by the Brigade Armourer Sergeant. Two inter-company	
			football matches were played. Much improvement was done to the camp during the ensuing period	
	5-6.10.17		Company training and football matches were the order of the day	
	7.10.17		There were Church parades in ERVILLERS for all denominations.	
	8-9.10.17		Company training and football games. The following officers went on	
			leave. On the 4th Lts H.A. HUNT, P.L. PALMER, and H.E. FLINN; on the 5th	
			Capt T.A. DILLON on the 8th Lts T. BOOTH and D.H. WICKHAM. The following returned	

D. D. & L., London, E.C. (A7883) Wt. W50?/M1672 350,000 4/17 Sch. 52a Forms/C/2118/14

October
~~September~~ 1917

Sheet 2.

6th Connaught Rangers

WAR DIARY

or

~~INTELLIGENCE SUMMARY.~~

(Erase heading not required.)

Confidential

Army Form C. 2118.

Instructions regarding War Diaries and Intelligence Summaries are contained in F. S. Regs., Part II. and the Staff Manual respectively. Title pages will be prepared in manuscript.

Place	Date	Hour	Summary of Events and Information	Remarks and references to Appendices
ERVILLERS			from leave:- on the 5th 2/Lt E.A.W. SMITH, on the 8th CAPT E.C. NORMAN on the 9th LT. M.H.S. TUITE	
Ref Sheet. 57c N.W			On the 8th Lt S.W. O'COFFEY returned from Brigade where he had been acting as signalling officer.	
	10-10-17		A practice attack in the morning was interfered with by rain.	
			2/Lt H.S. KIRKWOOD went on leave. 2/Lt D.D. BECKETT left the battalion to join the 47th Trench Mortar Battery.	
	11-10-17		A practice attack took place in the area occupied by the camp. Two companies advanced behind a barrage 1 coy mopped up and the remainder of the battalion including the snipers formed the opposition. Booby traps were formed and a well conceived counter attack was launched.	
	12-13.		Company training was proceeded with. 2/Lts J.A.V. KENT and B.S.F. PICKARD returned from a course on the 12th.	
	14		There were Church Parades for all denominations after which the final of intercompany football tournament was played. In the afternoon a boxing and sports programme was carried out.	
	15.		Company training. In the afternoon the battalion football team beat	

D. D. & L., London, E.C. (A7853) Wt. W593/M1672 350,000 4/17 Sch. 52a Forms/C/2118/14

October 1917 Sheet 3

Instructions regarding War Diaries and Intelligence Summaries are contained in F. S. Regs., Part II, and the Staff Manual respectively. Title pages will be prepared in manuscript.

WAR DIARY
or
~~INTELLIGENCE SUMMARY.~~
(Erase heading not required.)

Army Form C. 2118.

Confidential

Place	Date	Hour	Summary of Events and Information	Remarks and references to Appendices
ERVILLERS Ref			the 6th R. IRISH REGT (4-1) in the first match of the Brigade League 2nd Lt	
Sheet 57c N.W.			J.P. CAFFERKEY was admitted to hospital 2nd Lt J.E. BARRY joined the battalion	
			from the 7th R.I. RIFLES (disbanded)	
	16·10·17		Baths parades and inspections were the order of the day Lts H.A. HUNT,	Appendix 1
			P.L. PALMER and 2/Lt HEFLINN returned from leave	Operation
The Line	17·10·17		The battalion relieved the 7th LEINSTER REGT in brigade support (Appendix 1)	Orders No 34
Ref Sheet	18·10·17		The 47th Infy Bde front was reorganised into two subsections as a result of which	Appendix 2
BULLECOURT			the 6th CR held a two company frontage from QUEENS LANE to PELICAN AVENUE (Appendix 2)	Operation
51B S.W. 4			When the relief was complete the battalion had the 6th R. IRISH REGT on its left and	Orders No 35
			the 2nd SUFFOLK REGT 76th Bde 3rd Divn on its right. On the 17th CAPT T.A. DILLON returned from leave	Appendix 3
	19-20		Normal days in the trenches Lts T. BOOTH and D.H. WICKHAM returned from leave	O.O. No 36.
	21		C & D Coys relieved B & A Coys in the front line (Appendix 3).	
	22		A quiet day. Lt G. HAWORTH was discharged from hospital and rejoined the	
			battalion Lt F.T. CHAMIER went on leave ~~2/Lt H.S. KIRKWOOD returned from leave~~	
	23.		A quiet day	
	24.		A heavy artillery bombardment on the enemy's trenches and [illegible] was	

D. D. & L., London, E.C. (A7883) Wt. W803/M1672 350,000 4/17 Sch. 52a Forms/C/2118/14

October 1917 Sheet 4.

Instructions regarding War Diaries and Intelligence Summaries are contained in F. S. Regs., Part II. and the Staff Manual respectively. Title pages will be prepared in manuscript.

WAR DIARY
~~or~~
~~INTELLIGENCE SUMMARY.~~
(*Erase heading not required.*)

Confidential

Army Form C. 2118.

Place	Date	Hour	Summary of Events and Information	Remarks and references to Appendices
The Line. Ref			carried out during the day There was little retaliation from his side. 2nd Lt O.T. McWEENEY	
Sheet 57c S.W.4			joined the battalion	Appendix 4
BULLECOURT	25th		A & B Coys relieved D & C Coys in the front line (Appendix 4) Lt J.P. PRAEGER was	O.O. No 37
			admitted to hospital.	
	26th		At 1.5 p.m. and 3 a.m. on the night Oct 26/27 our stokes mortars sent over gas	
			shells on the enemy front line. Artillery and M. Guns cooperated. Retaliation was	
			slight. 2/Lt J.S. JENNINGS returned from a platoon commander's course. 2nd Lt F.C. WOODS on patrol found the enemy holding his line strongly	
	27th		A normal day. Lt R.H. FRENCH went on leave. Lt F.R. CUMMINS on patrol entered the ~~German~~ trenches & was challenged but the patrol returned without casualties	
	28th		Another quiet day. 2/Lt McWEENEY took out a patrol & returned with a dead Hun killed on the previous night	
	29th		C & D Coys relieved A & B Coys in the front line (Appendix 5). At 4.45 p.m. the 49th Bde	Appendix 5
			carried out a successful raid. Our heavies field guns and Machine guns cooperated	O.O. No 38
			in the barrage. There was some retaliation on the enemy's part.	
	30th		A quiet day. Lt J.P. PRAEGER was discharged from hospital & rejoined the battalion.	
	31st		~~From 11 till ... the enemy shelled the battery positions on Croix Road for about an hour~~	
			~~intentionally or otherwise many of these fell near Headquarters.~~ Lt J.H. McDONNELL	
			went on leave.	

[illegible] Lt Col
Comdg 1/ Comdt

D. D. & L., London, E.C. (A7883) Wt. W5o3/M1672 350,000 4/17 Sch. 52a Forms/C/2118/14

Appendix 1

No.34.

OPERATION ORDERS
BY
LIEUT COLONEL R.C FEILDING D.S.O.
COMMANDING 6TH BN THE CONNAUGHT RANGERS

17th SEPT.1917.

1. The Battalion will relieve 7TH LEINSTER REGT in the BRIGADE SUPPORT today 17th Inst.

2. "A" Coy will relieve "C" Coy and 2 platoons "D" Coy LEINSTER REGT, in RAILWAY RESERVE (South)
"B" and "D" Coy's & "C" less 2 platoons will relieve "A" and "B" Coy's and 2 Platoons "D" Coy LEINSTER REGT, in RAILWAY RESERVE. (North)
2 Platoons "C" Coy, together with "A" (less 2 platoons) 6th RL. IRISH REGT, will relieve a company of the 1st RL. MUNSTER FUSILIERS in STRAY SUPPORT.

3. Coy's will move off by platoons at 5 mins interval in the following order "C" "A" "B" "D" Coy's, the leading platoon of "C" Coy not to cross the ST. LEGER -VRAUCOURT ROAD before 6-45 pm.

4. Advance parties consisting of 1 Officer per coy and 1 N.C.O. per platoon will report to H.Qrs. LEINSTER REGT at 2-30 pm. LIEUT S.E. O'COFFEY and 1 N.C.O. will take over for Hd Quarters.

5. Trench Store receipts, which must be carefully checked will be forwarded to Bn Hd Qrs by 10 am 18th Inst.

6. Completion of relief will be reported to Bn Hd Qrs by wire Code word will be Coy Commanders name & strength of his Coy e.g. BRETT 105.

7. Each Company will take in 4 Officers (including the Coy Commander)

8. Packs will be taken in.

(sd) F.T. CHAMIER LIEUT.

A.ADJUTANT 6TH BN THE CONNAUGHT RANGERS.

Appendix 3

S E C R E T O P E R A T I O N O R D E R **No. 36.**

by

LIEUT COLONEL R.C. FEILDING D.S.O.
COMMANDING 6TH BN THE CONNAUGHT RANGERS.

20th Octr.1917.

1. The following reliefs will take place tomorrow 21st Inst.

2. "C" & "D" Coy's will relieve "B" & "A" Coy's respectively in the front line.

3. On completion of relief the battalion will be disposed of as follows:-

"A" COY	RAILWAY RESERVE. (South)
"B" ..(2 platoons)	MAN SUPPORT
do. (2 platoons)	RAILWAY RESERVE (north)
"C" Coy.	LEFT FRONT LINE.
"D" Coy	RIGHT FRONT LINE.

The relief will commence at ~~[illegible]~~ 2.30pm and will be parties of 5 men at 100 yards distance.

4. Completion of relief to be reported to Bn Hd Qrs, code word-INK.-

5. Trench Stores will be carefully handed over.

6. "A" and "B" Coy's will take over working parties as from 6pm. 21st Inst.

(sd) F.T. CHANIER. LIEUT
A.ADJUTANT 6TH BN THE CONNAUGHT RGS.

Appendix 2

O P E R A T I O N   O R D E R   No. 35.

by

LIEUT COLONEL R.C. FEILDING D.S.O.
COMMANDING 6TH BN THE CONNAUGHT RANGERS

18th Octr.1917.

1. The 47th Inf Bde front will be re-organised today into two subsections. The dividing line will be QUEENS AVENUE and LEG LANE, which are common to both subsections.

2. The following reliefs will take place - "A" & "B" Coy's will relieve 2 Coy's of 6th RL.IRISH REGT in the front line, commencing at 2 pm. "C" Coy (less 2 platoons) and "D" Coy will relieve "A" Coy in RAILWAY RESERVE., commencing at 2-30pm.

2 Platoons of "C" Coy at present in STRAY SUPPORT will be relieved under arrangements to be made by O.C. 6TH RL.IRISH REGT and will then proceed to occupy MAN SUPPORT.

3. "A" Coy will occupy the front line from the present right of the Brigade front to Post No. 16, about U.20.d.7.0. inclusive.

"B" Coy will occupy from Post No. 16 (exclusive) to the top of QUEENS AVENUE.

4. All movement to be by parties of 5 men only at not less than 300 yards distance.

5. Copies of trench store receipts to reach Bn Hd Qrs by 10am. 19th Inst.

6. Completion of relief to be wired to Bn Hd Qrs - CODE WORD TUG-OF-WAR.

7. Bn Hd Qrs will move at 4 pm.

8. O.C. "C" & "D" COY's will arrange with R.E., if possible, to have their working parties relieved in time.

(sd) F.T. CHAMIER. LIEUT
A.ADJUTANT 6TH BN THE CONNAUGHT RANGERS

SECRET.

Appendix 4.

OPERATION ORDER No. 57.
by
LIEUT COLONEL R.C. FEILDING D.S.O.
COMMANDING 6TH BN THE CONNAUGHT RANGERS.

24th Octr.1917.

1. The following reliefs will take place tomorrow the 25th Inst.

2. "B" & "A" Coy's will relieve "C" & "D" Coy's respectively, in the front line.

3. On completion of relief the battalion will be disposed of as follows:-

D Coy.	Railway Reserve (South)
C Coy.	Man Support. (2 Platoons).
..	Railway Reserve.(2platoons) North
B Coy	Left front line.
A Coy	Right front line.

The relief will commence at 2-30pm. and will be by parties of 5 men at 500 yards distance.

4. Completion of relief will be reported to Bn Hd Qrs, code word - YUKON.

5. Trench Stores will be carefully handed over, receipts to reach B.H.Qrs by 9 am 26th Inst.

6. "D" & "C" Coy's, will take over all working parties as from 6.pm. 25th Inst.

7. Coy Comdrs will make arrangements with R.E. Officers to have their parties returned in sufficient time so as to move with their companies.

(sd) T. BOOTH LIEUT

A.ADJUTANT 6TH BN THE CONNAUGHT RANG:

Appendix 5.

OPERATION ORDER No. 38.

by

LIEUT COLONEL R.G.F FIELDING D.S.O.
COMMANDING 6TH BN THE CONNAUGHT RANGERS.

28thOctr.1917. 28th

1. The following reliefs will take place tomorrow 29th Inst.

2. "C" & "D" Coy's will relieve "B" & "A" Coy's respectively in the front line.

3. On completion of relief the battalion will disposed of as follows.

"A" Coy.		RAILWAY RESERVE.(South)
"B" Coy.	(2 Platoons)	MAN SUPPORT
	(2 Platoons)	RAILWAY RESERVE (South).
"C" Coy.		LEFT FRONT LINE.
"D" COY.		RIGHT FRONT LINE

The relief will commence at [illegible]-30pm. and will be by parties of 5 men at 300 yards distance.

4. Completion of relief will be reported to Bn Hd Qrs, code word - INK.

5. Trench Stores will be carefully handed over.

6. "A" & "B" Coy's will take over working parties as from 6 pm. 29th Inst.

(sd) T. BOOTH LIEUTENANT.

ADJUTANT 6TH BN THE CONNAUGHT RANGERS.

W A R   D I A R Y

FOR MONTH OF NOVEMBER, 1917.

VOLUME :- 2pt

U N I T : - 6th Connaught Rangers

November Sheet 1. 6th Connaught Rangers Confidential Army Form C. 2118.

WAR DIARY
or
~~INTELLIGENCE SUMMARY.~~
(Erase heading not required.)

Instructions regarding War Diaries and Intelligence Summaries are contained in F. S. Regs., Part II. and the Staff Manual respectively. Title pages will be prepared in manuscript.

Place	Date	Hour	Summary of Events and Information	Remarks and references to Appendices
In the line	1.11.17		The battalion were in occupation of the front line from QUEEN'S LANE to PELICAN AVENUE C (on the left) and D Coy (on the right) were in front with B and A in support in RAILWAY RESERVE. Between 11 a.m and 5 p.m about 400 shells (5.9"s with a few 8.2"s) were fired at battery position in CRUX ROAD. Between 2 and 3 p.m many of these fell short, intentionally or otherwise, near RAILWAY RESERVE	
Ref Sheet BULLECOURT 51B S.W.4				
	2.11.17		The battalion were relieved in the line by the 7th LEINSTER REGT and proceeded to DYSART CAMP (See Appendix 1.)	
ERVILLERS				Appendix 1
Ref Sheet	3.11.17		A day of rest. The usual inspections took place	Operation
57C N.W.	4.11.17		Church parades as usual for all denominations.	Order 32
	5.11.17		Baths and musketry on the Rifle Range constituted the day's programme. On the 4th Lt F.T. CHAMIER returned from leave and on the 5th Lt A.H.E. RUSSELL returned from a Coy. Com's course	
	6-7.11.17		Company training. On the 7th 2/Lt T.F. GILMORE left on leave	
	8.11.17		The battalion paraded in mass formation and was inspected by the Divisional Commander at 11 a.m.	

D. D. & L., London, E.C.
(A7883) Wt. W803/M1672 350,000 4/17 Sch. 52a Forms/C/2118/14

November 1917. Sheet 2

Instructions regarding War Diaries and Intelligence Summaries are contained in F. S. Regs., Part II. and the Staff Manual respectively. Title pages will be prepared in manuscript.

WAR DIARY
or
INTELLIGENCE SUMMARY.
(Erase heading not required.)

Confidential

Army Form C. 2118.

Place	Date	Hour	Summary of Events and Information	Remarks and references to Appendices
ERVILLERS	9-11-17		Company training. Lt R.H. FRENCH returned from leave.	
Ref Sheet 57C N.W.	10-11-17		The battalion paraded at 9 am. in fighting order and proceeded to the training ground on the ERVILLERS – GOMIECOURT Road. The attack on TUNNEL TRENCH was practised twice. In the afternoon the finals of the Brigade Boxing Championship took place. Of 6 contests two – the Light and Middle Weights were won by the battalion	
	11-11-17		Church parades as usual. At 11·30 am the battalion was formed up in a square and addressed by the Brigadier who congratulated it on its good work in the trenches and in camp. Special mention was made of its sniping and patrol records. In the afternoon the R. DUB. FUS. were beaten at football 6-1 and the officers defeated the sergeants 4-1. Lts D.H. WICKHAM, U.A. MOORE, C.J. WAITES and H.E. FLINN left for various courses	
	12-11-17		The attack on TUNNEL TRENCH was rehearsed 3 times in the morning. In the afternoon the 6th R. IRISH REGT were defeated 6-1 in a League Football match	

D. D. & L., London, E.C. (A7883) Wt. W5031/M1672 350,000 1/17 Sch. 52a Forms/C/2118/14

November, 1917. Sheet 2

WAR DIARY
or
INTELLIGENCE SUMMARY.
(*Erase heading not required.*)

Confidential.

Army Form C. 2118.

Instructions regarding War Diaries and Intelligence Summaries are contained in F. S. Regs., Part II. and the Staff Manual respectively. Title pages will be prepared in manuscript.

Place	Date	Hour	Summary of Events and Information	Remarks and references to Appendices
ERVILLERS. Ref Sheet 57c N.W.	13.11.17		The attack on TUNNEL TRENCH was practised twice in the morning in the presence of the Brigadier and Divisional Commander	
	14.11.17		The attack on T.T. was practised 4 times in the morning. In the afternoon the Rangers Football team beat the 1st R. MUNSTER FUSILIERS 5-0 in a league match. 2/Lt G.D. BARRON left for the 12th Squadron R.F.C. on a course of instruction in contact aeroplanes. 2/Lt J.E. BARRY left on leave.	
	15.11.17		The attack on TUNNEL TRENCH was rehearsed twice in the presence of the Brigadier.	
	16.11.17		Companies were at the disposal of Company Commanders. In the afternoon the Rangers sustained their first defeat at football, its team which was by no means up to full strength being beaten 1-0 by the 2nd R. IRISH REGT in a friendly match.	
	17.11.17		The attack on TUNNEL TRENCH was practised 4 times. Lt J. McDONNELL returned from leave & 2/Lt G.D. BARRON from a course. Baths parades in the afternoon.	

D. D. & L., London, E.C.
(A7883) Wt. W807/M1672 350,000 4/17 Sch. 52a Forms C/2118/14

November 1917. Sheet 4

WAR DIARY
~~or~~
~~INTELLIGENCE SUMMARY.~~

(*Erase heading not required.*)

Instructions regarding War Diaries and Intelligence Summaries are contained in F. S. Regs., Part II. and the Staff Manual respectively. Title pages will be prepared in manuscript.

Army Form C. 2118.

Confidential.

Place	Date	Hour	Summary of Events and Information	Remarks and references to Appendices
ERVILLERS Sheet 57C N.W	18.11.17		Church parades as usual in the morning. In the afternoon the battalion moved up to the front line to the relief of the 7th LEINSTER REGT (see Appendix 2). At the conclusion of the relief D Coy occupied the front line from QUEEN'S LANE to U.20.d.9.4. The 1st ROYAL MUNSTER FUSILIERS were on their left and the 4th ROYAL FUSILIERS (8th Bde 3rd Divn) on their right. C Coy occupied MAN SUPPORT and A & B Coys were in RAILWAY RESERVE. Capt R.T. ROUSSEL ~~left~~ left for LE TOUQUET on a Lewis Gun course.	Appendix 2 O.O. No 3
In the line Ref Sheet BULLECOURT 51B S.W.4	19.11.17		On the night of Nov 19-20 took up its position for the attack as set down in Operation Orders No 1. (Appendix 3). The	Appendix 3 O.O. No 1
	20.11.17		zero hour was 6.20 a.m. Nov 20. At the same time the 3rd Divn advanced opposite BULLECOURT and down South the main attack on CAMBRAI commenced. The RANGERS were on the exposed right flank of the Divisional front with the 1st R. MUNSTER FUSILIERS on their left. A full account of the Operations is given in the special report by the Commanding Officer. (Appendix 4).	Appendix 4 Special Report

D. D. & L., London, E.C. (A7883) Wt. W807/M1672 350,000 4/17 Sch. 52a Forms/C/2118/14

November 1917. Sheet 5

WAR DIARY
~~or~~
~~INTELLIGENCE SUMMARY.~~
(*Erase heading not required.*)

Confidential Army Form C. 2118.

Instructions regarding War Diaries and Intelligence Summaries are contained in F. S. Regs., Part II. and the Staff Manual respectively. Title pages will be prepared in manuscript.

Place	Date	Hour	Summary of Events and Information	Remarks and references to Appendices
In the line			Casualties incurred and prisoners taken are also given in	Appendix 5
Ref Sheet			Appendix 4. Capts T.M.H.S. TUITE, M.C. and C.A. BRETT and Lt R.H. FRENCH	Congratulatory
BULLECOURT			were admitted to hospital wounded (Appendix 5)	Letter
51B S.W.4.			In the evening of the 22nd the battalion was relieved in	Appendix 6
	22-11-17		TUNNEL TRENCH by the 7th LEINSTER REGT and on completion C Coy	O.O. No 36
			occupied our old front line from Mebu 5 to Post 18 and A B & D	
			Coys were in reserve (Appendix 6) 2/Lt T.F. GILMORE returned from leave	
	23-11-17		At 7 p.m. the Leinsters recaptured JOVE and D Coy [illegible] dug	
			a communication trench during the night from JOVE to NOR SAP	
			By ~~the evening~~ 11 pm this afforded good cover (Appendix 7) Until finally	Appendix 7
			relieved on the 26th the Coys in reserve obtained little rest being	O.O. No 37
			continually employed in working parties.	
	25-11-17		D Coy relieved C Coy in the front line (Appendix 8) Lt J.S. DRYDEN	Appendix 8
	~~26-11-17~~		returned from the Tunnelling Coy & Lt D.H. WICKHAM from a bombing course	O.O. No 38
	26-11-17		The battalion was relieved and returned to DYSART CAMP	Appendix 9
			(Appendix 9)	O.O. No 39

D. D. & L., London, E.C. (A7883) Wt. W509/M1672 350,000 4/17 Sch. 52a Forms/C/2118/14

November 1917 Sheet 6

Instructions regarding War Diaries and Intelligence Summaries are contained in F. S. Regs., Part II. and the Staff Manual respectively. Title pages will be prepared in manuscript.

WAR DIARY
~~or~~
~~INTELLIGENCE SUMMARY.~~
(Erase heading not required.)

Confidential

Army Form C. 2118.

Place	Date	Hour	Summary of Events and Information	Remarks and references to Appendices
ERVILLERS	27 & 28.11.17		Time was occupied by resting refitting and cleaning up.	
Ref Sheet	~~28.11.17~~		On the 27th ~~inst~~ Capt R.T. ROUSSEL returned from a course & 2/Lt J.T. O'NEILL	
57C N.W.			left on leave	
	29.11.17		There was a Church parade for R.Cs at 8.45 am. At 10 a.m. the	
			battalion paraded in mass formation and was inspected by the	
			Commanding Officer who afterwards addressed the men. In the	
			afternoon the 7th LEINSTER REGT were beaten in a League match 7-0.	
			This completed our six matches all of which were won by us.	Appendix 10
			In the evening C & D Coys went to RAILWAY RESERVE (NORTH)	S.O. No. 39
			to be in reserve (Appendix 10.) Lt E.K. CUMMINS left on leave.	
	30.11.17		In the morning A & B Coys and Battalion Headquarters	
			were inspected by the Commanding Officer after which all	
			paraded under the Adjutant for drill.	

Rowland M. Feilding Lt Col
Comdg 6th Connr Rangers

D. D. & L., London, E.C. (A7883) Wt. W5o3/M1672 350,000 4/17 Sch. 52a. Forms C/2118/14

Appendix I

SECRET. No. 34.

OPERATION ORDER
BY
LIEUT COLONEL R.G. FEILDING D.S.O
COMMANDING 6TH BN THE CONNAUGHT RANGERS.

1st Novr.1917

1. The 7th LEINSTER REGIMENT will relieve the battalion in the front line and Support Lin tomorrow the 2nd Inst, commencing about 6-30pm.

2. On relief the battalion will proceed to DYSART CAMP at ERVILLERS.

3. Movement will be by ~~small~~ parties of 5 by the ~~usual~~ SPINE ROAD route until the ST LEGER -VRAUCOURT road is reached - and then by platoons at 200 yards distance.

4. All trench stores will be carefully handed over, receipts obtained and sent to O.Room by 9 am 3rd Inst.

5. Completion of relief will be reported to Bn Hd Qrs by wire in the case of "C" & "D" Coy's and by runner in the case of "A" & "B, code word - C O N O B.

6. All working parties will be handed over on relief.

7. The Qr Mr and C.Q.M's S. will take over DYSART CAMP from 1st RL.MUNSTER FUSILIERS, arrangements to be made with C.O. that battalion, by the Qr Mr.

8. The Transport Officer will have the necessary transport at CRUX CIRCUS BY 5-30pm.
All companies will have material for removal ready for loading at CRUX CIRCUS by 5-30pm.

(sd) T. BOOTH LIEUT

ADJUTANT 6TH BN THE CONNAUGHT RANGERS.

Appendix 2

No. 35.

O P E R A T I O N   O R D E R S
BY
LIEUT. COLONEL. R.C. FEILDING. D.S.O.
COMMANDING 6TH BN. THE CONNAUGHT RANGERS.

17th November, 1917.

1. The Battalion will relieve the 7th LEINSTER REGIMENT in the Right Sub Sector to-morrow, the 18th inst.

2. "D" Company will ~~relieve "A" Company LEINSTER REGT. in~~ take over the ~~Right~~ Front Line, from BULL ROAD. U20 d 9.4. to QUEENS LANE.
"C" Company will ~~relieve "B" Company LEINSTER REGT. in the Left Front Line~~, take over MANN. SUPPORT.
"B" Company will relieve "C" Company LEINSTER REGT. in the Left Reserve, Railway Reserve.
XXXXX "A" Company will relieve "D" Company LEINSTER REGT. in the Right Reserve, Railway Reserve.
Battalion H.Q. will relieve H.Q., LEINSTER REGT. in Railway Reserve, South.

3. Companies will move off by Platoons at 5 minutes interval in the following order:- H.Q., "D", "C", "A", "B".
The leading Platoon of "D" Company will not cross the ST. LEGER - VRAUCOURT ROAD before 4.45 p.m.

4. Advance parties of 1 Officer per Company & 1 N.C.O. per Platoon, No.1 Lewis Gunners and 1 Officer & 1 N.C.O. from H.Q. will report to H.Q. 7th LEINSTER REGT. at 3 p.m.

5. Completion of relief will be reported to Battalion H.Q. as follows:- Company Commander's name followed by strength of Company (e.g., TUITE. 120.)

6. 1 Limber will be at the disposal of each Company for Lewis Guns, Officers trench kits & Mess kits.
2 Limbers will be at the disposal of H.Q. for taking Officers kits, Orderly Room kit, etc.

7. Trench Store receipts will be handed into Orderly Room by 9 a.m. the 19th inst.

8. All Officers surplus Kits to be handed into Quartermaster's Stores by 2 p.m., and Officers valises will be ready for removal by 2 p.m.

(SD) T. BOOTH. LIEUT.

ADJUTANT 6TH BN. THE CONNAUGHT RANGERS.

Appendix 3

SECRET.

X.1

OPERATION ORDER (No.1).
BY
LIEUT.COLONEL. R.C. FEILDING. D.S.O.
COMMANDING 6TH BN. THE CONNAUGHT RANGERS.

18th November, 1917.

Reference Map. Special Sheet 1/10,000 U.1 to C.6.

1. At a date and time to be notified later the Battalion will Capture and consolidate a portion of TUNNEL TRENCH.

2. The Assault will be made by "A" Company, on the right, and "B" Company on the left; supported by "D" Company.
The 1st Royal Munster Fusiliers will co-operate on our immediate left. Beyond them the 48th & 49th Infantry Brigades will co-operate, and the 3rd Division will attack East of BULLECOURT.

3. Final Objective:-
"A" Company :- JOVE (U.20.b.50.70) to MARS Exclusive.
"B" Company :- MARS - inclusive - to a point (U.14.d.10.32) opposite KNUCKLE AVENUE.

4. Dispositions for the Assault:-
Prior to the Assault the Battalion frontage will be from BULL ROAD (U.20.d.90.43) to QUEENS LANE (U.20.a.98.57), and will be held by "D" Company. From QUEENS LANE to KNUCKLE AVENUE (U.14.c.70.10) will be held by the 1st Royal Munster Fusiliers.
At least one hour before Zero, "A" Company will have assembled in MARTIN ROAD, with its right on MONKSAP, and "B" Company will have occupied the front line between KNUCKLE AVENUE and QUEENS LANE, the Royal Munster Fusiliers and "D" Company 6th Connaught Rangers, side-slipping outwards, temporarily, to make way for them. Immediately "B" Company has left the trench the Royal Munster Fusiliers and "D" Company 6th Connaught Rangers will re-occupy their former positions.
All Companies to be 120 strong. Any surplus over this number, together with "C" Company will be held in local reserve, in MAN SUPPORT.

5. Dress :-
Fighting Order; i,e, haversack, ground sheet (rolled on back of belt), Steel helmet, Box Respirator, 170 rounds S.A.A., 2 Mills bombs (No.5), full water-bottle, 3 sandbags, 2 white aeroplane flares, iron ration, and ration for one day, including a slab of chocolate.
Every alternate man will carry a shovel or pick, in the ratio of 3 shovels to one pick. WATSON FANS, wire Cutters & breakers, Very pistols, S"O"S" signals, etc., will also be carried.
All bayonets and equipment will be dulled.

6. WIRE:-
1 Section 156th Field Company R.E. assisted by infantry wiring & carrying parties will wire the front of TUNNEL TRENCH. They will also wire the right flank from JOVE for a distance of 50 yards South towards NOB SAP.

7. Blocks:-
(a) A trench block will be made in TUNNEL TRENCH E. of JOVE by a party to be detailed by O.C."A" Company, assisted by 156th Field Company R.E.
(b) Directly the TUNNEL TRENCH has been cleared a Tunnel Block will be made E. of JOVE by No.1 PARTY 174th Tunnelling Company R.E. O.C. "A" Company will tell off a Covering party for this work.

Sheet 2.

NOTE :- Directly TUNNEL TRENCH has been reached sentries will be posted at each Tunnel Entrance, and two parties to be detailed by O's.C. "A" and "B" Companies respectively, will proceed to clear the Tunnel, commencing at the Southern Extremity of each Company frontage, and working Northwards.

As the Royal Munster Fusiliers will be working Southwards towards him it will be nexessary for O.C. "B" Company to makexarrangements with the Company Commander on his left, whereby any risk of the two parties bombing into one another is avoided.

8. LEWIS Gun Posts:-

3 Lewis Gun Posts will be constructed in Tunnel Trench by Lewis Gun Detachments, assisted by details of 156th Field Company R.E. as follows:-

(a) N. of and close to JOVE.

(b) E. of MARS.

(c) N. of MARS, at about U.14.d.21.05.

9. Communication Trenches:-

(a) JOVE LANE:- This will be dug by 11th Hants(P) Regt; route NOB SAP (U.20.b.2.5) to a point in Tunnel Trench just N. of JOVE (U.20.b.5070). Length 180 - 200 Yards.

True bearing from NOB SAP = 49°

Firebays will be constructed at intervals on the right or South side of this trench for flank defence.

(b) BOW LANE:- This will be dug by special infantry parties under 156th Field Company R.E. supervision.

Route S.E. corner of BEAUMANS LOOP (U.14.c.46.57) to point in Tunnel Trench S. of FAG ALLEY (U.14.c.90.80). Length 250 - 270 Yards.

True Bearing from U.14.c.46.57 = 83° 30'.

10. Reconnaissance of Tunnel:-

The removal of booby traps will be undetaken by a party of the 174th Tunnelling Company R.E., which will work Southwards, commencing from the left of the Brigade front, after the Tunnel has been cleared.

11. R.E. Dumps:-

(a) U.20.b.2.5. (MARTIN ROAD).

(b) U.14.c.6.1. (off KNUCKLE).

(c) U.20.a.7.4. (QUEENS LANE).

Pioneer Dump:-

U.20.a.85.50. (QUEENS LANE).

12. BATTLE Headquarters:-

(a) 47th Brigad :- Railway Reserve (North).

(b) 6th Connaught Rangers:- Queens Lane (U.20.a.22.28).

(c) Assaulting Companies:-. Queens Lane (U.20.a.90.52).

(d) Support Kompany:- Mebu 3 (U.20.b.35.17).

(e) Reserve Company:- MAN SUPPORT.

(f) 1st Roy.Munster Fus:- STRAY SUPPORT (U.19.b.88.38).

(g) Artillery Group:- (B.4.d.35.20).

(h) 156th Field Co. R.E:-(U.19.a.2.3.).

The Brigade Intelligence Officer will occupy Mebu 9.

13. BARRAGE:-

(a) At Zero a barrage will be placed on Tunnel Trench for 4 minutes.

(b) At Zero & 4 minutes this barrage will commence to lift to the protecting barrage line at the rate of 100 yards every 4 minutes.

(c) From the time of reaching the protective barrage line till Zero & 1 hour, 18 pdr Batteries will fire a proportion of smoke shell.

(d) At Zero & 1 hour fire on the protective barrage line will cease except in case of S.O.S.

(e) A light smoke screen to simulate a lethal shell bombardment will be placed, by 4" Stokes Mortars, in front of

Tunnel Trench from Zero to Zero & 30 seconds.

(f) A similar screen will be placed in the valley N.E. of BULLECOURT from Zero to Zero & 1 minute.

(g) A heavy smoke barrage will be plaeed E. of Tunnel Trench from Zero & 30 seconds to Zerp & 15 minutes to cover objectives from the East.

NOTE:- The above smoke barrgges will xxxxxxxxx take place in any wind.

(h) A heavy Smoke screen will be placed in the Valley N.E. of BULLECOURT from Zero & 1 minute to Zero & 16 minutes, if the wind is favourable.

14. Advanced Company Headquarters:-
O's.C. "A" and "B" Companies will follow their Companies and establish advanced Headquarters in Tunnel Trench, at or near JOVE and MARS, respectively each leaving an Officer to represent him at Company Battle Headquarters in Queens Lane.

15. Signal Communicatons:-
The means available will be
(a) By fullerphone.
(b) By visual.
(c) By pigeons.
(d) By runners.

An Advanced Battalion Signal Station will be established at MARS by the Battalion Signalling Officer, Immediately after the capture of Tunnel Trench.

6 pairs of pigeons will be available to the Battalion, and will be distributed as follows:-

1 pr with Commander of each Assaulting Coy.	2 prs.
1 pr at Advanced Battalion Signal Station.	1 pr.
Support Company Headquarters.	1 pr.
Battalion Headquarters.	2 prs.
	6

In all cases, sparing use should be made of runners, while other means are available, but when runners are sent, full use should be mad of them.

16. Overhearing by Enemy:-
It is unlikely that any listening sets the enemy may have will be affected by the operations, so the usual precautions against overhearing must be taken.

17. Maps and papers:-
(a) All Officers will be provided with the Special Sheet U.1. to C.6. which will be the only map carried. Positions of assembly and of our emplacements and Headquarters will not be marked on this map.

(b) No papers or orders will be carried by anyone into Tunnel Trench.

18. B.A.B. Code:- Is not to be used in advance of our present front line. All such books will be handed into Orderly Room before Zero.

19. Tracer Bullets:-
Arrangements will be made by the LEWIS Gun Officer to have two magazines per gun loaded with 1 tracer bullet in 5, for use against aeroplanes.

20. Contact Aeroplanes:-
The usual signals will be given immediately, if called for by a Contact Aeroplane.

21. Light for Tunnel:-
Electric torches will be carried for the use of those employed in clearing the Tunnel.

Sheet 4.

22. Enemy Wires:- All telephone xxxxx or other wires seen will be cut immediately.

23. Booby Traps:- All ranks are warned against booby traps. Prisoners should be employed to test any "doubtful" Souvenir.

24. P.Bombs:- Owing to the High inflammability of the timber in the Tunnel and the danger of fouling the air "P" Bombs should be used most sparingly.

25. Patrols and Covering Parties:- Patrols and snipers covering wiring parties will not go more than 100 yards beyond Tunnel Trench.

26. Great-coats:- These will be stored in the drying room in Railway Reserve (South).

27. Assembly for Attack:- In assembling for the attack absolute silence must be maintained. Troops will move up in parties of five, and bayonets will not be fixed till the man are in position.

28. Scaling Ladders:- 16 Scaling ladders will be drawn under arrangements to be made by O.C. "B" Company from PORTER'S Dump, at junction of LEG LANE and BULL ROAD.

29. Stragglers Posts:- The Battalion Provost Sergeant will maintain the following Stragglers Posts, which will prevent straggling, and take the name of all Connaught Rangers leaving the front line, whether wounded or otherwise.

(a) Queens Lane opposite Battalion Headquarters.

(b) Pelican Avenue, opposite M.G. Dug-out.

All Connaught Rangers prisoners will also be checked and noted by these posts.

30. Walking Sticks:- Officers will not carry Walking Sticks.

31. Officers Equipment:- All Officers will carry whistles, compasses, note books and field glasses.

32. S.O.S. Rockets:- Each Assaulting Company will carry 12 S.O.S. Rockets, to be drawn from LEG LANE Brigad Stores under Commany arrangements.

33. Observers:- The Battalion Intelligence Officer will arrange for observers to watch the operations from the following O.P's.

(a) BRAGANZA POST.

(b) PENGUIN TRENCH.

(c) PELICAN.

34. Penguin Trench:- O.C. "C" Company will detail 2 LEWIS guns and teams for employment in PENGUIN TRENCH.

35. Casualty Lists & Recommendations:- The Commanding Officer particularly hopes that Company Commanders will send these in as soon as possible. They should be carefully prepared and carefully written.

36. Special Parties:-

(a) 3 N.C.Os and 30 men to carry for R.E.

(b) 1 N.C.O. & 10 men to carry Stokes bombs.

(c) 2 Parties, each of 2 N.C.Os and 12 men, to carry ammunition, water, etc., under the direction of the R.S.M.

37. Advanced Ammunition Store:- Advanced S.A.A. and bomb Stores will be established in Tunnel Trench at, or near, MARS and JOVE.

Sheet 5.

38. Prisoners of War:- All Prisoners of War will be evacuated by Queens Lane, and marched to Brigade Headquarters in Railway Reserve (North).

(SD) T. BOOTH. LIEUT.

ADJUTANT 6TH BN. THE CONNAUGHT RANGERS.

Appendix 4 War Diary

SECRET.

Headquarters,

47th Infantry Brigade.

Herewith I beg to forward report describing the operations of 20-11-17, in so far as they affected the Battalion under my Command.

1. The Attack was made on a frontage of 350 yards, the objective being the Tunnel Trench, from MEBU "JOVE" to U.14.d.10.[illegible]., inclusive.

2. The Assaulting Companies were lined up, ready for battle, by 5.20 a.m., i.e., one hour before ZERO; "A" Company (on the right) in HARTIN ROAD, a sunken raod well out in front of our front line trench, and only about 75 yards distant from the MEBU "MARS".

"B" Company (on the left), having no dead ground in which to assemble in front of our front line, jumped off from the trench itself.

3. Previous experience having shown that the impetuosity of these men in the attack often carries them forward into our own barrage, "A" Company which had 75 yards to go, was ordered to start at Zero plus 3 minutes, i.e., at 6.[illegible] a.m. and "B" Company, which had [illegible]25 yards to go, at Zero plus 1 minute; i.e. at 6.21 a.m.

All watches had been synchronized three times during the night, the last time at 5 a.m., and I myself was in the front line at Zero and checked the start.

The Barrage, which started at Zero, remained on the German Front Line (the Tunnel Trench) for 4 minutes, and it was calculated, by the above arrangements, that the assaulting Companies would reach the objectives as soon as it was safe to do so.

The above instructions were carried out to the letter, and Tunnel Trench was reached and occupied almost without casualties, at Zero plus 4½ minutes, i.e. at 6.24½ am

No casualties were sustained from our own barrage.

Our smoke barrage had evidmmtly deceived the enemy and led them to believe that gas was being sent over, as they had on their gas masks.

They appeared to be in a very dazed condition. There were a few sentries in the Saps, and a number of men groupdd in the Tunnel entrances, who were forthwith shot or bayoneted.

4. Immediately the Tunnel Trench had been occupied, the MEBUS - JOVE and MARS - were approached from behind in accordance with plan, both surrendering after slight resistance.

Simultaneously, a sentry was posted at each Tunnel entrance, and parties were sent down the Tunnel to clear it of the enemy.

Capt. T.M.H.S. TUITE. M.C., commanding the left Company, then established his Headquarters in "MARS"; and Capt. C.A. BRETT, Commanding the right Company, began to make arrangements to do the same in "JOVE", he having himself led the party which rushed that MEBU, and shot at least one of the garrison with his revolver.

5. An Advanced Battalion Signal Station was set up at "MARS" and FULLERPHONE communication obtained between that point and our old Front Line. Subsequently though the wires were frequently cut, they were always repaired by our linesmen, often under heavy fire.

The ladder-wire was found impracticable as it got caught up in the barbed wire and piquets in No Man's Land, and it was almost immediately abandoned for ordinary D.I. wire.

6. The Tunnel was cleared and, up to 7.30 a.m., 121 prisoners had been counted. Further captures subsequently increased this number to 152.

7. At about 7.10 a.m. the enemy began to counter-attack our right flank, which was in the air, in a very determined and persistent manner, bringing up an overwhelming superiority in men, bombs and ammunition through the tunnel

from

from the South, which afforded them an uninterrupted communication with their rear, the R.E. tunnellers having failed to make the block which had been pre-arranged, their officer having been killed just as he reached the MEBU "JOVE".

8. These counter-attacks were repeated over and over again, the fighting becoming very fierce and continuing almost hand to hand for several hours. Its severity may be gauged by the fact that the Commander and 26 out of 28 other ranks of the right flank platoon became casualties.

Our men fought with the most heroic determination in spite of a failing and finally disappearing supply of bombs, supplimenting the limited supply which they had brought over with them with German bombs which they picked up in the Tunnel Trench.

At a most critical period 8006 Pte. K. WHITE rushed close up to a traverse from behind which the enemy was bombing, and actually catching many of their bombs in mid-air, threw them back before they had exploded.

After an hour, Capt BRETT having been wounded, and the bomb supply having run out, our men began slowly to fall back upon "MARS", continuing to hold the enemy back with LEWIS gun and rifle fire, yielding their ground only inch by inch, and leaving a trail of dead behind them.

9. At 7.50 a.m. a gap was reported on our left but this was subsequently filled and contact established with the 1st Royal Munster Fusiliers.

10. At 8.30 a.m. I began to reinforce Tunnel Trench, sending over first 1 platoon of "D" Company and subsequently 2 platoons of "C" Company, 6/Conn.Rangers.

No Man's Land at this time had become passable only with the greatest difficulty owing to machine gun and shell-fire.

Supplies of bombs were also got over, a party of the 7th Leinster Regiment giving us very gallant and valuable assistance in this matter.

11. At.

11. At 9.45 a.m. Capt. T.M.H.S. TUITE, M.C. was reported severely wounded.

12. At 10.30 a.m. the 7th Leinster Regt. relieved us in the Old Front Line, and I sent the remainder of the Battalion, under Captain E.C. NORMAN, to reinforce Tunnel Trench, with the exception of 2 Lewis guns which were left behind near PENGUIN TRENCH to cover our Right Flank.

13. Shortly after 1 p.m. I myself visited Tunnel Trench and found that a firm defensive flank had been formed along the sap connecting "MARS" with TUNNEL TRENCH, and that considerable progress had been made towards consolidating our position.

14. During the night this sap was dug through to our old Front line at MONK SAP by the 11th Hants Pioneers, and communication was thus extablished with the rear.

15. The following Casualties were sustained:-

	Killed.	Wounded.	Missing.
Officers.	—	3	—
Other Ranks.	34	106	~~8~~ —
	Total 143		

16. The advance to the attack across No Man's Land was made precisely according to programme, the front line of the first wave in extended order, firing LEWIS Guns and rifles as they went forward. The remainder of the assaulting troops advanced in artillery formation, in sections, in file.

The direction had been taped out the night before, and all platoon commandersand sergeants carried compasses.

The great majority of the casualties were incurred in the defense of the exposed Right Flank,

"JOVE" was re-captured by the 7th Leinster Regiment on the evening of 23-11-17., and many of our dead were found, and recovered from around the MEBU and from the

Parapet

Parapet of Tunnel Trench, both to the N. and S. of it. One of our dead was actually found locked in grips with a dead German.

R C Feilding.

Lieut.Colonel.

25-11-17. Commanding 6th (S) Bn. The Connaught Rangers.

Appendix 4

Head Quarters,
47th Inf Bde.

ORDERLY ROOM
37
27 NOV. 1917
6th SER. Bn. CONN. RANGERS

I wish to report that all men hitherto reported missing during the operations commencing 20.11.17, have now been traced. The figures now stand at :-

	Killed.	Wounded	Missing	Total.
Officers	-	3	-	3
O.RKS.	~~33~~ 34 *	~~107~~ 106	-	140
	~~33~~ 34	~~110~~ 109	-	143

Will you please amend the figures given in my report of the 26.11.1917, as it is important that the casualties should be correctly reported.

* A patrol of the 6/R.I. Regt found one of the men reported wounded, dead, in Nomans Land. 30.11.17 [initials]

Lieut Colonel.

28.11.17. Commanding 6th Bn The Connaught Rangers.

COPY. *Appendix 5*

Headquarters,

16th (Irish) Division.

November 22nd 1917.

My dear Feilding,

Many thanks for your letter. Indeed I congratulate you and your gallant Connaughts who have so worthily upheld the traditions of Guillemont. I am sorry indeed that you have had such heavy casualties.

Yours ever,

(sd) W.B. Hickie.

To-

O.C. 6th Connaught Rangers.

Last night I received a letter from the G.O.C. stating he had received a letter from you, "very proud of his men and in good spirits." He says: "I don't attach much importance to the loss of JOVE, provided you are satisfied over the block in the TUNNEL and outside it. The Connaughts must have fought splendidly and upheld the GUILLEMONT traditions."

(sd) G. PEREIRA, Brig-Gen.,

Comdg. 47th Infantry Brigade.

SECRET. Appendix 6 No 36.

OPERATION ORDERS
BY
LIEUT.COLONEL. R.C. FEILDING. D.S.O.
COMMANDING 6TH BN. THE CONNAUGHT RANGERS.

22nd November, 1917.

1. The Battalion will be relieved to-night by the 7th LEINSTER REGIMENT, commencing at 6 p.m.

2. On relief the Battalion will be disposed of as follows:-
"C" Coy. Old Front Line from Mebu 5 to Post 18.
"A" & "B" Coys Railway Reserve South.
"D" Coy. Railway Reserve North.
Headquarters. Railway Reserve South.

3. The 4 right Lewis Gun Posts of the Battalion may be relieved by daylight.

4. All movement will be via MARS LANE Parties must move in silence and must not be more than 10 strong. They will move at 100 yards distance.

5. Completion of relief to be reported by O.C. Front Line to present Battalion H.Q. by Codeword PLUM.

6 Each Coy. will send a billeting Officer in advance.

(SD) F.T. CHAMIER. LIEUT.
A/ADJUTANT 6TH BN. THE CONNAUGHT RANGERS.

Appendix 7.

SECRET.   No.37.

OPERATION ORDERS
BY
LIEUT. COLONEL R.C. FEILDING. D.S.O.
COMMANDING 6TH BN. THE CONNAUGHT RANGERS.

23rd November, 1917.

1. 7th LEINSTER REGIMENT will capture and consolidate TUNNEL TRENCH from U.20.b.50.72 to present block at U.20.b.30.88.

2. Zero hour will be about 7 p.m. to-night. Exact hour will only be notified to those concerned. Artillery, ~~XXXXX~~, T.M's and Machine Guns will co-operate.

3. "C" Company with 30 other ranks and 2 Lewis Guns and teams from "B" Company will hold VALLEY TRENCH from U.20.b.12.50 to U.20.d.95.45. The party from "B" Company will report to O.C. "C" Company at 5 p.m.

4. A communication trench will be dug between U.20.b.40.70 and our old front line by this Battalion. O.C. "D" Company will detail parties for this work as follows:-
   (a) 1 Sergt & 20 men to rendezvous at junction of QUEENS LANE and front line at 5.30 p.m.
   (b) 1 Officer & 60 other ranks to rendezvous at 6.30 p.m. in old front line, head of party at SUB SAP facing North.
   These Parties will carry one shovel per man, to be drawn from Battalion Headquarters.

5. All parties from this Battalion will report that they are in position by runner to Battalion Headquarters.

6. Lewis Guns will not shoot North or West of line U.20.b.4.2. - U.20.b.60.75. - U.20.b.50.98.

7. A C K N O W L E D G E.

(SD) F.T. CHAMIER, LIEUT.

A/ADJUTANT 6TH BN. THE CONNAUGHT TANGERS.

SECRET. Appendix 8 No.38.

7

OPERATION ORDERS
BY
LIEUT.COLONEL. R.C. FEILDING. D.S.O.
COMMANDING 6th Bn. THE CONNAUGHT RANGERS.

25th November.1917.

1. The following relief will take place to-day (25-11-17.).

2. "D" Company will relieve "C" Company in our old front line from Mebu 5 to Post 18.

3. On relief "C" Company will proceed to the CHALK PIT (U.19.a.2.3.).

4. Relief will commence at 8 p.m. and will be by parties of 5 at 100 yards distance.

5. Completion of relief to be reported to Battalion H.Q. by wire. Codeword:- SATISFACTORY.

(SD) F.T. CHAMIER. LIEUT.

A/ADJUTANT 6TH BN. THE CONNAUGHT RANGERS.

Headquarters,

16th(Irish) Division.

O.C. 6th Connaught Rangers.

I must express to you, to the Officers, N.C.Os and men who took part in the attack of the 20th November, and especially to all ranks who were engaged in the heavy fighting round the MEBU JOVE on the right flank, my extreme appreciation of the spirit and gallantry shown by all ranks. The capture of the main objective which was strongly held and stubbornly fought for by the Germans is a fitting sequel to the capture of the quarries at GUILLEMONT on the 3rd September 1916.

I wish you to convey to all ranks my thanks and apprec--iation.

(sd) W.B. HICKIE Major-General,

25.11.17. Commanding 16th (Irish) Division.

Appendix 9

SECRET. **No.[illegible].**

9

OPERATION ORDERS

BY

LIEUT.COLONEL. R.C. FEILDING. D.S.O.

COMMANDING 6TH BN. THE CONNAUGHT RANGERS.

26th November,1917.

1. The Battalion will be relieved to-night, 26th inst. and on relief will proceed to [illegible] CAMP.

2. 2 Companies of 1st Royal Munster Fusiliers will take over our old front line from BULL ROAD to [illegible] AVENUE, thus relieving "D" Company of this Battalion.
"A" and "B" Companies will be relieved by 1 Company 1st Royal Munster Fusiliers.
"C" Company will not be relieved, but may march out at 4.15 p.m.

3. The leading platoon of 1st Royal Munster Fusiliers will not cross the ST.LEGER - VRAUCOURT Road till 4 p.m.

4. Movement will be by platoons at 200 yards distance as far as the ST.LEGER - VRAUCOURT Road, where Companies will close up and will be met by at least 1 piper per Company.

5. Trench Stores will be handed over and receipts handed in to Orderly Room by 9 a.m. 27th inst.

6. Completion of relief to be reported to Battalion Headquarters by runner, except by O.C., "D" Company, who will report by wire. Code-word [illegible].

7. The Transport Officer will arrange for the same number of limbers as were allotted to Headquarters and Companies, when moving into the line on [illegible]th inst. Mess-cart and limbers for Headquarters and "C" Company will be at the usual rendezvous at 4.30 p.m., remainder at 5 p.m., by which time the first lot must be clear.

8. A C K N O W L E D G E.

(Sd) F.T. [illegible], LIEUT.

A/ADJUTANT 6TH BN. THE CONNAUGHT RANGERS.

Appendix 10

O P E R A T I O N   O R D E R   No. ~~39~~ 40.

by
LIEUT COLONEL R.C. FEILDING D.S.O.
COMMANDING 6TH BN THE CONNAUGHT RANGERS.

29th Novr.1917

1. "C" & "D" Companies will parade at 5-30pm this evening and proceed to the Dug-outs at the Eastern end of MAIDA VALE (RAILWAY RESERVE NORTH), where they will be kept in reserve.

2. One limber per company will report at 5.pm. at the Company Lines.

3. The Companies will be accompanied by 2 Field Kitchens and 1 Water Cart.

(sd) T.BOOTH Lieut Colonel
A.ADJUTANT 6TH BN.THE CONNAUGHT RANGERS

La. 25E

WAR DIARY,

FOR MONTH OF DECEMBER, 1917.

VOLUME :- 24

UNIT :- 6th Connaught Rangers.

Vol 24

December 1917. Sheet 1

6th/The Connaught Rangers

Army Form C. 2118.

Confidential.

WAR DIARY
or
~~INTELLIGENCE SUMMARY.~~

(Erase heading not required.)

Instructions regarding War Diaries and Intelligence Summaries are contained in F. S. Regs., Part II. and the Staff Manual respectively. Title pages will be prepared in manuscript.

Place	Date	Hour	Summary of Events and Information	Remarks and references to Appendices
ERVILLERS Ref Sheet. France 57c. N.W.	1.12.17		C and D Coys were in reserve in RAILWAY RESERVE (NORTH) and A and B Coys were in DYSART CAMP. A & B Coys paraded at 9 a.m. for drill under the Adjutant. Lt F.K. CUMMINS left on leave.	
GOMIECOURT	2.12.17		Church parades for all denominations took place in ERVILLERS in the morning. In the evening the 16th Division was relieved by the 40th Division and the battalion proceeded to camp in GOMIECOURT (Appendix 1.). Lt B.S.F. RICKARD was admitted to hospital.	Appendix 1. Operation Order No 40.
BEAULENCOURT Ref Sheet. France 57c.	3.12.17		The battalion paraded in full marching order at 1.30 p.m. and proceeded via BAPAUME to BEAULENCOURT.	
	4.12.17		Orders to proceed to LECHELLE were cancelled and the battalion remained in camp at BEAULENCOURT. 2/Lt G.E. MAGUIRE went on leave.	
TINCOURT Ref Sheet France 62c.	6.12.17		The battalion marched to TINCOURT in heavy marching order stopping near MOISLAINS for dinner and arriving about 5 p.m. when it was billeted in huts and houses (Appendix 2.).	Appendix 2. Operation Order No 42.
	7.12.17		Lt J. M. FORBES rejoined the battalion and 2/Lt T.S. JENNINGS went on leave.	

(A7092). Wt. W12839/M1293. 750,000. 1/17. D. D. & L., Ltd. Forms/C.2118 14.

December 1917. Sheet 2.

Instructions regarding War Diaries and Intelligence Summaries are contained in F. S. Regs., Part II. and the Staff Manual respectively. Title pages will be prepared in manuscript.

WAR DIARY
or
~~INTELLIGENCE SUMMARY.~~

(Erase heading not required.)

Confidential.

Army Form C. 2118.

Place	Date	Hour	Summary of Events and Information	Remarks and references to Appendices
TINCOURT. Ref Sheet France 62C.	8.12.17		There was a Church Parade for Roman Catholics in TINCOURT Church at 9am. 2/Lt H.S KIRKWOOD left the battalion to join the 180th Tunnelling Company, R.E. Lt V.A. MOORE returned from a course.	
	9.12.17		Church parades were held in the morning for all denominations. At 10am. the battalion paraded in Church Order and letters from the Divisional General were read out by the Commanding Officer. Lt E. HAWORTH left the battalion to act as Assistant Town Major, TINCOURT.	
LEMPIRE Ref Sheet France 62 C.	11.12.17		The 47th Infy Bde relieved the 48th Infy Bde in the right sector of the Divisional front. The CONNAUGHT RANGERS relieved the 2/R. DUB. FUS. in support in LEMPIRE (Appendix 3.) 2/Lt H.E FLINN returned from a course and 2/Lt F.C. WOODS was admitted to hospital.	Appendix 3 Operation Orders. No 43
	12-16.12.17		The battalion in support were chiefly occupied in working parties under R.E. supervision and in improving the strong points and defence positions of LEMPIRE and RONSSOY. There were	

(A7092). Wt. W12839/M1293. 750,000. 1/17. D. D. & L., Ltd. Forms/C.2118/14.

December 1917 Sheet 3

Army Form C. 2118.

WAR DIARY
or
~~INTELLIGENCE SUMMARY.~~
(Erase heading not required.)

Confidential

Instructions regarding War Diaries and Intelligence Summaries are contained in F. S. Regs., Part II. and the Staff Manual respectively. Title pages will be prepared in manuscript.

Place	Date	Hour	Summary of Events and Information	Remarks and references to Appendices
LEMPIRE Ref Sheet France 62C.			practically no casualties during this period except for one unlucky shell which killed 3 and wounded 6 of A Coy on the 16th.	
			On the 14th 2/Lt J. J. O'NEILL returned from leave	
			On the 16th MAJOR R.M. RAYNSFORD (LEINSTER REGT.), who had commanded the 5th Battn CONNAUGHT RANGERS in SALONIKA, joined the battalion as 2nd in command. Lt F.K. CUMMINS returned from leave & Lt B.S.F. PICKARD was discharged from hospital and rejoined.	
	17.12.17		The battalion relieved the 1st R.M.F in the left subsection of the front line (Appendix 4). On our right were the 6th R. IRISH REGT and on the left the 2nd R.D.F.	Appendix 4 Operation Orders No 45.
	18.12.17		A quiet day in the line but owing to the snow on the ground and the extreme cold conditions were trying throughout the tour.	
	19.12.17		In the evening two patrols under 2/Lt D.T. McWEENEY and 2/Lt J.M. GARRET respectively were out in the foggy weather. The former reconnoitred the enemy post in CRELLIN AVENUE which was found to be occupied.	
	20.12.17		C and D Coys relieved A and B in the front line (Appendix 5). Between 3.15 and 4 am. on the night Dec 20/21 the enemy put down a heavy T.M. barrage on our front line under cover of which a patrol of	Appendix 5 Operation Orders No 46.

(A7092). Wt. W12839/M1293. 750,000. 1/17. D. D. & L., Ltd. Forms/C.2118/14.

December 1917. Sheet 4

Instructions regarding War Diaries and Intelligence Summaries are contained in F. S. Regs., Part II. and the Staff Manual respectively. Title pages will be prepared in manuscript.

WAR DIARY
~~or~~
~~INTELLIGENCE SUMMARY.~~
(Erase heading not required.)

Confidential

Army Form C. 2118.

Place	Date	Hour	Summary of Events and Information	Remarks and references to Appendices
In the line Ref Sheet France 62c			about 10 men attempted to ~~attack~~ enter COCHRAN POST held by C Coy; they were dispersed by rifle and bomb and next afternoon an enemy rifle and several 'stick' bombs were discovered outside our wire and brought in. During the T.M. bombardment D Coy suffered casualties - 2 killed and 4 wounded.	
	21.12.17.		Two patrols went out at night. One, under Lt J. H. McDONNELL found KNOLL TRENCH occupied and one under Lt E. A. W. SMITH confirmed the occupation of the enemy post in CRELLIN AVENUE.	
	22.12.17		Capt J. M. FERGUSON, R.A.M.C. was killed in the afternoon by shell fire. His place was filled by Lt M. LYONS, M.O.R.C., U.S.A. 2/Lt F. C. WOODS was discharged from hospital and rejoined the battalion.	
	23.12.17		At 5.20 a.m. a patrol under 2/Lt G. D. BARRON went out to reconnoitre certain pits shown on an Aeroplane Photo. They proved to be an old unoccupied line of small trenches. Lt Col R. C. Feilding, D.S.O. went on leave and Major R. M. RAYNSFORD took command. In the evening the Brigade was relieved by the 49th Infy Bde and the battalion proceeded by train to TINCOURT to its old billets (Appendix 6.)	Appendix 6 Operation Order No 46

(A7092). Wt. W12839/M1293. 750,000. 1/17. D. D. & L., Ltd. Forms/C.2118/14.

December 1917 Sheet 5.

Army Form C. 2118.

Instructions regarding War Diaries and Intelligence Summaries are contained in F. S. Regs., Part II. and the Staff Manual respectively. Title pages will be prepared in manuscript.

WAR DIARY ~~or~~ INTELLIGENCE ~~SUMMARY~~.

(Erase heading not required.)

Confidential

Place	Date	Hour	Summary of Events and Information	Remarks and references to Appendices
TINCOURT Ref Sheet France 62C	23.12.17		Lts J. H. McDONNELL and LT J. M. FORBES were admitted to hospital	
	24.12.17		The usual inspections were held during the day Capt I. P. PRAEGER and Lt M. LYONS, M.O.R.C, U.S.A were admitted to hospital. REV F. F. DUGGAN. C.F. joined the battalion.	
	25.12.17		XMAS DAY. Church parades for all denominations were held in the morning. At 1 p.m there were Xmas dinners for the battalion in 2 large huts. All were in festive mood. Lt J. A. V. KENT proceeded on leave.	
	26.12.17		Companies were inspected by the Commanding Officer. There were also Baths parades and rifle inspection by the Armourer Sergeant.	
	27.12.17		The battalion paraded for drill at 9.30 a.m. and the usual classes for specialists were held	
	28.12.17		Drill under the adjutant at 9.30 a.m. and box respirator drill in the afternoon. 2/Lt J. J. CONLON was admitted to hospital Capt D. H. WICKHAM joined the Brigade as Bombing Officer and Lt J. H. McDONNELL rejoined from hospital.	

(A7092). Wt. W12839/M1293. 750,000. 1/17. D. D. & L., Ltd. Forms/C.2118 14.

December 1917 Sheet 6

WAR DIARY
or
~~INTELLIGENCE SUMMARY.~~
(Erase heading not required.)

Confidential

Army Form C. 2118.

Instructions regarding War Diaries and Intelligence Summaries are contained in F. S. Regs., Part II. and the Staff Manual respectively. Title pages will be prepared in manuscript.

Place	Date	Hour	Summary of Events and Information	Remarks and references to Appendices
Bde Reserve Ref Sheet Fanca 62c.	29.12.17		The 47th Bde relieved the 48th Bde in the line on the left section of the Divisional front. The 6/Connaught Rangers relieved the 2nd R.Dub.Fus. in reserve where the companies were billeted in huts and bivouacs along the light railway cutting between VILLERS FAUCON and St EMILIE (Appendix 7). Capt I.P. PRAEGER rejoined from hospital & 2/Lt T.T. ONe[illegible] left on a course. 2/Lt S.O.C. MALLINS & 2/Lt I.J. KELLY joined the battalion with a draft of 55 men from the Divisional Reinf. Depot.	Appendix 7 Operation Orders No 48
	30 & 31		The companies were employed, chiefly under the supervision of 180 Tunnelling company & 11th Hants Pioneers, in improving the accomodation.	

R M Raynsford Major
Cmdg 6th Conn Rangers

(A7092). Wt. W12839/M1293. 750,000. 1/17. D. D. & L., Ltd. Forms/C.2118/14.

OPERATION ORDER No.40.

BY

LIEUT COLONEL R.C. FEILDING. D.S.O.
COMMANDING 6TH BN THE CONNAUGHT RANGERS.

2nd Decr.1917.

1. The 47th Infantry Bde will be relieved by 119th I.Bde on the night of 2nd/3rd Inst.

2. 6th R.IRISH Regt will be relieved by 17th WELSH Regt in the Left Sub. Sector.

3. 1st R.MUNSTER FUS will be relieved by 19th WLESH Regt in the right SubSector.

4. "C" & "D" Coy's 6/CONNAUGHT RANGERS will be relieved ny 2 Coy's of 12th S.W.B.

5. On completion of relief 6th R.IRISH and 1st R.MUNSTER FUS and 2 Coy's 6/CONNAUGHT RANGERS will march to ERVILLERS & embus at B.13.b.3.4.,proceed by Bus to GOMMIECOURT.

6. The remainder of the battalion will be ready to fall in as soon as relieved, in M.Order,(probable time 5pm.) and march to GOMMIECOURT.

7. All trench maps of 1/10,000 and 1/20,000 scale,Air Photos Trench stores,plans for future work and defence schemes will be handed over and receipts obtained, and handed into O.Room by 12 noon 3rd Inst.

8. Movement on and West of BAPAUME - ARRAS Road will be at intervals of 200 yards between companies: and Battalion Transport.

9. On relief Brigade H.Qrs will be opened at GOMMIECOURT CHATEAU.

(sd) T. BOOTH LIEUT.

ADJUTANT 6TH BN THE CONNAUGHT RANGERS

No. 42.

OPERATION ORDERS
BY
LIEUT. COLONEL. R.C. FEILDING. D.S.O.
COMMANDING 6TH BN. THE CONNAUGHT RANGERS.

5th December, 1917.

REVEILLE	6 a.m.
BREAKFAST	7 a.m.
SICK PARADE	8 a.m.
O.OFFICER	Lieut. A.H.E. RUSSELL.
NEXT FOR DUTY	Lieut. E. HAWORTH.
COY IN WTG.	"D" COY,

Reference Sheet 57c and 62c. 1/40,000,

1. The 47th Infantry Brigade Group will move by march route from BEAULENCOURT to TINCOURT to-morrow, the 6th inst.

2. Route taken will be ROCQUIGNY - MANANCOURT - MOISLANS - TEMPLEUX-LA-FOSSE, distance about 14½ miles.

3. The Battalion will parade in Marching Order at 9 a.m. between A and B Camps. Steel helmets will be worn covered with canvas.

4. The usual advance parties, under Lieut S.W.O'COFFEY, will parade at Orderly Room at 7 a.m., and will meet Staff Captain at the Cross Roads N. of TINCOURT. J.18.C. at 12 noon.
   The advance parties will meet the Battalion at this point.

5. The Brigadier will inspect the Battalion as it passes the starting point.

6. Dinners will be cooked en-route, and will be served on arrival in camp.

7. Huts and Camp must be left scrupulously clean.

8. All kits will be ready for removal by 7.30 a.m.

(SD) T.BOOTH. LIEUT.

ADJUTANT 6TH BN. THE CONNAUGHT RANGERS.

O.P.E.R.A.T.I.O.N. O.R.D.E.R. No.[illegible]

by

LIEUT COLONEL R.G.FEILDING D.S.O.

COMMANDING 6TH BN THE CONNAUGHT RANGERS.

11th Dec. 1917.

1. 47th Inf Bde will relieve the 48th Inf Bde by day of 11th and night of 11th/12th.

2. After relief the 47th Inf Bde will be disposed of as follows

Bde H.Qrs	ST EMILIE
LEINSTER RGT	-Front line, Right sub section
R.MUNS FUS	Left front line left sub section.
6 CN RGR	Bde Support LEMPIRE
R.IR.RGT.	Bde Reserve ST EMILIE.

3. The battalion will relieve 2nd RI.DUBLIN FUSRS in Bde Support in LEMPIRE.

"A" & "D" Coy's will relieve "A" & "D" COY's 2nd R.DUB FUS in LEMPIRE. These companies will take their dinners with them. "B" & "C" Coy's will relieve the two remaining companies 2nd R.DUB.FUS in LEMPIRE. These Coy's can take their cookers into the valleys in X.[illegible] and F.24.c., one company in each.

4. Companies will parade at [illegible]-15 am ready to move off. They will march off in the following order A.D.B.C.

5. Company guides will be at F.24.a.[illegible] at [illegible] am and Platoon guides at F.24.c.[illegible] at 12 noon.

6. Movement West of ST EMILIE will be by companies at 500 yards,
" East " " " " Platoons "

7. Completion of relief will be reported by runner to Bn Hd Qrs code word [illegible].

8. Lewis Gun Limbers will accompany companies to ST EMILIE, from where L.G. will be man handled.

9. Each Company will leave 1. N.C.O. and 4 men to clean up the billets and hand over.

(sd) T. [illegible] LIEUT

ADJUTANT 6TH BN THE CONNAUGHT RANGERS.

OPERATION ORDER No. 45.

by

LIEUT COLONEL R.C. FEILDING D. S. O.
COMMANDING 6TH BN THE CONNAUGHT RANGERS.

Field. 16th Decr.1917.

1. The battalion will relieve the 1st R.MUNSTER FUSRS in the left subsection tomorrow the 17th Inst.

2. Relief will not commence before 4-30pm.

3. "A" Coy will relieve "W" Coy R.M.F. in right front line.
"B" .. "X" .. left .. ..
"C" .. "Z" .. SART LANE.
"D" .. 1 Platoon of "Y" Coy,R.M.F.in LEMPIRE, near Battalion Hd Qrs.
2 Platoons of "Y" Coy in WRAFTER POST.
1 Platoon .. .. LEMPIRE EAST.

4. Batalion Head Quarters will be at LANCASTER HOUSE.

5. All Work,trench stores etc.,will be handed over. Copies of trench store receipts will be handed into O.Room by 9 am 18th Inst.

6. Completion of relief will be reported to Batn: Hd Qrs, code Word - M O O N.

(sd) T. BOOTH LIEUTENANT.
ADJUTANT 6TH.BN.THE CONNAUGHT RANGERS.

OPERATION ORDER No. 46.
by
LIEUT COL NEL R.C. FEILDING D.S.O.
COMMANDING 6TH BN THE CONNAUGHT RANGERS.

20.12.1917.

1. The following releifs will take place today 20.12.17.

2. "C" COY will relieve "A" COY in the right front line.
"D" COY .. "B" COY .. left .. ..

3. On completion of relief "A" & "B" COY's will be disposed of as follows:-

"B" COY H.Qrs & 2 Platoons	WRAFTER POST.
2 Platoons in	RANGER VILLAS (LEMPIRE).
"A" COY in SART LANE	

4. Relief will not commence before 4-30pm.

5. All working parties will be handed over on relief.

6. All trench stores will be handed over and copies of trench stores receipts will be sent to Bn Hd Qrs by 9 am 21-12-17.

7. The relief will not be allowed to interfere with the punctual rendering of the Daily Work report, or with the daily R.E. working parties

8. Completion of relief will be reported to Bn Hd Qrs, - CODE WORD - S E T.

(sd) T. BOOTH LIEUT.

ADJUTANT 6TH BN TH E CONNAUGHT RANGERS.

SECRET.

OPERATION ORDER No. 47.

by.

LIEUTENANT COLONEL R.C. FEILDING D.S.O.
COMMANDING 6TH.BN. THE CONNAUGHT RANGERS

22nd Decr.1917.

1. 1. The 47th Inf Bde will be relieved by the 49th Inf Bde on the night 23/24th Decr.17.

2. The battalion will be relieved by the 7th (S.I.H.) Bn R.IRISH RGT. as under:-

"C" COY will be relieved by	"B" Coy S.I.H.	in	Right Front line.
"D"	"C"		Left .. ..
"A"	"A"		SART LANE
2 Platoons "B" Coy ..	2 Platoons S.I.H.		WRAFTER POST
.. "B" ..	2 Platoons S.I.H.		LEMPIRE EAST.
Bn.H.Q. ..	Bn.H.Q. S.I.H.		LANCASTER HOUSE.

3. On relief the battalion will proceed to TINCOURT, by train as far as HAMEL. Details of entrainment will be issued later.

4. Advanced parties will be guided to companies by H.Q. Runners and will arrive about 3-30pm.

5. 1 Officer each from A.C. & D Coy's, 2 Officers from B Coy, 1 N.C.O. per Platoon and 1 from Hd Qrs will report at Bn HD Qrs at 4.15 pm to guide the main bodies.

6. All trench stores, work in hand and proposed, maps and defence schemes but not aeroplane photographs, will be handed over in writing on relief. Copies of Trench Store Receipts will be handed into O.Room by 9 am 24th Inst.

7. 1 Limber per company, 2 Limbers for H.Qrs, Mess Cart and Maltese Cart, and the usual limber for the Cook Sergeant, will report at the ration dumps immediately after dark.

8. Relief complete will be reported to Bn Hd Qrs by Code word "OMAR" and arrival in billets by runner to O.Room.

9. Major T.A. DILLON and the 4 Company C.Q.M.S. will take over the billets in TINCOURT tomorrow

(sd) T. BOOTH LIEUT.

ADJUTANT 6TH BN THE CONNAUGHT RANGERS.

[illegible]

[illegible] joint [illegible]

[illegible]

1. The [illegible] Inf [illegible] - in [illegible], [illegible] Section, on the [illegible] inst.

2. The Battalion will relieve the [illegible] on [illegible] in the [illegible] [illegible]

3. Coy's will move off in the following order [illegible] A, B, C, D, HQ Coy, and will [illegible] [illegible] via [illegible]

4. Advanced parties of 1 Officer per Coy, 1 N.C.O. per platoon and 1 N.C.O. from HQ Coy will report to [illegible] Bn HQrs [illegible] on the [illegible] inst.

5. Lewis Gun limbers and Field Kitchens will accompany companies... Mess Cart, Maltese Cart and [illegible] will report to [illegible]

6. Blankets and Officers kits will be ready for removal by [illegible] The Quartermaster will make the necessary arrangements to have Blankets sent up to the Companies and the kits removed to store.

7. Each Company will leave behind 1 N.C.O. [illegible] to clean [illegible] hand over their billets. When this has been done, they will rejoin their companies. Clean billets certificates will be obtained.

8. All [illegible] stores, [illegible] and programme of work will be taken over and [illegible] handed into [illegible] will not be taken over.

9. Completion of relief will be reported [illegible] code word - [illegible].

[illegible]

[illegible]

WAR DIARY

FOR MONTH MOF JANUARY, 1918.

VOLUME :- 26.

UNIT :- 6th Connaught Rangers.

Sheet 1. January 1918. 6th (S) Bn The Connaught Rangers. Confidential

WAR DIARY or ~~INTELLIGENCE SUMMARY.~~

(Erase heading not required.)

Army Form C. 2118.

Instructions regarding War Diaries and Intelligence Summaries are contained in F. S. Regs., Part II. and the Staff Manual respectively. Title pages will be prepared in manuscript.

Place	Date	Hour	Summary of Events and Information	Remarks and references to Appendices
Ref Map EPEHY 67.c.N.E.2	1-3		The 47th Infy Bde were holding the right sector of the Divisional front. The 6th Connaught Rangers were in Brigade Reserve and situated in the Light Railway cutting at E 24 a.1.5. The time was occupied in building huts and foundations for the same and in continuing three mine shafts. On the 1st Lt A.H.E. RUSSELL went on leave and Lt E.A.W. SMITH and 2/Lt P.S.C.L. PALMER went on courses. On the 3rd 2nd/Lts A. RIBBONS, T.C. SLOWEY, S.J. WHITAKER, H.E. TAGGART, and H.E. HALL joined the battalion. Lt. J.H.O'C. de C. MACDONNELL was admitted to hospital	
	4th		The battalion relieved the 1st R.M.F in the right sub-section of the front line. On conclusion of relief A Coy held GRAFTON POST, B Coy ~~the~~ HEYTHROP POST, C Coy – LEMPIRE RD and MULE TRENCH and D Coy YAK and ZEBRA POSTS and SANDBAG ALLEY. Battn HQ were at F.10.c 44.44. (see Appendix 1). Capt E.C. NORMAN was admitted to hospital. On the right of the battalion were the 2nd R.D.F and on the left the 6th R. IRISH. REGT.	Appendix 1 Operation Orders No 50

January 1918. Sheet 2

Instructions regarding War Diaries and Intelligence Summaries are contained in F. S. Regs., Part II. and the Staff Manual respectively. Title pages will be prepared in manuscript.

WAR DIARY

~~or~~

~~INTELLIGENCE SUMMARY.~~

(Erase heading not required.)

Confidential

Army Form C. 2118.

Place	Date	Hour	Summary of Events and Information	Remarks and references to Appendices
Ref Map EPEHY 62c N.E.2 Front line	5th		Two patrols went out at night. One, under Lt F.K. COMMINS, reconnoitred NO MAN'S LAND, S. of BIRD LANE and one on the left, under Lt B.S. PICKARD, reconnoitred N. of BIRD LANE. Recent wheel marks of, apparently, an enemy hand ambulance were found just outside our own wire.	
	6th		A small patrol found CATELET COPSE to be unoccupied.	
	~~7th~~		LEMPIRE ROAD near C Coy's HQ was shelled between 6 p.m and 12 midnt and 5 men were wounded by 1 shell.	
	7th		C Coy relieved B in HEYTHROP POST and D Coy relieved A in GRAFTON POST	
	8th		Lt/Col R.C. FEILDING, D.S.O returned from leave and resumed command of the battalion. Capt J.H.R. DICKSON was admitted to hospital.	
	9th		Capt I.P. PRAEGER went on leave & Lt J.A.V. KENT, M.C. returned from leave.	
	10th		At 4.5 a.m an enemy raiding party under cover of a bombardment of 7.7 cms attempted to enter our advanced L.G. post in LEMPIRE ROAD which they bombed wounding three of our men. The enemy were however repulsed with L.G. and bombs without being able to get within our wire. In the evening the 47th Brigade were relieved by the 49th Bde (see Appendix 2) and the battalion proceeded to billets in VILLERS FAUCON.	Appendix Operation Orders No 51

(A7092). Wt. W12839/M1293. 750,000. 1/17. D. D. & L., Ltd. Forms/C.2118 14.

Sheet 3. ~~1918~~ January 1918.

Instructions regarding War Diaries and Intelligence Summaries are contained in F. S. Regs., Part II. and the Staff Manual respectively. Title pages will be prepared in manuscript.

WAR DIARY
or
~~INTELLIGENCE~~ SUMMARY.

(Erase heading not required.)

Confidential.

Army Form C. 2118.

Place	Date	Hour	Summary of Events and Information	Remarks and references to Appendices
VILLERS FAUCON Ref Sheet EPEHY 62c N.E. 2	11th		A day of rest. The usual inspections took place under company arrangements. During the whole of the rest period the battalion were largely occupied in working parties, chiefly on wiring the BROWN LINE and in clearing ground near Divisional HQ in VILLERS FAUCON for a new battalion camp. Four L.G. anti aircraft emplacements and a battalion Observation Post were also built and permanently occupied. Bomb proof ~~huts~~ walls for the company huts were put up. Bombing and Lewis Gun classes were held whenever possible.	
	12th		Baths parades were held during the day. Six officers attended a lecture on the field cypher by the Brigade Signalling Officer in Hamel.	
	13th		Church parades were held for all denominations. Major R.M. RAYNSFORD went on leave.	
	14th		At 1.30 p.m. the battalion paraded in Drill Order and were inspected by the Commanding Officer. Lt V.A. MOORE went on leave. Capt E.C. NORMAN was discharged from hospital and returned to the battalion.	
	15th		2/Lt M. McKIERNAN joined the battalion.	

(A7092). Wt. W12839/M1293. 750,000. 1/17. D. D. & L., Ltd. Forms/C.2118/14.

January 1918 . Sheet 4

Instructions regarding War Diaries and Intelligence Summaries are contained in F. S. Regs., Part II. and the Staff Manual respectively. Title pages will be prepared in manuscript.

~~WAR~~ DIARY
~~or~~
~~INTELLIGENCE SUMMARY.~~
(Erase heading not required.)

Confidential.

Army Form C. 2118.

Place	Date	Hour	Summary of Events and Information	Remarks and references to Appendices
VILLERS FAUCON Ref Sheet France EPEHY 62c N.E 2	16th		Lt S. W. O'COFFEY gave a lecture on the field cypher to all available subaltern officers. Lt A. RIBBONS was admitted to hospital. Capt A MASSEY, R.A.M.C left the battalion and Lt A STRAUSS, M.O.R.C, U.S.A took his place.	
	17th		The battalion inspection by the brigadier was cancelled on account of bad weather	
	19th		Lt A.H.E RUSSELL returned from leave & 2/Lt J. J. KELLY was attached to the 180th Tunnelling Coy, R.E.	
	20th		Church parades were held for all denominations. 2/Lt H.E. FLINN	
	21st		left on a course. 2/Lt J.M. GARRETT, M.C went on a course 2/Lt T.F GILMORE was attached to the 56 Coy R.E.	
RONSSOY	22nd		The 47th Infy Bde relieved the 48th Infy Bde in the right sector of the line. The CONNAUGHT RANGERS relieved the 10th R.D.F in Bde support in RONSSOY (see Appendix) and took over the LEMPIRE DEFENCES	Appendix 3. Operation orders No 14.
	23-28		The time was chiefly occupied in working parties under R.E supervision and in the improvement of our defence positions.	
	23rd		2/Lt P.S.C.L PALMER returned from a course.	
	24th		Capt T. BOOTH, M.C and 2/Lt M. McKIERNAN went on leave	
	25th		Lts D.P.J. KELLY, M.C & O.H. ACTON joined the battalion	
	28th		Lt D.P.J KELLY, M.C was admitted to hospital & 2/Lt J.J. CONLON was discharged from hospital.	

(A7092). Wt. W12839/M1293. 750,000. 1/17. D. D. & L., Ltd. Forms/C.2118/14.

January 1918. Sheet 5.

Instructions regarding War Diaries and Intelligence Summaries are contained in F. S. Regs., Part II. and the Staff Manual respectively. Title pages will be prepared in manuscript.

WAR DIARY

~~or~~

~~INTELLIGENCE SUMMARY.~~

(Erase heading not required.)

Army Form C. 2118.

Confidential.

Place	Date	Hour	Summary of Events and Information	Remarks and references to Appendices
EMPIRE Ref Sheet 62c N.E.2.	28th		The Connaught Rangers relieved the 1st R.M.F. in the left sub-sector of the front line (see Appendix 4) The 6th R. IRISH REGT were on our right and the 7/8 R INNIS. FUS. on our left.	Appendix 4 Operation Orders No 15.
	29th		A patrol under 2/Lt H. E. HALL reconnoitred the hostile post in CRELLIN AVENUE but did not get into contact with the enemy, who were not occupying the post. Major R. M. RAYNSFORD returned from leave.	
	30th		A Coy relieved C Coy on the right of the front line & B Coy relieved D Coy on the left (see Appendix 5) A patrol under 2/Lt T. C. SLOWEY reconnoitred the enemy's wire from the KNOLL to LOWLAND POST.	Appendix 5 Operation Orders No 16.
	31st		Capt E. C. NORMAN was admitted to hospital. A patrol under 2/Lt H. E. TAGGART reconnoitred the enemy's wire from CRELLIN AVENUE to TOMBOIS ROAD	

R.M. Raynsford Major
Cmdg 6/Connaught Rangers.

(A7092). Wt. W12839/M1293. 750,000. 1/17. D. D. & L., Ltd. Forms/C.2118/14.

OPERATION ORDER No. [illegible]

by

MAJOR R.F.R. [illegible]

COMMANDING [illegible]

[illegible]

1. The Battalion will relieve the 1st [illegible] FUSILIERS in the right subsection tomorrow the 8th inst.

2. "A" Coy will relieve "[illegible]" Coy 1st [illegible] FUSILIERS.

3. Relief will not commence until [illegible]pm. and Coy's will move off in the following order and times.

"A" Coy [illegible]. "[illegible]" Coy [illegible].
"[illegible]" Coy [illegible]. "[illegible]" and [illegible].

4. All movement will be in small parties at 200 yards distance. The ST. [illegible] road will not be used.

5. Working parties will be found up to [illegible] day of relief.

6. Copies of Trench Store receipts, handed and taken over will be sent to O.Room by [illegible].

7. The Transport Officer will arrange for the necessary transport for LEWIS GUNS and [illegible], etc.

8. Completion of relief will be reported to Bn HQ [illegible] STAFF being used followed by Company Commanders name.

[illegible] Lieut.

[illegible] THE [illegible]

SECRET. OPERATION ORDER No 51 Copy No 7

BY

LT COL R.C. FEILDING, D.S.O., COMDG 6th (S) Bn CONNAUGHT RANGERS.

---

(1) The 47th Inf Bde will be relieved in the Left Subsection by the [illegible] Inf Bde on the day [illegible] and the night [illegible] Jan [illegible].

(2) The Bn will be relieved by the S.I.H. and on relief will proceed by March Route to VILLERS FAUCON, [illegible].

(3) On completion of relief the Bde will be disposed as follows:-

Bde H.Q.	....	TINCOURT, (J.24.[illegible])
6th Conn.Rangers.	....	VILLERS FAUCON
7th Leinster Rgt.	....	HAMEL (K.19.[illegible])
1st R.M.F.	....	.. (K.19.a.10.9[illegible])
6th R.I.Rgt.	....	TINCOURT. (J.[illegible].b.[illegible])
47th T.M.B.	....	.. (J.24.b.[illegible])

(4). The following will be handed over and receipts obtained:-

(a). All trench stores.
(b). Written Defence Schemes.
(c). All documents connected with the line (except air photos, which will not be handed over)
(d). All work in progress and proposed (in writing).

Trench store lists to be in Orderly Room, by 9am the 11-1-18.

(5). A.Coy will be relieved by C.Coy, S.I.H.
B.Coy .. .. B.Coy, S.I.H.
C.Coy .. .. A.Coy, S.I.H.
D.Coy .. .. B.Coy, S.I.H.

(6). Relief complete will be reported to Bn H.Q. the code word will be CANDLE. followed by the Coy Cadre name.

(7). One guide per platoon from D.Coy will meet the platoons of B. Coy S.I.H. at 4pm at junction of TOMBES ROAD - LONDON ROAD.

One guide per platoon from A.B.&C Coys will report to Bn H.Q. at 5pm.

(8). The Transport Officer will make all necessary arrangements for transport of Lewis Guns, Blankets, Officers kits, and Mess kits.

(9). Clean trench certificates will be obtained from relieving unit.

In the Field.
9-1-18.

Sd T.BOOTH. Lt & Adjt.
6th (S) Bn Connaught Rangers.

SECRET. Copy No. 8

OPERATION ORDER No. [illegible]
by
LIEUT COLONEL R.C. F E I L D I N G D.S.O.
COMMANDING 6TH. BN. THE CONNAUGHT RANGERS

21st January 1918.

1. [illegible]
The 47th Inf Bde will relieve the 48th Inf Bde in the Right Section on the day 22nd and night 22/23rd Jan.1918.

2. On completion of relief the 47th Inf Bde will be disposed of as follows:-

Bde H.Qrs.........................ST. EMILIE.
7/LEINSTER RGT....................Front line Right Subsection.
1/R.MUNSTER FUSRS................. .. .. Left ..
6/CONNAUGHT RANGERS...............Bde Support (Lempire)
6/RL.IRISH RGT....................Bde Reserve (ST EMILIE).
47th T.M.BATTERY..................Line.

3. The Battalion will relieve the 10th RL.DUBLIN FUSRS [illegible] in Bde Support (LEMPIRE).
"A" COY will relieve "D" Coy 10th Rl.Dub Fusrs, H.Q. at F.21.a.5.05
"B" COY .. .. "A" .. .. SANDBAG ALLEY
"C" COY .. .. "B" .. .. do do
"D" COY .. .. "C" .. .. F.15.d.70.85.
Bn.Hd.Qrs will be at F.[illegible].

4. Companies will move off in the following order, "D"."A"."B"."C",H.Qrs. leading company must not cross level crossing at E.[illegible].d.5.9. before 6-30pm. The ST EMILIE - RONSSOY road must not be used E. of road junction F.[illegible].b.8.[illegible].

5. The usual advance parties, with Nos.1. of Lewis Gun teams will leave here at 1.pm.

6. Anti Aircraft Lewis Guns protecting wagon lines will be relieved by 48th Inf Bde by 12 noon 22.1.18.

7. All work in progress and proposed must be taken over and handed over in writing.

8. All trench stores and Gum Boots must be carefully checked before giving receipts. Trench store receipts to be rendered to O.Room by 9 am 23rd Inst.

9. All billets must be left scrupulously clean and certificates obtained.

10. Transport Officer will make the necessary arrangements for Transport of Lewis Guns, 1 Blanket per man, Officer's Kits, Mess Kits. One Blanket will be carried on the man.

11. Completion of relief will be reported to Bn.H.Q. by Runner.

(sd) T. BOOTH. CAPTAIN.
ADJUTANT 6TH BN THE CONNAUGHT RANGERS.

SECRET. OPERATION ORDERS No.15.

No 8 Copy

by

LIEUT COLONEL. R.C. FIELDING D.S.O.
COMMANDING 6TH.BN.THE CONNAUGHT RANGERS

27.1.1918.

1. The Battalion will relieve the 1st R.MUNSTER FUSRS.in the Left subsection tomorrow the 28th Inst. Relief will not commence before 4-30pm.

2. Coy's will relieve in accordance with table bwlow. This is calculated on the basis of 3 Platoons in each Company.

Coy of CONN RANG	COY OF R. M. FUS.	PLACE.
2 Platoons "A" Coy	3 Platoons "Y"Coy (less 1 L.G. team.)	SART LANE
1 Platoon "A" Coy	1 Platoon "Y" Coy	WRAFTER POST.
2 Platoons "B" Coy	3 Platoons "Z" Coy (less 1 L.G. team)	F. 16.a.9.8.
1 Platoon "B" Coy	1 Platoon "Z" Coy	LEMPIRE EAST. (F.10.d.6.2.)
"C" Coy (Plus 1 L.G. and team from "A" Coy	"W" Coy, with an extra L.G. & team.	RIGHT FRONT LINE.
"D" Coy(Plus 1 L.G. and team from "B"Coy.	"X" Coy, with an extra L.G. & team.	LEFT FRONT LINE.

Bn. Hd.Qrs will be at LANCASTER HOUSE.

3. The usual advance parties will proceed at 2pm. Attention is directed to the letter recently circulated with regard to patrolling during a relief.

4. All Work, Defence Schemes and Trench Stores, will be carefully handed and taken over. Copies of trench Stores lists to reach Bn.Hd.Q. by 9 am 29th Inst.

5. "C" & "D" COY's will take no Blankets into the line, - "A" & "B" Coy's will take 2 per man.

6. Rations will be delivered as early as possible after dark to the New Ration Dumps. The Limbers can then be used for moving Officer's Mess Kits,etc., from the old to the new Hd.Qrs.

7. The Transport Officer will make the necessary arrangements for the removal of "A" & "B" Coy's blankets to their new positions & of those of "C" & "D" Coy's to the Transport Lines. The Mess Cart & Maltese Cart will report at Bn Hd Qrs at Dusk.

8. Working parties in the present Area will be found up to 1pm.

9. Completion of relief will be wired to Bn Hd Qrs, - Code Word - A U N T I E.

(sd) F.T. CHAMIER LIEUTENANT.

A.ADJUTANT 6TH BN THE CONNAUGHT RANGERS.

SECRET

OPERATION ORDER NO 1? Copy No....7..

BY

LIEUT-COLONEL R.C. FEILDING D.S.O.

COMMANDING 6TH BN THE CONNAUGHT RANGERS.

31st January 1917.

1. The following reliefs will take place to-morrow 1.2.18., commencing at 5 pm.

"C" Coy will relieve "A" Coy in the Right Front Line.

"D" Coy .. .. "B" Coy .. Left .. ..

2. On relief "A" & "B" Coys will withdraw to SART LANE & LEMPIRE EAST respectively.

3. "A" & "B" Coys will take over all working-parties as from 6 pm 1.2.18. onwards.

4. Blankets and Trench Stores will be carefully handed over. Copies of Trench Store Lists to reach Battn H.Q. by 9 am 2.2.18.

5. "A" & "B" Coys will send out a protective patrol of 1 officer and 10 O.R. each immediately after dark. These patrols will not withdraw before 8 pm.

Completion of relief to be wired to Bn H.Q. Code word NICELY.

(sd) F.T. CHAMIER LIEUT.

A/ADJUTANT 6TH BN THE CONNAUGHT RANGERS.

Vol 26

L.B. 27E

WAR DIARY.

FOR MONTH OF FEBRUARY, 1918.

VOLUME:- 27.

UNIT:- 6th Connaught Rangers.

February 1918 Sheet 1. 6th (S) Bn The Connaught Rangers. Confidential

Army Form C. 2118.

Instructions regarding War Diaries and Intelligence Summaries are contained in F. S. Regs., Part II. and the Staff Manual respectively. Title pages will be prepared in manuscript.

WAR DIARY
or
~~INTELLIGENCE SUMMARY.~~

(Erase heading not required.)

Place	Date	Hour	Summary of Events and Information	Remarks and references to Appendices
Front line Ref Sheet LEMPIRE	1st		The battalion was holding the front line in the left sub-sector of the right sector of the Divisional front. The 6th R. IRISH REGT were on our right and the 7/8 R. INNIS FUSILIERS on our left. In the evening C and D Coys relieved A and B in the line. Lt J.A.V. KENT, M.C. and a patrol of 7 other ranks inspected the enemy's wire in front of LOWLAND POST and WILLOW TRENCH.	Appendix 1 O.O. No 16.
	2nd		The battalion was relieved by the 1st R.M.F and proceeded to Brigade Reserve at ST EMILIE (see Appendix 2). Lt Col R.C. FEILDING, D.S.O left for a course with a French Army School of Instruction and Major R.M. RAYNSFORD took over command. 2/Lt J.M. GARRET returned from a course.	Appendix 2 O.O. No 17
ST EMILIE	3rd		There were Church parades in VILLERS FAUCON for all denominations in the morning and the usual inspections were held under Company arrangements. Lt V.A. MOORE and 2/Lt J.T. O'NEILL returned from courses	
	4th		A and B companies were inspected by the Commanding Officer in Marching Order and afterwards kits were laid out.	
	5th		C and D companies were inspected by the Commanding Officer. Lt B.S.F. PICKARD was discharged from hospital and returned to the battalion	
	6th		HQ Coy were inspected by the C.O. Lt E.A.W. SMITH returned from a course.	

(A7092). Wt. W12839/M1293. 750,000. 1/17. D. D. & L., Ltd. Forms/C.2118/14.

February 1918 Sheet 2

Army Form C. 2118.

Instructions regarding War Diaries and Intelligence Summaries are contained in F. S. Regs., Part II. and the Staff Manual respectively. Title pages will be prepared in manuscript.

WAR DIARY
~~or~~
~~INTELLIGENCE SUMMARY.~~
(Erase heading not required.)

Confidential

Place	Date	Hour	Summary of Events and Information	Remarks and references to Appendices
St EMILIE	7th		There were baths parades in VILLERS FAUCON for all. Capt R.T. ROUSSELL left on leave and Lt H.E. TAGGART went on a course.	
Front line	8th		The battalion relieved the 1st R.M.F in the left subsector (Appendix 3).	Appendix 3 O.O. No 18.
	9th		A patrol of 1 N.C.O and 4 O.R. examined FLEET ST CRELLIN AVENUE and TOMBOIS RD. No enemy patrol was encountered. 2/Lt J.J. CONLON joined the 180th Tunnelling Coy. R.E.	
	10th		C and D Coys relieved A and B in the front line. A patrol examined No MAN'S LAND between COCHRAN and CRELLIN AVENUES. No enemy was met with but the patrol was fired on by a M.G. from the enemy front line. Capt T. BOOTH, M.C and 2/Lt M. McKIERNAN returned from leave.	
	11th		Lt S.W. O'COFFEY left the battalion to take up the duties Adjutant, 47th T.M.B.	
	12th		A fighting patrol of 16 O.R under 2/Lt J. MEENAGHAN met no enemy in No MAN'S LAND; the wire opposite BEEL LANE was examined. 2/Lt T.S. JENNINGS went on leave.	
	13th		2/Lt M. McKIERNAN and a patrol of 5 O.R examined the wire opposite WILLOW TRENCH.	

(A7092). Wt. W12839/M1293. 750,000. 1/17. D. D. & L., Ltd. Forms/C.2118/14.

February 1918. Sheet 3.

Instructions regarding War Diaries and Intelligence Summaries are contained in F. S. Regs., Part II. and the Staff Manual respectively. Title pages will be prepared in manuscript.

WAR DIARY

~~or~~

~~INTELLIGENCE SUMMARY.~~

(Erase heading not required.)

Confidential.

Army Form C. 2118.

Place	Date	Hour	Summary of Events and Information	Remarks and references to Appendices
Front Line	14th		A and B Coys relieved C and D in the front line. (Appendix 4)	Appendix 4
	15th		2/Lt D.T. McWEENEY and 8 O.R went on a fighting patrol with the object of entering the enemy's line near BEEL LANE and obtaining an identification. They found the line strongly held and the enemy alert. Three separate occasions were made to cut his wire but each time the party was discovered and fired on. It finally returned without casualties after being out for 5 hours.	O.O. No 20.
	16th		The battalion was relieved by the 2nd LEINSTER REGT and proceeded (less D Coy) to Brigade support where it occupied the LEMPIRE Defences. D Coy were attached to the 1st R.M.F and were put into the front line to hold the GILLEMONT FARM sub-sector for the next 4 days. (Appendix 5) 2/Lt J.M. GARRETT was admitted to hospital.	Appendix 5 O.O. No 21.
	17th – 20th		The battalion was occupied with working parties throughout the period. On the 17th Capt T. BOOTH, M.C, went to PERONNE on a Sanitation Course & Lt B.S.F. PICKARD went on leave. On the 18th Lt F.T. CHAMIER went on leave. On the 19th Lt F.C. WOODS returned from leave.	
	20th		The battalion relieved the 1st R.M.F. in the right subsector of the line (see Appendix 6.) 2/Lt J.T. O'NEILL was admitted to hospital.	Appendix 6. O.O. No 22.
	21st		A heavy barrage was put down on our line at 5.30 am killing 2 men. Capt T. BOOTH, M.C returned from his course.	

KJ8

(A7092). Wt. W12839/M1293. 750,000. 1/17. D. D. & L., Ltd. Forms/C.2118/14.

February 1918 Sheet 4.

Instructions regarding War Diaries and Intelligence Summaries are contained in F. S. Regs., Part II. and the Staff Manual respectively. Title pages will be prepared in manuscript.

WAR DIARY

~~or~~

~~INTELLIGENCE SUMMARY.~~

(Erase heading not required.)

Army Form C. 2118.

Confidential

Place	Date	Hour	Summary of Events and Information	Remarks and references to Appendices
Front Line	22nd		A patrol of 1 N.C.O. and 4 O.R. examined No Man's Land opposite MILL LANE	
	23rd		A patrol of 1 N.C.O and 4 O.R examined the enemy wire for a distance of 200 yds S. of BREAD LANE. Lts O.H. ACTON & P.S.C.L. PALMER went on courses and Lt J.M. FORBES left on leave.	
	24th		B and D Coys relieved A and C Coys in the front line. 2/Lt H.S. KIRKWOOD was discharged from hospital and returned to the battalion. 2/Lt T.C. SLOWEY left on a course.	
	25th		Capt R.T. ROUSSEL returned from leave.	
	26th		2/Lt D.T. McWEENEY left on a course	
	27th		A patrol of 1 N.C.O and 2 O.R examined the enemy's wire from WICK LANE to BREAD LANE. Lt Col R.C. Feilding, D.S.O., returned to the battalion from his visit to the French Army & Lt A. RIBBONS was discharged from hospital and returned to the battalion.	
	28th		Operation Orders concerning the relief of the 16th by the 21st Division were cancelled and the battalion was relieved by the 2nd LEINSTER REGT and returned to Brigade Support to occupy the LEMPIRE Defences. (Appendix)	Appendix 7 O.O. No 24.

(A7092). Wt. W12839/M1293. 750,000. 1/17. D. D. & L., Ltd. Forms/C.2118/14.

[signature] 2/Lt Comdg 1st Conn Rs

SECRET.

OPERATION ORDER No. 7

by
LIEUT COLONEL R.C. FEILDING D.S.O.
COMMANDING 6TH BN THE CONNAUGHT RANGERS.

2nd Feby. 18.

1. The Battalion will be relieved by the 1st RL. MUNSTER FUSRS today the 2nd Inst, and on relief will proceed to Bde Reserve at ST EMILIE. The Relief will not commence before [illegible]pm.

2. "A" COY will be relieved by "W" COY 1/R.MUNS FUSRS.
"B" .. .. "X" ..
"C" .. .. "Y" ..
"D" .. .. "Z" ..

3. Advance parties of the 1st R.M.FUS will arrive about [illegible]pm.
A. patrol of 1 Officer and [illegible] O.R. from each of "Y" & "Z" Coy's 1.R.M.FUS will come up during daylight and will patrol the front after dark to protect the relief.

4. All work, trench stores and defence schemes will be carefully handed over. [illegible] Copies of Trench Store Lists to reach Bn Hd Qrs by [illegible] on 2nd Inst. Clean trench certificates will be obtained from the relieving unit.

5. Completion of relief to be wired to Bn Hd Qrs, - Code word - THAMES. Arrival in new positions to be reported to Bn.H.Qrs. by runner.

6. Advance parties of 1 N.C.O. per Company, 1 man per platoon and 1 N.C.O. from Hd Qrs will meet LIEUT A.W. O'CONNOR, at ST EMILIE (F.24.b.9.1.) at 4pm.

7. The Transport Officer will arrange for the removal of L.Guns, Officers' Mess Kits, "A" & "B" Coy's Blankets, etc.

(sd) F.T. CHAMIER LIEUT.

A.ADJUTANT 6TH BN THE CONNAUGHT RANGERS.

SECRET.

OPERATION ORDER No. 18.
by
M A J O R R .M. R A Y N S F O R D
COMMANDING 6TH BN THE CONNAUGHT RANGERS.

7th Feby.1918.

1. The Battalion will relieve the 1st Rl.MUNSTER FUSRS in the Left Subsection tomorrow the 8th Inst.
2. The Relief will take place as under:-

Coy of C.RGS.	Coy of R.M.FUS.	PLACE.
"A" Coy plus 1 L.G. of "C" Coy.	"Y"COY. plus 1 L.G. of "W" Coy.	Right front line.
"B" Coy. plus 1 L.G. of "D" Coy	"Z" Coy plus 1 L.G. of "X" Coy.	Left front line..
"C" COY les 1 L.G.	"W" COY less 1 L.G.	SART LANE & WRAFTER POST
"D" Coy less 1 L.G.	"X" Coy. less 1 L.G.	LEMPIRE EAST.

3. Companies will move off in the following order, "A","B","C","D", & Hd Qrs. All movement will be by Platoons at 500 yards distance. "A" Coy will not move off before 5pm.

4. "A" & "B" Coy's will each send up a Patrol of 1 Officer and 20 other ranks by daylight. They will patrol the front from dark until 10 pm. to protect the relief.

5. The usual advance parties will report to the Coy H.Qrs of the 1st Rl.Munster Fusrs at 4pm.

6. All Work,Defence Schemes and Trench Stores will be carefully taken over, Copies of trench store lists will reach Bn Hd Qrs by 9 am 9th Inst.

7. Completion of relief will be wired to Bn Hd Qrs, CODE WORD - S T U C K.

8. "C" & "D" Coy's will.take up 2 blankets per man. "A" & "B" will not take blankets.

9. All valises Blankets. etc. for the Transport Lines must be ready for removal by 2pm. Lewis Guns Blankets etc, for the line will be ready by 4pm. The Transport officer will.make the necessary arrangements for teir conveyance.

10. Table of working parties attached for those concerned.

11, All billets will be left scrupulously clean and certificates obtained from the incoming unit (7th LEINSTERS).

12 Surplus Officers will reportto the TOWN MAJOR,VILLERS FAUCON for accomodation.

(sd) F.T. CHAMIER LIEUTEMAMT.

A.ADJUTANT 6TH BN THE CONNAUGHT RANGERS.

SECRET. OPERATION ORDER NO. [illegible] Copy No. 7

BY

MAJOR [illegible]

COMMANDING 6TH BN THE CONNAUGHT RANGERS.

13th February [illegible].

1. The following reliefs will take place to-morrow 14th. Inst.-
"A" Coy will relieve "C" Coy in the Right Front Line.
"B" Coy. " " "D" Coy. " Left " "

2. Relief will not commence before 5 pm.

3. On relief, "C" & "D" Coys. will withdraw to the positions vacated by "A" & "B" Coys respectively.

4. "A" & "B" Coys will send up a patrol of 1 officer and 15 O.R. each. These will patrol the front during the relief and will not withdraw before 6 pm. They will not be sent up to the front line before dusk.

5. All blankets, Trench Stores and Work in progress & contemplated will be carefully handed over. Copies of Trench Store Lists to reach Battn H.Q. by [illegible] 15th Inst. "C" & "D" Coys will take over all Working-parties as from 6 pm 14th.

6. One Lewis Gun and team of "B" Coy. will be attached to "A" Coy during the latter's tour of duty in the line.

7. Completion of relief to be wired to Bn H.Q. Code word - GALA.

(sd) F.T. [illegible] LIEUT

A. ADJUTANT 6TH BN THE CONNAUGHT RANGERS.

SECRET | OPERATION ORDER NO. 21 | Copy No. 10

BY

MAJOR R.M.RAYNSFORD

COMMANDING 6TH. BN. THE CONNAUGHT RANGERS

16 th February 1918

1. The Battalion will b e relieved toonight by the 2nd BN. Leinster Regt. Relief will not commence before 6 p.m.

2 On relief the Battn.(less "D" Coy.) will become the Battn in Bde.Support,and will be disposed as follows:

"A"Coy. will occupy Area "D" Coy H.Q. at the Cit adel
"B"Coy. " " Area "C" " " at GILLEMONT LODGE (F.15.d.75.85.)
"C"Coy. " " Area "A" " " at SANDBAG ALLEY

3. On relief "D" Coy. will proceed to KEN LANE, and come under the orders of O.C. 1st.ROYAL MUNSTER FUSILIERS.

4 The usual patrols will come up from the 2nd. Leinsters, to protect the relief.

5. Advance parties of 1 N.C.O. per Coy. 1 man per platoon, and 1 N.C.O. from Bn. H.Q., will report to thee Coy.H.Q. of the Coy. they are relieving, at 4 p.m.

6. All Trench Stores and Work in prog ress and contemplated will be carefully handed and taken over. Copies of Trench Store Receipts to reach Bn. H.Q. by 9 a.m. 17th Inst.

7. Rat ions will be dumped in the new positions. Coys will arrange to meet the limb ers, and unload them at once.

8. The Transport Officer Will arrange for the conveyance of L.G's, Officers Mess Kit s,and "C" & "D" Coys blankets as soon after dark as possible. The Q.M. will send up "A" & "B" Coys blankets to them.

9. Completion of relief will be wired to Bn. H.Q. Code Word-TIRED. "A""B" &"C" Coys will report their arrival in support by runner to Bn. H.Q.

(Sd) F.T.CHAMIER LIEUT.
A/ADJUTANT 6TH. BN. THE CONNAUGHT RANGERS

4

SECRET

OPERATION ORDER NO. 82

Copy No 10.

By

MAJOR R.M. RAYNSFORD

COMMANDING 6TH. BN. CONNAUGHT RANGERS

20th February 191

1. The Battalion will relieve the 1st Royal Munster Fusiliers in the Right Sub-section to-day, the 20th inst.

2. The relief will take place as follows:-

"A" Coy. will relieve the right front line Coy. (1st. R.M.F.)
"C" Coy " " " left " " " "
"B" Coy. " " " Coy in DUNCAN POST
"D" Coy. " " " Coy. in KEN LANE

"D" Coy. will send an advance party to take over KEN LANE

3. Coys will move off in the following order "C" "A" "B" "D" "HQ".
All movement will be by Platoons at 300 yards interval.
"C" Coy will not move off before 6.p.m.

4. "A" Coy will send up a patrol of 1 Officer and 20 O.R. by daylight. They will patrol from dark to 9 p.m. to protect the relief.

5. The usual advance parties will report to the Coy. H.Qs. of the 1st. Royal Munster Fusiliers by 4 p.m.

6. All work, defence schemes, and Trench Stores will be carefully taken and handed over. Copies of Trench Store Lists will reach Bn. H.Q. by 9 a.m. the 21st inst.

7. Completion of relief will be reported to Bn. H.Q. by runner

8. Table of Working parties attached for those concerned.

9. Front line Companies will carry 1 blanket per man. O.C. Coys will send back to to Transport Lines the 2nd. blanket. This can be done by means of the rations waggons under the supervision of the Transport Officer.

10. Coys in support will on inter Coy relief hand over their 2nd blanket to the relieving Coy.

11. All billets will be left scrupulously clean and certificates obtained from the incoming unit (1st. R.M.F.)

(Sd) M. O'LOUGHLIN 2nd Lt.
A/Adjutant 6th. Bn. CONNAUGHT RANGERS

Operation Orders No 24
by
Major W.M. RAYNSFORD. Cmdg 6th Conn. Rangers

I The Battalion will be relieved in the right subsection tonight, commencing at 6.30pm, by the 2nd LEINSTER RGT.

II A Coy LEINS' RGT will relieve B Coy CONN RANGERS
B D
C C
D A

III On relief the Bn will proceed to BRIGADE RESERVE and will be disposed as follows:- A Coy CITADEL, B Coy GUILLEMONT LODGE, C Coy SANDBAG ALLEY (former [illegible]) D Coy SANDBAG ALLEY.

IV Coys will send advance parties to take over at once.

V All trench stores etc of the battalion will be [illegible] obtained, receipts to be forwarded to Bn H.Q. by 9am 1st March.

VI Completion of relief will be reported to present Bn H.Q. by runner. Code word 'SOLD' followed by Coy Commanders name. Arrival of the [illegible] will be reported to NEW Bn H.Q. by runner.

28.2.18.

J Booth Capt
6 Conn [illegible]

47th Brigade.

16th Division.

The War Diary is missing; this file contains the Report by O.C. Battalion 21st-27th March.

6th BATTALION

CONNAUGHT RANGERS

MARCH 1918

16 Div

6th CONNAUGHT RANGERS

1918

21st-28th March.

OFFICIAL REPORT RENDERED TO BRIGADE BY LIEUT.-COLONEL R.C.FEILDING

April 1918.

EPEHY Sheet 62.C.N.E. 2 Edition 2A
FRANCE " 62.D. Edition 1.

Headquarters,
47th Infantry Brigade.

Herewith I beg to submit report on the hostile offensive operations which began on 21.3.18, in so far as they affected the battalion under my command. The period covered expires on the evening of 27.3.18, when I became a casualty and handed over the command of the battalion to Captain Richie Dickson.

21.3.18:

1). At 4.30 a.m. the enemy's preparatory bombardment commenced. The great intensity and the extensive character of this bombardment are well-known, and it is sufficient to say that Villers Faucon where we were in divisional reserve, came in for its full share. In spite of the fact that the enemy had not previously registered, and in spite of a heavy fog, a very large number of shells fell upon the village.

At 8.30 a.m. my battalion headquarters, which were alongside the ruins of the church, received a direct hit, which slightly wounded Major Rainsford, Second in command, and Lt. Chamier, asst. adjutant, besides shaking the building to such an extent as to render it unsafe. Ithen shifted my headquarters to the Mount 150 yards to the north of the church.

As soon as the nature of the bombardment had been realized, the companies had been scattered as far as possible, the men being ordered by sections to take cover in the trenches which formed part of the anti-air bomb defences surrounding the huts, and which fortunately I had caused to be deepened a few days previously against such an emergency as this. Sections of men were also distributed wherever the contour of the ground or standing walls provided any sort of cover.

The result that no casualties were suffered during the ~~bombardmen~~ morning, and though on one occasion a large shell hit the limber of a field kitchen, throwing the cook, the latter picked himself up and continued cooking the men's breakfast.

2) While the men were having dinners Ronssoy was reported lost, and I received orders to man the Brown Line. At 12.53 p.m. the battalion marched off in the following order, C Coy, D Coy, A Coy B Coy. The route taken was by the narrow gauge railway to St. Emilie. The enemy was shelling heavily, and several casualties were incurred by us on the way up.

I first of all established my headquarters in the narrow gauge cutting, opposite the building known as the Crystal Palace; From here I sent Major Rainsford (who had pluckily carried on in spite of his shaking of the morning) to report to Br.-General ~~Lawford~~ Leveson Gower, commanding 49th Inf. Bde., under whose orders I had been directed to place myself and my battalion.

3) Shortly afterwards, I received orders to report personally at 49th Brigade Hqrs. On the way I met Lieut.-Col. Kane comdg. 1/R.M.F., who told me that he had been ordered to make an immediate counter-attack upon the enemy in conjunction with myself. Upon reaching 49th Bde. Hqrs. I received orders from the Brg.-General to counter-attack Ronssoy to the left of the St. Emilie road with as little delay as possible. He added that the 1/RMF would co-operate on my right. I asked that the time at which this counter-attack was to be made should be specified in order to insure effective co-operation between the two battalions. The Brigadier, however, desired me to carry on independently of the 1/R.M.F., and I therefore made straight for the Brown Line, to give the necessary orders.

This trench was being very heavily and effectively shelled,

as I reached it, and one of my company commanders - Captain Wickham - already lay wounded. severely.

The counter-attack was delivered at 3.45 p.m. by two companies: D Coy on the right and A Coy on the left. C Coy followed in support with B Coy. in reserve.

It was pressed with the greatest gallantry, and had it been supported on the right, as arranged, it is possible that it would at least have resulted in a local set-back to the enemy's advance. A and D Coys. reached the sunken road bounding the western edge of Ronssoy wood. As C Coy under Captain Normal advanced they saw what at first they thought was the 1/RMF but soon discovered to be the enemy. lining the factory ridge to their right front, as well as parties of the enemy approaching along the Ronssoy St. Emilie Road, evidently with the object of getting round the flank of D Coy. C Coy immediately engaged the enemy, forming a defensive flank along the Ronssoy - St. Emilie road, but all the officers and the greater part of the company becoming casualties, they were soon compelled to fall back on the Brown Line, together with the few that remained of A and D Coys, who also had suffered very severely, Captain Crofton having been killed while gallantly leading forward A Coy, which he commanded, whilst Lieut. Ribbons, who had succeeded Captain Wickham in the command of D Coy. was missing.

The two tanks which, prior to the attack, it had been arranged should co-operate with the battalion under my command, apparently received fresh orders, since one of them went forward independently while my men were assembling for the counter-attack. I did not see the other, though I was informed that it also made a bold and independent assault upon the enemy, but both were soon knocked out.

4) At 5.15 p.m. I received orders from Hqrs. 47th Bde. to move my hqrs. to the Right Brigade H.Q. at the chateau, St. Emilie. I therefore moved my hqrs. from the Brown line.

On my arrival the Brigadier-General commanding 49th Bde. informed me that the orders for the counter-attack should have been cancelled: he added that they had been cancelled in the case of the 1/RMF, but that he had not been able to communicate with me in time.

The 47th Bde. was in the act of moving as I arrived, and I now came under the orders of the 47th Bde. whose hqrs. had moved to the Quarry, St. Emilie.

5) I reported the situation over the telephone, and it was arranged that I should get into personal touch with the OC. St. Emilie defences (Lieut.-Colonel Crockett), there being no telephonic communication with him. I found him in the narrow gauge railway cutting, and with him the OC 1/RMF. This being more accessible and a more suitable location for battalion Hqrs. than the deep dug-out under the Chateau, I decided, after consultation with Colonel Crockett, to move my hqrs. there, and notified the bde. to this effect.

6) Later in the evening the 1st Hertfordshire arrived as a reinforcement, the commanding officer establishing his hqrs. at the Quarry (HQ. 47th Inf. Bde.). Three companies were sent to the Brown Line - two to the left of the narrow gauge cutting and one to the right of the St. Emilie Ronssoy road. One company was kept in reserve in the Quarry.

7) During the night I visited 47th Bde.Hqrs. in the Quarry with Col. Crockett, who proposed, in view of the probable renewal of the attack by the enemy in the morning, that a preventive counter-attack should be delivered during the night on the left of the narrow gauge cutting.

The acting Bde. Cmdr. (Lieut.-Colonel Watson) had just

received orders to move his hqrs. from the Quarry back, and he was leaving as we arrived.

On my return to my headquarters I sent Major Rainsford to the Brown line to visit all the posts occupied by the battalion under my command.

The night and early morning passed quietly.

22nd March 1918:

8) At 3.30 a.m. all stood to. There was a thick fog, and daylight arrived without any sign of activity on the part of enemy.

About 6 o'clock three German prisoners (an officer and 2 other ranks) were sent back from the Brown Line, having been captured while on aptrol. They spoke English and upon being questioned stated that it was intended to resume the attack during the morning. This news was immediately sent back by telephone via the Quarry. A quarter of an hour or so later, the hostile bombardment was renewed on a similar scale of intensity to that of the preceeding day, and the machine-gun fire being also very heavy and there being no communication trench to the Brown line, the companies were completely cut off.

At 7.30 a.m. with Col. Crockett, I moved my hqrs. along the narrow gauge railway to the right of the St. Emilie - Villers Faucon road.

About the same time parties of the 2/Leinster Regt. began to fall back, stating that the enemy had broken through the Brown line on the right of this road.

The 13/R. Sussex (39th Div.) were lining the Narrow Gauge Railway (south).

About 8.30 a.m. the troops were falling back freely from the right of St. Emilie, and I established a straggers post at the junction of the Broad Gauge railway and the Villers Faucon - St. Emilie road (east of Villers Faucon), and in conjunction with Col. Crockett (commanding 11/Hants Pioneers) and Lt. Col. Kane (comdg. 1/RMF) manned the bank which crosses the road at this point as well as the ridges on either side, with headquarter signallers, police, pioneers, etc. and stragglers from other regiments whom we had collected.

Enemy machine guns were now sweeping the road where we were.

About 9.15 a.m; two runners whom I had despatched at 7.45 to try and get in touch with the front line having failed to return, I sent 2/Lt. McWeeny with Pte. Walsh, a battalion observer, to reconnoitre the situation. He duly reported later that he had been nearly into St. Emilie without seeing the enemy, but that the latter had apparently broken through between the 16th and 66th Divisions (on our right).

About 11 a.m. one of the two runners whom I had despatched at 7.45 a.m. returned. He had been wounded while passing through St. Emilie, his companion - Pte. Feeny - having been killed. He brought a short note from Capt. Roussell, commanding in the front line, with whom he had succeeded in getting into contact. This note was timed 8.55 a.m.and stated that Capt. Roussell was holding from the narrow gauge railway to the Ronssoy - St. Emilie road. (Note: A later message said that he was still holding on at

abt 11/ 9.30). A message arrived almost simultaneously/from the 11th Hants who had garrisoned St.Emilie to the effect that a block had been established across the St. Emilie - Villers Faucon road; but a short time later Capt. Howson of the same battalion arrived personally and reported that the enemy had forced his way past him on either side of the road and that he had therefore withdrawn his men to Villers Faucon.

The enemy shelling of Villers Faucon and the ridges around which had been severe for some time, had now become very intense and with Col. Crockett and Col. Kane I withdrew my hqrs. to the ridge west of Villers Faucon.

The troops were now slowly falling back in large numbers, though without any sign of panic. In most cases the officers seemed to have the men well in hand.

9) Orders were now received providing for a withdrawal to the Green line in front of Tincourt, and after a conference with the other battalion commanders present, the movement was carried out successfully in spite of a certain amount of enemy shelling which caused some casualties.

The battalion under my command was now represented by the battalion headquarter coy. and a few runners, and with these I manned a section of the Green line with my right on the Tincourt - Villers Faucon road. Every single officer who had been doing duty with the companies had become a casualty.

10) During the afternoon I received orders to leave the Green line and to march my men to the Tank Camp in the small wood in the angle between the Péronne and Templeux la Fosse roads, where the brigade was being reorganized, and where 34 stragglers from the companies rejoined.

At dusk I was ordered to line the Tincourt - Templeux la Fosse road (my left on the edge of Tincourt Wood), with the 1/RMF on my left and the 2/Leinster on my right, the latter being temporarily placed under my command. My instructions were to cover the retreat of the 49th Bde. should it be compelled to fall back from the Green line, allowing them to pass through my ranks; then to follow after them and take up a position on the Doingt - Bois des Flacques - Bussu line before Péronne.

23rd March 1918.

11) The 49th Bde. began to fall back shortly after daybreak and the arrangements for the withdrawal to the Bois des Flacques line were carried out without difficulty and in good order. The operation was assisted in its initial stages by a fog, and the retirement was covered by a number of tanks, as well as by a heavy artillery barrage.

12) Behind us in the xlxax plain to the west of our new position which capped the summit of a step ridge lay Doingt and Péronne. Already some buildings were blazing in both places and I also noticed one or two explosions, suggesting that preparations were being made for a further retreat.

13) Early in the afternoon the enemy's line of skirmishers topped the sky-line some 2,000 yards in front of our position. These were followed by his assault troops, who soon had gathered in large numbers in the woods and wherever the ground offered cover. Simultaneously, a heavy long-range machine-gun fire was opened upon us, which, owing to the steep angle of descent of the bullets and the shallowness of the trenches wexx were occupying, was uncomfortable, though its effect was trifling. The leading skirmishers were very bold and in the face of a moderate fire from us - I had given orders to economize ammunition till they got close - persisted in their advance across the very exposed valley which separated us.

14) About this time an enemy aeroplane flew low over our line and dropped a flare. This was evidently mistaken by our artillery for one of our own signals, as shrapnel was put over killing
/my two of/men and wounding a third.

15) About 1 p.m. I saw the 1/RMF, who were on my immediate left, leaving the trenches in a body, and I sent a runner to ask for an explanation. The 2nd in command returned personally with my runner and informed me that he had received orders from the bde. to fall back. I suggested that there must be some mistake and he replied that he would go to Bde. Hqrs. and ascertain definitely the acting brigadier's wishes. Seeing no reason for a retirement, I then ordered two platoons of the 13/Sussex, who

happened to be available, to fill the gap vacated by the 1/RMF. I also asked Col. Crockett if he could help me with men, but this he was unable to do as all his men were already occupied in holding line. When later I saw the O.C. 1/RMF he informed me that when he withdraw, the troops of the 48th Bde. on his left had already left the trenches, leaving his left in the air.

16) As I was returnèng to the front line I was met by my Adj., who informed me that during my absence an order had come from the Bde. to evacuate the line we were holding and to fall back on Biaches, and that Major Rainsford had gone to make the necessary arrangements. Major Rainsford has since informed me that he passed on the order in writing to the 2/Leinster and to the 6/Connaught Rangers, but when I saw him at the time he had just been severely wounded and was being carried back under considerable difficulties on a ground sheet.

17) I formed up the Connaught Rangers on the edge of the village of Doingt at the foot of the hill, and in conjunction with Col. Crockett and Major Whittall R.E. a considerable fire was brought to bear upon the enemy, who were already descending, and whose machine guns were firing down from the ridge we had so recently occupied.

18) We then fell back through Doingt and Péronne, halting parties at convenient points to cover the withdrawl of the remainder of the troops. In this connexion the 11/Hants (P) rendered good service, and though our retirement was followed by the enemy's machine gun and shell fire, the reply was so effective and the enemy's advance consequently so hesitating that we were able to reach the old line of trenches crossing the Herbecourt road just west of Biahces almost without casualties.

These trenches we manned facing east, in the following order: (1) on the right 1/RMF, forming a defensive flank; (2) 11/Hants (3) 6/Connaught R. (4) Major Whittall's RE details, forming a defensive facing left.

A R.E. officer was waiting at each bridge in Péronne ready to blow it up after the passage of the infantry. At the first, i.e. that nearest the enemy, I left four men to assist inthis operation and at his own request, I also left Capt. Ritchie Dickson, my adj. All rejoined the battalion safely during the evening.

<u>24th March 1918</u>:

19) At midnight I received orders through Col. Crockett to march back towards Bray, and at 6.30 a.m. we reached and bivouacked in a field a few hundred yards east of the village, where we found the 47th Bde. hqrs.

During the day the battalion was reorganized in two coys. AB and CD. By the addition of stragglers and officers and men returned from courses, leave, etc., the fighting strength of the battalion was increased to 7 officers and 180 other ranks.

20) During the afternoon Br.-General Gregorie cmdg. the 47th Inf. Bde. returned from leave and I was ordered to move to Sailly Lorette, to guard the bridges, it being reported that enemy cavalry had crossed the Somme south of Péronne and were making their way in a westerly direction. We got into position about 10 p.m. During the night sappers placed gun cotton slabs in position to blow up the bridges in case of necessity.

<u>25th March 1918</u>:

21) In the early morning the evacuation of the village by the civilian inhabitants was ordered by the French authorities, and was soon in active progress. No arrangement appeared to have been made

by the French for policing the village or safe-guarding the abandoned houses, many of which contained large stocks of wine, etc., so I made arrangements to have this done, with the gratifying result that I neither observed a sign nor heard of a single case of looting or drunkenness throughout the day.

22) In the afternoon I received orders to move to Cerisy and to guard the two bridges at that village, it being reported that the enemy was now threatening from the north side of the river. As at Sailly Lorette arrangements had been made to destroy the bridges in case of necessity.

During the day the division was transferred from the VII. to the XIX. Corps.

26th March 1918:

23) During this day six Lewis guns were issued to the battalion, the whole establishment having been lost or destroyed at St. Emilie.

24) During the morning I received orders to send a digging party of 100 men and 2 officers to Proyart, leaving 6 men and a Corporal on each bridge to assist the sappers. I was ordered to make my hqrs. at Morcourt, but almost immediately after arrival there was sent forward to take up a line in front of Proyart with the 1/RMF on my left and the 2/Leinster on my right. The line heldby the battalion under my command was the railway in R.21.a my right being on the Proyart-Chuignes road.

25) A gap on the right of the 2/Leinster was filled at my request by a detachment of the 1/Herts. Regt. under 2/Lt. Knew, which had been left behind as a covering party, beyond them being the 13/Gloucester (P), and the 17/KRRC - both battalions of the 39th Division. The line to the left of the L/RMF I was advised would be held by the 48th Bde.

26) At 3.50 p.m. it was reported, and it soon also became apparent from his enfilade fire, that the enemy had broken through the 66th Division, on our right, and this was confirmed shortly afterwards by an officer - 2/Lt. McWeeny - whom I sent to get in touch with the Os C's of the 13/Gloucester and 17/KRRC. Later the position on this flank improved, but it was then reported that the 48th Bde. on our left had left the trenches. This I reported to Bde. and I was ultimately informed that the gap would be filled before dawn.

27) The battalion frontage was patrolled continuously throughout the night. The enemy was observed digging some 800 yards in front of our line, and I sent forward a Lewis gun under 2/Lieut. Slowey to hamper them.

28) At 2.30 a.m. my line was visited by Capt. Monk GSO2 of the 16th Division, who told me that strong French reinforcements had already arrived at Lamote and would be passing through us to the counter-attack within next 6 hours.

29) Before dawn some men were reported to have returned to the gap on the left of the 47th Bde, but these appear to have left again almost immediately, and as soon as it was light enough to see, small parties of the enemy could be observed between us and the Somme making their way towards Maricourt and Morcourt. When I first saw this movement on the part of the enemy I sent a message to

Captain Goodland 1/RMF, who was on the left, asking him to send out a patrol to intercept it if possible, and I also asked a section of field artillery and two Vickers guns to sweep the ridge (R.9 Cent.) Later, as the movement continued, and the parties of the enemy passing round our flank grew larger and bolder, I sent a Lewis gun under 2/Lt. McWeeny to try and get round them.

30 For several hours the enemy continued to stream through the gap on our left in ever increasing numbers, and at 10.15 a.m. the position had become so acute that the OC. 1/RMF reported that he had been compelled to accommodate himself to the new situation which had arisen and was retiring. A conference was then held, as the result of which Lt. Col. Weldon ordered a withdrawal in echelon, commencing from the left to a position in the line Morcourt-Frammerville.

The withdrawal which, so soon as it was observed by the enemy provoked a considerable shell fire and heavy machine-gun fire, was successfully carried out, the right covering the retirement of the left, during the initial stages and covering parties being left behind as the withdrawal continued. That the retirement had become necessary was proved by the heavy machine-gun fire which met us, as we fell back, from the direction of Morcourt, in which locality large bodies of the enemy had already collected.

31) On reaching the line arranged I occupied an old trench crossing the road at R.25.c.3.8 and at 11.40 a.m. reported my position to Bde. I myself then went forward towards Proyart to look for Col. Welldon, who, being on my right, had retired after me. Having found him to be safe, I returned to my own men, and as a general retirement was by this time in progress, I formed them in in threes on the main Amiens road, together with the 1/RMF, who had become detached from their Col. and a good many stragglers from other regiments who had attached themselves to us. With this force, which must have been close on 400 strong, I then reported to Br.-Gen. Bellingham (comdg. 118th Bde.), whom I found on the road, offering my services pending receipt of a reply to my message to my own bde.

At his request I lined up with the 39th Div. in 3 lines of old trenches which cross the main Amiens road about 200 yds. west of the road junction (Q.30.d.90.30).

Here, until I left some 4 or 5 hours later, we held up and inflicted heavy losses upon the enemy, who advanced repeatedly in force through the villages of Raincourt and Framerville in front of us

A considerable number of aeroplanes, both enemy and British, took part in this action, and assistance was rendered by the artillery, and in particular by a section of field artillery, who took up their position immediately behind us, and whose shelling soon set fire to the villages.

About 3 p.m. a counter-attack was delivered on our right by about two fresh companies brought up by motor lorries for the purpose. The enemy began to fall back and in doing so offered some good targets, which were taken full advantage of. It was in rushing forward to get the Lewis guns on to a bunch of the enemy that I had observed retiring at about 4.15 p.m. that I fell over some hidden trip wire, and dislocated my elbow. About half an hour later I handed over the command as already stated.

32) A list of the casualties incurred has been prepared independently of this report, and the names of officers and other ranks deserving of special mention have been dealt with similarly.

R.C. Feilding, Lt. Col.
Comdg. 6th Battn. Con.Ran.

N.B. The total casualties (killed, wounded and missing) 21st-27th March were 22 officers and 618 other ranks.

Sheet 1.

1st April — ~~31st May~~ 20th Apl 1918

6th Bn The Connaught Rangers 47/16

Instructions regarding War Diaries and Intelligence Summaries are contained in F. S. Regs., Part II. and the Staff Manual respectively. Title pages will be prepared in manuscript.

WAR DIARY
or
INTELLIGENCE SUMMARY.

(*Erase heading not required.*)

Confidential

Vol 28

Army Form C. 2118.

Place	Date April 18	Hour	Summary of Events and Information	Remarks and references to Appendices
AUBIGNY	1st		5 officers and 150 other Ranks (approximately) were situated at AUBIGNY forming a Company of the 47th Bde Composite Battalion. Captain J H R Dickson was in command. Lt Col. A J DIGAN D.S.O. and Bn Headquarters being at the Transport Lines, BLANGY-TRONVILLE. The 47th Inf. Bde were in reserve.	
HAMELET	2nd		Orders were received about noon to proceed to HAMELET at once. On arrival there Lt Col. A.J. DIGAN D.S.O. came up.	
SALEUX	3rd		The 47th Inf Bde was relieved by the [illegible] Inf Bde, and the Battalion proceeded to SALEUX by motor lorry.	
BLANCHY	4th		The Battalion entrained at SALEUX and proceeded to [illegible] where it detrained and marched to FRANICOURT.	
FRANICOURT	5th – 9th		The Battalion was re-organised into two Companies. On the 5th Lieut. J.H. McDONNELL rejoined the Battalion and on the 8th Lt T. E. GILMORE rejoined. On the 9th the Battalion marched to ST. QUENTIN arriving there about 4 p.m. At 10 p.m. it marched to EU and entrained for ARQUES.	
WARDREQUES	10th		On arrival at ARQUES the next morning the Battalion detrained and marched to WARDRECQUES.	

D. D. & L., London, E.C. (A8004) Wt W1771/M2031 750,000 5/17 Sch. 52 Forms/C2118/14

April 1918

Sheet 2

Instructions regarding War Diaries and Intelligence Summaries are contained in F. S. Regs., Part II. and the Staff Manual respectively. Title pages will be prepared in manuscript.

WAR DIARY

or

~~INTELLIGENCE SUMMARY.~~

(Erase heading not required.)

Confidential

Army Form C. 2118.

6TH CONNAUGHT RANGERS TRAINING STAFF.

No. C/23

Date 6.6.18

Place	Date	Hour	Summary of Events and Information	Remarks and references to Appendices
MERCK ST LIEVIN	11th 12th		The Battalion marched to MERCK ST LIEVIN where it was billeted for 2 nights	
DRIONVILLE	13th		The Battalion marched to DRIONVILLE where orders were received that all officers and men with the exception of Headquarters and transport were to be transferred to the 2nd Leinster Regiment. This was done. Lt Col A J DIGAN DSO CAPT J H R DICKSON. LIEUT H.A. HUNT. Lt E.A.W. SMITH. LIEUT J M FORBES 2nd LIEUT T.F. GILMORE 2nd LIEUT D T McWEENEY remaining with the Headquarter Staff and transport. CAPTAIN R.E. BOWEN MC. LIEUT J.H. McDONNEL, LIEUT P.S.C.L. PALMER. LIEUT J.J. CONLAN & LIEUT. A. McMAHON and 281 other ranks joined the 2nd Leinster Regiment.	
REMILLY WIRQUIN	14th		The remnants of the Bn marched to REMILLY WIRQUIN	
	16th - 26th		while at REMILLY WIRQUIN orders were received to form a Training Staff. For this purpose Captain Bowen MC and 12 ~~other~~ NCOs were re-transferred from the 2nd Leinster Regiment on the 20th	

D. D. & L., London, E.C. (A8004) Wt W1771/M2031 750,000 5/17 Sch. 52 Forms/C2118/14

April 1918 Sheet 3

Instructions regarding War Diaries and Intelligence Summaries are contained in F. S. Regs., Part II. and the Staff Manual respectively. Title pages will be prepared in manuscript.

WAR DIARY

~~or~~

~~INTELLIGENCE SUMMARY.~~

(Erase heading not required.)

6TH CONNAUGHT RANGERS TRAINING STAFF. No. C/23 Date 6.5.18

Army Form C. 2118.

Confidential

Place	Date	Hour	Summary of Events and Information	Remarks and references to Appendices
REMILLY WIRQUIN	15th – 26th Cont		On the 19th Lt J L HARDY reported for duty from the Base On the 20th 2/Lt G.D. BARRON returned from base On the 18th 2nd LT D.T. McWEENEY went on a Lewis Gun Course On the 21st Lieut +W.S. JOURDAIN AND LIEUT S.W. O'COFFEY reported for duty On the 22nd Lt J.L. HARDY was transferred to the 2nd Innniskillings and Lt E.A.W. SMITH was transferred to the 2nd Royal Irish. 2nd Lieut McWEENEY was instructed to report to the O.C. 2nd Royal Irish Regiment on the conclusion of the course. On the 22nd Lieut JOURDAIN became Adjutant On the 22nd CAPT J H R DICKSON AND CAPT R.E. BOWEN, MC went on a 4 day Refresher Course in Musketry.	
BLEQUIN	26th – 30th		The Connaught Rangers Training Staff and Transport marched to BLEQUIN on the 26th and the time was there employed in Tactical Schemes under the Commanding Officer. On the 29th a Lecture on the General principles governing the action of a Company in the attack.	

A. J. Dixon
COMDG. 6th (S) Bn. THE CONNAUGHT RANGERS TRAINING STAFF.

[illegible] (S) Bn. THE CON[illegible] TRAINING STAFF.

D. D. & L., London, E.C. (A8004) Wt W1771/M2031 750,000 5/17 Sch. 52 Forms/C2118/14

May 1918. Sheet 4 6th Bn The Connaught Rangers Training Staff

Confidential

Vol 29

Instructions regarding War Diaries and Intelligence Summaries are contained in F. S. Regs., Part II. and the Staff Manual respectively. Title pages will be prepared in manuscript.

WAR DIARY

~~or~~

~~INTELLIGENCE SUMMARY.~~

(Erase heading not required.)

Army Form C. 2118.

Place	Date	Hour	Summary of Events and Information	Remarks and references to Appendices
BLEQUIN Ref map HAZEBROUCK 5A	1st – 14th		The Training Staff was stationed at BLEQUIN and the time was chiefly employed in musketry training and tactical schemes. The following lectures were given. On the 1st "Indents and Supplies" by Lt G.E. WELCH. On the 2nd Capt J.H.R. DICKSON on Advance Guards. On the 7th 'Requisitions and the Chain of Supplies' by Lt G.E. WELCH. On the 8th the Divisional Gas Officer and on the 13th the Corps Gas Officer lectured on Gas. On the 14th Lieut J.M. FORBES lectured on 'Fire Discipline'.	
			On the 1st 2/Lt G.D. BARRON proceeded on a course at the First Army S.O.S. School at LINGHEM and returned on the 11th. On the 2nd Lt J.M. FORBES went on a Lewis Gun Course and returned on the 11th. On the 11th Capt R.E. BOWEN and Lt F.W.S. JOURDAIN went on an Infantry Course and Lt J.M. FORBES took over the duties of Adjutant.	

D. D. & L., London, E.C. (A6004) Wt W1771/M203: 750,000 5/17 Sch. 52 Forms/C2118/14

May 1918. Sheet 8

Army Form C. 2118.

Confidential

Instructions regarding War Diaries and Intelligence Summaries are contained in F. S. Regs., Part II. and the Staff Manual respectively. Title pages will be prepared in manuscript.

WAR DIARY
or
~~INTELLIGENCE SUMMARY.~~
(Erase heading not required.)

Place	Date	Hour	Summary of Events and Information	Remarks and references to Appendices
DESVRES Ref Map CALAIS 13.	15th		The Training Staff and other details of the 47th Infy Bde proceeded by route march to DESVRES where they were billeted in the town and remained for three days.	
	18th		At 2 p.m. the Connaught Rangers proceeded by route march to DOUDEAUVILLE.	
DOUDEAUVILLE	19th –31st		While waiting for the arrival of the Americans, work for the Training Staff consisted mainly of an hours drill under the Adjutant followed by Tactical Schemes.	

A. J. Dugan Lieut Col
6th Connaught Rangers

D. D. & L., London, E.C. (A8004) Wt W1771/M2031 750,000 5/17 Sch. 52 Forms/C2118/14

June '18 Sheet 1. 6th Bn The Connaught Rangers Training Staff

Confidential

Army Form C. 2118.

Instructions regarding War Diaries and Intelligence Summaries are contained in F. S. Regs., Part II. and the Staff Manual respectively. Title pages will be prepared in manuscript.

WAR DIARY
or
~~INTELLIGENCE SUMMARY.~~
(Erase heading not required.)

VA 30

Place	Date	Hour	Summary of Events and Information	Remarks and references to Appendices
DOUDEAUVILLE Ref Map CALAIS 13.	1st		The final detachments of the 39th Regiment, ~~and~~ 4th Division, U.S. Army arrived in the area.	
	2nd		Church parade for Roman Catholics took place at 8.45 a.m	
	3rd		N.C.O instructors were divided amongst the three American battalions and commenced training at 1.30 p.m.	
	4th - 6th		The training of the N.C.Os of the 1st Batta of the 39th Regt U.S. Army in Musketry, Lewis Gun, Bombing, Scouting, Signalling and Bayonet fighting was carried out in DOUDEAUVILLE. The hours of instruction were 8 a.m – 12 noon and 2–4 p.m. On the 5th, Lieut G. E. WELCH proceeded on ~~the~~ leave to the United Kingdom. On the 6th General HORNE G.O.C 1st Army inspected the training in the evening.	
	7th		The 39th Regiment marched to SAMER to exchange their British rifles for those of the SPRINGFIELD pattern.	

D. D & L., London, E.C. (A8004) Wt W1771/M2031 750,000 5/17 Sch. 52 Forms/C2118/14

June 18. Sheet 2. 6th Bn The Connaught Rangers Training Staff

Army Form C. 2118.

WAR DIARY
~~or~~
~~INTELLIGENCE~~ SUMMARY.

(*Erase heading not required.*)

Confidential

Instructions regarding War Diaries and Intelligence Summaries are contained in F. S. Regs., Part II. and the Staff Manual respectively. Title pages will be prepared in manuscript.

Place	Date	Hour	Summary of Events and Information	Remarks and references to Appendices
DOUDEAUVILLE Ref Map CALAIS 13	8th		No training was carried out as the American troops were preparing to depart.	
	9th		The Americans left the Area in the morning. At 8.45 am there was a Church Parade for Roman Catholics in DOUDEAUVILLE Church. G.P.D.	
	16th		One battalion of the 317th Regt 80th Division, U.S. Army arrived in the area and on the following morning the remainder of the Regt under Col PERRY arrived. Regimental Headquarters were stationed in DOUDEAUVILLE & the battalions in BEAUCORRY, HODICQ and BEZINGHEM.	
	18th-31st		The training of the N.C.Os of the 1st and 3rd battalions commenced and continued till the end of the month. G.P.D.	

D. D. & L., London, E.C.
(A8004) Wt W1771/M2031 750,000 5/17 Sch. 52 Forms/C2118/14

July 1918. Sheet 1. Confidential Army Form C. 2118.

WAR DIARY

~~INTELLIGENCE SUMMARY.~~

(Erase heading not required.)

Instructions regarding War Diaries and Intelligence Summaries are contained in F. S. Regs., Part II. and the Staff Manual respectively. Title pages will be prepared in manuscript.

29

Place	Date	Hour	Summary of Events and Information	Remarks and references to Appendices
DOUDEAUVILLE	1st–3rd		The training of the 317th Regt, 80th Division, U.S. Army continued as before.	
Ref. Sheet CALAIS 1/100,000.	4th		Independence Day was celebrated by the American troops and the attached Cadres.	
	5th		The 317th Regt left the area by March Route commencing at 2 a.m.	
			No further American troops arrived during the month and on the 31st the Cadre received orders that the Battalion was broken up and the personnel to proceed to the 5th Battalion The Connaught Rangers on August 1.	
	31st		Lt-Col. A.T. Brown D.S.O. was under orders to proceed to the reinforcing Officers pool at ETAPLES.	

John H. Ritchie Dobson Capt
O.C. 6th Bn Conn Rangers

www.ingramcontent.com/pod-product-compliance
Lightning Source LLC
Chambersburg PA
CBHW081432300426
44108CB00016BA/2357

* 9 7 8 1 4 7 4 5 0 9 9 8 5 *